Gender and Power Relations in Nigeria

Gender and Power Relations in Nigeria

Edited by Ronke Iyabowale Ako-Nai

LEXINGTON BOOKS
Lanham • Boulder • New York • Toronto • Plymouth, UK

Published by Lexington Books
A wholly owned subsidiary of The Rowman & Littlefield Publishing Group, Inc.
4501 Forbes Boulevard, Suite 200, Lanham, Maryland 20706
www.rowman.com

10 Thornbury Road, Plymouth PL6 7PP, United Kingdom

British Library Cataloguing in Publication Information Available

Library of Congress Cataloging-in-Publication Data
Gender and power relations in Nigeria / [edited by] Ronke Iyabowale Ako-Nai.
p. cm.
Includes bibliographical references and index.
ISBN 978-0-7391-7778-5 (cloth : alk. paper) — ISBN 978-0-7391-7779-2 (ebook) 1. Women—Nigeria—Social conditions. 2. Women's rights—Nigeria. 3. Women—Legal status, laws, etc.—Nigeria. 4. Women—Political activity—Nigeria. 5. Sex role—Nigeria. 6. Feminism—Nigeria. 7. Sexism—Nigeria. I. Ako-Nai, Ronke Iyabowale.
HQ1815.5.G456 2013
305.4209669—dc23 2012037647

∞™ The paper used in this publication meets the minimum requirements of American National Standard for Information Sciences—Permanence of Paper for Printed Library Materials, ANSI/NISO Z39.48-1992.

Printed in the United States of America

This book is dedicated to my lovely children
and
women of Nigeria

Contents

PART IV: FEMINISM AND SOCIAL MOVEMENT

List of Contributors

Adedeji, Ogunleye J. (PhD) and **Sulaiman O. Adebayo** (PhD) are both with the Department Psychology, Faculty of the Social Sciences University of Ado-Ekiti, Nigeria

Adesoal, Funso (PhD) is a senior lecturer at the Department of International Relations, Obafemi Awolowo University, Ile-Ife, Osun State, Nigeria

Ako-Nai, Ronke Iyabowale (PhD) is a lecturer at the Department of International Relations, Obafemi Awolowo University, Ile-Ife, Osun State, Nigeria

Aransi, I.O. (PhD) is a reader at the Department of Local Government Studies, Faculty of Administration, Obafemi Awolowo University, Ile-Ife, Nigeria

Coker, Adesina (LL.M, MBA) is a senior lecturer at the Department of Public Law, Faculty of Law, Obafemi Awolowo University, Ile-Ife, Nigeria

David, I. D. is a doctoral student at the Department International Relations, Obafemi Awolowo University, Ile-Ife, Osun State, Nigeria

Erhun, Mercy Onaodowan is a lecturer at the Department of Public Law, Obafemi Awolowo University, Ile-Ife, Nigeria

Faleti, Stephen A. (PhD) is a lecturer at the Peace & Conflict Studies Programme Institute of African Studies University of Ibadan, Ibadan, Nigeria

Idowu, A. A. (PhD) is a senior lecturer and the current acting head, Department of Public Law, Faculty of Law, Obafemi Awolowo University, Ile-Ife

Osun State, Nigeria. His major areas of research are constitutional jurisprudence and human rights, all within the purview of public law.

Iwilade, Akin is a doctoral student at the Department of International Relations, Obafemi Awolowo University, Ile-Ife, Nigeria

Kuteyi, Oluwafisayo Semiu (LLB LLM BL) is a senior lecturer at the Department of Business Law, Faculty of Law, Obafemi Awolowo University, Ile-Ife, Nigeria

Modupe, Adu Funmilayo is a lecturer at the Department of History and International Studies Faculty of Arts, University of Ado–Ekiti

Okome, Mojúbàolú Olúfúnké (PhD) is a professor of political science at Brooklyn College, New York

Okwechime, Iwebunor is a lecturer at the Department of International Relations, Awolowo University, Ile-Ife, Nigeria

Oladoyin, Anthony M. (PhD) is reader at the Department of Public Administration, Obafemi Awolowo University, Ile-Ife, Osun State, Nigeria

Ologunde, A. O. (Mrs.) is a lecturer at the Department of Management and Accounting, Obafemi Awolowo University, Ile-Ife, Nigeria

Omotosho, Mashood is a lecturer at the Department of International Relations, Obafemi Awolowo University, Ile-Ife, Nigeria

Oni, Michael Abiodun and **Rachael Iyanda Oluseye** are both with the Department of Political Science & Public Administration, Babcock University, Ilesan Remo, Ogun State, Nigeria

Sehinde, Benson Kunle (PhD) is a lecturer at the Department of Public Administration, Obafemi Awolowo University, Ile-Ife, Osun State, Nigeria

Foreword

The struggle for female emancipation and hence women's empowerment in all areas of human endeavors reached its climax in the twentieth century. The debt trap and its overhang constituted a clog in the wheel of the development of the third and Nigeria is one of such.

Led by the United Nations, studies have confirmed that women's participation and the recognition of such are a sine qua non in the development process. Hitherto, traditional encumbrances and gender inequality of access to productive resources as well as the skewed division of labor in the household have made women poor. The result of this has been marginalization in the process of decision making. The good news, however, is that most developing countries of the world have now realized that policies made without the contribution of women do not achieve their goals. It is also heartening to know that Nigeria is a signatory to the UN affirmative document on gender mainstreaming in the development process. Nigeria's desired 35 percent of political participation for women is an evidence of this. It is in regard to the contribution of this book to this cause of women's empowerment that I appreciate the various contributors. It is an appropriate document for the introduction of newcomers to the campaign of gender equality and a reminder of the salient steps to take for the existing vanguard of gender mainstreaming.

The sections are well organized with chapter one discussing the perceived universalization of gender oppression and its remedies. Part I confirms the existence of constitutional and legal support for women's rights in the Nigerian polity. Part II traces the origins and patterns of women's marginalization in the development of Nigeria. Part III confirms through the various contributions, the need for policy supports for mainstreaming gender in the country while Part IV highlights the relevance of women's activism in the democratization process of Nigeria. The richness of the various contributions makes the book a "must read" for all genuine promoters of development in Nigeria.

Professor Omolara Olusi
Department of Economics
Faculty of Social Sciences
Obafemi Awolowo University

Acknowledgments

To God be the glory for my life which according to His plan is moving forward. I am particularly grateful to those that have made my journey tolerable and this book possible. Special thanks to Dr. Orobola Faseun who suggested this project and is always looking out for me. To my colleagues who assisted me in various ways in the production and preparation of this book: Professor Tale Omole, Dr. Olugbemi Mololoye, Dr. Funsho Adesola, Mr. Iwebunor Okwechime and Mr. Mashood Omotosho, I say thank you. To David Ibukun David, an extraordinary graduate student who worked tirelessly in the production of this book, great job and thank you. To my husband, my siblings, and members of their families who are always with me through thick and thin, I say a big thank you.

1

Western Feminist Theories

How Applicable to Africa?

R. I. Ako-Nai

ABSTRACT

Theories are developed for better understanding of events. Feminist theories are based on the need to free women from bondage. Mingst (2004:3) says "political scientists develop theories or frameworks both to understand the causes of events that occur in the international system and to answer the fundamental questions in the field." The study of international relations uses theories and concepts in its explanation and developing answers to global phenomena and developments, which also applies to women's struggle for emancipation and empowerment. This is a global struggle that has permeated all nations in respect of religion, culture, or political ideology and it is not a size-fit-all situation. In addition feminist theories are meant to be applied to daily lives; they are not expected to be abstract as they are to reflect the conditions of lives as well as gender roles in a given society. The various chapters in this book demonstrate the position of women in various walks of life vis-a-vis men in Nigeria. The goal of this chapter is to put forward the desire of feminists, which essentially is to identify the different modes of oppression as well as find solutions. The significant conclusion is that there are differences among women worldwide, and these differences make it imperative that the universalization of their "liberation" as proposed by Western feminists and international agencies must be looked into for any meaningful change.

INTRODUCTION

In view of the Western orientation of writings and documentation, Western concepts and theories dominate the field of feminism and are the basis for the interpretation of developments even in Africa where values and beliefs differ. The inappropriateness of Western concepts is the differences in culture, values and experiences and time. The nature of oppression and victimization differ from region to region even within the same environment. Although the various systems are exploitative and oppressive, they differ in many ways. However, as a result of the global nature of the international system, issues tend to be addressed through similar paradigm without adequate reference to the individual nature of the various entity or society.

No doubt, women are oppressed which is the result of the common call for emancipation. However, the nature of the oppression is not universal, which calls for the refinement of theories for meaningful change.

The struggle for women's empowerment in Africa, and in a patriarchal society such as Nigeria has variously been explained using theories deducted from Western society, a society whose antecedent greatly differs from that of Africa. The history and experiences of Africans have influenced their resistance, organizations and struggles, and the feminist struggle is not different. This explains the reaction of African women to the imposition of Western gender values on Africa. The differences in the mode of oppression call for a revisit of the existing theories when considering non-Western societies. The need for a theory that will embrace developments in Africa could also be seen in the work of Ferguson (2009:84–101), who pushes differences between men and women beyond political activities and power, that is, a "culturalist model." Jones (2000) highlights the role of culture in women's nature. She also highlights the view that on the issue of women and their oppression: "there is no one position but many, they move off in many directions . . . covering a broad sweep of disciplines within feminist studies." The diverse nature of feminist oppression shows that its study needs diverse tools to analyze the problems and related issues, if appropriate result is to come out of the current global campaign for women's emancipation and empowerment.

In most states of the world, human rights as defined and conceived by the West are rejected or, more accurately, are meaningless and not accepted. Many critiques hold the view that the Western concept is inapplicable and irrelevant to their environment. Inasmuch as this could be considered an extreme view, the protest of many nations to issues of human rights could be seen in this light. Ann Oakley, a British sociologist, sees culture as a major determinant of gender roles and holds the view that sexual division of labor is not universal as culture differs from place to place.[1] This does not preclude the fact that the current feminist struggle for emancipation and empowerment in Africa borrow from developments in the West, and that there are some similarities in the mode of oppression.

A CRITICAL LOOK AT SOME FEMINIST THEORIES

Liberal Feminist Theory

Liberal feminism has its roots in the sixteenth and seventeenth centuries with the ideals of liberty and equality based on man's rationality and the premise of sharp demarcation between public and private spheres, and that the individuals are paramount. Stamp (1983) and Bryson (1992) separately argue that the primary object of any study in liberalism is the individual. Women as individuals possess reason and as such are entitled to full human rights and they should therefore be free to choose their role in life and explore their full potential in competition with men. This was the guiding principles during the first wave of feminism period when women demanded for the right to education, employment, property and the vote. Unfortunately, liberal feminism does not analyze all the structures of oppression. This "theory" is inadequate even for women in the West or in Africa, as it has not met the goal of legal equality.

Even in African societies, for example Nigeria, the aspirations and desires of women differ. The differences are based on religion, ethnic and religious values among others. A similar situation existed in the United States of America as the earlier feminist struggle recognized the various classes, race and others. Liberal feminism ignores biological differences between the sexes and the fact that women have interests opposed to that of men. It is important to bring out clearly the differences between men and women in order to correct the anomalies. A sex blind theory dictated by men will not produce a good result.

Traditional Marxist Feminist Theory

The traditional Marxist theory is based on class oppression. It rejects biological differences as a basis for varying gender roles. The theory is based on family, private property and the state which result in the defeat of the female sex, the subjugation of mother-right and the establishment of the family.

The view that it is, only under modern conditions of production that women could realize their potential for free autonomous action has been criticized extensively. For instance, Amadiume (1995), criticizing Marx and Engels in her work on "gender, political systems and social movements," says that women's oppression does not arise solely from the division of society into classes. She rejects biology as a basis for gender differences, a position that is clearly seen even in modern day Africa, where in spite of the introduction of modern means of production, women still do not have a fair share of government or executive appointments. This theory concentrates on states, family and class structures of oppression. Amadiume argues that this theory does not fit Africa as it speaks about the elimination of the patriarchal family, a family structure that is still very much in practice in most African counties. Most African women are particular about their families whatever their achievements.

Another criticism of this theory is that Marx did extend his analysis to gender as done by feminist theory today. It deals more with conflicts between social classes with the dominant class—bourgeoisie—oppressing the other classes—proletariat. Contrary to this, women's interests unite them in a common sisterhood that transcends the division of class or race as the current movement cuts across borders and women issues are considered and articulated locally and internationally.

Although Marxist feminism sees women in a class struggle, it cannot adequately explain the situation of women in Africa as the African's dual-sex and other non-Western issues must be considered. Therefore a more holistic concept must be adopted which will be more embracing and capture the experiences of the African woman.

Radical Feminist Theory

On the other hand, radical feminism that uses Marxist language of oppression sees women as an oppressed class, an oppression based on patriarchy. Pereira (1997) questions the classification of all women into class. This theory is based on the assumption that patriarchy is universal as it is in Europe. According to Bryson (1992) patriarchy is the key term. This claim is wrong as can be seen in Africa, where patriarchal, matriarchal and matrilineal lineages exist. The single sex system (one man, one wife) of Europe does not hold in Africa. For example, the Akans of Ghana are matriarchal and there exist the matrilineal Arochukwu clans of Nigeria.[2] Hence, theorizing on Africa, based on the patriarchal theory is faulty, and such conceptualization will only produce unreliable results, as it reduces cultural diversity, and impedes feminist progress especially in the Third World, to which Africa belongs.

Social Feminist Theory

Social feminism, which does not give priority to class or gender oppression, is of interest as it embraces the historical, materialist method of Marx and Engels with the radical feminist idea that the personal is political and that gender oppression cuts across class lines. The fact that it considers gender differences in its concepts and female biology endeared it to many. It is based on the fact that an individual's life is shaped by her sex and gender assignment, and that politics cannot be separated from economics (Pereira, 1997). Unlike others, it does not give priority to class or gender oppression.

Feminist Political Economic Theory

The manner in which gender politics is articulated and played out varies widely across the different types of states. Significant differences in the politics and legal status of women across different political systems in the world predispose the use of the same theoretical framework in analyzing different peoples. The feminist political economy theory is more embracing as it is more adaptable. It is not based solely on Western cultures and beliefs. It could be adapted to African situations, as Africans, like many, would not like to accept Western notions without ensuring their practicability in their respective societies.

Feminist Political Economy Theory (FPET) that builds on socialist theory is more encompassing and pluralistic in its approach. It involves more non-Western categories than others. It incorporates ethnocentrism and economics as well as African experiences including colonialism, thus making it more acceptable. While Marxist feminism sees capitalism as the primary cause of gender differential treatment, and radical feminism sees men as the oppressors who refuse to see gender inequalities in the arena of public life, FPET addresses the social, economic, political and cultural inequalities in women's lives. It represents the concrete aspirations and struggles of women including African women, and points to certain experiences and realities that are not sufficiently accounted for by other theories. FPET is didactically engaged with other forms of consciousness and struggles.

FPET is pluralistic and captures diverse interests and societies. It recognizes that feminists could differ in their analysis of the causes of gender inequalities, which should influence the various recommendations for change. This theory is more suitable as it does not rely on concepts that are simplistic and narrow in scope. It utilizes a holistic approach to the study of pre-capitalist and capitalist societies of the Third World to which Africa belong.

In spite of the qualities of FPET, and judging from the above, a combination of theories such as the socialist and liberal theories will be appropriate for the study of African feminism.

WOMEN'S RIGHTS AND ITS CONTRADICTIONS

At the Beijing conference in 1995, similar to the development at the Mexico conference in 1975, African women condemned the use of Western paradigm in dealing with the situation of African women.

This brings up the issue of the relativity of human rights which is still very much a point of contention in the contemporary international system and a source of major conflicts. Human rights, which can be defined as the rights of individuals or groups protected by law and are inalienable, have attracted a lot of controversies. It is seen in certain cultures and by some groups as the imposition of Western values on a non-Western world as culture and justice vary from society to society. It has been argued that prior to the emergence of human rights on the world stage various communities had ways of maintaining rights and human dignity. However, attempts have also been made to distinguish human rights from human dignity. One of the major concerns is that different cultures differ in their perception of human rights and especially the rights of women, as this varies from place to place. Mahmoud (2004) argues that differences in culture and perceptions bring up the question of whether the same theory could apply to societies with different cultures and religions. For instance to the West, Islam encourages the submission of women to men. However, in the Muslim world such "submission" is perceived as men protecting their women. The present clash of civilization and unending acts of terror attest to this view.

FEMINISM AND RELIGION

In the West, which is largely Christian, men are leaders in the church. Although some women like Mary Magdalene played an important role in the history of Christianity, the mantle of leadership has always been with men. Paradoxically, leadership of the cults and shrines in African cosmology does not lie solely with men. The priestesses were and are still important in the sociopolitical lives of the people. The goddesses were revered in their respective societies, and their priestesses had a voice in the organization and development of the communities. Cosmological context of many African traditional religions depicts a situation in which women and men play vital roles in the economic, social and political lives of their people, a contrast to the Western religious practices in which men were the dominant actors, while women played mainly peripheral roles in the church. The emergence of women as leaders in the Christian world is a late twentieth century development, and it is a situation that is still critically challenged in many orthodox churches. The Catholic Church, in spite of the need for men to hold leadership positions in the church, is still vehemently opposed to the ordination of women to play the same role as men. An attempt to forcibly ordinate women met with excommunication.[3]

As mentioned earlier, in many African societies, religion and politics go hand in hand. In the precolonial era the rulers were the custodian of culture and the messengers of the gods, and governance was done through them. As much as African states would like to claim secularity, religion cannot be completely ruled out of the political discourse. The application of Western feminist theories to Africa's feminist movement and strategy must be carefully looked into, since the influence of religion on politics cannot be easily wished away, as it is still a potent political instrument in Africa. For example, in spite of years of interaction between the major religious groups in Nigeria, religion is still a major factor in the polity and politics of the state.

Unfortunately for the female gender, since colonization, the major religions in Nigeria, as in most African countries, preach male superiority and domination. On the other hand, religion was an important factor in America's national life, but by 1940, religion was watered down, as religious observance was relegated to the homes and churches. By the 1950s public places and even schools no longer observed religious practices. This gives credence to the views of scholars such as Amali et al that criticize the concept of gender in political studies. They condemn and do not accept universalizing and homogenizing feminist theorizing, as perception differs from place to place.

THE RIGHTS OF WOMEN DENIED

In recent time much has been said about the rights of women. They are topical issues at national and international fora, while the United Nations has become the major actor in the campaign for the rights of women worldwide, an attempt to universalize the rights of women. However, the literature shows that there are differences in the emergence of women's struggle against oppression, even with women within the same environment. In the United States in the 1950s, while the black women wanted their men carried along, white women who dominated the discourse on feminism wanted freedom from their men. Presently, there is a marked difference between the "old model" movement, which was tied to political parties and the new autonomous organizations that represents the interests of all women. These heterogeneous groups are autonomous from state apparatus and political parties and are no longer tied to the apron strings of male dominated parties.[4] This explains and differentiates the feminist struggles by time as the demand varies from a period in history to the other. This view strengthens the need for different theoretical approaches in dealing with issues that concerns various history and ideology. The early struggle in Nigeria such as the Aba women's riot of 1925 and the uprising led by Mrs. Kuti in Abeokuta were to address economic oppression of women. These are different from the current struggle as they are better organized and heterogeneous in nature and demands. They are not ad hoc, but a continuous and well articulated struggle. In Nigeria, for example, there are various nongovernmental organizations networking internally and internationally to ensure women's emancipation and empowerment in various fields.

On a daily basis, news media are filled with discussions on various aspects of women's rights and empowerment programs. The international community more than before is concerned with gender relations as it affects women. Although the United Nations Human Rights Declaration of 1948 has been explicit on women's rights, the emergence of women's rights on the world stage gained momentum in the 1970s, focusing on women's "common oppression." However, it has been well documented that although women are oppressed all over the world, the phrase "common oppression" should be subjected to further debate, making the use of same theories questionable as culture, time and place differ. hooks (2000), writing on feminism in the American experience, notes that common oppression was only used at building solidarity as even women in the United States had different experiences: white versus black and poor versus rich. Similarly, women in the West have had distinctive experiences from women in other parts of the world such as Africa. Evidence has shown that even women within the same environment are not necessarily subjected to the same form of oppression as Muslim women's experiences are different from Christian women. This is also applicable to women in Africa and even in Nigeria where religion and culture play prominent roles in the socialization process, the girl-child and the male-child learn their roles in society. The needs, interests and desired rights of the various groups are critical variables that differ from place to place and as periods in history change. Privileged women knew there were differences even among American women, as they were asking women to organize around their own oppression. In her book, hooks highlights how race, money and states affected the feminist movement in the United States (ibid). This contradiction in the feminist movement within the same society and people shows that applying the same theoretical explanations to different cultures, values and religions might produce faulty results. The current feminist struggle, and that of Africa cannot be driven by only old theories; new ones must emerge to take care of the interests of the various cultures, ideologies, race, religion and the home, which are major factors in women's struggle in Africa.

This brings to mind Africa's socialization process in a patriarchal and matriarchal environment where polygyny is still very much part of the society. Islam is a major religion and it supports a man having more than one wife. In addition, some Christian sects also embrace polygamy. This might not be taken care of by Western-based and value-loaded theories that originated in a system that only support a Christian monogamy. In view of the diverse cultures and socialization processes, human rights as perceived by the West has come under numerous attacks, challenging the existing theories that are in place to explain the subjection and marginalization of women worldwide. These Western-based models have constantly been challenged and criticized as neocolonial. This is one of the reasons why Ake (1992) says that African countries rather than "try to reproduce should share new institutional forms and practice appropriate values and principles."

CONCLUSION

The argument is that no single theory can explain women's positions, as highlighted in the above theories, as each touches different aspects of women's problems. Women come from various classes, races and cultures; these are powerful variables and therefore create differences that must be taken into account. The category "women" is pluralistic, as the socialization and gender assignment vary from society to society. Treating women as a homogenous group is conceptually inappropriate. Recent developments in the world has shown that what some societies hold sacred is held with levity in others. Mahmoud (2004), writing on gender and culture, questions the universality of women's rights. She even argues that "Islam is affected by the culture of the societies into which it is introduced . . . ." She further questions the possibility of having an international women's law as championed by the United Nations (ibid).

Even in non-Islamic societies, some of the views held high in the West do not hold. In Africa, the nature of religious observance still determines the marriage system and polygamy is still widely practiced. Islam accepts it and traditional religion upholds it, and some Christian sects still practice and accept polygamy. Matrilineal culture also gives women both reproductive and productive responsibilities. Ashanti (Akan) women along with the Queen mothers were powerful in precolonial Ghana.[5] The opposition of African women to some issues at the Mexico conference of 1975 and the Beijing conference of 1995 to the imposition of Western gender values on Africans is indicative of their concern for preservation of their culture and opposition to imposition of a gender agenda determined in the West. It affirms the African view that they have a different socialization from the West which should be respected and not relegated to the background.

Women all over the world do not have the same attributes and experiences; as a result of which international standards that do not reflect the African experience cannot be said to be universal. African women do not support the idea of the universality of causes of subordination. Western feminism was designed to meet the needs and aspirations of white women; a feminism, which Africans believe, is characterized by racist arrogance. These theories are limited in their explanation of the oppression of women. They lack a universal applicability and fail to consider the diverse nature of women's lives.

This chapter maintains that the general trends in the oppression of the female gender must not be taken for granted as there are several common causes of female exploitation that cut across culture. A hold on cultural relativity will be an excuse for female oppression. While ensuring that certain aspects of a society's culture are not trampled on, cultural imperialism must be rejected in totality. Feminist theories must allow for differences among women as they are from diverse cultures, ideology and religion, among others. While African women activists and scholars criticize Western feminist theories, they must also note that there are negative and positive aspects of African culture, which international instruments and actions could help to change.

Finally, we uphold the view of Vasquez (1996:59) that "concepts and theories used to construct explanations are leading scholars in the wrong direction," which should not be. This also brings up the view of Mingst (2004:3) that theories are not static:

> theory is situated in a particular time and place, conditioned by ideology, cultural sociological influences. There is no single objective reality, only multiple realities based on individual experiences and perspectives.

Human cultures and ideologies are diverse and issues must not be looked at from narrow Western views only.[6] In addition, most of the feminist theories are formulated by men for women and some like Marxism were not expected or drawn up for women's struggle.

NOTES

1. For more on gender and power relations in Nigeria see R. I. Ako-Nai (2010) *Women, Governance and Democratization in Nigeria and Ghana: A Comparative Study*, VDM, Publishing House Ltd., Berlin.

2. Women's movement in the pre- and past-independence era were majorly focused on welfare and domestic issues. However, women operating with a favorable international environment are demanding equitable share of political power with their men.

3. For more on religion and human rights, see *African Notes*, May/June 2004.

4. bell hooks says bourgeois women only supported their class interests by the ideology of "common oppression."

5. The matrilineal Akam people of Ghana constitute about 50 percent of the population of Ghana. The female leaders were powerful, a position the colonial masters almost destroyed as result of the imposition of British value system of the colonized territory.

6. For more on this see M. Haralambos, with R. M. Heald, *Sociology: Themes and Perspectives*, Bungay, Suffolk: Richard Clay (The Chaucer Press) Ltd., pp. 373–375.

REFERENCES

Amadiume, Ifi (1995) *Gender, Political Systems and Social Movements: A West African Experience.* Dakar: CODESRIA Book Series.
Ake, C. (1992) *The Feasibility of Democracy in Africa.* Ibadan: CREDU.
bell hooks (2000) *Feminist Theory: From Margin to Center.* Cambridge, MA: South End Press.
Bryson, V. (1992) *Feminist Political Theory.* London: Macmillan Press Ltd.
Ferguson, A. (2009) Empowerment, Development and Women's Liberation, in *The Political Interests of Gender Revisited,* A. G. JonasdoHir and K. B. Jones (eds). Manchester, UK: Manchester University Press.
Jones, S. (2000) *Feminist Theory and Christian Theology.* Minneapolis, MN: Augsburg Fortress.
Mamdani, M. (1995) A Critique of the State and Civil Society Parading in Africanist Studies, in M. Mamdani and E. Wemba-dia Wamba (eds), *African Studies in Social Movement and Democracy.* Dakar: CODESRIA Book Series.
Mingst, K. A. (2004) *Essentials of International Relations.* New York: W. W. Norton and Company.
Mohmoud, F. A. (2004) Are Human Rights Universal? Issues of Gender and Culture. *African Notes.*
Oakley, A. (1997) Who is Afraid of Feminism?: Seeing through the Backlash, in M. Halambos *Sociology: Themes and Perspectives.* Slough, UK: University Tutorial Press Limited.
Pereira, C. (1997) Introduction to Gender Studies: An Overview of Concepts, in *Concepts and Methods for Gender and Women's Studies in Nigeria.* Report of the Network for Gender and Women's Studies in Nigeria, No. 2.
Stamp, P. (1983) *Technology, Gender and Power in Africa.* Ottawa: International Research Centre.
Vasquez, J. A. (1996) *Classics of International Relations.* Upper Saddle River, NJ: Prentice-Hall, p. 59.

Part I

WOMEN'S RIGHTS UNDER THE LAW

2

An Overview of the Rights of Nigerian Women under the Laws

Oluwafeyisayo Semiu Kuteyi

ABSTRACT

This chapter seeks to examine the rights accruable to the female gender under the Municipal and Customary Laws of Nigeria. The International Statutes, which confer recognizable rights on the female gender, is also examined. Under the 1999 Constitution of Nigeria, the Criminal Code Act and the Penal Code Act as well as the Labor Laws, some recognition is given to the female gender. Such rights include the right against discriminations, the right of access to court, the right against sexual harassment, among others. These laws are similarly protected under international laws. However, this chapter observes that some customary practices under the various communities in many parts of Nigeria are oppressive to woman. For example, widows pass through some barbaric acts after the death of their husbands while in some communities, inheritance and the right to private ownership of property are denied the female gender. It is further discovered that some old judicial decisions by the Nigeria Court consigned the female gender to the mercy of culture. Also discussed are some recent judgments of the higher courts in Nigeria that have recognized that some cultural practices against women are contrary to the doctrine of equity and the prevailing municipal and international laws. The chapter concludes with the advice to women to harness their political powers recognized under the aforementioned laws as well as other rights granted to them through international laws to unite and forge a common goal in their quest to realize their rights to equal treatment in Nigerian society.

INTRODUCTION

Over the years, the clamor for global recognition of the special role of the female gender in human societies has become loud. From all parts of the globe, the female gender seems to have suddenly found their voices through conferences, seminars, workshops, and symposiums. The common agenda has been the need to tackle the male gender over the perceived unfair treatment of the female sex. Accusations have been made; general and sweeping condemnations have been aimed at men. The male gender has been subjected to the massive attack by women for their perceived role in female discrimination. In fact, at times nature (if not God) has not been spared the attack on the plight of women. Hence, in the opening address at the conference organized by the Constitutional Rights Project (CRF), and the Friedrich Naumann Foundation in Nigeria,[1] Mr. Justice G.G.I. Ojiako[2] has expressed the sentiment that

> At times nature seems to lend a helping hand to this discrimination (against women) starting with the Holy Book, when Adam and Eve, our first parents fell out of God's grace to grass. God Sentenced Eve thus: I shall give you intense pain in childbearing; you will give birth to your children in pain, your yearning will be for your husband and he will dominate you (Genesis 3:16) Jerusalem Bible.[3]

Sometimes in the struggle for recognition, the female gender often sound confused in conceptualizing what their struggle is all about. While this struggle is referred to as "women's rights" or feminism, in one breath, on the other breath, the shout that the struggle is about human rights would rend the air.

Charlotte Bunch tries to explain the confusion when she stated

> When we first began to conceptualize our rights we called our struggle "Women's rights or Feminism." We did not think in terms of "human rights" because we were trying to understand what was distinct in women's experience. Having Conceptualized women's rights, we now know what is missing in the mainstream definition of human rights. Our demand that "women's right is human right" is a return to the mainstream, but not to fit ourselves in on the old terms, but to transform the very definition of human rights.[4]

Whichever angle the women looked at to deal with the female gender, the conclusion has always been that the women are abused, oppressed, intimidated, and are made to be inferior to men.[5] However, the question I seek to address in this chapter is whether there are laws especially made under the Nigerian laws that protect the female gender to the exclusion of the male. In answering this question focus was made on the Municipal Laws of Nigeria, the international legislation on the women's rights, which

Nigeria is a signatory to, and finally the judicial approach to the customary law practices.

RIGHTS IN THE NIGERIAN MUNICIPAL LAWS

Here I shall examine some salient provisions of the Nigerian 1999 Constitution, the criminal as well as the penal codes, and the Labor Act as these provisions relate to the female gender in general.

The 1999 Constitution

The Nigerian Constitution is presently the highest law in the land. During the period of military administration[6] the country witnessed the era of promulgation of military decrees and edicts that whittled down the effect of any existing constitution in the country. However, with the passage of the Nigerian Constitution when democracy was restored in Nigeria,[7] the sacrosanct of the letters of the constitution have become imperative. The provision of S.42 (I)[8] (a) of the Constitution provide thus:

> A Citizen of Nigeria of a particular Community, Ethnic, Group, Place of Origin, Sex, Religions or Political Opinion shall not, by reason only that he is such a person
>
> {a} Be Subjected either expressly by, or in the practical application of any Laws in force in Nigeria or any executive or administrative action of the government, to disabilities or restrictions to which Citizens of Nigeria of other Community, Ethnic Groups, Place of Origin, Sex, Religions or Political Opinions are not made Subject.

This singular, unambiguous, and clear provision of the Constitution means that there should be no discrimination between the male and female gender under the Nigerian context (Kuteyi, 2000:1). With this provision, the female gender is at liberty to access the Court of Law in Nigeria to complain of any discrimination on the ground of sex.

However, it is a sad commentary to note that years after coming into effect of the provision and similar provision under the 1979 Constitution[9] in Nigeria, women have either pretended to be ignorant of the enormous power available under this law or are too complacent to utilize or appropriate the provision of the Constitution to ensure such to their benefit. What we rather see is the daily complaint of discrimination against women that the constitution specifically outlawed. There is yet to be a decided case by the Nigerian Court that sided with men on the issue of discrimination against women.[10] It is my view here that the reality created by the provision of the Constitution is being rendered a myth by the carefree attitude of women.

Criminal Code[11]

Under the Nigerian criminal code there are various provisions that are basically female oriented. Section 218 of the code makes it an offense for anyone to defile girls less than 11 years of age. Under sections 221 of the same code, an attempt to have carnal knowledge of a girl less than 13 years of age carries two years imprisonment. The provision of sections 222, 222^{A}, 223, 224, 225^{A}, 225^{B}, 226, and 227 of the code lists various offenses seeking to protect the female gender from indecent sexual experiences. Under section 222^{B} it is an offense to keep a child under the age of thirteen in a brothel. However, despite the penal consequences of these criminal practices, some men still persist in the act, which is contrary to the above provisions of the law. Again, the sad commentary is that many women are totally ignorant of the provisions of the law made to protect them from some unlawful sexual harassments. Where the criminal acts persist, some women often refuse to voice the outrageous act.

Their silence indirectly condones the shameful acts, thereby encouraging the continuous and persist acts. Both the criminal code and the penal code (Ashiru, 2004:250), which is based on the Sudanese code and was adopted by Northern Nigeria because of its Islamic flavor,[12] contained a provision that make rape a serious criminal offense. The Nigerian Code still considers rape a female affair. This is despite the sentiment now being expressed that rape is gender neutral and nondiscriminatory since both the male and female equally stand the risk of being raped. One can be raped through the vagina, anus, or mouth. No wonder the English Sexual Offences Act 2003[13] has updated the law to make it nondiscriminatory against a male or female.[14] While the law in Nigeria is awaiting to be amended, the provision still persists that only the female gender is protected from the offense of rape in Nigeria. Despite this female-oriented provision, women daily suffer from cases of rape. Hardly can one week pass in Nigeria without a reported case of this ignoble and criminal act being perpetrated against the female gender.

Under the penal code,[15] a conviction for an offence of rape carries a life imprisonment together with a payment of a fine, whereas under the criminal code, the penalty is similarly life imprisonment as well as the possibility of caning.

From the penal provisions discussed above, it can be seen that the female gender are given special protection by the Nigerian laws relating to the commission of sexual offenses against them, yet the penal protection has not yielded the desired protection against sexual abuse as anticipated. It therefore stands to reason that we can conclude that, despite the penal laws and enactments put into place in Nigeria, women and the entire female gender have not benefited very much from the laws especially made to benefit them.

Labor Act

The Labor Act[16] consolidates the law relating to labor in Nigeria. The provisions of sections 54–56 of the act is appropriately termed "Employment of the women" while the provision of section 54 specifically deals with maternity protection for a women before and after the birth of her child. In section 54(5), "child" includes both legitimate and illegitimate children.[17] By virtue of Circular No. 12 of August 2, 1979, the provision of 554 ensures the benefit of both married and unmarried women[18]; under the act[19] a woman with an infant may not enter into any contract to work at night (Emiola, 2000:43) in an industrial or agricultural undertaking except when the woman is a nurse or a woman holding managerial positions in which she would not perform manual labor.[20]

This provision is solely for the benefit of the female gender in the Nigerian legal system. But the problem is that an average employed woman in Nigeria is ignorant of this law that protects her working conditions.

THE RIGHTS OF WOMEN UNDER THE INTERNATIONAL LAWS

Apart from the municipal laws, Nigeria as a member of the international community is a signatory to many international laws and conventions as a contracting party. Graciously enough, many of these laws seek not only to create equality between men and women, there were also specific laws made to protect women as well. Some of these laws shall now be considered.

The United Nations Charter and Universal Declarations of Human Rights[21]

This charter is a basic[22] provision of International Human Rights Law. It ensures freedom from racial, sexual, and religious discrimination in a variety of ways. Articles 1 and 2 are direct protections against discrimination based on sex. For example, Article 1 states as follows:

> All human beings are born free and equally in dignity and rights. . . .

While Article 2 provides inter-alia thus

> Everyone is entitled to all the right and freedom set forth in this declaration without distinction of any kind such as race, color, sex, language, religion, political or other opinions, national or social origin, property, birth or other status.

Article 21 covers the political rights of all sexes. The provision states that

> Everyone has the right to take part in the Government of his Country directly or through freely chosen representative.

By this singular provision, it is an abuse of rights of women if they are barred from personally exercising a voting right[23] or when they are not allowed to contest elections into elective positions or not permitted to occupy political posts. Closely associated with the provision of Article 21 of the charter in context and spirit is the United Nation Convention on Political Rights of Women.[24]

The convention is a means of encouraging contracting parties to the convention who desire to implement the principles of equality of rights for men and women contained in the 1948 Charter of the United Nations. Article 1–3 of the charter encourages women to be entitled to vote in all elections on equal terms with men without any discrimination. Women are eligible for election into all publicly elected bodies as well as entitled to hold public offices and to exercise all public functions.

Apart from the above, there are other international conventions relating to protection of the female gender.[25] At the Vienna conference, women were especially recognized as being vulnerable in the international community; no wonder the conference confirmed that the full and equal participation of women in political, civil, economic, social, and cultural life at all national, religious, and international forum as well as eradication of all forms of discrimination on the grounds of sex was an important objective. The Vienna Conference coincided with the Universal Declaration on the Elimination of Violence against Women.[26]

The 1995 Beijing Declaration

Perhaps the loudest and most vocal conference on the rights of women in which the Nigeria government encouraged the Nigerian women to attend and participate was the September 1995 Fourth United National Conference on Women held in Beijing, China.

Chapter 1 of the Mission Statement of the conference is titled "An Agenda for Women Empowerment."

The focus was on actions to eradicate poverty, eliminate violence and inequality in education, promotion of women rights, and easy access to relevant health care systems.

Much has been said and written about the 1995 conference. However, the salient spirit behind the conference is to further draw the attention of women to their rights, which is internationally recognized. Their focus was similarly drawn to the relevant laws and opportunities provided for the female gender under the existing laws in their various countries.

The Africa Charter on Human and People's Rights[27]

This Charter on Human and People's Right is an African affair. It is a continental treaty binding on all states that have signed, ratified, or assented to it. Nigeria is one of such states. The charter was entered into force officially on October 21, 1986. Some of the earlier recognized United Nation Rights are restated in the charter; Article 13 provides for the right to participate directly or through chosen representatives in political matters.[28] Article 17 provides for the right of education as a duty of the state to the citizenry without any discrimination. And Article 18 provides for the family as the natural unit and basis of society and protection of women's rights.

Apart from the provisions of the 1995 Beijing Declaration, Nigeria is also a signatory to the other international statutes relating to the rights and protection of women. Some of these are:

i. Convention on the Elimination of All Forms of Discrimination Against Women.[29]
ii. Declaration on the Elimination of Discrimination Against Women.[30]
iii. Convention on Consent to Marriage, Minimum Age for Marriage and Registration of Marriage which came into force in December 1973.[31]

The salient point that this chapter strives to do is project the fact that Nigerian women have always been recognized by all the enabling municipal and international statutes in which Nigeria is a signatory as a protected species and one that qualifies for special attention and protection.

The Nigerian government dares not openly deny the projected and protected rights of women without encountering the problem of international accusation and condemnation. However, a cursory look at the various customary law and practices in Nigerian communities may lead to the conclusion that Nigerian women are not protected at all from abuse of their inanimate rights and privileges. Similar observation may also be seen in the area of religious practices among the Nigerian communities. To this end, the focus of this chapter shall turn to the customary laws and religious practices in Nigerian communities.

NIGERIAN WOMEN UNDER THE CUSTOMARY LAWS IN NIGERIA

Generally, the customary law is the traditional but unwritten law of the people. It is generally handed down from one generation to another.[32]

The test of the validity of a custom is that it should not be repugnant to natural Justice, Equity, and Good conscience. It must not be incompatible either directly or indirectly with any written law in force and which is not contrary to public policy. It is sad to note that the various rights that are accruable to the women are not so recognized under the Customary Laws of various communities in Nigeria. The reality on ground may then be that rights of women as contained in both the municipal laws and international statutes may well be considered as a myth rather than a reality. The truth is that some customary practices have eroded the dignity of women by the reason of their barbaric practices. Although there is nothing inherently bad in the cultural belief of the communities in Nigeria. Many, however, are changing as a result of global interaction. Indeed Rev. Father Matthew H. Kukah stated[33] that

> Culture is dynamic and the barometer for gauging any society's progress is the extent to which it can decide on what to borrow and what to retain or throw away.[34]

However, a perusal of some of the cultural practices would reveal the bastardization of the inalienable rights of the female genders in the name of culture. For[35] example, Jane Osagie, while examining the case of widowhood in South West Nigeria, is of the opinion that

> Many practices harmful to women's health are still being widely carried out in the name of widowhood rites.

On her own part, while writing on the religious, culture and tradition in Cross River State of Nigeria, Akpo Offiong Bassey[36] presented two different scenarios.

Firstly, where a woman has a still birth, she is made to scrape her hair, trek into the evil forest at dawn and sacrifice to appease the gods of the land. No one is concerned with the trauma of neither the pangs she had passed through nor keen on consoling her. In order words, she is not seen as a human being. If she fails to do these, she is not allowed to visit pregnant women or women who had just had babies. The second situation is the widowhood practice. Where a man of consequence dies, his wife or wives are forced into seclusion. They are not to have their bath nor change their apparels. They are to rub cow dung and palm oil on their body. The hair must be kept bushy. They sleep on hard floor and eat from broken earthen plates. They are expected to cry every morning throughout the mourning period. All these are said to be ways of showing her love and appreciation for the man. On the day of burial, the wives and children are beaten mercilessly by the Ekpe cult and their associate. The wives are to wear black apparels for about two years before changing to other colors. In some areas like AGOI[37] and BOKI,[38] she is expected to refund her bride price and go back home. On the contrary, to the above, the men are not bound by this traditional practice. Men are not to mourn their deceased wives. They are encouraged and expected to look for replacements during the mourning period. Indeed, amongst some tribes in Yoruba Land, a widower is expected to sleep with another woman the night preceding his dead wife's burial.

According to Sam Egwu[39] the Igala women of Kogi State of Nigeria and the Tiv people of Benue State have little in common in matter relating to the ownership of land. While the Igala women are not allowed to engage in agricultural venture in whatever form, she is totally disallowed from owning land. Farming is seen as a predominantly men's occupation. The labor of women is only required during the harvesting period.

Apart from the little that is offered as compensation over which she has no control, men claim exclusive control over the proceeds of the farm. On the other hand, the Tiv women have access to sufficient farmland but only as long as they remain married and live with their husband. Tiv women on their own do not and cannot enjoy ownership of the family land. On cultural and traditional practices relating to ownership and succession right of the Ikeduru Local Government Area of Imo State in the South Eastern part of Nigeria, May Victoria. Mbu[40] wrote that the birth of a male child is welcome more than that of a female child. To an average Igbo man (of the South East) it is better to have all male children than to have all female children who will eventually leave the home for marriage. Traditionally, a woman is from birth made to realize and feel that she is inferior to men. Women are not expected to own property. The role is limited to being the workforce in the farms. She has no right to sell or lease farmland. She cannot inherit property in either her father's house or in her husband's house. Her ownership of property starts and ends with her personal domestic animals, and the only way a women can have a share in her husband's property is by having a male child.

A woman is regarded as property to be inherited alongside[41] her husband's property. The eldest son and not the widow will inherit his entire father's property.

The widow's right to continue living in her husband's home depends on whether or not she has a son, and if her children are too young, the eldest male relative of the husband inherits the property.

The picture above no doubt depicted an inherent belief of the people from different parts of Nigeria. The troubling part of the scenario was that the earlier judicial attitudes favored this position. Until recently[42] judicial pronouncement of the Nigerian courts gave accent to the rights of women being subsumed in her husband or child right. For example, in March 1999, to mark the United Nations International Women's Day, the Zones International Club, Ibadan Oyo State of Nigeria, organized a lecture on the inheritance right of women. The club invited Hon. Justice M. O. Onalaja JCA[43] (now retired) as the guest lecturer. The honorable justice of the Nigerian Court of Appeal examined the vexed issue of the inheritance right of the women under the Customary Laws as compared with the Muslim Law of

Succession. He confirmed that the Muslim laws are more liberal and more favorable to women than the Customary Laws. Relying on the old case of *Nezianyan v. Okegbu*,[44] which decided that if the husband of a woman dies without any male issues, his real property descends to his family. Upon evidence of good behavior she may be allowed to continue to occupy the deceased's husband's house. If the woman does not remarry to any members of her deceased husband's family but remains in his family, she can only cultivate a portion of her husband's farmland. This decision accentuated the Onitsha Customary Law of the South Eastern part of Nigeria.

Under the Bini and Ishan Customary Law of the South South Geo-Political Zone of Nigeria, inheritance is governed by the principle of progenitor whereby the eldest son succeeds his father's real, personal and intangible assets and all disposal properties.[45]

This position was re-echoed as recently as in 1997, by the Nigerian Supreme Court. In the case of *Akinnubi v. Akinnubi*[46] the court still held on to the old judicial attitude of consigning women to the mercy of culture. The court held that[47]

> Under the Yoruba Customary Law, a widow under an intestacy is regarded as part of the estate of her deceased family, she could neither be entitled to apply for a grant of letters of Administration nor to be appointed as Co-Administration of her deceased husband's estate.[48]

A decision like this undoubtedly gives a gloomy picture of the future of the desire of women to harness the benefits inherent in the various laws. However, other judgments of the Nigerian Court of Appeal[49] seem to tacitly have postdated this earlier judicial position.

In the case of *Mojekwu v. Mojekwu*[50] the Court of Appeal in Nigeria declared that the "Oli-Ekpe" Customary Law of Nnewi (South East Nigeria), which permits the son of the brother of a deceased person to inherit his property to the exclusion of his female child, as discriminatory and therefore inconsistent with the doctrine of equity.

In this judgment generally regarded as a landmark,[51] Hon. Justice Niki Tobi JCA (as he then was) stated as follows:

> We need not travel all the way to Beijing to know that some of our Customs, including the Nnewi's "Oli-Ekpe" Custom are not Consistent with our Civilized world in which we all live today, including the appellant. In my humble view, it is the monopoly of God to determine the sex of a baby and not the parents. Although the scientists would disagree with this divine truth, I believe that God the creator of human being is also the final authority of who should be male or female. Accordingly, for a Custom or Customary Law to discriminate against a particular sex is to say the least an affront on the Almighty God Himself. Let nobody do such a thing. On my part, I have no difficulty in

holding that the "Oli-Ekpe" Custom of Nnewi is repugnant to natural justice, equity and good conscience.

While we unreservedly adopt this landmark pronouncement of the Honorable Law Lord, we submit that the Oli-Ekpe Custom is a violent violation of the spirit of S.42 of the Nigeria 1999 Constitution which prohibits discrimination on ground of ethnic group, place of origin, sex, religion and political opinion.

Another judgment of the Nigerian Court of Appeal which adopted the ratio and spirit of the Mojekwu's case is the case of *Nnanyelugo v. Nnanyelugo*[52] delivered on July 12, 2007 by the Enugu Division of the Court of Appeal.[53] The court came out boldly to hold that

> A legend has it that around this jurisdiction when a man dies intestate, his family members especially the male members of his extended family always and invariably claim to be the owners or as in this case co-owners of his property. There is usually the grand desire to manipulate the widows and sometimes the offspring's of the deceased if they are young and tender.[54]

In the case, the two brothers of the deceased husband of the respondent had insisted that the respondent, being a widow, had no business being involved in her late husband's property. The court went further to hold that:

> The trial judge's perpetual injunction granted to the 1st Respondent is a step in the right direction of ensuring that justice is done to widows with their children in accordance with the law. This action will go a long way to reduce the plight of dispossession of widows and their children to the deceased husband's property. At the root of this case is the gross economic deprivation of Stephen Nnanyelugo Family and indeed most deceased husbands who had not left a Will as regards the disposition of his estate. . . . The Courts now are posed to do substantial justice and not allow repugnant Traditions, Customs and Traditional Law of inheritance or even technicalities distract them from achieving substantial justice. . . . After a careful and exhaustive analysis of the attitudes of dejection and economic deprivation meted out to widows in this Country (Nigeria) generally and in particular in this jurisdiction, that gave rise to such decisions as in MOJEKWU V MOJEKWU (Supra) it behoves this Court to commend the decision of the trial Court in this case.[55]

It is submitted that the decision of the Nigerian Court of Appeal is a welcome development in the new globalized clamor for the enforcement of the spirit of the laws that tend to give equality to both the male and the female genders. The fact that the Nigerian Supreme Court is yet to finally lay to rest this all important issue. However, the pronouncement of the Court in Nnanyelugo will for a long time remain a reference point.

THE POLITICAL RIGHTS OF THE NIGERIAN WOMEN

Nigerian society is socially stratified into two groups. These are the educated and the illiterates. Similarly, the society is predominantly polarized into two religions groups which are Islamic religion and Christian religion. The traditional region is gradually giving way to these two dominant religions.

No doubt, the political rights of the female gender are contained in both the municipal as well as the international statutes to which Nigeria is a signatory. While the educated (non-Muslim) are easily able to access and harness provisions of these laws to their benefit, many illiterate majority are not so able.

Thus education has afforded the few minority women to access their political rights in Nigeria in all ramifications. The majority being illiterate only limited their exercise of political power to voting on election period. Even then, their power may be subjected to the directives of men.

However, the Muslim women[56] are not so encouraged to exercise these political rights, their level of education notwithstanding. Justifying this restriction Adeniyi O. Adewola,[57] citing copiously from the Holy Quran, reiterated the belief that generally, Muslim women are not supposed to lead the men folk. Their leadership role is limited. But when it comes to participation in political campaigns, it is forbidden for women to "engage in political campaigns or rallies" since it is forbidden for her to intermingle with men. She may express her political belief in a write-up. She is an object of concealment. According to Adeniyi, the Prophet abhors a woman being the leader of the society. Islam, she says, forbids women to rule over men or a community of men and women. She gave example of Sahir Bulshari who on being told that the people of Persia made a female their queen retorted: "Never would such Nation succeed which makes a woman their ruler." Adeniyi made reference to the Biblical Queen of Sheba[58] who was a good ruler and allegedly relinquished her position of the Queen when she converted to the Islamic religion.

Giving some reasons such as subjection to husband's wishes, pregnancy and sucking and even menstruation as inhibitions to women being able to climb the leadership ladder, she concluded that the participation of women in active politics and in jobs outside the home has often lead to disintegration of the home and break ups in marriages. As lofty as the reasons given above may seem, it is submitted that Adeniyi has not given enough logical reasons that would explain why the provisions of the laws should be subjected to religious limitation. In fact earlier on in her thesis, under the sub-topic "feminism," she wrote that

> The cruelty or injustice against women over the years in different society fueled the agitation by women for their rights to be recognized in the society.

> This gave rise to feminist movement, seeking to improve the quality of life for women.[59]

And under the specific sub topic "Islamic Feminism,"[60] she stated that

> Islamic feminism gleaned from the writing and work of Muslim protagonists as a feminist discourse and practice that derives its understanding and mandate from the Quran, seeking rights and justice within the framework of gender equality for women and men in the totality of their existence. Islamic Feminism explicates the idea of gender equality as part and parcel of the Qur'an notion of equality of all human beings and calls for the implementation of gender equality in the state, civil institutions and everyday life. . . . Islamic feminism aims to recover the notion of gender equality.

With the above scenario, it is humbly submitted that if Islamic feminism is aimed at what Adeniyi projected it to be, it is wrong to have the latter affirmed that women's participation in politics is a disservice and a taboo to the Islamic norms.

CONCLUSION

In this chapter, we have been able to examine some laws in Nigeria made to favor the female gender. International statues have also been examined. The cultural and traditional belief of the people have been focused on. The limitation placed on political rights of women has also been examined. It is the view of this chapter that there are numerous legislation which have accorded the female gender the necessary platform to insist on their rights. Where there is religious bigotry, attempt should be made to be more proactive and follow the drift of the globalized world. However, there is a need for a cohesion of various female empowerment movements and organizations. Women as a body should press forward to champion a bill in the National Assembly to call for the ratification of all the existing international conventions on the rights of women.

Women should learn to work together as a body. The feminist nature and pettiness which is a bane of oneness should be discarded. They can tap from their enormous influence on the male gender by asking for a favorable atmosphere for development. They can similarly mobilize for sensitive and powerful political position. Already within a span of nine years of democratic rule in Nigeria[61] women have been made a Minister of Finance and Speaker of the House of Representatives. Sensitive positions have been given to them in Nigerian political, economic[62] as well as social[63] spheres. They should strive to improve on their agitation and while basking in the euphoria of this achievement, move forward to press for more.[64]

It is our submission that when all these suggestions are considered and implemented, then it may be concluded that the rights of Nigerian women under the laws are a reality and not a mere myth. It is a great achievement that the Nigerian society has moved from the 1935 position in which the Chief Secretary to government, in a reply to Lady Abayomi's representation that "both sexes must be equally and fairly educated and equally paid" said "Women don't make good Saleswomen and since women don't have the financial responsibilities as men, they should[65] not receive equal salaries."

This unfortunate preindependent colonial Nigeria pronouncement has gone into oblivion, the women folks should ensure that the interred body of this negative sentiment is never allowed to be resurrected.

NOTES

1. At the Concorde Hotel Oweri, Imo State, Nigeria between May 15 and May 16, 1995.
2. The Chief Judge of Imo State of Nigeria.
3. See the report of a conference organized by CPR and the Friedrich Naumann Foundation published in December 1995 at P.1.
4. Director, the Centre for Global issue and women's leadership, Rutgers, New Jersey, quoted in *Women's Rights Is Human Rights* by Isabella Okegbue, associate professor and director of research at the Nigeria Institute of Advanced Legal Studies (NIALS), occasional paper series (1996), P.1.
5. See, for example, Joy Ngozi Ezello, *The Law and Women in Nigeria; Ifeoma Unobagha, Women, the Law and Women* etc. and their contribution to the CRD Conferences at Oweri, Nigeria, in 1995.
6. Basically, since 1966 to 1999 with an interregnum of 1979 to December 1983, when there was a civilian administration.
7. For instance, May 29, 1999.
8. See S. 39 (1) (a) of the 1979 Constitution which is *parimateria* with the provision of S. 42(1) (a) of the 1999 Constitution.
9. See, for example, *Nnanyelugo v. Nnanyelugo* (2008) All F.W.L.R pt 401 at p. 897; *Mojekwu v. Mojekwu* (2000) SNWLR Pt 657.
10. Cap 77 LFN 1990.
11. CAP 189 Laws of Northern Nigeria 1963.
12. The Sexual Offences Bill received the Royal Assent and came into force in England in May 2004.
13. See M. O. A. Ashiru (Supra) who viewed that the law of rape in Nigeria is archaic and needs to be amended to apply to both male and female gender.
14. CAP 189 Laws of Northern Nigeria 1963.
15. CAP 198 LFN 1990.
16. By provision of S.42 (2) of the 1999 Constitution of Nigeria the dichotomy between legitimate and illegitimate child has been removed.
17. See law relating to maternity leave by Emeka Chiannu (1997), chapter 3.
18. Section 55.

19. Section 55 (1).
20. Approved by Rebohition 217 A (III) of the General Assembly, December 10, 1948.
21. Human Right in International Law and Policy issues. Edited by Meron, p. 309.
22. Article 21 of the Charter covers the political rights of all sexes.
23. As it was the position during the First Republic in Nigeria when some Northern Nigerian Muslim women were not allowed to vote by their husband due to their religious beliefs.
24. Approved by Resolution 640 (VII) of the General Assembly, December 20, 1952. It entered into force on July 7, 1954.
25. See, for example, the 1979 Convention on the Elimination of All Forms of Discrimination against Women.
26. See *International Law* by Rebecca M. N Wallace, 3rd Ed. (1997) pp. 216–218.
27. CAP 10 Laws of the Federation of Nigeria 1990.
28. See manual on *Gender Specific Right Litigation and Protection Strategies*, edited by Eze Onyekpere, Chapter 5.
29. Adapted by the U.N. General Assembly Resolution 34/180 of December 1979 and entered into force on September 3, 1981.
30. U.N. General Assembly Resolution 2263 (XXII) of November 7, 1969.
31. Proclaimed by the General Assembly Resolution 3318 (XXIV) of December 14, 1974.
32. See S26(I) of the High Court of Lagos State CAP 1973 CAP 62 and see Obilade.
33. Discrimination, Religion and Culture. A Theoretical Approach—Eliminating Discrimination against Women—Constitutional Rights Project, 1995 P.20.
34. Ibid, p. 21.
35. *The Case of Widowhood in South West Nigeria*, ibid, p. 23.
36. *Religion, Culture and Tradition in Cross Rivers State*, ibid., pp. 24–25.
37. One of the tribes of Tiv of Benue state.
38. Another tribe of the Tiv Kingdom of Benue State.
39. *Womanhood among the Tiv of Benue State and Igala of Kogi State*, ibid., p. 28.
40. *Cultural and Traditional Practices: The Ikeduru* example, ibid., p. 30.
41. See also BAOBAB for Women's Human Rights Legal Literacy Series 1. Against Violence against Women (2000), p. 7.
42. Possibly from the case of *Mojekwu v. Mojekwu* (1997) NWLR, p. 572.
43. Formerly of the Court of Appeal Ibadan Division.
44. (1967) I All NLR 352.
45. See *Nigeria Tribune* of Monday, March 8, 1997, p. 7.
46. (1997) 46 LRCN 137.
47. See also *Bolaji v. Akapo & Ors* 2FNR 241 at 245 and *Aileru & Ors v. Anibi* 20 NLR 46.
48. At p. 155.
49. See, for example, *Mojekwu v. Mojekwu* (1997) 7(NWLR) pt 512, p. 283 and *Nnanyelugo v. Nnanyelugo* (2008). All F.W.L.R. pt 401, p. 97.
50. Supra.
51. See O. S. Oyelade, infra note 67.
52. Supra.

53. Per Denton, West JCA.
54. At p. 908.
55. At pp. 915–916.
56. Mostly from the northern part of Nigeria.
57. See Adeniyi and Omotayo Adeola, Women's Rights under the Shariah, an essay submitted in partial fulfillment of the requirement for the award of bachelor of law degree (LLB) of the Obafemi Awolowo University Ile-Ife Nigeria (2007).
58. The Holy Bible: 1 King 10 1–13.
59. At p. 67.
60. At p. 73.
61. For instance, since May 29, 1999.
62. For example, the Director General of the Nigerian Stock Exchange is a woman while the Nigerian Administration of Foods and Drugs (NAFDAC) is men.
63. The current head of the Economic and Financial Crime Commission (EFCC) is a woman.
64. NAPTIP, i.e., National Agency for the Prohibition of Traffic in Persons and Other Related Matter, is a law designed to eradicate the trafficking of the female gender for commercial sex purpose outside the shore of Nigeria to Europe and other countries. The law makes it a criminal offence to engage in such activities. The Executive Secretary Mrs. Carol Ndaguba is also a woman. Indeed some wives of states governors, e.g., Edo State have made the challenge to this social problem a pet project to which they supervise personally.
65. Quoted by Oyelade O. S Women's Human Rights in Africa: Myth or Reality seminar presented at the faculty of Law Obafemi Awolowo University Ile-Ife Nigeria.

3

Women's Rights, Violence, and Gender Discrimination

The Nigerian Circumstances

A. A. Idowu

ABSTRACT

This chapter examines women's rights, violence, and gender discrimination within the context of Nigerian socioeconomic, cultural, educational, and political circumstances. This approach was with a view to appraising how far, the relevant governmental, non-governmental authorities and other stakeholders had complied with domestic laws, international legal instruments and best practices to recognize, protect and advance the rights and freedom of women in Nigeria. The author relied on quantitative and theoretical methods of research assisted by primary and secondary sources of information. The data obtained were subjected to content analysis. It was found that despite a sizeable number of laws and constitutional provisions outlawing women's violence, gender inequality and discrimination in Nigeria, not much success had been recorded. There were still instances of violence against women such as rape, forced marriage, discrimination, assault, battery, trafficking and a host of other abuses. The essay concluded that the present sorry state of women's rights in Nigeria cannot pave a way for the actualization of the much acclaimed 35 percent affirmative action of women involvement in governance toward the 2020 Millennium Development Goals.

INTRODUCTION

Over the ages, students of history and sociology had maintained that certain groups of people who were vulnerable to abuses and violations of their rights existed in each epoch and every society. A sizable number of such groups were the peoples under colonial regimes who formerly had no rights of their own but later allowed by virtue of the United Nations Charter to exercise their rights of self-determination.[1] However, there are still groups of human beings who are particularly vulnerable to arbitrary and wanton deprivation of their rights and fundamental freedoms. In view of their disabilities probably arising from physical challenges, old age, minority, sex, religion and background; such people are not always in a position to assert their rights and defend themselves (Gasiokwu, 2003:140). Examples of these persons are women, children, disabled, mentally retarded persons of different ethnic, religious and linguistic groups, those who are born out of wedlock, aliens and members of indigenous populations.

Fortunately, some international legal instruments under the auspices of the United Nations Organization had emerged over the years proclaiming equality of rights and basic freedoms for all persons.[2] There are also other International Regional Declarations which confirm that those vulnerable class of human beings should have special treatments and guidance as may be necessary to develop their skills, manage their abilities and maximize their potentials so as to enable them to contribute their quotas to the development of their various societies.[3] Aside from the issue of protection of the rights of vulnerable groups, most nations have also entrenched provisions safeguarding such rights in their national constitutions and statutes. In Nigeria for instance, fundamental rights provisions have always appeared in various constitutions for the purpose of protecting all categories of human beings including vulnerable groups.[4] There are also sections of Nigerian statutes which forbid various offences against individual existence, safety and fundamental freedoms in the society.[5] In addition, Nigeria has also ratified many international treaties, conventions and declarations with other international communities through the umbrella of the United Nations Organization bordering on the rights and freedoms of vulnerable peoples.[6] Laudable as the above development appears to be, efforts at carrying out effective legal reforms and ensuring adequate prevention of violence and discrimination against women in Nigeria have been fruitless. For example, the National Assembly of Nigeria has not passed two of the oldest bills pending before it on Violence against Women and Freedom of Information Bill as at November 2010. Over the years, all efforts at providing a better and workable legal framework for protecting women and other vulnerable groups like children and the disabled have failed. It is quite unfortunate to recount that the federal government of Nigeria had, on one occasion, either knowingly or unknowingly, to note that:

> Nigeria law has copious provisions to safeguard the rights of women against abuse of all forms of maltreatments. Assault and battery have been made subjects of both civil and criminal laws, with the criminal aspects attracting very

stiff and severer penalties. *There is, therefore, no need for a special law on violence against women.*[7]

Giving the above purported position of the federal authority, there is no doubt that the issues of safeguarding women and other vulnerable groups from violence, abuses and all sorts of deprivation are almost relegated in Nigeria. Fortunately, the new trends in governmental agenda border on national rebranding, Affirmative Action for women's participation in governance and aspiring toward the Millennium Development Goals. There is no way by which Nigeria can realize her dreams in this respect without taking concerted efforts at following the footsteps of other advanced nations for advancing the rights and freedoms of the people. This essay begins with abstract followed by an introduction. It embarks on theoretical framework for some key words and phrases in the topic before appraising the nature of women's rights, violence and gender discrimination as well as causative factors.

RIGHTS OF WOMEN AND OTHER VULNERABLE GROUPS

The foundations of human rights in general are rooted in certain philosophical and ideological principles relating to different customs, traits, traditions and religions of peoples with diverse ethnic and tribal affiliations in Nigeria just as it is, in other multi-cultural societies of Africa, America and Asia (Engels, 1884). Despite the differences in peoples' culture, customs and traditions, recognition, protection and advancement of human rights have become issues of universal application throughout the world especially in the newly independent nations. Although there are some fundamental species of human rights common to all peoples irrespective of their backgrounds, certain specific notions of rights have also been attributed to women and other vulnerable groups. Women are regarded as adult female human beings (Hornby, 2000:1373), but for the purpose of this essay, the word "women" is taken to mean female human beings in general, such as female children, who by their sex and age are not as strong, rugged or vibrant enough to withstand much external rigors or violence like their male counterparts.

The phrase "vulnerable groups" refers to classes of human beings who are open to attack[8] or susceptible to confrontations, abuses or violence by other groups of people in the society or by their surrounding climatic or physical circumstances. These are human beings who, by reasons of their tender nature and age, cannot resist much pressure from external influence. Vulnerable groups are also persons who are minorities under different political authorities where they have no opportunities to express their opinions, freedoms and right of self-determinations.

In both domestic and international laws, certain fundamental rights have been recognized which are common to all categories of human beings including women. These include: rights to life, dignity of human person, personal liberty, fair hearing, private and family life, freedom of thought, conscience and religion, freedom of expression and the press, peaceful assembly and association, freedom of movement, freedom from discrimination and rights to property.[9] Apart from these species of fundamental rights, many constitutions of prominent nations also contain another category of rights bordering on obligations of governments toward citizens, duties of citizens and privileges expected to be enjoyed by the people through effective governance. This category of rights as contained in the Constitution of the Federal Republic of Nigeria, 1999 refers to fundamental obligations of government; relationship between government and the people; political objectives; economic objectives; social objectives; educational objectives; environmental objectives; foreign policy objectives; directive on Nigerian cultures; obligation of the mass media; national ethics and duties of the citizens toward the State.[10]

It is important to note that while all classes of human beings including vulnerable groups are both entitled to the foregoing enumerated species of human rights, vulnerable groups by virtue of their special difficult and imperfect circumstances also enjoy certain set of rights already recognized under various domestic and international laws. Some of them are: rights to equality; security; freedom from slavery and forced labor; torture or degrading treatment; recognition as a person to seek a remedy before a competent court or tribunal; political participation; freedom from forced and premature marriage; marriage inheritance; sexual decisions; freedom of women to demand fidelity from their husbands; education; freedom from harmful traditional practices like female genital mutilation; adequate food and clean water; social security and reproductive rights (Schulera, 1997: 8-12).

VIOLENCE AGAINST WOMEN OR DOMESTIC VIOLENCE

The word "violence" has been legally defined as the use of physical force usually accompanied by fury, vehemence or outrage (Garner, 2004:1601). In the context of this chapter, the expression "violence against women or domestic violence" is the unlawful use of physical force to gain an advantage or realize a particular objective. It is violence between members of a household, usually spouses such as an assault or battery committed by one member of a household against another. Domestic violence can also be expressed as the infliction of physical injury or the creation of a reasonable fear that physical injury or harm will be inflicted by a parent or a member of family against a child or by a husband against his wife and vice versa.[11]

Violence against women can also be seen as physical, verbal or emotional abuse by one member of a family to another which is reported to be common at present and more dangerous to the stability of the society. The damage that domestic violence inflicts has serious debilitating effects on the structure of the society while it equally destroys the victims. According to Itoro Eze-Anaba (2009:44), "it is generally agreed that when there is a war in the streets, you run to the house for safety; but when there is war in the house, where do you run to." Violence within the home among members of the same family who are expected to be bound together by a fortified code of love, affection and compassion leaves psychological scars on other members of the family, which may prove difficult to erase.

In Nigeria at present, despite governmental efforts at domesticating international legal instruments for the protection of women's rights like the United Nations Convention on the Eradication of all forms of Discrimination against Women (CEDAW), domestic violence remains an increasing burden on female folks due to its persistence and galloping phenomena. The problem of domestic violence in Nigeria has a wide intersection between other problems confronting women such as their economic, social, educational and political disempowerment. Other perennial problems are inequality, personal development and reproductive and inheritance rights.

Violence against women has many notable effects and implications. These include: high level of mortality, permanent injuries, bruises, cuts, concussions and somatic complaints. Violence may come in the form of physical harm, psychological attacks, threatening behavior, forced sexual acts like rape and harassment. Abuse in the nature of violence also leads to miscarriage, serious impairment, damage to joints, partial loss of hearing or visions, burns, bites and wounds. The psychological effects of violence on women can also include anxiety, fatigue, post-traumatic stress, sleeping and eating disorder, depression, sexual dysfunction and premature menstrual periods. In some cases, researchers have also confirmed that violence engendering forced sexual acts, put women at risk of sexuality transmitted infections including HIV/AIDS, unwanted pregnancies and obstetric complications (GDW, 2003:11). It may also prevent women from using appropriate contraceptives thereby, increasing the risk of reproductive health hazards and even death. Unfortunately, in a developing nation like Nigeria where healthcare services are inadequate, prompt attention to abused women is often impossible.

GENDER DISCRIMINATION AND INEQUALITY

Immediate sense of awareness about issues of discrimination and gender inequality was noticed as far back as 1948 when the United Nations Universal Declaration of Human Rights was written. The first draft of Article 1 of the Declaration provided that "all men are . . . equal in dignity and rights." In order to ensure that this statement would not be understood to mean that women are excluded, the female members on the Drafting Commission insisted that the language be changed to what now appears in the Article was "all human beings are born free and equal in dignity and rights" (Awake!, 1998:9). The pertinent question is whether the change effected in the language of the Article had ever changed the position of women in Nigeria and other developing nations. It is important to stress that the phenomena of discrimination against women and gender inequality had been firmly entrenched in the cultures of many societies.

The word "gender" refers to the fact of being male or female (Hornby, 2000:492). It is used in this essay to refer to women or female folks especially in Nigeria. Discrimination has been expressed as the effect of a law or established practice that confers privileges on a certain class or that denies privileges to a certain class because of race, sex, religion etc. (Garner, 2004:500). Gender discrimination within the purview of this chapter therefore, means discrimination or all forms of denials based on gender, especially against women. Equality on the other hand is defined as the quality or state of being equal, especially in power, political, social or economic status (ibid.). It goes without saying that the phrase "gender inequality" portends a situation of imbalance between the positions of men and women in the society. It refers to various forms of preferential treatments tilting favorably toward men at the disadvantage of the women folks. In other words, it can also be expressed as the inability of women and other vulnerable groups to stand on the same socioeconomic, cultural, political and educational pedestals with their male counterparts in the society.

Historically, the societies and cultures of Nigeria are pervaded with skepticism toward any attempt by the womenfolk to go beyond traditional limits to women's self-expression, let alone competing with and leveling up with men. It is often said that "a women's place is in the kitchen," This belief positions women as domestic servants who are of no relevance in the society. In fact, a woman who ventures into the public, takes part in politics, assumes a public office or joins a religious ministry as a clergy risks discrimination even from other women (Iboro, 2010:87). Studies on traditional socialization practices in Nigeria, according to Nelson, show that they are male-biased. Male children are trained to become heads of families, breadwinners and decision makers, while female children are taught how to be loyal, faithful, diligent and subservient to their husbands. Male children are given some freedom of speech and movements outside their homes while their female counterparts are preoccupied with domestic chores and their movements closely monitored (ibid.). In the northern parts of Nigeria, seclusion of women and restriction of their movements are serious practices due to Islamic purdals tradition. These restrictions on women and female folks have made it difficult for them to acquire relevant skills through effective education.

According to Jennings, social scientists on gender issues have offered three major explanations for the disparity between men and women's access to socioeconomic and political power in Nigeria:

(a) the situational explanation which examined different roles played by women at each stage of their adult life. These include the burdens of motherhood and the role of housewife, both of which discouraged political participation and the struggle for economic independence.
(b) the structural explanation is based on the existence of gender inequality in other sectors of society such as economy, law and education. It was argued that the lack of control by women in these sectors reduced the resources of women and their input into various life careers.
(c) the socialization explanation analyzed the childhood socialization process of males and females into different participatory roles and argued that adult socioeconomic, cultural and political expressions by males were basically internationalized by society. (Kent, 1985)

On the basis of the foregoing, gender discrimination and inequality between men and women in various Nigerian circumstances can be appreciated.

NIGERIAN CIRCUMSTANCES

Circumstances are conditions and facts that are connected with and which affect a situation, an event or an action. They can be regarded as conditions of a person's life or situations or events that affect and influence a person's life beyond his or her control (Horby, 2000). The term "Nigerian circumstances" here is used as those conditions and situations in which women and other vulnerable groups found themselves in Nigeria. It also refers to situations, events and actions from other human beings or the environment which affects or influences the behavior, utterances and physical existence of women and other vulnerable groups in Nigeria. Most prominent of the existing circumstances, situations, conditions and facts which engender or encourage gender discrimination and inequality can be itemized as follows:

Discriminatory Laws

There are still some discriminatory statutes in different parts of Nigeria. The most notorious of them in the northern parts of Nigeria is section 55(1) (d) of the penal code which permits a man to beat his wife for the purpose of correcting her subject only to any native law or custom in which such correction is recognized as lawful and provided that the result does not amount to infliction of grievous hurt. The worrisome aspect of this law is that bringing charges of wife-battering and similar crimes to court is difficult since the entire system of justice reflects gender bias that permits domestic violence.

Obnoxious Aspect of Sharia Law

The gravamen of provisions in the Sharia Law on marriage is parental consent to enable a man to get married to a woman irrespective of the requirement for maturity age of 18 years and above. In the unfortunate case of Yerima Bakura, the senator of the Federal Republic of Nigeria was reported in May 2010 to have married a 13-year-old Egyptian girl. Responding to public odium on this issue, Senator Yerima argued that he had not done anything to violate Sharia Law. It may be difficult to find any common law which permits such a marriage as applicable to other southern parts of Nigeria. This development not only endangers the life of such a female individual, it also brings about discrimination and inequality in social status between female individuals within the same geographical entity.

Harmful Traditional Practices

Harmful traditional practices like female genital mutilation, tattoos, using female children as house help, putting children into slavery etc., are quite common among different tribes in Nigeria. Apart from the health hazards involved, women folks and children from the areas of the country where the practices are most prevalent tend to loose their personality and rights to dignity. They also appear to differ in character and feature from their counterparts who are not subjected to such harmful practices in other parts of Nigeria or beyond the shores.

Widowhood Rites

Widows are women who have lost their husbands. This class of persons have emerged as one of the most marginalized, vulnerable and victimized groups of women in Nigeria. In most cultures, the following restrictions are often imposed on a widow during the period of transition:

1. abstinence from sexual intercourse;
2. protracted period of confinement;
3. silence and;
4. restriction of movement and from eating certain classes of food. (Offrey, cited in Iboro, 2010:67)

Apart from the above, widows under the inheritance laws of the South East and South-South areas of Nigeria also have very few, if any, rights to a share in their deceased husbands' property even though they may have contributed substantially toward the acquisition of such property while their husbands were alive.

Women and the Nigerian Economy

The marginalization of women in Nigeria is best explained within the context of productive relations (Ityaryar, 1992:54). Women's experience in the economy has been largely discriminatory. It has been established that women form an active and reserved labor force, but they rarely own the means of production. They are often denied rights of land ownership, even when they make up about 80 percent of Nigeria's agricultural labor force (Iboro, 2010:68). In modern industrial sectors, women are hardly found at the top of the hierarchy of any establishment. They are mostly concentrated in the service sectors such as health, education, social welfare and banking industry.

Women and Politics

The level of illiteracy among Nigerian women is quite high while the enrolment rate of female students especially, in the Northern part of the country at all levels of education, has been unsatisfactory. Owing to their low level of education, most women lack critical self-awareness, knowledge of their environment, their socioeconomic conditions as well as other problems militating against their status. Most of them are also incapable of articulating meaningful positions on issues affecting their welfare; neither can they be easily mobilized to struggle with their men counterparts for effective enhancement of women's aspirations (ibid.). This is why they are regarded as the most subdued and oppressed members of the society. The next issue to be addressed borders on factors or determinants of violence and discrimination against women in Nigeria.

FACTORS OR DETERMINANTS OF VIOLENCE AND DISCRIMINATION AGAINST WOMEN

Traditional Overlook over Women Abuse

The culture of silence over women's discrimination, abuse and inequality in Nigeria has actually propelled the problems related thereto. Culture of silence in this regard refers to the whole range of normative practices obscuring, legitimating and concealing abusive treatment of women and representing it as a private matter, which cannot be inquired into or beyond debate by members of the public. For example in Nigeria, except where cases of rape and wife-battering have caused serious injuries or death, they are never reported to the police let alone getting to courts of law for proper adjudication. The situation is that traditional systems of gender relations seriously collude with institutions of the family and religion to maintain the status quo, making it difficult for women to escape violence, discrimination and gender inequality.

Obnoxious Cultural Practices

Certain old and wicked cultural traditions and practices still abound among many tribes in Nigeria. For instance, it is strongly believed in certain parts of Nigeria that a female person must undergo female genital mutilation to suppress her desire for sexual intercourse (Hedley and Dorkeno, 1992:61). Also, wife-battering and other forms of domestic violence have been widely acknowledged in many parts of Nigeria as means of focusing women into submission to the authority or sovereignty of their husbands.

Women's Low Social Status

The rather low status of most women in Nigeria limits their decision-making ability and undermines their capacity to determine the patterns of their own lives. Women's economic dependence on men, their limited access to socioeconomic resources and constant fear of violence are factors which compel them to yield control over sexual relations or physical abuses to men. Also, the tender age of most women at marriage position, decreases their power of thought and imagination as well as exposes them to abuse in the hands of their partners. Early marriage, for instance, makes many female folks unable to complete their formal education and this further prevents them from the acquisition of sound skills capable of enhancing their personality and standard of living.

Masculinity and Power over Women

The popular notions of masculinity and imbalance of power between men and women is another factor which encourages discrimination and violence against women in Nigeria. In most Nigerian societies, children are taught that men should be in control while women submit to the authority of men. They also learn that violence is an acceptable means of asserting power and settling disputes. While male children learn that aggression and violence constitute appropriate male behavior, female children are trained to tolerate men's violence and yield control over sexual relations to them (Counts and Brown et al., 1999:77).

Weakness in the Law

Another serious factor which brings about violence against women, discrimination and inequality is inadequate legislation and effective enforcement of laws. For instance, the Child Rights Act, 2003, which is a federal law containing many attractive provisions against child abuse has not yet been domesticated by many states in Nigeria. Also, even though Lagos State had taken a giant stride in 2007 to enact the Protection against Domestic Violence Law, the abuse of women still strives in the State. While Nigeria was also a party to CEDAW and Beijing Platform of Action for protection of women's rights, no pragmatic step has been taken by various governments to implement the recommendations of the United Nations Organization in that respect.

CONCLUSION

In the perspective of their overriding reproductive status, women are known to be the highest common factors for the establishment of families whose products are eventual members of the society. Hence, the importance of women in global affairs cannot be underestimated. Women in Nigeria are acknowledged as primary processors of food and healthcare for families and their communities. In fact, it has been recorded that women provide an estimated 60–80 percent of labor input in agriculture, especially in food production, processing and marketing.[12] By virtue of their creation, women have maintained their overwhelming influence in their sociocultural relationship with men and this continues to sharpen the patterns, configurations and dynamics of all socioeconomic, cultural and political affairs of the nation. It is often said that "the ultimate secret of a powerful man lies in the hands of his wife." Women have also been recognized as harbingers of peace through their efforts at resolving crises in the society.

Notwithstanding the foregoing statements about the importance of women in the society, especially in Nigeria, it is observed in the course of this essay that women's rights in Nigeria have been seriously neglected in the face of the overgrowing incidents of domestic violence and gender discrimination. It is also observed that gender issues in development received little attention in national planning in Nigeria until the Declaration of the United Nations Decade for women.[13] Hitherto, women's reproductive, productive and community management roles and potentials were marginalized and left out of the system of national accounting. Hence, development planning since the colonial period had been gender insensitive due to continuous interaction between the indigenous culture and the inherited traditions and capitalist ideologies of the colonial administration.

Until the last decade and a half, the gains of women from development were minimal and temporal. Although the United Nations Decade for Women increased awareness about the strategic and practical needs of women, there was little commitment to incorporate these into national policies in Nigeria until the mid-1980s. Between that time and 2010, it would appear that increased yearnings for a National Women in Development Policy have been developed to facilitate full integration of women into the social, economic and political life of the nation. The development has been anchored by the efforts and intervention of many international organizations, regional bodies, federal, state and local governments, non-governmental and individual organizations. In spite of all the above stated trends in the development of women, it is sad to observe that with the present status of Nigeria as a sovereign, independent and democratic nation women and other vulnerable groups like children and the physically challenged are still passing through the valley of the shadow of death in terms of frequent violence, discrimination, deprivation and inequality against them.

In other to achieve the millennium development goals set for 2015 and emerge as one of the 20 largest economies by the year 2010 as stipulated by the present administration till November 2010, governments should focus their attention seriously on the following recommendations:

1. Priority must be given to various issues relating to security of life and property in Nigeria. Prolonged culture of insecurity assisted by malfunctioning law enforcement agents has paved a way for unrestricted incidents of violence, discrimination and inequality against women in the country.
2. Harmful cultures and traditions which enhance violence against women and increase the rate of their being abused should be discouraged through effective laws capable of being enforced by responsible law enforcement agencies and being applied by an independent judiciary.
3. All provisions of the Constitution which aid discrimination against women like section 39(3) (b) of the 1999 Constitution which allows men to confer citizenship on their foreign spouses should be amended at the Constitution review exercise still in progress as of November 2010. All other laws and religious/cultural practices which encourage early marriage for females should also be amended or removed from the nation's books.

4. Governments at all levels in Nigeria should intensify their efforts at removing all legal, constitutional and traditional barriers which inhibit greater participation of women in politics and direct promotion into leadership positions. The Indian solution concerning the integration of a quota for women into the Constitution should be practically emulated by Nigeria instead of paying lip service to the proposed 35 percent Affirmative Action for Women Participation in public positions.
5. Current government policies which address the problems of widows should not be restricted to harmful and discriminatory treatments of widows but should also take cognizance of their more complex problems of poverty, ill-health, unemployment and lack of accommodation. In this respect, all governmental authorities should pay more particular attention to proper implementation of various objectives enshrined in the National Economic Empowerment Development Strategies (NEEDS).
6. Education is the mother of inventions and it has been recognized over the ages as a veritable instrument against poverty, disease and ignorance. Governments in Nigeria should further revamp their efforts at providing qualitative, sound and productive education to all Nigerians, especially women and other vulnerable groups so that they will be in a position to recognize, assert and defend their rights against violence, discrimination and inequality.
7. Finally, I submit that concerted emphasis on women's rights and assertion of their freedoms in the society is good but must not be overdramatized beyond the natural positions of their male counterparts as defined by God. In matrimonial causes, women who entered into a monogamous marriage should know that it is a contract in which obligation is placed on them to respect their husbands and subject themselves to their authority. The book of Ephesians chapter 5 verse 21 to 28 stress that wives should subject themselves to their husband, who in turn, is expected to love their wives. In Islamic religion as well, the Holy Quaran (Surah An-Nisa verses 34–35) mandated the wives always to obey their husbands and take instructions from them. According to Justice Malins in *Re- Agar–Ellis* v. *Lascelles (1875) L. R. 10 C. Dgat* page 55:

> By the Laws of England, by the laws of Christianity and by Constitution of Society, when there is a difference of opinion between husband and wife, *it is the duty of the wife to submit to the husband.* (ital mine)

In the same vein, John Nox, in his book, *Divine Relationship Between Spouses,*[14] was of the view that "women are ordained in their perfection to serve men *and their refusal to do so is a rebellion against Jehova.*"

NOTES

1. Article 73 of the United Nations Charter.

2. The Preamble of the United Nations Charter provides in part that; ". . . and to reaffirm our faith in fundamental human rights, in the dignity and worth of human person, *and in the equal rights of men and women and of nations large and small. . . .*"

3. United Nations International Covenant on Civil and Political Rights 1966, and International Covenant on Social, Economic and Cultural Rights 1966.

4. Chapters Four of the 1960, 1963, 1979 and 1999 Constitutions of the Federal Republic of Nigeria.

5. See sections 306–372 of the Criminal Code Act, Cap. C 38, Laws of the Federation of Nigeria 2004 dealing with all manners of criminal offences and civil actions which are *actionable per se.*

6. These include, the United Nations Charter; the United Nations International Covenants on Civil and Political Rights 1996; International Covenants on Social, Economic and Cultural Rights 1966; African Charter on Human and Peoples' Rights 1979; African Charter for Popular Participation in Development and Transformation 1990; the United Nations Convention on the Elimination of All Forms of Discrimination Against Women; the UN Convention on Rights of the Child etc.

7. See *Vanguard* (Nigeria) December 4, 2010 at p. 4, www.vanguardngr.com

8. *Webster's Ninth New Collegiate Dictionary* (1985). Merriam Webster Inc. Publishers, Massachusetts, p. 1323.

9. See sections 33–44 of the Constitution of the Federal Republic of Nigeria, 1999.

10. Ibid., sections 13–24.

11. See Violence Against Women Act, USA, 2000 or the case of *United States v. Morrison* (2000) 529 U.S. 598.

12. See *National Policy on Women* (2004) edited by the Women's Aid Collective (WACOL), New Haven, Enugu, p. 16.

13. Ibid., p. 1.

14. Above all, it is hereby reiterated that if Nigeria intends to maintain her dignity and fame among the respected community of nations, domestic violence and all forms of discrimination and inequality against women and other vulnerable groups should always be seen as anathema to sustainable development and *ipso facto*; be made as sacrificial lambs' at the altar of effective protection of women's rights.

REFERENCES

Awake! (1998) *Will There Ever Be Human Rights For All.* Benin, Nigeria, November 22, p. 9.

Counts and Brown et al. (1999) *To Have and to Hit*, Chicago, University of Chicago Press, p. 77.

Engels. F. (1884) *The Origin of the Family, Private Property and the State*, Enrich, XXI.

Garner, B. (2004) *Black's Law Dictionary*. St. Paul, MN: Thomas West Publishers, p. 1601.

Gasiokwu, M. O. U. (2003) *Human Rights: History, Ideology and Law.* Jos, Nigeria: Fab Educational Books, p. 140.
Group for the Defence of Women (GDW) (2003) *Domestic Violence Against Women in Nigeria: A Nation-wide Survey*, Enugu, pp. 11–22.
Hedley and Dorkeno (1992) *Violence Against Women.* Berlin: Adrienne Press, p. 61.
Hornby. A. S. (2000) *Oxford Advanced Learner's Dictionary of Current English.* London: Oxford University Press, p.1373.
Iboro, E. N. (2010) Violence Against Women in Nigeria: The Factors and the Dynamics, *The Constitution: A Journal of Constitutional Development*, Vol. 10, No. 2, p. 87.
Itoro-Eze-Anaba (2009) Stopping Violence Against Women, 10 years after (2), *Vanguard*, Friday, December 18, 2009, at p. 44, www.vanguardngr.com (accessed December 18, 2009).
Ityaryar Denis et al. (1992) *The State and Women in Nigeria.* University of Jos Press, p. 54.
Kent, J. M. (1985) Gender Roles and Inequalities in Political Participation: Results from an 8 Nation Study, *Western Political Quarterly*, Vol. 36, No. 5.
Schulera, Margaret. A. et al. (1997) *Women's Human Rights Step by Step.* Washington, D.C.: Women, Law and Development International Publications, pp. 8–12.

4

1999 Constitution and Gender Analysis of Elective and Appointive Positions in Nigeria

Michael Abiodun Oni and Rachael Oluseye Iyanda

ABSTRACT

Series of efforts have been made at the global level to enhance and promote the rights of women with a view to protecting them against discriminations. These efforts at protecting and promoting women against discriminations are pervasive, cutting across socioeconomic and political abuse. Specifically, the Beijing Conference resolution of 1995 stated that there is the need to frown against inequality between men and women in the sharing of power and decision making at all levels.

Consequent upon this vital resolution, nations of the world including Nigeria are expected to incorporate non-discriminatory mechanisms in her statue book to ensure equality of the gender in the sharing of offices. This is expected to be reflected in the national constitution. Hence, this study examines the conference resolution of guarding against inequality between men and women in the sharing of power and decision making at all levels.

The study which examines the compliance of Nigeria is the 1999 Constitution with resolution adopted documentary method. The study concentrated on the appointment at the federal level as study cases. It discovered that the 1999 Constitution did not after all put effective mechanisms in the form of section and sub-section to guard against discriminations against women gender in appointments in Nigeria.

The study recommended that until mechanisms are put in place stating clearly the sharing formula between men and the women gender in both the elective and appointive positions, the discrimination against women in Nigeria may continue unabated.

INTRODUCTION

Women have from time immemorial being discriminated against in power sharing and decision making and have been sidelined in both appointive and elective positions. These discriminations have brought sharp inequalities between the male and female gender in positions both in the developed and developing nations.

However, to assuage the feeling and sense of discriminations against females, a series of conferences and convention have been held where various resolutions and policies were recommended to bridge the gap of gender inequality. Toward this end, apart from the efforts of women activities to either close or end gender equality, the United Nations as the universal organisation had facilitated conventions from where declarations were made as regarding the mending of discrimination against women. Some of these conventions at the global level to eliminate gender inequality are the International Convention on Civil and Political Rights (ICCPR) and International Convention on Economic, Social and Cultural Rights (ICESCR).United Nations also organized a convention on the Elimination of All Forms of Discrimination Against Women (CEDAW). In the summary of the Convention's resolution, it is described as "an international bill of rights for women and a framework for women's participation in the development process."

The most popular and outstanding effort to promote the right of women to positions in the form of power sharing and decision making was the Fourth World Conference on Women held in Beijing, China. The conference popularly known as Beijing Conference passed a number of resolutions on how to end discriminatory practices against women worldwide. The resolutions at the conference were expected to be incorporated into the nations' constitutions to promote equality. This study therefore examines the provisions of the 1999 Constitution vis-a-vis attempts to bridge the gender gaps in the appointment into position in Nigeria between 1999 and date. This is however limited to the federal level. Again, it examines the attempts by the operators of the constitution in ensuring gender balancing in appointments into positions at this level.

However, there is the need for the discussion of the two concepts relating to the study. These are constitution and gender.

CONSTITUTION

Constitution is the body of law codified or not codified in a document specifically designed to control the action of the state and regulate the behaviour of its citizens. It is an instrument specifically meant to guarantee law and order by specifying the rules and regulations for both the states and the people. It also spells out the powers and limitations of the ruled and the rulers.

Constitution is therefore the norms, conventions, customs and usages which set the structural format on how a state is to be governed. It defines the intended relations between the governed and the government, outlines the major institutional framework, the rights and duties of citizens.

Whearse (1966) sees constitution as:

> The whole system of government of a country, the collection of rules which establish and regulate the governed and the government.

Paine, a contributor to the French constitution of 1793, states that the constitution is:

> not the act of a government but of people constituting a government and a government without a constitution is power without right.

Moreover, the *Encyclopaedia of Social Sciences* defines constitution:

> as the fundamental principle according to which a state, nation or group is constituted and governed.

For the purpose of this chapter, constitution is defined as both an instrument for and guiding spirit of governance which states and defines the rules and regulations, rights, duties and powers of government and those of the governed in a given state.

There are various sources (natural and unnatural) from where the body of fundamental laws for the governing of state can be generated.

According to Anyaegbunam (2007), the following are the sources of a nation's constitution: customary norms and laws, country's historical experience, constitutional conferences and constitutional assemblies, legal, political and social writings/public opinions, the influence of successful foreign countries.

In this discussion of sources of Nigerian constitution, Oni (2006) listed the following as sources of a nation's constitution. These are: customs, conventions and usages, colonial experiences, Nigeria's personal, historical and political experiences, judicial reviews, laws made by the parliament, inspirations from other countries, writing and pronouncement of eminent jurists, international treaties and conventions.

Concerning the imperatives of constitution in any political system, Ayeni-Akeke (2008) says they include: ensuring certainty and due process, prevention of arbitrariness, prevention or mitigating conflict, setting out the basic rights and duties of citizens, guides as to the creation of basic political structure of a state including their powers and functions.

For the purpose of this chapter we adopt Ayeni-Akeke's conceptualization of constitution as an integrative instrument in a heterogeneous society. According to him:

> A constitution promotes a sense of community among members of a political system especially in countries made up of heterogeneous groups. Where a constitution is a product of collective deliberation, its contents or provisions tend to be distillations of the rules, interests and aspirations of the various groups making up the state.

GENDER

Gender as a concept refers to responsibilities of men and women in our society or cultures. This includes the expectation of behaviours of both feminity and masculinity (UNESCO, 2003). Over the years, the concept assumes different interpretations to explain cultural differentiation that has been associated to men and women. Gender is now widely used to designate to culturally defines, socially formed identities of men and women that are highly variable across cultures and are continually subject to change. The concept is also used to explain social analysis, it reveals how women's subordination (or men's domination) is socially constructed.

Enemuo (1999) described the social analysis of gender to mean unequal perceptions, views, role and relevance, rewards, that a society assigns men and women through its culture. He stated further that gender is constructed inequality between men and women.

In the light of the chapter, the conception of gender in a Nigerian context has culturally impacted to mean submission, illogical, passive, emotional, easily moved to tears, while men are suggested to be logical, competent, outstanding, powerful, independent etc. With this view in mind, men and women have been reflected as a line within a continuum that is highly distinct from each other or rather that there are desirable qualities that men possessed while women have undesirable ones.

1999 CONSTITUTION AND FIGHTING AGAINST DISCRIMINATION PRACTICES

Section 17(1) states that the need to ensure social justices in the Nigerian state, pressure crystalline discriminations with a view to ensuring equality.

The section states that "the social order is founded as ideas of Freedom, Equality and Justice."

In furtherance of this objective of the social order, SUS section 2 a, b, c, d state thus:

a) Every citizen shall have equality of rights, obligations and opportunities before the law;
b) The sanctity of the human person shall be recognized and human dignity shall be maintained and enhanced;
c) Government actions shall be humane.

Based on the provisions of this constitution, this study measures the compliance in the appointive and elective positions in the Nigerian Fourth Republic.

On the strength of gender, when the President of the Federation had the cause to change the nation's ministerial list, gender composition is presented here.

Table 4.6 is a list of the replaced and incoming ministers against their gender.

BACKGROUND TO 1999 CONSTITUTION

After the collapse of the Second Republic in December 1983, not less than two attempts were made to fashion another constitution for the nation. The first was in 1989 by the General Ibrahim Babangida-led military administration and the second was in 1995 under General Sani Abacha's military junta.

However, the two constitutions did not see the light of day because of two interruptions, one natural and the other artificial. The annulment of June 12, 1993, did not allow Babangida's constitutional attempt to run its full swim. The death of General Abacha did not allow the constitution making he started to fruition.

The nation was at a crossroad when General Abdulsalam Abubakar took over the reign of government in 1998. The military man, who was never attracted by the aroma of office to want to sit tight, was in a hurry to hand over power to a democratically elected government; he was, however, faced with difficulties with which constitution to adopt within the shortest time.

The regime set up a Constitution Debate Committee (CDC) under the chairmanship of Justice Niki Tobi of the Supreme Court. The CDC sampled the opinions of Nigerians. At the end of the day, the preference of Nigerians was for the 1979 constitution. Therefore, the regime adopted the 1979

Table 4.1 Gender and 1999 Ambassadorial Appointment by the Federal Government: Appointees by State

	Name of Appointed Ministers	*State*	*Female*	*Male*	*State*
1	M.G. Samaki,	Adamawa	-	3	3
	Wilberforce Juta	,,			
	Amb. Na Amb. Na	,,			
2	Amb. S.J. Edem	Akwa Ibom	-	1	1
3	Amb. G.S. Akunwafor	Anambra		3	3
	Amb. A.A. Anopuechi				
	Chief Sam Okechukwu				
4	Amb. M.M. Bauchi	Bauchi	-	3	3
	ADEMN Jimba				
	Bappa Lawal Toro				
5	Emmanuel Otiotio	Bayelsa	-	1	1
6	Amb. A.A. Agada	Benue	-	3	3
	Amb. G.O. Ajonye				
	Dr. Ogbe O. Bande				
7	Alhaji Baba Jidda	Borno	-	1	1
8	Akapan Ade Obi Odu	Cross-River	-	1	1
9	Amb. K.O. Olisemeka	Delta	-	3	1
	A.T. Nanna				
	Chief Ray Inije				
10	Ogbonaya Nwachukwu	Ebonyi	-	1	1
11	Prince Iheneden Erediawa	Edo		2	2
	Amb. P.I. Ayewoh				
12	Amb. S.A. Otuyelu	Ekiti		2	2
	Chief Dare Bajide				
13	Amb. C. Anigbo	Enugu		2	2
	Dr. Cyril Igwe				
14	Ayuba Ngbako	FCT-Abuja		1	1
15	Alhaji Saidu Mohammed	Gombe		2	2
	Alhaji Yerima Abdulahi				
16	Chief Greg Mbadiwe	Imo		3	3
	Senator Emeka Echeruo				
	Dr. George Obiozor				
17	Alhaji Daudu S. Hadejia	Jigawa		1	1
18	Dr. Shehu Lawal Giwa	Kaduna		3	3
	Alhaji Sule Buba				
	Amb. L.A. Munir				
19	Alhaji Kabiru Rabiu	Kano		2	2
	Gen. Sarki Mukthar				
20	Amb. K. Ahmed	Katsina		2	2
	Alhaji Mogaji Mohammed				

Table 4.1 Continued

	Name of Appointed Ministers	*State*	*Female*	*Male*	*State*
21	Amb. B. Adu Alhaji Sani Kangiwa	Kebbi		2	2
22	Amb. E.A. Aina Amb. J.K. Shinkaiye Alhaji Usman E. Bello	Kogi		3	3
23	Amb. M.S. Abdul-Wahab Dr. Tunji Olagunju	Kwara		2	2
24	Amb. (Mrs.) O.O. Harrison Obafemi Dr. R.A. Sule Dr. (Mrs.) Tokunbo Awolowo Dosunmu	Lagos	2	1	3
25	Amb. A.M. Bage Alh. Buba Ahmed Engr. Polycarp Azige	Nassarawa	-	3	3
26	Amb. (Mrs.) A.O. Oyesola Amb. (Mrs.) F.A. Ukonge Chief (Mrs.) Ebun Oyagbola	Ogun	3	-	3
27	Amb. E.O. Aderele Amb. A.A. Ilemia Chief Bayo Yusuf	Ondo	-	3	3
28	Amb. (Miss) A.A. Ayorinde Chief Gunju Adesakin	Osun	1	1	2
29	Chief Yomi Akintola Mrs. Ronke Adefowope Amb. E.O. Oladeji	Oyo	1	2	3
30	Amb. A.B. Rinap Fidelis Tapgun Bagudu Itirse	Plateau	-	3	3
31	Amb T.D. Hart Chief Ignatius Ajuru Mrs. Ine Kurubo	Rivers	1	2	3
32	Alhaji Mohamed Maradun Alhaji Ibrahim Wambai	Zamfara	-	2	2
33	Senator Laden Shuni Alhaji Abdulqadir Sani Dr. Mohammed Wali	Sokoto	-	3	3
34	Idris Waziri Amb. J.L. Umaru	Taraba	-	2	2
35	Lawan Gana Guba	Yobe	-	1	1
	TOTAL		8	70	78

Percent of male appointed 70/78 x 100/1 = 90%.
Percent of female appointed 8/70 x 100/1 = 10%.

Table 4.2 Gender and Composition of the Federal Government 1999–2003

		Male	Female
President	South-West	1	-
Vice President	North-East	1	-
Secretary to the Federal Government	South-South	1	-
Senate President	South-East	1	-
Deputy Senate President	North-Central	1	-
Speaker, House of Representatives	North-West	1	-
Deputy Speaker, House of Representatives	South-South	1	-
Total		7	0

Percent of male elected 7/7 x 100/1 = 100%.
Percent of female elected 0/7 x 100/1 = 0%.

Table 4.3 Gender Composition of the Federal Government, 2007

		Male	Female
President	North-West/ South-South	1	-
Vice President	South-South/ North-West	1	-
Secretary to the Federal Government	North -East	1	-
Senate President	North-Central	1	-
Deputy Senate President	South-East	1	-
Speaker, House of Representatives	South-West	1	-
Deputy Speaker, House of Representatives	South-East	1	-
Total		7	0

Percent of male elected 7/7 x 100/1 = 100%.
Percent of female elected 0/7 x 100/1 = 0%.

constitution for the transition program and the present regime. The constitution was only minorly amended to meet the present realities.

SUMMARY OF FINDINGS, CONCLUSION, AND RECOMMENDATIONS

The study shows that appointment at the federal level particularly as regards the composition of the federal government from 1999 to 2010 reflect a hundred percent male domination. The only time when a female was elected as the Speaker, House of Representatives in 2007, she was threatened to resign consequent upon an allegation of fraud arising from the renovation of her official residence.

Table 4.4 Gender and Composition of Ministerial Appointment, 1999–2003

		Male	*Female*
Mr. Ojo Maduekwe	Abia	1	-
Mr. Nnyeabo Obi	Anambra	1	-
Alhaji Waziri Korfi	Bauchi	1	-
Chief E. Bamyo	Bayelsa	1	-
Dr. Iyorchia Ayu	Benue	1	-
Alhaji I. Bonu	Borgo	1	-
Chief C. Agbobu	Delta	1	-
Chief Tony Anenih	Edo	1	-
Prof. T. Adeniran	Ekiti	1	-
Alhaji D. Goje	Gombe	1	-
Mrs. K. Chikwe	Imo	-	1
Alhaji Sule Lamido	Jigawa	1	-
Mr. Isaiah Bala	Kaduna	1	-
Mr. Kanu Agabi	Cross River	1	-
Hon. Dobem Onyia	Enugu	1	-
Alhaji Musa Gwadabe	Kano	1	-
Alhaji Sani Zongo Daura	Katsina	1	-
Dr. (Mrs.) Ndalolo	Kwara	-	1
Chief Dapo Sarumi	Lagos	1	-
Chief Solomon Ewuga	Nasarawa	1	-
Engineer Mustapha Bello	Niger	1	-
Chief Jubril Martins Kuye	Ogun	1	-
Dr. Olusegun Agagu	Ondo	1	-
Chief S.M. Afolabi	Osun	1	-
Alhaji Haruna Elewi	Oyo	1	-
Mr. Damisi Sango	Plateau	1	-
Chief Precious Ngelala	Rivers	1	-
Alhaji Mohammed Arzika	Sokoto	1	-
Chief Bola Ige	Osun	1	-
Mrs. Dupe Adelaja	Ogun	-	1
Dr. Tim Menakaya	Anambra	1	-
Dr. Mrs. Bekky Ketebu Igwe	Bayelsa	1	-
Chief Tonye Graham Douglas	Rivers	-	1
Prof. Jerry Gana	Niger	1	-
Mrs. Pauline Tallen	Plateau	-	1
Alhaji Lawal Bitarurawa	Katsina	1	-
Alhaji Hassan Adamu	Katsina	1	-
General Theophilus Danjuma	Taraba	1	-
Alhaji Wakili Adamawa	Adamawa	1	-
TOTAL		34	5

Percent of male appointed 35/40 x 100/1 = 87%.
Percent of female appointed 5/40 x 100/1 = 13%.
Total: 40

Table 4.5 Gender and 2003 Ministerial List

Name	*State of Origin*	*Male*	*Female*
Dr. Ngozi Okonjo-Iweala	Abia	-	1
Mr. Chukwuemeka Chikelu	Anambra	1	-
Mallam Adamu Bello	Adamawa	1	-
Mrs. Rita Akpan	Akwa Ibom	-	1
Dr. Iyorchia Ayu	Benue	1	-
Chief Broderick Bozino	Delta	1	-
Mrs. Binta Musa	Borno	-	1
Mr. Roland Oritsejafor	Delta	1	-
Chief Franklin Ogbuagu	Ebonyi	1	-
Prof. Turner Isoon	Bayelsa	1	-
Elder Odion Igbesia	Edo	1	-
Mr. Frank Nweke	Enugu	1	-
Chief Samuel Babalola	Ekiti	1	-
Alhaji Shehu Sahel	Jigawa	1	-
Chief Cornelius Adebayo	Kwara	1	-
Prof. Eyitayo Lambo	Kogi	1	-
Chief Adeseye Ogunlewe	Lagos	1	-
Mr. Fabian Osuji	Imo	1	-
Chief (Mrs.) Mobolaji Osomo	Ondo	-	1
Chief Bamidele Dada	Oyo	1	-
Ambassador Oluyemi Adeniji	Osun	1	-
Chief Akin Olujimi	Oyo	1	-
Mallam Nassir El-Rufai	Kaduna	1	-
Dr. Rabiu Kwankaronzo	Kano	1	-
Col. Musa Mohammed (rtd.)	Gombe	1	-
Dr. Precious Sekebo	Rivers	1	-
Mr. Oseni Akwanga	Benin	1	-
Alhaji Mukhtar Shagari	Sokoto	1	-
Mrs. Rita Akpa	Cross River	-	1
Mr. Nyel Imoe	Cross River	1	-
Mrs. Funke Adedoyin	Kwara	-	1
Mr. Isa Yuguda	Bauchi	1	-
TOTAL		26	6

Percent of male appointed 26/33 x 100/1 = 79%.
Percent of female appointed 7/33 x 100/1 = 21%.
Total: 33

Table 4.6

Outgoing Minister	*State*		*Incoming*		*State*
Chief Mrs. Mobolaji Osomo	Ondo	F	Olusegun Mimiko	M	Ondo
Dr. Chukwuemeka Chikelu	Anambra	M	Mrs. Obiageli Ezekwesili	F	Anambra
Funke Adedoyin	Kwara	F	Mrs. Halima Tayo Alao	F	Kwara
Elder Odion Ugbesa	Edo	M	Dr. Joseph Odidilitoh	M	Edo
Mrs. Obong Rita Akpan	Akwa Ibom	F	Chief Mrs. H.O. Ezuene	F	Akwa Ibom
Hajia Bintu Musa	Borno	F	Mrs. Maryam Aroma	F	Borno
Col. Mala Manile (rtd)	Zamfara	M	Yahaya Abdulkarim	M	Zamfara
Alhaji Shehu Sahel	Jigawa	M	Hon. Ahmed Abdulhamed	M	Jigawa
-	-	-	Mr. Fidelis Tapgun	M	Plateau
			Bayo Ojo		
Prof. Fabian Osuji	Imo	M	Prof. Chinewe Osuji	M	Imo
Chief Akin Olujimi	Oyo	M			

Number of ministers dropped: 10.
Number of ministers replaced: 10.
Number of males removed: 6.
Number of females removed: 4.
Number of males replaced: 6.
Number of females replaced: 4.
Percent of males removed and replaced 6/10 x 100/1 = 60%.
Percent of females removed and replaced 4/10 x 100/1 = 40%.
Total: 10.

Table 4.7 Gender and Composition of Ministers in Nigeria, State of Origin and their Ministry (2007)

S/No	*Name*		*Ministry*	*State of Origin*
1	Chief Mike Aondoakaa	M	Minister of Special Duty	Benue State
2	Dr. I. Abba Ruma	M	Min. of Agriculture & Water Resources	Katsina State
3	Mrs. Fidelia A. Njeze	F	Minister of State, Agriculture & Water Resources	Ebonyi State
4	Mr. Babatunde Omotoba	M	Minister of Aviation	Ekiti State
5	Senator Bello J. Gada	M	Minister of Culture & Tourism	Sokoto State
6	Dr. Shettima Mustapha	M	Minister of Defence	Borno State
7	Mr. Ademola Seriki	M	Minister of State, Defence	Lagos State
8	Dr. Sam Egwu	M	Minister of Education	Ebonyi State
9	Hajia Aishatu Dukku Agada	F	Minister of State, Education	Gombe State
10	Mr. John Oddey	M	Minister of Environment	Cross River State
11	Senator M. Aliero	M	Minister of the Federal Capital Territory	Kebbi State
12	Mr. J.S. Odom	M	Minister of State, Federal Capital Territory	Abia State
13	Mr. Remi Babalola	M	Minister of State, Finance	Oyo State
14	Mr. Ojo Maduekwe	M	Minister of Foreign Affairs	Abia State
15	Alhaji Jubril Maigari	M	Minister of State, Foreign Affairs I	Yobe State
16	Ambassador Bagudu Hirse	M	Minister of State, Foreign Affairs II	Plateau State
17	Prof. B. Osotimehin	M	Minister of Health	Ogun State
18	Dr. A.I. Hong	M	Minister of State, Health	Adamawa State
19	Prof. Dora Akunyili	F	Minister of Information & Communication	Anambra State
20	Alhaji Aliyu Ikra Bilbis	M	Minister of State, Information & Communication	Zamfara State
21	Godwin Abe	M	Minister of Interior	Edo State
22	Chief Adetokunbo Kayode	M	Minister of Justice	Ondo State
23	Mrs. Deziani Allison Madueke	F	Minister of Mines & Steel	Bayelsa State
24	Dr. Shamsudeen Usman	M	Minister of National Planning Commission	Kano State
25	Elder G. Orubebe	M	Minister of State	Delta State
26	Dr. Rilwanu Lukman	M	Minister of Petroleum	Kaduna State

Table 4.7 Continued

S/No	*Name*		*Ministry*	*State of Origin*
27	Mr. O. Ajumogbobia	M	Minister of State	Rivers State
28	Dr. I.Y. Lame	M	Minister of Police Affairs	Bauchi State
29	Arch. Nuhu Waya	F	Minister of State, Power	Kaduna State
30	Dr. A.B. Zaku	M	Minister of Science & Technology	Taraba State
31	Engr. S.M. Ndenus	M	Minister of Sport	Niger State
32	Alhaji Ibrahim Bio	M	Minister of Transport	Niger State
33	Mrs. S.H. Sulaiman	F	Minister of Women Affairs	Kebbi State
34	Dr. Hasan M. Lawal	M	Minister of Works & Housing	Nasarawa State
35	Mrs. Grace Ekpiwher	F	Minister of State, Works & Housing	Delta State
36	Sen. A. Olasunkanmi	M	Minister of Youth Development	Osun State
37	Amb. A. Kazaure	M	Minister of Special Duties	Jigawa State
38	Chief Ufort Ekaette	M	Minister of Niger-Delta Affairs	Akwa-Ibom
39	Dr. Muktar Mansur	M	Minister of Finance	Kano State
40	Chief Archike Udenwa	M	Minister of Commerce & Industry	Imo State
41	Mr. Rilwan Babalola	M	Minister of Power	Osun State
42	Abdulrahman Adamu	M	Minister of State, Interior	Adamawa State

Gender Composition:
Male: 36
Female: 6
Total: 42
Gender analysis of ministerial appointment:
Percent of males appointed 36/42 x 100/1 = 86%.
Percent of females appointed 6/42 x 100/1 = 14%.
Total: 42

Moreover, the compositions of the executives, particularly the ministers, also show a male dominated appointment. For example in the appointment of ambassadorial appointees, seventy were male and eight female, representing ninety two (92) percent and eight (8) percent, respectively. In the composition of the federal government in 1999 and 2007 out of the seven members in both the executive and legislative arms that composed the membership, all were male representing 100 percent and female gender 0 percent. In the appointment of the ministers in 1999, out of the forty appointees 35 were male representing 87 percent and five female representing 13 percent. In 2003, out of the thirty-three ministers appointed 27 were male and 6 were female representing 87 and 13 percent, respectively. Even when some ministers were dropped in a cabinet reshuffle the equal number of male and female that were dropped six male and four female were returned. In the composition of the ministerial list in 2007, out of the 42 ministers that were appointed, 36 were male and six female representing 86 and 14 percent, respectively.

CONCLUSION

Apart from the fact that there are no effective provisions in the 1999 constitution to safeguard feminine gender and ensure equality in sharing of powers and decision-making, the operators of the constitution did not help matters. The argument against women in the elective position was because of being passive in politics; however, the data adapted for this study was the appointive positions, yet women's percentage of representation falls below the Beijing affirmative action. Hence, it is concluded that the 1999 constitution gives no pride of place to gender in the appointments into offices. The operators did not also help the situations; women are sidelined in appointments.

The future constitution must state unambiguously the sharing formula and percentage analysis of allocating positions at all levels in Nigeria between men and women. A situation where this is left to be determined by the operators in a male dominated policy is not the best. Therefore, this study calls for an institutionalized mechanism to guard against discrimination in the appointment into public offices.

REFERENCES

Abiodun, A. (1998) The Making of Political Parties. *The Guardian*, September 11, 1998.

Anifowose, R. (1999) Constitution and Constitutionalism in Remi Anifowose and Francis Enemuo (eds) *Elements of Politics*. Lagos: Malthouse Press Ltd.

Awolowo, O. (1996) *Path to Nigeria Greatness*. Ibadan: Oxford University Press OUP.

Ayeni-Akeke, O. A. (2008) *Foundation of Political Science*. Ibadan: Ababa Press.

Enemuo, F. (2005) Gender and Women Empowerment in Remi Anifowose and Francis Enemuo (eds) *Elements of Government*. Lagos: Sam Iroanusi Publications.

Ihnovbere, J. O. (2002) *Towards a New Constitution in Africa*. CDD, Occasional Papers Series, No 4, London.

Iroanusi, Sam O. (2000) *The Making of the Fourth Republic*. Lagos: Sam Iroanusi Publications Inco.

Nwabueze, B.O. (1978) *Constitutionalism in the Emergent States*. London: C Horsts and Co.

_________ (1982) *A Constitutional History of Nigeria*. Ibadan: Longman Press.

Roberts, F. O. N. and Obioha, E. E. (2005) Electoral Violence and Role of Political Party.

United Nations Development Programme, Nigerian Development Report, 1999. Lagos: UNDP.

5

An Appraisal of the Protection of Women's Rights under Nigerian Laws

Mercy Onaodowan Erhun

ABSTRACT

Females are the most vulnerable members of society, and most victims of human rights violation are females. Nigerian women are facing problems of discrimination, abuse, economic and sexual exploitation, neglect, extreme poverty, illiteracy, homelessness trafficking, prostitution, just to mention but a few. These problems are major challenges that require protective measures in order to ensure an effective redress.

This chapter sets out to assess the situation of the rights of women against the existing legal framework in Nigeria.

INTRODUCTION

Women form a sizeable proportion of the country's population and constitute a potent productive force and hold a numerical majority. Yet women face the battle of combating power imbalance with the society because of their gender. Post independent Nigerian State can be characterized as patriarchal. This is attributable to the effects of the colonial and post-colonial state on women which strengthened the powers of men over women. The civil rights of Nigerian women are at the mercy of the patriarchal order which is in operation in Nigeria.

Nigerian women face problems of disadvantage, discrimination, abuse and exploitation sometimes in appalling circumstances. Traditionally, the role of the woman is that of child bearing, child-raising and home-making. It was once asserted that "from the historical necessity and division of labor, there gradually developed the myth that the woman is a creature, the purpose of whose creation was limited to kitchen and the home. Tending the kitchen and the children thus became her quintessential role and fulfillment. . . . Outside of domesticity she lacks meaning (Olatunbosun, 2003:83)." Women thus face both physical and attitudinal constraints which have served to curtail their self-advancement in no small measure. They face various forms of discrimination which limit their aspirations and opportunities to develop to their full potentials on the basis of equality with men.

Although women have been given equal rights and opportunities for full participation in theory and in legal terms, there is a wide disparity between acclaimed recognition of women's rights and the accrual of these rights in fact. These are more honored in words than observance thus perpetuating inequality of all types. The position of women is still inferior as they are treated as chattel. Women remain in subordinate and subservient positions. Despite the fact that the Nigerian constitution guarantees every male and female the same fundamental rights, there are certain legal provisions and procedures which tend to undermine this equality.

This chapter sets out to assess the situation of the rights of women against the existing legal framework in Nigeria.

RIGHTS

Rights represent the interest which is accorded legal recognition and which confers on the recipient certain freedom to act or to expect others to act toward him/her in the manner and within the scope prescribed by law (Onifade, 1989). The word "right" has been defined as "an interest recognized and protected by law, respect for which amounts to a duty and disregard of which is a wrong."[1] Right means that which the law directs for the protection or for the advantage of an individual (Oputa, 1997:5). Women's rights have been defined (Augie, 1993:235) as the protection guaranteed to women by law in order to enable them to participate on an equal status with men in political, legal, social and economic institutions of the State.

According to Akinola Aguda (1985), fundamental rights are vehicles for obtaining justice. Although the constitution puts in place freedom from discrimination on grounds of sex and pronounces the right to be free from torture and human indignity, most rights enshrined in our constitution are nothing more than empty words to millions of Nigerians, women in particular.

All are declared[2] equal before the law and are entitled without any discrimination to equal protection before the law. All human beings, male or female are born equal into a free world and are expected to participate freely without any inhibition on ground of sex.

The right and freedom of every one without distinction of any kind such as race, color, sex, language, religion, social origin has been guaranteed,[3] just as the right to recognition everywhere as a person before the law.[4] The right of all to participate in the governance of one's country either directly or indirectly,[5] and the right to equal access to public service in one's country[6] are well enunciated. In spite of this, the existence of customs all over Nigeria which discriminate against womenfolk and which regard them as inferior to the menfolk have been acknowledged.[7]

The family is recognized as the natural and fundamental group unit of society and is entitled to protection by society and the State.[8] The woman, as a member of society, has the right to social security and is entitled to realization through national efforts and international co-operation and in accordance with the resources of such state, of the economic, social and cultural rights indispensable for her dignity and the free development of her personality.[9] As Oputa J.S.C. put it,[10] nature made no distinction between men. We are all given the same humanity. Therefore it is illogical to make any distinction between men as a group and women as a class. There ought to be equality of treatment to produce justice.

Since the inception of the Women's Liberation Movement, attention given to women's rights have increased. At the global scene there is a demand for equal opportunity and even equal access to various institutions such as employment, education, etc. by women. This has brought about significant changes particularly in developed countries. Nigeria must be repositioned to reflect these changes in her laws. A right is not a concession from the State. It is an authority to a claim and demand. The point must be made that women's rights are human rights which every woman is entitled to on an equal footing to the full protection of their rights and freedoms for the mere fact that they are human beings. There is an urgent need to improve the legal status of women under Nigerian laws by accentuating those rights peculiar to women.

FAMILY LAW AND WOMEN IN NIGERIA

In Nigeria, women are subjected to several types of family laws which are in operation in this country such as customary law, Islamic law and statutory law. The issue of women's rights is much affected by the competing values of this multi-system of law which govern the family circle in Nigeria. Each of the systems has its own view on the role of women in the family. Rights accruing upon dissolution of marriage are governed by these different normative systems. The triple system of marriage laws in Nigeria has resulted in a plurality of legal provisions and precedents regarding property rights and inheritance. Women are not accorded any status except under statutory law. Inheritance rights are governed by these systems of law with much complication upon the demise of one of such parties. Contrary to the increase in demand for the recognition of the right of the women to a fixed portion of the husband's property, a wife under the Nigerian customary law cannot inherit the husband's estate. Where a couple contracts their marriage under native law and custom that permits the chastisement of women as obtained in the northern part of Nigeria, the man can plead that as a defense against assault.[11] Where such acts are criminalized, women find it difficult to convince law enforcement officials to take action. There is therefore an urgent need to modernize and improve the legal status of women under Nigerian laws in order to enhance the status of women.

CUSTOMARY MARRIAGE

Marriage under the native law and customs is governed by customary law of the place of marriage. Customary marriage is potentially polygamous as far as the husband is concerned. A marriage celebrated under customary law precludes a wife from validly marrying another man under either system but the husband is allowed to validly marry other wives.[12] It has been asserted that there are as many customary marriage contracts in a polygamous household as there are wives (Obi, 1966:155).

Nigerian law recognizes the validity of any marriage contracted under or in accordance with any customary law.[13] While the man is entitled to inherit the property of the wife, a wife under customary law cannot inherit the husband's estate because devolution of property follows the blood,[14] and since she is regarded as chattel to be inherited by a relative of her husband,[15] she is precluded from inheriting the husband's estate under customary law. In allowing the man to inherit the woman's property, the rule that devolution of property follows the blood is thrown away. The Nigerian woman is far from liberation from the indignities of the law especially in the area of customary law and practice despite the obligation of states to ensure the protection of women's rights.[16] Women are debased and exploited as a means of making money or amassing wealth. They are degraded and treated without dignity, thus derogating from her fundamental human right which accrues to her as a human being.

ISLAMIC MARRIAGE

Under Islamic law marriage, child marriage is permitted thereby preventing the child from developing her talents and making her useful contribution to society. It also exposes the girl-child to the yoke of sexual intercourse before the physical and anatomical growth is developed enough to accommodate the stresses which endanger the health of the child, thus shortening the life expectancy of the child. Under Islamic marriage in Nigeria, the bride to be is subjected to pudah or seclusion contrary to many Moslem states of the world thereby preventing women in Nigeria from contributing to the development of their society. This system of marriage entitles the wife to a portion of her husband's/parents' estate,[17] but there is discrimination in quantum of entitlement along sexual lines. While a widower inherits a whole estate, the widow is entitled to only half of the net estate of the deceased wife.[18] This is rather unfair.

Islamic law recognizes women as legal entities[19] with the right to hold property on their own during or after marriage.[20] Despite this they do not enjoy independent land rights since the tendency is for them to be economically dependent on their husbands. Under Islamic law, women are considered incapable of managing their property. She cannot give away or donate more than one third of those properties which are exclusively hers without the approval of her husband. Despite the rhetorics of the recognition of women as legal entities and their rights to acquire and earn property under Islamic law, it has been stated that a women can have independent thinking only when she is divorced and does not have surviving parents or male kin (Abdullah and Hamza, 2003:147).

STATUTORY MARRIAGE

Statutory marriage is viewed as being superior to customary and Islamic marriages.[21] Marriage under the Marriage Act is essentially monogamous in nature. It is an offence to contract any customary marriage during the subsistence of a statutory marriage.[22] This amounts to the commission of an offence termed bigamy. It is painful to note that these provisions are more honored in their breach than in their observance.

Under the Matrimonial Causes Act of 1970 the courts can rule that women have a share of property in the event of divorce on equity grounds. However, petition for a decision for termination of marriage or legal separation may be initiated by a person domiciled in Nigeria.[23] This act thus establishes one domicile for matrimonial causes. Where the husband resides outside Nigeria, the High Court is empowered to hear her case and the woman is entitled to claim dissertation in a divorce petition so long as:

1. She can establish that she has been residing in Nigeria for a period of not less than three years before her petition;
2. She can prove her status of abandonment at the time of petition.

The point must be made, however, that women who are married under customary and Moslem laws are handicapped by the requirement of domicile since the Matrimonial Causes Act does not protect them. This makes the issue of divorce difficult for them. The Evidence Act makes women married under statute to enjoy some form of protection from domestic violence since it offers them some form of legal recourse.[24] Women married under customary and Islamic Laws remain unprotected from domestic violence.

LEGAL PROTECTION OF WOMEN IN THE STATUTE BOOKS

The Nigerian Constitution

Constitutional equality of women is not a novel thing. The Nigerian constitution,[25] while outlawing discrimination on the basis of sex and women's employment, emphasizes equality of persons before the law and professes gender neutrality. By the same constitution[26], every woman is assured equal pay for equal work without discrimination on account of sex or on any ground whatsoever.[27] There is also a provision in the Nigerian constitution[28] which states that no person shall be held in slavery or servitude. In order to advance the social order it states that every citizen shall have equality of rights, obligations and opportunities before the law.[29] The constitution also stipulates that every Nigerian citizen shall have the right to acquire and own immovable property anywhere in the country.[30] In spite of these constitutional rhetorics, the political system in Nigeria appears to erect barriers in the economic and political development of the average Nigerian woman. This ought not to be so.

Labor Law

Under the Nigerian Labor Law, there are provisions devoted exclusively to regulating the employment of women. According to the law, a pregnant woman is entitled to stay away from work for a period of six weeks before delivery, and another six week period after delivery. No pregnant woman may be given notice of termination of her employment during pregnancy or the nursing of her baby.[31] These provisions cannot but meet with admiration. However, despite the legal protection accorded women under the Labor Law, Nigerian women are far from enjoying equal rights in the labor market. The legal protection has little or no practical effect especially in the informal sector such as agriculture and domestic services where the vast majority of women are employed (National Planning Commission, 2001:179).

The Criminal Code

The Criminal Code of Nigeria makes it an offence to procure a woman or girl to have unlawful carnal connection with a man either by threat or intimidation[32] or by false pretense.[33] Such an offender is guilty of a misdemeanor, and liable to punishment of 2 years imprisonment.[34] It is unfortunate to note that a person cannot be convicted for that offence upon the testimony of one witness. The testimony of one witness must be corroborated before a person can be convicted for that offence.[35] Under the Nigerian Criminal Code, couples married under statute are accorded some rights and privileges as defense against criminal charges by the Evidence Act and the Criminal Code. As stated in the code, a married woman is not free from criminal responsibility for doing or omitting to do an act merely because the act or omission takes place in the presence of her husband. But a wife of a Christian marriage is not criminally responsible for doing or omitting to do an act which she is actually compelled by her husband to do and which is done or omitted to be done in his presence. But where the act or omission constitutes an offence punishable with death or an offence of which grievous harm to the person of another or an intention to cause such harm is an element, the presence of her husband is immaterial.[36] A husband and wife of Christian marriage are not criminally responsible for a conspiracy between themselves alone.[37] According to the code, a husband and wife are each criminally responsible for any act done with respect to the property of the other which would be an offence if they were not husband and wife. But when a husband and a wife of a Christian marriage are living together, neither of them incur any criminal responsibility for doing or omitting to do any act with respect to the property of the other. There are two provisos to this namely, an act or omission with intention to injure or defraud some other persons, i.e. where a third party is involved, and an act done by either of them while leaving or deserting the other, for instance, where a spouse took the property of the other spouse while deserting or intending to desert the other.[38] Such spouses are exempted from criminal liability so long as they are living together. Consequently, couples under this type of marriage can make use of the property of the other anyway, without prior approval or consent. Where a spouse decides to dispose of the property of the other without consent, so long as they still live together, an aggrieved spouse cannot start criminal proceedings against an erring spouse. The code accords a woman the right to own property in her own name against all other persons, including the husband. She has the same remedies and redress by way of criminal proceedings for the protection and security of her own separate property as if such property belonged to her as an unmarried woman.[39] This privilege does not extend to married women under customary or Islamic law. Criminal Code of Southern Nigeria categorizes indecent assaults on females as a lesser offence (misdemeanor) while similar assaults on males are categorized as felonies[40] and the Penal Code of Northern Nigeria allows for chastisement of the wife by her husband.[41]

Rape was described (Ashiru, 2004:250–263) as one of the most brutal and atrocious gender-based form of violence that can be committed against women. The Criminal Code which prohibits rape states as follows: "Any person who has unlawful carnal knowledge of a woman or girl without her consent or with her consent, if the consent is obtained by force or by means of threats or intimidation of any kind, or by fear of harm, or by means of false and fraudulent representation as to the nature of the act, or in the case of a married women by personating her husband is guilty of an offence called rape."[42] Consent is vitiated if it is given as a result of threat[43] or where it is given in an unconscious state.[44] Where the accused honestly believes that the victim consented, he will not be convicted. The law of rape is archaic and needs amendment in order to make it applicable to current day situations. In a bid to prohibit a woman from committing abortion, the Nigerian Criminal Code states: "Any woman who, with the intent to procure her own miscarriage, whether she is or is not with child, unlawfully administers to herself any poison or other noxious thing or uses any force of any kind, or permits any such thing or means to be administered or used to her, is guilty of a felony, and is liable to imprisonment for seven years."[45] The law prohibiting abortion did not take cognizance of situations of rape, especially where two or more persons are involved, thus making it difficult to ascertain the real father of the child, and the stigma that goes with the birth of a fatherless child or even issues of infected or abnormal fetus (Olaseeni, 2004:392-400).

The criminal justice system is not adequately protective of women victims of sexual offences because of the requirement of corroboration entrenched in the Nigerian Law of Evidence.

Customary Law of Nigeria

Customs cause a lot of misery and underdevelopment in Nigeria. The laws that produce sex discrimination are mostly reflected in customs. The Nigerian Customary Law emanates from the ideology of patriarchy and conservation, encouraging the subservience of women. It excludes women from land ownership and encourages their dependence on men, thus depriving women of essential personal rights. Women who marry under customary law face a lot of hardship. They are deprived of any right of inheritance of their husband's estate. Most of the customary laws are pro-male, according a man the right to bride price refund from his wife upon dissolution of marriage.

Under customary law, a woman is granted no property right.[46] It is stated that a woman has no right to personally acquire landed property. She must acquire such property through her husband.[47] Women were regarded as having no property status in the community. They were seen simply as creatures of man to be exploited and degraded—his laborer (Livingstone, 1918:22). According to the Customary Law Manual, where a woman acquires movable property while she is married, such property belongs to her exclusively, but like her own person, is subject to the overall control of her husband.[48] She has no right to dispose of such property in any way whatsoever without the prior consent of her husband.[49] She must first obtain her husband's consent before she can give away any property she acquired during marriage (movable or immovable) to any person other than her child in her lifetime or by will.[50] The capacity of a wife to acquire and own property under customary law is questionable since she cannot deal with the property the way she likes without the prior consent of the husband. A married woman was once regarded as having no legal capacity to acquire, own and dispose of property in her own right and in her own name under customary law (Obi, 1966:357). She was considered to be perfectly incapable to acquire land in her personal capacity by purchase, gift, pledge or otherwise (Nwabueze, 1972:171). While there is a regime of customary law rules which regulates the acquisition and ownership of property by wives of customary law marriages (Akande, 1968:15), the capacity of a customary law husband to acquire and own property has never been rendered questionable.[51]

The prevailing customary laws in operation in most parts of Nigeria make women to have very limited or no property rights. There has been a submission (Akintola, 2004:312) that the customary rule of inheritance which denies a surviving spouse the rights of inheritance or benefits over the property of his or her deceased partner is repugnant to social justice, equity, fair play and good conscience. This should be made practicable in Nigeria.

The Married Women Property Act

The Married Women Property Act was enacted in England in order to improve the status of the English wife under the Common Law in respect of property rights. A married women is entitled to have and to hold as her private property, and to dispose of any real and personal property which belongs to her at the time of marriage,[52] or which she acquires in any employment or which she carries on separately from her husband, or by the exercise of any literary, artistic or scientific skill[53] without the intervention of any trustee. According to the act,[54] in any matter between husband and wife as to or possession of property, either party may apply by summons or otherwise in a summary way to any judge in the High Court of Justice for an order and the judge may make such order with respect to the property in dispute as he dims fit. The wife is authorized by the act[55] to sue her husband for the recovery of her personal property detained by him.

The Married Women Property Act 1882 is generally enforceable by virtue of the general importation of English Law into Nigeria (Nwogugu, 1974) on any question relating to the property rights of spouses who are married under statute. This is also the position of the courts in Nigeria.[56] It has force and validity in Nigeria[57] as a statute of general application. The 1882 act was revised in 1893. The English Act was described (Park, 1963:51) as inappropriate to many Nigerian situations. Consequently, the government of the then Western Regions enacted the Married Women's Property Laws, 1959.[58] The 1959 act was enacted as a result of the growing dissatisfaction with the operations of the pre-1900 "English" acts in Nigeria (Marshall, 1965:151). There is thus the Married Women Property Law of Nigeria of 1958 which confers liberty on a married woman in a legally accepted monogamous marriage to dispose of her real property as she desires. Upon divorce, her rights may be enforced through court processes. It provides that all properties which belong to a married woman by marriage shall be hers as if she were unmarried. This act liberates a married woman from all the legal restraints of contracts which tends to incapacitate her legally. It empowers her to sign contracts and other legal requirements independent of her husband. She can file a suit against any, and can be sued independent of her husband.[59] In postmarital contracts she can sue and be sued by her husband or other persons connected with contractual responsibilities. Under the 1958 act, couples cannot sue each other in tort.[60] Under the Nigerian Law, a claim in detinue for the release of personal effects will fail[61] because such a claim is considered incompetent. The position that neither a husband nor a wife can sue the other in tort is adhered to by the courts.[62]

There is no discrimination between spouses by the courts in England in the distribution of property.[63] Fairness, having regard to all the circumstance of the case and equality remain the yardstick which guide the courts in the distribution of property in England, unless there is good reason to depart from this.[64] According to the courts in England, whatever the division of labor chosen by spouses or forced on them by circumstances, fairness requires that neither party should be disadvantaged when considering their contributions. There should be no bias in favor of the party who earned the money and against the homemaker and the child carer. In Nigeria, there is the tendency to feel that the man is always the breadwinner and the earner of every resource in the home. This is reflected when making decision as to distribution of property. Nigerian courts can learn from the position in England by making fairness their guiding spirit in the distribution of property between spouses without putting the women in any disadvantaged position.

SUCCESSION RIGHTS OF A WIFE

Nigerian social norms do not regard the Nigerian women as an individual but an appendage of a father or mother (Omonubi-McDonnel, 2003:130). Customary legal system approves of the subordinate status of women who contracted customary law marriages. Nigerian customary laws accord males succession privileges in land and other properties and deprive women such rights. As a matter of tradition, a wife is deprived of succession rights in her husband's estate. A wife has no right to possess or administer a deceased husband's estate under customary law. Only male descendants or relatives have such rights. Even where the husband voiced his wishes to make the wife inherit his property, the relatives or male descendants have the right to circumscribe the unwritten wishes of the deceased, and to evict the widow out of her late husband's home.

Be that as it may the type of marriage contracted determines intestate disposition of a deceased person's property. In intestate succession, property may be succeeded to a widow if a valid bequest has been made to her. As a general rule, where wills are written, customary law does not limit women's right to inheritance. The Marriage Act accords a widow an unequivocal right to a portion of her husband's estate in intestate succession.[65] It does not matter whether she had children by the man or not. She is entitled to one third of the deceased husband's estate while the remaining two-thirds are shared equally among the offspring, if any. Where there is no offspring, the widow takes one-half of the estate while the other half goes to his parents. In the absence of a widow, the estate devolves in equal proportion to the children.[66] Thus a widow under statutory marriage and her offspring have a right to her deceased husband's estate. This provision does not however protect a woman who is married under customary law.

RECOMMENDATION

All laws must be a reflection of the social consciousness of people who live under it. The changing socioeconomic and political conditions must inevitably affect the legal order. Contrary to the increase in demand for the recognition of the right of women to a fixed portion of the husband's property, a wife under the Nigerian customary law cannot inherit the husband's estate. With increased social contact and political advance, there has to be an irreversible urge to improve the body of customary rules of conduct as well as the evolution of a modern legal system which will define the extent of a woman's right and status in society in general in better and clear terms. There is therefore a need to improve the legal status of women under Nigerian laws.

Women's rights must be made the focus of Nigeria's political agenda. We must discourage discrimination and gender inequality and acknowledge women's contribution while all barriers to women's equal rights to access economic goods and services must be removed. The tendency to feel that the man is always the breadwinner and the earner of every resource in the home should be put aside especially when making decisions as to distribution of property. Nigerian courts can learn from the position in England by making fairness their guiding spirit in the distribution of property between spouses without putting the women in any disadvantaged position.

One of the most likely casualties of social development is polygamy. Society has grown from the age when polygamy was cherished because of the economic usefulness and social purpose it once served. Polygamy is no longer fashionable as the procreation of more children to provide labor on the farm is fast disappearing. The time has come for us in Nigeria to borrow a leaf from Angola where town residents are forbidden from taking and having more than one wife,[67] and other places where the practice of polygamy is totally bound.[68] Polygamy breeds hatred, evil practice, untimely death etc. It is not economical. It breeds disharmony in the family and unhealthy rivalry and undue competition. It is not suitable for any modern society. Any law which encourages polygamy must be discarded with. Our customary law which encourages the practice of polygamy must be regarded as repugnant to natural justice, equity and good conscience and done away with.

CEDAR has been ratified by this country, yet its provisions are yet to be domesticated into Nigerian laws. As a result, those rights given voice to in CEDAR cannot be upheld in a court of law in Nigeria. There should not only be domestication of the provisions of CEDAR, there should be the development of a local CEDAR in order to ensure the protection of the rights of women in Nigeria.

CONCLUSION

Women are central to the development of Nigeria. They constitute a potent production force and hold a numerical majority. Nigerian society is male dominated and highly stratified by class and gender. In spite of the number of legal supports for women's rights and legal protection in Nigeria, there are yet inequalities many of which are consequences of contemporary laws. Despite the array of available legal rights as reflected in laws, gender specific legal rights in Nigeria remain inadequate. We all have a responsibility to join hands in order to create a future in which all forms of discriminations against women would cease. If positive results of achieving real recognition of the fundamental rights of women to freedom from discrimination and right to human dignity are to be achieved, there must be the generation of more awareness among the people by way of education. There must be a remedial measure aimed at re-orientating the minds of the people with respect to their attitude to the role and rights of women in the society. The protection of the civil rights of women in Nigeria which is currently at the mercy of the patriarchal order would have been placed on the principle of law.

Nigerian women constitute the largest female population in Africa. The Nigerian sociocultural and political systems encourage subjugation, relegating women to the bottom rung of the political and economic ladder. They are often treated as a minority in the Nigerian patriarchal social order. Social justice and self-reliance cannot be guaranteed without the elimination of all forms of oppression, discrimination and subordination of women. The rights of Nigerian women as an oppressed social group need a system of protection in order to ensure that their freedom to pursue economic, social and political opportunities are protected by the laws and regulations of the land. This will serve to ensure that the civil rights of women in Nigeria are removed from the mercy of the patriarchal order and to place them on the principle of law. The best way to achieve this is to ensure that the protection of the rights of women is enshrined in our laws rather than maintaining gender neutrality.

Nigeria is an egalitarian society. As a civilized society, there should be no place for discrimination against women. Any custom which discriminates should not only be regarded as unconstitutional but should be regarded as repugnant to natural justice, equity and good conscience. The time is now to put in place measures to abolish those customs and practices which serve to promote discrimination against women.

NOTES

1. Salmond on Jurisprudence.
2. Article 7 of the Universal Declaration of Human Rights (1948).
3. Article 2 of the Universal Declaration of Human Rights (1948).
4. Ibid., Article 6.
5. Article 21(1) Married Women Property Act.
6. Ibid., Article 21(2).
7. *Augustine N. Mojekwu v. Caroline M.O. Mojekwu* (1997) NWLR (pt 512) 283 at 304-305 – Par Niki Tobi, JCA.
8. Article 16(3) of the Universal Declaration of Human Rights (1948).
9. Ibid., Article 22.
10. Oputa J. S.C., Womanhood and the Human Side of Justice, in the 2nd Annual Graham.
11. Douglas Memorial Lecture.
12. The Nigerian Penal Code.
13. The Customary Marriage Manual 1977, p. 266.
14. *Sogunro-Davies v. Sogunro Davies and Ors,* (1929) 2 N.L.R. 79 at 80 p Per Beckley J.
15. *Suberu v. Sunmonu* (1957) 2 F.S.C. 31 per Jibowu F.I.
16. United Nations Convention on the Elimination of all Forms of Discrimination Against Women: African Charter.
17. Qur'an 4.

18. Buxton, Maliki Law (1916).
19. Holy Qur'an, Chaper 2:56.
20. Holy Qur'an, Chaper 4:32.
21. Constitution of Federal Republic of Nigeria.
22. Section 33(1) of the Marriage Act.
23. Section 2(2) of the Matrimonial Causes Act 1970.
24. Section 160(1)(c) of the Evidence Act.
25. Section 41 Article 1(a)(b), Section 41 Article 3.
26. Section 18 Article 3(e).
27. Section 18 Article 3(c).
28. Chapter iv, Section 33(1b) of the 1989 Constitution.
29. Section 18 Article 2(a) of the Constitution.
30. Article 43 of the Constitution.
31. Sections 54 – 58 of the Labor Law.
32. Section 224(1) of the Criminal Code.
33. Section 224(2) of the Code.
34. Section 224(3) of the Code.
35. Ibid.
36. Section 33 of the Code.
37. Section 34 of the Code.
38. Section 36 of the Criminal Code.
39. Section 14 of Criminal Procedure Act.
40. Section 353 of the Criminal Code of Southern Nigeria.
41. Section 55 of the Penal Code of Northern Nigeria.
42. Section 357 of the Criminal Code.
43. Section 75 of the Sexual Offences Act 2003.
44. Section 76 of the Sexual Offences Act 2003.
45. Section 229 of the Criminal Code.
46. The Customary Law Manual, 1977, para. 321, p. 266.
47. Ibid., para 321(3)(b) p. 266.
48. Para. 322(1) of the Customary Law Manual 1977.
49. Ibid., Para 322(2).
50. Ibid., Para 322(3).
51. Customary Law Manual (1977) para. 323, p. 267.
52. Section 1(1) of the Married Women Property Act 1882.
53. Section 2 of the Married Women Property Act 1882.
54. Section 17 of the 1882 and 1959 Act.
55. Section 12 of the Act.
56. *Ogedengbe v. Ogedengbe* (1964) LLR 209.
57. Section 3(2) of the Revised Edition (Authorized Omissions) Order 1990.
58. Laws of Western Region of Nigeria 1959 Cap. 76.
59. Section 2 of the Married Women Property Act 1958.
60. Section 10 Married Women Property Act 1893.
61. *Asomugha v. Asomugha*, C.C.H.C.J./12/72, 91.
62. *Edet v. Edet*, Suit No. E/6D66 of 8/8/66s.
63. *McFarlane v. McFarlane* (2006) UKGL 24.
64. *White v. White* (2000) 2 FLR 981.
65. A situation where a person dies without a will.

66. Section 36 of the Marriage Act.
67. Phillips: An Introductory Essay in Survey of African Marriage and Family Life.
68. Tunisian Law of Personal Status, 1956; Law of personal status for Iraq. Law 18 of 1959.

REFERENCES

Abdullah, H. J. and Hamza, I. (2003), Women and Land in Northern Nigeria: The Need for Independent Ownership Rights in I. M. Wanyeki (ed) *Women and Land in Africa: Culture, Religion and Realizing Women's Rights*. Cape Town: David Philip Publishers, pp. 133–147.

Aderinto, F. O. A. and Fashoyin, T. (eds.) (1986), *Manpower Development and Utilization in Nigeria: Problems and Policies*. Lagos: Lagos University Press.

Aguda, A. (1985) A New Perspective in Law and Justice in Nigeria, Text of Lecture Delivered at NIPPS, Kuru, October 25, 1985.

Akande, J. O. (1968) The Rights of Women in Property in Nigeria, Vol. 2, p. 15.

Akintola, S. O. (2004) A Focus on Female Discrimination and Seclusion in Nigeria, Ife Juris Review, *A Journal of Contemporary Legal and Allied Issues*, Vol. 1 IFJR Part 2, pp 312–320.

Amina, A. Augie (1993) Women's Rights in Law and Practice: Special Welfare in Akintunde O. Obilade (ed), *Women in Law*, Southern University Law Center and Faculty of Law, University of Lagos, p. 235.

Ashiru, M. A. O. (2004) Preserving the Dignity of Women in Ife Juris Review, *A Journal of Contemporary Legal and Allied Issues*, Vol. 1 IFJR Pt. 2, pp. 250–263.

Ashiru, M. O. (2007) Gender Discrimination in the Division of Property in Nigeria, *Journal of African Law*, 51, 2 (2007), School of Oriental and African Studies, Printed in the United Kingdom.

Boserup, Ester (1970) *Women's Role in Economic Development*. London: George Allen and Unwin.

Boulding, E. (1977) *Women in the Twentieth Century World*. New York: John Wiley and Sons.

Dworkin, Ronald (1977) *Taking Rights Seriously*. Cambridge, MA: Harvard University Press.

Fried, E. (1975) *Women and Men: An Anthropological View*. New York: Holt, Rinehart & Winston.

Godwin, D. D., and J. Marlowe (1990) *Farm Wives Labor Force Participation and Earnings Rural Sociology*, Vol. 55, No. 1, Spring.

Hall, W. W. (1862) *Health of Farmer's Family*, United States Department of Agriculture Annual Report.

Hart, H. L. A. (1961) *The Concept of Law*. Oxford, UK: Oxford University Press.

Hodges, A. (2001) Children and Women's Rights in Nigeria: A Wake-Up Call. A UNIFECS Publication, National Planning Commission, Abuja.

Livingstone, V. P., Mary Slessor of Calabar, 1918, p. 22.

Mann, D. S. (1984) No Way to Treat a Lawyer: Female Lawyers in South Carolina, *Women Lawyers Journal*, Vol. 70, No. 2, Winter.

Marshall, O. R. (1965) A Critique of the of the Property Legislation of Nigeria *1 Nig. L.J.* 151.

National Planning Commission (2001) *Children's and Women's Rights in Nigeria: A Wake-Up Call*, A UNIFECS Publication, National Planning Commission, Abuja, p.179.

Nwabueze, B. O. (1972) *Nigerian Land Law*, p. 171.

Nwogugu, E. I. (1974) Problems of the Dissolution of Customary Law Marriages in Nigeria, A Seminar Paper on New Direction in African Family Law, presented in 1974.

Obi, S. N. C. (1966) *Modern Family Law in Southern Nigeria*. London: Sweet & Maxwell, p. 155.

Obilade, A. O. (1993) *Women in Law*, Southern University Law Center and Faculty of Law, University of Lagos.

Ogungbe, M. O. (2003) *Nigerian Law: Contemporary Issues*. Essays in Honour of Sir, Chief (Dr.) Gabriel Osawaru Igbinedion, The Esama of Benin Kingdom & Chancellor, Igbenidion University, Okada.

Olarinde, E. S. (1997) *Contemporary Issues in Nigerian Legal System*. Nigerian Bar Association, Ibadan.

Olaseeni, O. O. (2004) The Nigerian Law of Abortion: The Need for a Change in Ife Juris Review, *A Journal of Contemporary Legal and Allied Issues*, Vol. 1 IFJR Part 2, pp, 392–400.

Omonubi-McDonnel, M. (2003) *Gender Inequality in Nigeri*a. Ibadan: Spectrum Books Ltd., p. 130.

Onifade, J. A. (1989) The Adequacy of Legal Rights of Women in Nigeria, in Akande and Osinulu, *Voter Education For Nigerian Rural Women*, Reports of Two Workshops.

Onokah, M. C. (2007) *Family Law*. Ibadan, Nigeria: Spectrum Books Limited.

Oputa, C. (2003) Equal Rights Under the Law: A Myth or Reality, cited by Adeniyi Olatunbosun. An Enquiry Into the Rights of Working Class Women in Nigeria, Nigerian Law: Contemporary Issues, Essay in Honour of Sir Chief (Dr.) Gabriel Osawaru Igbeinedion, College of Law Igbinedion Univerity, Okada, Benin City, pp. 76–87 at p. 83.

Oputa, C. (1997) Equal Rights Under the Law: A Myth or Reality, in *Contemporary Issues in Nigerian Legal System*, Nigerian Bar Association, Ibadan, pp. 1–25 at p. 5.

Park, A. E. W. (1963) Sources of Nigerian Law, p. 51.

Ransome-Kute, F. (1961) The Status of Women in Nigeria, *Journal of Human Relations*, No. 1.

Rawls, J. (1971) *A Theory of Justice*. Cambridge, Mass.: Belknap Press of Harvard University Press.

Rosaldo, M. Z., and L. Lamphere (eds) (1975) *Women, Culture and Society*. Stanford, Calif.: Stanford University Press.

Schlegel, Alice (ed) (1977) *Sexual Stratification: A Cross Cultural View*. New York: Columbia University Press.

Uchem, R. N. (2001) *Overcoming Women Subordination*. An Igbo African and Christian Perspective: Envisioning an Inclusive Theology with Reference to Women. Dissertation.com Parkland, U.S.A.

Wanyeki, I. M. (ed) (2003) *Women and Land in Africa: Culture, Religion and Realizing*. London: Zed Books.

Wilson Joan, H. (1989) The Negative Impact of the American Revolution, in *Major Problems in American Women's History*, Mary Beth Norton, 90–101, Washington, D.C: D.C. Heath and Company.

Women's Rights. Cape Town: David Philip Publishers, 2003.

6

Critical Appraisal of Domestic Violence in Nigeria

Adesina Coker, LL.M, MBA

ABSTRACT

The problem of domestic violence cuts across national boundaries as it is a problem of global concern. There is the erroneous belief that only women are victims of domestic violence but this is not entirely true. It must be quickly pointed out that there is ample evidence in our homes to show that men too (even though in less proportion), children and the elderly are vulnerable to domestic violence. This chapter looks at domestic violence on women under the pretext of marriage.

It looks at the physical and mental assault elements as the crux of the matter in the nature of domestic violence. The writer proceeded to characterize the problem as encompassing violence against women, child abuse, be it physical, psychological or sexual violence between siblings, abuse or neglect of the elderly and abuse of parents by children.

This article concludes that attempts must be made to amend our laws particularly the Criminal Code to take care of the domestic violence at home as it is now settled that marriage does not constitute a license to assault a spouse against his or her will and the old common law doctrine which allows a husband to beat his wife provided "he used a stick not thicker than his thumb" has since been consigned to the museum of legal folklore.

INTRODUCTION

Fundamentally, the problem of domestic violence cuts across national boundaries as it is a problem of global concern and consequently, there is no shortage of modern authority that defines the nature and attempt to state the limits and frontiers of the problem.[1]

There exist this widely held but erroneous impression (even alluded to in the United Kingdom Law Commission's Report) that wives are the only victims of ill treatment and domestic violence, particularly in our society. This conclusion in a society where sociocultural and traditional patterns and norms place unwarranted and limitless power on men over women and even give them the latitude to treat wives as mere chattel and in some cases wards deserving strict marital supervision administered by husbands is not out of place.

It must be quickly pointed out that there is ample evidence in our homes to show that men too (even though in less proportion), children and the elderly are vulnerable to domestic violence.[2] However, the position that women and children are the main victims remain unassailable as the family unit is one social unit in which there are strong dependency relationships whereby some family members such as the wife and the children depend on the husband /parent so much in terms of physical, material and psychological security.

The varieties of domestic violence prevalent in our society[3] today as noted earlier are incapable of any exhaustive classification and attempt will not be made in this direction, but suffice it to say however that certain acts of violence are common today which has emerged a more urgent social problem, in the sense that the victims may not be able to do anything to himself or herself. This urgent social problem is the abuse (both sexual and other forms) of children in particular either as dependants of their parents or young and underaged brides in general. Today, such a child is a victim of innumerable hazards (both at home as a wife and as a dependant child) ranging from violent domestic assaults, which can be manifested in either physical assault and battery or sexual abuse of the child.

In any society where such degree of violence reigns, it is expected that institutions of state must be utilized to check and control the spate of such aberrant tendencies. The keen but curious silence or near silence of the law in this area do not confer any advantage; neither does it reflect extant global effort to redress the inequalities of the human race.

Currently, Nigeria is a signatory to the United Nations on the Elimination of All Forms of Discrimination against Women (CEDAW),[4] an international convention which amongst other things enjoins state parties to condemn discrimination against women in all its forms, agree to pursue by all appropriate means and without delay a policy of eliminating discrimination against women.

According to a writer (Nwankwo, 1992: 50), domestic violence generally is the "physical or mental assault of one member of the family by another member, that is, where the victim and the perpetrator have some form of personal relationship or where they have had such a relationship in the past." Having identified the physical and mental assault elements as the crux of the matter in the nature of domestic violence, the writer proceeded to characterize the problem as encompassing violence against women, child abuse, be it physical, psychological or sexual violence between siblings, abuse or neglect of the elderly and abuse of parents by children.

The above definition embraces substantially the pity and substance of the problem of domestic violence in our society. For as the United Kingdom's Law Commission pointed out, "domestic violence can take many forms." The term according to the commission's report has a wider meaning (in addition to the narrower meaning of the use or threat of physical force) "which extends to abuse beyond the more typical instances of physical assault to include any form of physical, sexual or psychological molestation or harassment which has a serious detrimental effect upon the health and well-being of the victim." Example of such "non-violent harassment or molestation cover a very wide range of behavior, common instances include persistent pestering and intimidation through shouting, denigration, threats or argument, nuisance telephone calls, damaging property, following the applicant about and repeatedly calling her home or place of work, installing a mistress into the matrimonial home with wife and children, filling car locks with super glue, writing anonymous letters and pressing one's face against a window whilst brandishing papers."[5]

The above definitions clearly show that there is no divergence of opinions on the fact that domestic violence in all its ramifications goes beyond the narrow concept of the use or threat of physical force to, other conducts which as pointed out have the effect of subjecting the victims to both mental, psychological and in most cases physical torture. With little exceptions which pertain to form only, both the violent and non-violent forms of domestic abuse exist in our society today. Acts ranging from wife beating, sexual abuse of wives and children to physical and emotional torture exist in varying degree in most Nigerian societies. The truth of the matter is that the extent of such conduct which must be classified as domestic violence is impossible to assess with exhaustive accuracy; there seems little doubt however that domestic violence is indeed widespread.

Marriage has been defined to be a "voluntary union for life of one man and one woman to the exclusion of all others."[6] It is assumed that a man and woman would live happily together as one happy family during the pendency of the marriage and till death do them part. However, this is usually not the case as some marriages become so bad that one of the couples would resort to violence. The focus of this chapter is on domestic violence in matrimonial homes.

One of the most dangerous symptoms of conflict in domestic relationships is when it escalates into domestic violence. Studies have shown that incidence of domestic violence is on the increase and spouse killings were found to occur almost exclusively against a background of severe marital discord.[7]

Love, care, understanding, mutual trust and mutual tolerance, all hitherto the hallmark of a prosperous marital union take flight and in their stead violence or at least threatened violence reigns supreme in such homes and there exists a steady degree of mutual intolerance. There is in fact an ascendancy of a charged atmosphere in a home where love has disappeared. In such circumstances, the affected couples gradually resort to violence as a means of settling their disputes.[8] Domestic disputes that were hitherto settled with little or no verbal altercation are now settled by resort to physical violence and in some bizarre cases sexual, psychological and mental violence (Edwards and Halpern, 1991). These disputes often go to the extreme when most often they lead to the commission of violent crimes.[9]

In *Kowalski*,[10] a husband and wife engaged in oral sex. At first the wife tolerated this practice but when she changed her mind, her husband refused to accept her decision. He burst on her while she was in the lavatory, threatened her with a sharp knife and forced her to have oral sex and vaginal intercourse. His (unsuccessful) defense against a charge of indecent assault was that in view of his wife's previous consent, oral sex had become permissible adjunct to the intercourse to which a wife was (at that time legally deemed to have consented).

Cases of domestic violence like the above-mentioned and others like wife beating, child molestation and abuse as well as marital sexual assault culminating in marital rape are not restricted or confined to certain peculiar societies or cultures. In fact, studies have shown that domestic violence occurs between people of all social classes, racial and religious groupings and in all age groups[11] and the practice in itself is not a modern or contemporary phenomenon (Cobbe, 1878). The truth of the matter is that crime and other statistics provide only a rough estimate of the nature and extent of the suffering which are endured by families behind closed doors, but there can be no doubt that parents and children living in households in which assaults take place are damaged by this behavior both physically and emotionally.

In Nigeria, just like other countries where people are more tolerant and civil, victims of domestic assaults do not complain of violence. This may be due to the fear of being further assaulted or because they are too embarrassed and ashamed to reveal their plight to professionals who might be able to assist them. Apart from the foregoing, sociocultural attitudes and even statutory provisions[12] tend to further make victims of domestic assault to refrain from complaining. In a society like Nigeria, cultural trends and attitudes see conducts or acts like wife and child beatings, sexual assaults and molestation by the husband as a necessary privilege flowing from his status as husband and this tends to undermine and stigmatize the usual female or wife victim of domestic violence. In these societies,[13] the relationship between husband and wife is considered as being analogous to that of parent/guardian, child/ward, schoolmaster/pupil and master servant. In fact, the relationship between a husband and wife in most of our communities is best exemplified by the common Chinese proverb that "a wife married is like a pony bought: I will ride her and whip her as I like."[14]

Against this uninhibitive sociocultural background, men generally in our society today have ample latitude and do take advantage of the reprehensible sociocultural attitude to unleash violence in the home and in most cases, they are sadly supported by our laws.

This chapter looks at whether marriage should constitute a license to assault a spouse or child of that union in a manner whatsoever against his or her will and whether crimes committed within the safe confines of "marriage" should go unpunished. Attempts shall be made to look at the current state of the law and the inadequacies in the existing legislation in the area of domestic violence in Nigeria.

DOMESTIC VIOLENCE

Nigeria's principal legislation on domestic relations, that is, the Matrimonial Causes Act[15] is bereft of any definition or description of the social problem known as domestic violence. It is noteworthy to say that the Act did define the term domestic violence. This legislative inadequacy or omission does not however relegate the problem of domestic violence to a second or third degree of social dilemma deserving little or no legal solution. In fact, studies have shown that the incidences of domestic violence in Nigeria are as rampant as many other social vices and exists as a societal problem of immense tragic proportion.[16]

One clear fall-out of this state of affairs, that is, the absence of any definite legislative framework on domestic violence is not only an exacerbation of the problem but also its transformation to that of an intractable social ill and the difficulty of our laws in detecting this challenge and the ability of our institutions to operate effectively (Besharov, 1985; Mosteller, 1992).

SEXUAL ASSAULT AND RAPE WITHIN MARRIAGE

Section 357 of the Criminal Code provides that "any person who has unlawful carnal knowledge of a woman or girl without her consent, or with her consent, if the consent is obtained by force or by means of threats or intimidation of any kind, or by fear of harm or by means of false and fraudulent representation as to the nature of the act, or in the case of a married woman, by impersonating her husband, is guilty of an offence which is called rape." Section 6 of the Criminal Code defines 'unlawful carnal knowledge as carnal connection which takes place otherwise than between husband and wife.'

The combined effect of S.6 and S.357 of the Act referred to above makes it abundantly clear that a husband is incapable of committing the offense rape against his wife. The rationale and justification for this (antiquated position of the law in England) is based on the old rule of common law proclaimed ex-cathedral[17] Sir Matthew Hale stating this absurd common law fiction said that ". . . the husband cannot be guilty of a rape committed by himself upon his lawful wife, for by their mutual matrimonial consent and contract, the wife hath given up herself in this kind unto her husband which she cannot retract."[18]

This common law position is also supported by the unity theory of Blackstone (Hary, 1986: 1255) that contends that the legal existence of the woman is suspended during the marriage and by their mutual matrimonial contract, the wife had given up herself without limitations to her husband. While the tide of legal opinion in the time of Hale seems to be in favor of the non-existence of the offense of rape within marriage, it is however clear that there was no unanimity among the judges of the Hale era.

In *Reg v. Clarence*[19] where there was non-consensual intercourse between the couple, Wills J. in his judgment said ". . . if the intercourse under the circumstances now in question constitutes an assault on the part of the man, it must constitute rape, unless, indeed, as between married persons rape is impossible, a proposition to which I certainly am not prepared to assent, and for which there seems to me to be no sufficient authority."[20]

Field J. also in the same case cast serious doubt on the position of Hale and the common law proposition when he said ". . . the authority of Hale C.J on such matter is undoubtedly high as any can be, but no other authority is cited by him for this proposition, and I should hesitate before I adopt it. There may, I think, be many cases in which a wife may lawfully refuse intercourse, and in which, if the husband imposed it by violence, he might be guilty."[21]

The above dicta show that as authoritative and preponderant as Hale's and the common law proposition might seem,[22] there existed no absolute consensus of opinion on the matter[23] but this theory held sway throughout the eighteenth and nineteenth centuries.

The long line of English cases clearly shows the introduction of criminal law into what would otherwise pass as purely domestic affairs. However Nigerian laws clearly demonstrate a reluctance to be drawn into the vortex of domestic disputes, a reluctance which cannot be justified today. According to a learned writer (Owoade, 1990), it is probably correct to say that the criminal law is not the best way of dealing with family matter, but that the exemption encourages reconciliation, intimacy and marital harmony is not altogether logical."

CONCLUSION

Our laws,[24] particularly some sections of the Criminal Code, clearly reflect a legal system that has and is still fanning the embers of an antiquated societal notion that sees no injury to a wife in a society when she is violated sexually while co-habiting with her husband. The truth is that if we view domestic violence as serious or repeated injury administered by one co-resident spouse to another, then we must be in line with the indisputable legal climate of opinion in other parts of the world that reject this proposition (which the law of marriage and crime had long rejected) and be prepared to accept that marriage is indeed not a license to commit rape.

Today in England, it is now settled that marriage does not constitute a license to assault a spouse against his or her will[25] and the old common law doctrine which allows a husband to beat his wife provided "he used a stick not thicker than his thumb" has since been consigned to the museum of legal folklore. Also, the old common law rule that was re-echoed by Hale C.J[26] in 1736 and codified by the criminal law[26] of Nigeria that a man could not be convicted for raping his wife has since been discarded.[27]

Obviously, our laws have failed to modify and our courts have also failed to sanction sociocultural patterns which are based on the superiority complex of men over women. The continuous retention of sections such as sections 6 and 357 of the Criminal Code and section 282 of the Penal Code in our statute books are indelible attestation to this fact and further demonstrates resolute but impolite refusal of our legislation to move away from a base and antiquated legal regime. It is this writer's opinion that these laws will encourage marital disharmony in the family and ultimately affect societal fabric, the family unit being the basic societal pillar.

While it may be true that these laws are indicative of the metes and bounds of our sociocultural values and therefore reflective of our long established social and traditional attitudes, I hasten to maintain that law as an instrument of social change must be used to affect a change from this base propensity of our laws to a more dignified and humane attitude effectively hinged on modern legislation. Man in every society has a propensity for change and this propensity must be permanent. To this end, legislation aimed at affecting a change in societal attitude will slowly but eventually change these present day repugnant sociocultural practices.

According to a learned writer, "specific rules of law will develop, great fields of law will be systematized, simplified, cleared of obscurity and technical obstacles will be swept away, and most of this must be accomplished under the sanction of legislation."[28]

The time has indeed come when prejudices of yester-years that have brought no good with them to give way to fresh, equal and protective attitudes ushered in by law to align our society with practices and dictates of the civilized world.

NOTES

1. Smith, L. J. F. (1989) *Domestic Violence: An Overview of the Literature.* UK Home Office Research Study No 107; Edwards, S. S. M., and A. Halpern (1991) Protection for the Victim of Domestic Violence: Time for Radical Revision, JSW & FL 940; see also the UK Law Commission Report on Domestic Violence and Occupation of the Family Home. Law Com. No. 207 1992; see also Marruagem, M. D. (1992) *Wife Beating and the Law in Victoria England.*

2. Obiageli Nwankwo op. cit at p. 51; see also Mary Hayes and Catherine Williams op. cit at p. 306.

3. www.whbw.org/important_information_about_domestic_violence.htm last visited on 23/01/2007.

4. Adopted and opened for signature, ratification and accession by the General Assembly on December 18, 1979. Entered into force on September 3, 1981. Ratified by Nigeria in 1985.

5. Report on Domestic Violence and Occupation of the Family Home: Law. Com. No 207 (1992) para 2:3.

6. Per Lord Penzance in *Hyde v. Hyde* 1860 L.R 1 P.D 130.

7. Wallace, A. (1996) *Homicide: The Social Reality,* Research Study No. 5 Bureau of Crime Statistic and Research, NSW Attorney General Department, p. 127; see also Graycar, R. and J. Morgan (1984) *The Hidden Gender of Law,* The Federation Press; Freeman, M. D. A. (1979) *Violence in the Home,* Farnborough, UK: Saxon House; Hayes, M., and C. Williams (1995) *Family Law, Principles, Policy & Practice.* London: Butterworth, p. 305.

8. Koyonda, S. O. (no date) A Contemporary Appraisal of the Law's Response to Domestic Violence in Nigeria, unpublished article.

9. The Law Reports from the Commonwealth Jurisdiction are full of such cases. See *R v. Brown* (1986) 8 Cr. App. R 323 where a sentence of three years at the lower court was upheld; *R v. Gotts* (1991) 2AllE.R 1, where a 16-year-old son attempted to kill his mother in response to a threat by his father that if he did not do so, the father would shoot the son.

10. [1998] 8 Cr. App 339.

11. Russel, M. (1989) *Taking Stock: Refuge Provisions in London in the Late 1980s,* South Council; United Nations Centre for Social Development and Humanitarian Affairs; *Violence against Women in the Family,* see Law Commission of England Working Paper No. 113 and Law Commission Paper No. 207, 1992 (Domestic Violence and Occupation of the Matrimonial Home).

12. S.6 of the Criminal Code of Nigeria (which is applicable to the Southern States of Nigeria) where the term unlawful carnal knowledge used in defining the offence of rape clearly excludes unlawful carnal knowledge which takes place otherwise than between husband and wife. See also S.5591 of the Penal code (which is applicable to the Northern State of Nigeria) which provides that "nothing is an offence which does not amount to the infliction of grievous hurt upon any person and which is done: (a) by a parent or guardian for the purpose of correcting his child or ward, such child or ward being under 18 years old; (b0 by a husband for the purpose of correcting his wife such husband and wife being subject to any native law and custom in which such correction is recognized as lawful."

13. See People from the Northern Nigeria, some parts of China, Papua and New Guinea.

14. Obiageli Nwankwo, Violence Against Women; see also Eliminating Discrimination against Women, op. cit. at p. 50.

15. Cap 221 Laws of Federation of Nigeria 1990 (formerly Matrimonial Causes Decree) 1970.

16. Ada Okwuosa, *Some Perspectives on Domestic Violence and the Law in Nigeria*; see also Pioneer newspaper February 10–16, 1992, where a man was reported to have set his wife ablaze following an argument when the man alleged his wife had insulted him and his family.

17. By Sir Matthew Hale in his Seminar work History of the Pleas of the Crown (1736) Vol. 1, Ch. 58.

18. Ibid. at page 629.

19. Ibid (1888) 22 Q.B.D 23.

20. Ibid. at p. 33.

21. Ibid. at p. 57.

22. In line with Hale's theory; Archbold, "Pleading and Evidence in Criminal Cases" (1822) p. 259, where it was stated that "a husband also cannot be guilty of rape upon his wife." Also in matrimonial cases, the theory was also accepted. See *Popkin v. Popkin* 1774 1 Hag ECC 765.

23. See the dictum of Byrne J in *Rex v. Clark* (1949) 2 All E.R 448.

24. See S.55 of the Penal Code Law of Northern Nigeria which provides that "nothing is an offence which does not amount to infliction of grievous hurt upon any person which is done by a husband for the purpose of correcting his wife, such husband or wife being subject to native law and custom in which such correction is recognized as lawful." S.241 of the same Penal Code defines the term "grievous hurt" to include emasculation, permanent loss of sight, ability to hear and speak. It is sad to state that the act did not include non-consensual intercourse within marriage as grievous hurt.

25. See *R v. Jackson* (1981) 1 Q.B 671 at 679; *R v. Reid* (1973) Q.B 299. The extent to which consent is capable of being a defense to a charge of sexual assault presents considerable difficulties. See *R v. Brown* (1994) A.C 214.

26. Hale op. cit.

27. See Ss 6 and 357 and S.282 of the Penal Code of Northern Nigeria.

28. See *Regina v. R* (1992) 1 A.C 599.

REFERENCES

Harv, L. R. (1986) *To Have and To Hold: The Marital Rape Exemption and the Fourteenth Amendment: A Note*, p. 1255.

Besharov, D. *Doing Something about Child Abuse: The Need to Narrow the Grounds for State Intervention.*

Cobbe, F. P. (1878) *Wife Torture in England.* Following a campaign drawing attention to the brutal treatment of many working-class women, S.4 of the matrimonial Causes Act 1878 in England gave a criminal court before which a man was convicted of aggravated assault on his wife the power to make a separation and maintenance order in her favour.

Mosteller, R. (1992) Child Abuse Reporting Laws and Attorney-Client Confidences: The Reality and the Specter of Lawyer as Informant. *Duke Law Journal*, Vol. 42, No 2.

Owoade, M. A. (1990) *A note on rape,* 1 O.S.U L.J 31.

Nwankwo, O., Violence Against Women: An Overview: Eliminating Violence Against Women, p. 50.

Edwards, S. S. M., and A. Halpern (1991) *Protection for the Victim of Domestic Violence: Time for Radical Revision.* JSW & FL 94.

7

An Overview of Legal and Implementation Framework of Nigeria's National Gender Policy

Benson Kunle Sehinde

ABSTRACT

This study assessed the legal and implementation framework of Nigeria's National Gender Policy (NGP). It also aimed at realizing Nigeria's national and international commitments as enshrined in policy and treaty documents promoting and protecting women's human rights in public and private places. It gives an overview of the National Gender Policy articulated by the Federal Ministry of Women Affairs which contains monitoring framework and indicators to ensure that women benefit from their implementations. The analysis revealed that the articulation and wide dissemination of the NGP is a significant achievement in the direction of gender mainstreaming in Nigeria. The study concluded that change is inevitable and the continued articulation and implementation of the legal framework and policy, no matter how slow, are steps in the right direction.

INTRODUCTION

The past three decades have witnessed a global emphasis on women's issues. This has been remarked by the decade for women (1975–1985) and international meetings on women's issues such as those in Nairobi (1985) and Beijing (1995). These meetings centered on the strategies for women's advancements in various countries and have had significant effects on the political agenda and social life of several nations. In Nigeria, for example, the Beijing conference increased to some extent the awareness for gender considerations in many issues. Phrases such as in the interest of Beijing have become a common slogan of the the Guardian on Sunday, April 27, 1997). It is interesting to note that many development agencies have also encouraged research and placed greater emphasis on gender and development issues from interdisciplinary and multidisciplinary perspectives.

Gender is culture specific, gender issues are not women issues alone, they are issues of men and women and the attendant power relations between the sexes. Gupta (2000) is of the view that gender refers to the widely shared expectations and norms within a society about appropriate male and female behaviour, characteristics and roles. It is a social and cultural construct that differentiates women from men and defines the ways in which men interact with each other.

In other to understand the concept of gender we must look at it in terms of the social construction and the allocation of roles and expectations to men and women in any given society. National gender policy is a document approved by the federal government of Nigeria containing its plans toward the equal fair treatment of men and women, its reason for the plan and what it hopes to achieve.

Promoting gender equality is now globally accepted as a development strategy for reducing poverty levels among women and men, imposing health and living standards and enhancing efficiency of public investments. The attainment of gender equality is not only seen as an end in itself and a human rights issue, but as a prerequisite for the achievement of sustainable development. The intention of this chapter is to assess the legal and implementation framework of Nigeria's National Gender Policy (NGP). This chapter is structured into six parts. Part one introduces the chapter, part two examines conceptual clarification, part three looks at policy direction and gender ideologies, part four focuses attention on gender misconceptions and persistent inequalities policy, part five deals with the assessment of legal and implementation framework of Nigeria's policy, while part six concludes the study.

Conceptual Clarifications: Gender, National Gender Policy, Gender Mainstreaming

According to UH-Habitat (2003), the term "gender" refers to economic, social and cultural attributes and opportunities associated with being male or female. There is no doubt that in almost all societies, women and men differ in their activities and undertaking, regarding access to and control over resources, and participating in decision making. Gender is a social institution, cultural construct and power tool.

However, there is a danger to confuse gender with women. Sen (1999) is of the view that the concept of gender is not limited to the male or female species, but goes further to assess the relations between them.

Gender analysis entails having knowledge of both women and men's roles and responsibilities, as it is the comparative analysis between these that will highlight the gender inequalities of any society. Gender inequality does not imply that all women are worse than men. Rather gender being male or female is an important social division characterized by inequality. Being a woman or a man influences people's perspectives and their social expectations. Canada-Ukraine gender fund (2004) means that women and men enjoy the same status and have equal opportunities for realizing their full human rights and potential to contribute to national, political, economic, social and cultural development, and to benefit from the results.

The concept of gender equality acknowledges that different treatment of women and men sometimes required to achieve sameness of results, because of different life conditions or to compensate for past discrimination. Gender inequality is a reflection of the disparities existing between the male and female sexes. These disparities are due to misconceptions of the natural differences and make-ups between men and women as designed by God. In Nigeria today the attitude toward women is such that it calls for serious concern.

National Gender Policy

The issue of national gender policy becomes imperative as treating women equally with men will bring development to the country in no small measures. The Millennium Development Goal no. 3 which is the achievement of gender and equality and women empowerment is the one needed to achieve all other MDGs. Section 2 of the Nigerian constitution stipulates that women are to be treated in the same fair manner as men, but the reverse seems to be the case. Section 43 of the 1979 constitution also allows women and men to own and acquire property, yet in many of our communities when land is shared women are not given, and when fathers die, daughters are barred from inheriting land or property.

Gender is not about women empowerment though it is inclusive; it is about empowering all the component members of the society but there is emphasis on women because of their importance in the society as equal partners in national development, as citizens of the world and as our mothers, wives and sisters. I cannot agree more that empowerment of women is smart economics. According to Robert (2008) investments in women yield large economic and social returns.

National Gender Policy (NGP) 2006/2007 articulated by the Federal Ministry of Women Affairs contains monitoring framework and indicators to ensure that women benefit from their implementation. It is one of the municipal (national) instruments aimed at realizing Nigeria's national and international commitments as enshrined in policy and treaty documents promoting and protecting women's human rights in public and private spaces. It is not a novel initiative as it is preceded by the National Policy on Women which came into operation in 2001. The contents and focus of the NGP are premised on Nigeria's aspirations for a) social justice (Chapter II of the 1999 Constitution); (b) inclusive democracy (CEDAW and the African Union Protocol on the Rights of Women in Africa); and c) participatory and sustainable development (MDGs) for all citizens irrespective of sex or circumstances. Overall, the NGP seeks to equip stakeholders with strategic skills for achieving the levels of social change for the empowerment and inclusion of all citizens. The challenge here is not the articulation of the policy document but in its implementation through the employment/application of values and global standards to formulate and assess its progress.

GENDER MAINSTREAMING

The third Millennium Development Goal (MDG) to promote gender equality and empower women is considered by the World Bank as a central component to its overall mission to reduce poverty and stimulate economic growth. Therefore concerns in ensuring gender equity through gender mainstreaming has been recommended and accepted in different instruments and conventions by member nations of international and regional organizations. For Nigeria, the most pertinent instruments are the United Nations Convention on the Elimination of All Forms of Discrimination Against Women (CEDAW), the Beijing Platform for Action (BPfA) and the African Union Protocol on the Rights of Women (AU Protocol). Thus gender in development has become a policy issue with the emphasis on framework and strategies in pursuing economic growth, social cohesion and stability, empowerment of constituent members of the society, enjoyment and protection of human rights of constituent members (World Bank, 2008).

POLICY DIRECTION AND GENDER IDEOLOGIES

The goal of the National Gender Policy is to build a just society devoid of all social groups regardless of sex or circumstances, promote the enjoyment of fundamental human rights and protect the health, social, economic and political well being of all citizens in order to achieve equitable rapid economic growth; evolve an evidence-based planning and governance system where human, social, financial and technological resources are efficiently and effectively deployed for sustainable development (National Gender Policy, 2006).

The attainment of the NGP above is premised in some of the below key principles

- The need to see gender issues central and critical to national development goals and objectives.
- Policies need to be reviewed to reflect gender implications and strategies as contained in line with the National Gender Strategic Framework.
- Commitment to gender mainstream as a development approach and tool for achieving the economic reform agenda and social transformation among others.
- Effective and results-focused policy implementation demands a cooperative interaction of all stakeholders.
- Promotion and protection of human rights, social justice and equity.
- Emphasis is laid on information and communication research and data as well as monitoring and evaluation as supportive strategies for achieving the policy goals.

The primary governance tools for integrating gender into development planning and sustainable national development is the 1999 constitution of the Federal Republic of Nigeria. Chapter two, fundamental objectives and directive principles stipulates particularly the political, economic, social and educational objectives of the state, which forbids any form of discrimination against women.

The rights of women under the constitution are complemented by a series of other global initiatives and national efforts aimed at building a just, rational, open and equitable society where women are not only recognized but also given their right dues as co-partners in the development process. Some of the global, regional, sub-regional and national initiatives which Nigeria has acceded their relevant provisions into sectoral policies impinging on the welfare of women among others:

- National policy on women
- The National Economic Empowerment and Development Strategy (NEEDS)
- The Millennium Goals
- The ECOWAS Gender Policy
- Declaration of the 1994 International Conference on Population and Development (ICPD)
- The African Charter on Human and People's Rights
- The United Nations Convention as the Elimination of All Forms of Discrimination against Women (CEDAN) which was signed in 1985 and ratified in 1991

- Declaration of the 1993 World Conference on Human Rights held in Vienna which articulated and unequivocally defined women's rights
- The 1999 Beijing Declaration and Platform for Action
- The New Partnership for Africa's Development (NEPAD)

Despite the long history of women empowerment in Nigeria, gender issues suffered by the majority of women still continues to be on the increase. All efforts through special legislation, state, by-laws and gender specific policies at all levels of government and of the civil society seem to have failed to deliver dividends of development to women and men equitably. The existing policy documents, including the extant national policy on women failed to challenge the structure, which continues to reproduce gender inequality and the overall disempowerment of women. In the absence of an equal opportunity commission in the country, and vibrant legislative structures to protect the rights of women, development opportunities will be far away from women. However, using a development-oriented approach, gender inequality is no longer seen only in human rights terms, but also as a cost to the development process.

Reconceptualizing gender ideologies especially gender equality not only from the context of legal equality and human rights but within a broad development context will have direct effect on overall development goals as well as gender justice. It is undisputable that the purpose of the gender policy is to bring a gender perspective into all aspects of planning policy, developing legislation and transformation activities in Nigeria. In other words, gender policy addresses the systematic inequalities between women and men in our society without ignoring the fundamental differences between them. It is also worthy of note that the gender policy prioritises the empowerment of women as an entry point to achieving gender equality, and seeks balance of power relations between men and women for the optimum benefit of both parties.

It has been observed that there are many constraints that hinder the implementation of gender policy in Nigeria. Culture features prominently, patriarchy follows as well as absence of legal instruments to drive actions. Also the lack of political issues as well as an inadequate number of gender advocacy groups are not left out. The few existing advocacy groups do not practice what they preach. The negative portrayals of females by the media are a worrying concern.

GENDER MISCONCEPTIONS AND PERSISTENT INEQUALITIES POLICY

The wrong perception of the concept of gender by policy makers, coupled with the responsibility for policy articulation and execution has been a challenge to the attainment of gender equality and women's empowerment goals; it is still obvious that gender issues is still exclusively about women as gender education has not cut across all level of the populace. In the same vein the impression that gender issues negatively challenges accepted norms and values of marriage, family and religion is rife. In addition many stakeholders believe that gender concerns should be addressed only within the Ministry of Women Affairs and Social Development.

There is no doubt gender inequalities to a reasonable extend limit women's access to, control over, and use of services and productive resources. Most especially they face challenges within the agricultural sector, lack of access to appropriate technologies, time, exploitation by marketers and lack of access to productive opportunities.

Gender-based differences also exist in relation to the use of forest resources. Men tend to utilize forest resources for the generation of immediate income such as logging wood for sale to furniture makers and other commercial users. However, women are becoming prominent in this area as a reasonable percentage of them are found in the saw mill selling planks to commercial users.

The role of women in promoting economic growth and social stability continues to be inadequately recognized and undervalued. This is as a result of the male dominated culture in Nigeria which gives women an inferior position in society. So do customs that forbid women from owning land, taboos, and the sexual division of labour which keep women subordinate to men and bring about the problem of unpaid productive activities performed by women at the domestic front. A remedy to these factors is that appropriate gender-sensitive policy that dismantles every form of discrimination against women in agricultural production and land use system will be a priority policy for implementation.

Gender-based marginalization can also be perceived in the unwritten norms and traditions which shape and influence organizational culture and practices. Failure to address the discriminating aspects of frameworks and policies in all sectors can spell doom to development goals. A gender audit of Nigeria's local laws and policies affirms that, until very recently, many legal instruments were discriminating and at best, gender blind. The existence of three legal systems, English law, customary law and Sharia law added more to violations of women's rights. The aftermath of which is numerous gender insensitive local laws that are not easily documented, hence difficult to monitor. Policy planners and implementers need to address this issue to foster development.

Assessment of Legal and Implementation Framework of Nigeria's National Gender Policy

The legal status of the policy thrust of the NGP is to promote gender sensitive and gender responsive culture in policy planning and national development. This presupposes a legal status that ensures compliance through enforceable mechanics and to an extent some form of redress for nonfulfillment.

The NGP as it is and even with the best articulated implementation framework may suffer the fate of its predecessor. There is therefore a need to propose and pursue legislative advocacy for an enabling act by the NASS to both affirm its status and cause enforcement and compliance with its provisions in all ramifications.

Prominent among the features of the NGP is the National Gender Policy. It has 7 objectives and 23 targets and are expected to guide the design and content of the strategic implementation framework. Key features of the discussions of the NGP focused on 16 thematic issues ranging from education to human rights. The National Gender Policy is exhaustive in its specific features and comprehensive discussion of issues with particular reference and statements on Reproductive Health and Gender Based Violence.

However, the statement of context and rationale (part 1, pages 1-2) of the National Gender Policy was fluid and in many instances statements of aspiration and impact were drowned. There was no clear statement of context of the political and economic dispensations in Nigeria being the basis of or in conformity with the global and regional instruments alluded to in Part I, Section 1.1, paragraphs 1 and 2 of the National Gender Policy. The language of the NGP is generic, lacking in firmness and direction/thrust to justifying provisions or guide accountability.

Data used in the situation analysis seem inadequate, only 3 sources were quoted, CIDA, GASS and NBS. Data and statistics from other sources such as the NDHS, UNICEF, UNIFEM and Nigeria CSOs were not referred.

A substantial number of the policy targets are ambitious in their timelines considering the weak political will, the low level of appreciation of the concept of gender mainstreaming, and the weak structures supporting current initiatives. Consequently it is proposed that the National Gender Strategic Framework (NGSF) should take these into account and align the time frames of outcome with Nigeria's 2020 vision and at the West of the MDG attainment of 2015.

Another issue is the need to recognize that some of the activities leading to the achievement of the set targets are subject to sector and global developments: For instance, Section 2.5.2; Objective (2) speaks on economic and political policies that may be subject to global trends. It would do well in drawing up the NGSF to extract and attach realistic and achievable timelines and progress evaluation that allows for mitigation of the impact of local and international developments.

Under 2.5.3 Objective 3(b) the ambition seems too high and a policy document should aim at substantial reduction as against total elimination. This will enable us to articulate benchmarks that begin with knowledge and shifts in attitudes and then reduction in prevalence of negative practices. The NGSF should therefore reasonably phase and measure achievable indices by 2020. With regards to institutional framework (pp. 27, fig. 3.1 and pp. 28), the National Gender Management System adopted by the NGP needs to be unpacked in the strategic implementation framework. Specific roles and linkages should be identified and designated to institutions (formal and informal). This is to aid disaggregation of the opportunities and gaps in capacity, budgeting and strategy development as well as the supply and demand index for a holistic gender management system as envisaged by the Commonwealth Secretariat and adopted by Uganda and others.

In respect of monitoring and evaluation (Section 3.1.7, p. 28), this section of the policy did not mention/address the gender assessment as well as the built-in benchmarks for monitoring and evaluation. The policy should have identified best practices and compatible/adaptable tools for systemic and sectoral performance reviews. This would facilitate the articulation of realistic benchmarks for activities and interventions. In addition to this, the coordination of roles and outputs of as contemplated in the gender management model will assist in monitoring stakeholder participation in the implementation of the policy while also harnessing technical and financial resources.

The legal and implementation framework of Nigeria's NGP notwithstanding has some problems and prospects. Some of these problems include the absence of requisite political will around gender issues to match words with actions on the part of the government. This is coupled with limited technical capacity of the current structures of governance to coordinate and evaluate gender mainstreaming initiatives as envisaged by the NGP.

The implication of this may be mitigated by deliberate funding, education and training at all levels for the appreciation of gender and the value for its mainstreaming. In addition, the dearth of gender disaggregated data in key sectors underscores the submission of discrimination and exclusion of women in particular and other vulnerable groups in society. Therefore the initiatives for gender mainstreaming are consistently challenged and placed low on the priority scale.

The cost (in terms of time and value judgements) of achieving an appreciation of gender needs and concerns to feed into the demand and supply index of budgeting and planning processes leading to positive shifts perceptions and attitudes. This necessarily slows down and reduces the impact of existing and new initiatives for gender mainstreaming. Also the high turnover of technocrats in structures of governance particularly the gender machinery draws back aspirations for sustainability in implementation of gender mainstreaming initiatives.

The issue of global acceptance of gender equality as a development strategy thereby providing an entry point for gender mainstreaming initiatives in programmes and development plans could be seen as one of the major prospects of legal and implementation framework of Nigeria's NGP. For Nigeria this is well demonstrated by the focus and content of NEEDS 2 and the utilization of Debt Relief Gains targeted at achieving the MDG goals. Others include the Role of Development Partners in programme and advocacy at all levels.

The strategy will be to create a synergy in the work of Development Partners and civil society organizations in order to deepen and consolidate the gains in gender awareness and appreciation. In addition, creation of a core of change agents to fast track endorsement and accountability for gender mainstreaming is also needed. The entry point will be formal and informal structures of engagement particularly amongst youth in secondary and tertiary formal institutions and the age group platforms in social structures. The cost of this must be borne by Development Partners to provide leverage for implementation of their core programmes. This is coupled with the legal reforms, the ongoing constitutional and electoral reforms provide an entry point for securing legal frameworks to recognize and create accountability on gender mainstreaming.

CONCLUDING REMARKS

National Gender Policy (NGP) to a reasonable extent has been able to promote gender sensitive and gender responsive culture in policy planning and national development. Promoting gender equality is now globally accepted as a development strategy for reducing poverty levels among women and men, improving health and living standards as well as enhancing efficiency of public investments. The attainment of gender equality is not only seen as an end in itself and human rights issue, but as a prerequisite for the achievement of sustainable development.

The articulation and wide dissemination of the NGP is a significant achievement in the direction of gender mainstreaming in Nigeria. Change is inevitable and the continued articulation and implementation of legal frameworks and policy are steps in the right direction. However, this must be complemented with sustained education and a move to impress on all the equality of opportunities for the overall well being of the Nigerian populace.

Some vibrant civil society groups are causing awareness in gender issues. The presence of some good role models in government presents an opportunity. These efforts, especially that of developing a National Gender Policy for Nigeria, has become imperative and commendable so as to effect a change in our attitude toward women.

There is need for government, school, mass media, the family, civil society, groups, non-governmental organizations, community based organizations to organize private sector, traditional and religion institutions as change agents to come together and support these transformatory and time enduring policy initiatives of the Federal Ministry of Women Affairs.

REFERENCES

Adegoroye, G. (2005) Gender Integration into Policy Reforms in Nigeria. Paper presented at 1st Annual Murtala Muhammed memorial summit. ECOWAS secretariat Asokoro Abuja.

Alamveabee, E. Idyorough (2005) *Gender Concepts and Issues in Nigeria*. Mankurah: Aboki Publishers.

Awe, B. (1994) *Nigerian Women in Historical Perspective*. Ibadan: Sankore/Bookcraft.

Canada-Ukraine Gender Fund (2004) Canadian Charter of Rights and Freedoms;

Concepts of Gender and Gender Relations; www.genderfund.com.ua

Federal Republic of Nigeria (2006) *National Gender Policy, Federal Ministry of Women Affairs and Social Development*.

Nigeria Country Report (1995) 4th World Conference on Women, Beijing.

Sunday Guardian, April 27, 1997.

Udegbe (2003) The Constitutional Conference, Political Restructuring and Women's Access to Power, in K. Amuwo, A. Agbaje, R. Suberu, and G. Herault (eds) *Federation and Political Restructuring in Nigeria*. Ibadan: Spectrum Books Limited.

World Bank Group (2008) Gender; http://World Bank.org/WEBSITE/EXTERNAL COUNTRIES/AFRICA EXT 1999 Constitution of the Federal Republic of Nigeria.

Zoellick, Robert B. (2008) *Ways to Bridge Gender Gap* on the sidelines of the IMF/WB spring meetings.

Part II

SEXISM AND WOMEN'S MARGINALIZATION

8

Masculinity in Gender Relations

The Nigerian Experience and Contribution to Sustainable Development

Adu Funmilayo Modupe

ABSTRACT

This chapter applies the theory of masculinity in a fluid form with emphasis on cultural relativity in Africa. The emphasis is the Nigerian case. Since masculinity existed since ancient times, the study sets out with the assumption that feminism is a reaction to masculinity. The history of creation has Adam as the first man and Eve as a creation from his ribs. It is believed that, nature gave men the superior edge over women. Male dominance also existed in other species of mammals. Masculinity in Africa was dominant and inculcated into the sociopolitical and economic life of the people. The spiritual was not left out in the categorization of jobs and distribution of rights within the different cultures. Resistance to masculine dominance started from Europe and spread to other continents. With globalized contact feminist ideals have spread to Nigeria and Africa at large. Nigerian ethnic variety also idealised societal values based on the superiority of men. Across the broad swath of the country men were idolised and worshipped. In pockets of cases where women were given important political and religious positions, important considerations were still accorded the male. The available cultural facts on male dominance is considered in this chapter in an attempt to bring to light better avenues to improve the promotion of gender equity. Sustainable development cannot be achieved without the contribution of about half of the population.

INTRODUCTION

Gender is the social organisation of sexual difference. It is the way society creates, patterns and rewards our understanding of feminity and masculinity or the process of ascribing roles to men and women (Shaw et al., 2001). Although biology makes the division, societal interpretations delienate into feminine and masculine people (ibid). Shaw further explains that notions of feminity and masculinity are socially constructed, created by social processes that reflect the various workings of power in society. She concluded that these notions are therefore culturally and historically changeable. Agreeing with the opinions of Nhiwatiwa (1989) Olusi Onuoha (1995) and Ogba (2006), Shaw further stressed that,

> There is nothing essential, intrinsic, or static about feminity or masculinity, rather they are social categories that might mean diferrent things in different societies and in different historical periods. Society shapes notions of feminity and masculinity through the subtle interactions between nature and nurture(2007:107). It is really impossible to speak of a fixed biological sex category outside of the sense that a culture makes of that category (ibid.).

Masculinity is the idea that the male is dominant, an ultimate creation, superior to the other gender. It is the dominant male nature in man or other organisms. It is supported with words and ideas such as "macho" representing masculine attributes. Masculine in different cultures vary in the level of dominance. In the Islamic culture for instance, the respect and responsibility accorded man is higher and totally different from that of the woman. An Afghan grandmother on the cable network refused to comment when interviewed and insisted she needed the permission of her grandson. The grandson in this respect would be the oldest available male in the family. Women in Islam are not allowed to leave the hidden places of the home without being covered. In the European culture,with generations of feminist ideas as opposed to masculinity, gender equity has grown to a fair level of comfort.

Religious, sociocultural acceptance and influence goes a long way in determining the situation of relations between gender. The African culture places a lot of importance on male dominance. In most parts of Africa, women are not allowed property inheritance, and in some parts, they are not consulted in the process of decision making, even when it boarders on their personal interest. Masculinity in Africa is culturally grounded. Different genders in the African society grow to learn a follow-up pattern of behavior. Any resistance to the norm is sanctioned from fine to death penalty for the ultimate violation. It is so terrible that women are not allowed to sit in the council of certain elders and are not allowed to join important secret societies, such organisations as the Egungun and Ogboni. They were not allowed to rule in most African societies and the backup idea is the attributed weakness believed to be biologically embedded in the female.

Masculinity describes the supernatural in the African tradition, the male gods are more violent and superior. For instance, such male gods as Ogun,

Shango, Orunmila, Aro-Oracle etc., are violent and superior in the Yoruba race of Africa. It structures the roles that African men and women play in the household; sociopolitical and economic arenas. The idea of male ally in gender empowerment is inhibited by masculine ideas. Our chapter discusses the traditions and existing cultures as it pertains to masculinity in relation to gender and its negative effects on gender equity to aid sustainable development. The popular theme among social scientists, policy makers and international agencies is the claim that the emancipation of women is a major solution to the problem of development. Women population has been estimated to about 50 percent of the world's population. Out of the 939 million rural poor, women represent the majority, that is 565 million (global development agenda). It is therefore necessary to have women's contribution to development. The chapter is subsequently structured as follows: theoretical considerations; masculinity in practice in Africa; impact of gender equity; and, sustainable development and conclusion.

THEORETICAL CONSIDERATION

Masculinity is a concept construed from the classical trait of intelligence, courage and honesty (Shaw et al., 2001:112), with two other dimensions; potent sexuality and an affinity for violence referred to as the "machismo element." According to Shaw (ibid.) machismo involves breaking rules, sexual potency, contexualised in the blending of sex and violence, and contempt for women (misogyny). Attributes such as weakness, softness and vulnerability are to be avoided at all cost.The second dimension is the provider role, composed of ambition, confidence, competence and strength. David and Brannon (1976:13-35) did an analysis into four categories of masculine dimensions:

1. No "sissy stuff": the rejection of feminity.
2. The "big wheel": ambition and the pursuit of success, fame and wealth.
3. The "sturdy oak": confidence; competence, stoicism and toughness.
4. "Give 'em hell": the machismo element.

Giving further explanations, Shaw et al. (ibid.) reveal that, although these scripts dictate masculinity in a broad sense, there are societal demands that construct masculinity differently for different kinds of men. They (ibid.) enlighten us to the fact that middle class masculinity puts an emphasis on the big wheel dimension, and the dictates of white masculinity often involve the sturdy oak, that men of colour often become associated with the machismo element. They insist some changes in the social construction of contemporary masculinity have allowed for a downplaying of the machismo element without a loss of sexual potency or societal control. A few steps into the land of the feminine, the machismo element is sometimes avoided by many who genuinely do not want to be constrained by its demand. knowing the avoidance does not mean a loss of power, but being a little more sensitive and vulnerable to please contemporary women, as the result of gender sensitization.

Gender is one of the most important features of one's identity, shaping the social life, informing attitudes, behaviours and the individual sense of self (ibid., 2001:109) (see also Akonai, 2004; Omoleke et al., 2004; and Oquaye, 1996) in line with Shaw's quotation noted that Lorber which reiterates the important point that, because gender is so central in shaping our lives, much of what is gendered we do not even recognise, it has been made normal and ordinary and occurs on the subconcious level. In emphasis she noted,

> In other words, the difference between feminity (passive, dependent, intuitive, emotional) and masculinity (strong, independent, in control, out of touch emotionally) are made to seem natural and inevitable despite the fact that gender is a social script that individuals learn . . . many of the skills and practices associated with gender involve privileges and entitlements . . . and limitations. (Shaw, 110)

Through a process of gender socialisation we learn to be a boy or a girl. Gender attitudes are learnt, internalised and rewarded or sanctioned when inappropriate. Culture is the bane on women career development. Culture places different behavioural expectations on men and women and how these expectations affect individual reactions to issues of gender. It is necessary like some countries of Africa, such as Uganda and Ghana, to have some offical gender parity laws and sustain them through affirmative action. It has been historically proven that women are able to achieve what men could not achieve in some fields of endeavour. Politically, women like Thatcher, Alele Williams (first Nigerian female vice-chancellor and woman leader), Ngozi Okonjo Iweala, Efunsetan, Moremi and other historical heroes have made marks on the sand of time. Biblically, women like Esther, Jezebel and Athaliah ruled their husbands and societies negatively and positively.

Traditional conceptions of masculinity put aside, gender equity would push forward and sustain society's development. Sustainable development cannot be achieved without the contribution of the better half of the population (Bruitland). The idea of cultural definition of roles was to increase awareness as to where power lies in the community. There is an emphasis on cultural forces which reinforces stereotype beliefs about gender but to which education and training cannot render immunity for women, especially in leadership. Scholarly and masculine writings in support of male dominance include Ezeaku (1990:104), who in support of masculinity, argued:

> History and religion have made man to look at women as passive human persons. History has placed women particularly the pre-modern (primitive) women as passive as it has never shown them as active in the world's economic, political, military and social activities. Religion which has recognised the world as divinely ordered has recognised them as the causes of all bad calamities, bad omen.

Ogba (ibid.) quoted Napoleon Bonaparte (1769–1821):

> Nature intended women to be our slaves . . . they are our property we are not theirs, they belong to us, just as a tree that bears fruits belong to a gardener. What a mad idea to demand equity for women . . . women are nothing but machines that produce children.

Onuoha (1995:2) also quoted Aristotle and Thomas Aquinas:

> an insufficient or defective creature whose entire psychosexual life was shaped by her having been deprived of a penis, and whose mortal and social existence was marked by every insincerity, and underdeveloped sense of justice and honour and incapacity for the higher human tasks.

Negative views about women in different fields of endeavour, Ogba concluded, are based on the cultural milieu of the scholar. He advised that, our claims about women should neither be culturally inductive nor based on the conclusions of scholars who have erred in history.

MASCULINITY IN AFRICA

Africa is a vast continent, it is therefore difficult to exhaust past and contemporary cultural and traditional perspectives on masculinity within the purview of an article. For our purpose therefore a brief survey of the important issues under sociocultural, religious and political perspectives will be perused. In the typical African society women are "meant to be seen and not heard" (Ogba, 92) In Zulu, Urudi Yoruba, Hausa, Ibibio, Itshekiri, and other tribes, a man is always the head of the family. Even in Asanti, with matrilineal inclinations, the male still holds a superior position of head. At the death of the head, his son takes over, no matter how young he is and if a man dies without a son, then the closest next of kin would be considered instead of a woman.

In traditional Yoruba culture the woman is not allowed to sit at the village council. She cannot also participate in certain religious festivals such as the Oro cult and the Egungun. In most African society, there is professional segregation. Men do not embark on the same trade with women.Their apartments are separated. In the traditional Igbo society, the male-female stead is separated and a woman does not visit the male stead uninvited. Ezeaku vividly portrayed this (1990:105):

> The husband's apartment is called the Obi, while the wife is called Mkpuke. There was wall with one small gate seperating the husband'obi and the wife's mkpuke. The main entrance into the compound brings visitors into the Obi. The Obi is very important and sancrosant movement is therefore restricted, conception was permissive only in the the obi. (ibid.)

The preference for a male child cuts across African traditions. Many African states are patrilineal. In extreme cases, selective abortion, foeticide and sex selection have been on record. The male child is given preferencial nutritional selection to ensure survival. Yolah (1996:5) recorded that a girl must toil more and even if permitted to attend school or any other useful venture, she must juggle school and housework and is likely to fall sick with poor nutrition. Scholarly research has recorded that in many countries such as Bolivia, Colombia, Iran, Philippines, Saudi Arabia and Nigeria, female mortality is recorded as high. The male head of the family determines and carries out traditional marriage laws which did not permit choice for a female and is usually too early in most parts of Africa. The 1990 Nigerian demographic and health survey put the median marriage for girls at seventeen years, which is too early. Africa can boast of about thirty-seven percent women literacy as opposed to ninety percent in Europe (ibid.: 6). Job opportunities are more readily available for men than for women. Law of bail did not permit women, property rights are also male inclined. The sociocultural background relegates women as appendages to their husbands. Their contributions in the home and nation is usually not recognised. The male inherits in Libya, Lesotho, Egypt, Morocco, Tunisia, Mauritius and others. Record of women political participation in Africa has not been encouraging. Masculinity in Africa is so culturally embeded, it ensures male dominance in every aspect of the sociopolitical and economic life and the African woman is accustomed to playing the role of second fiddle.

MASCULINITY AND SUSTAINABLE DEVELOPMENT IN NIGERIA

Masculinity in Nigeria vary from culture to culture in terms of concentration. Nigeria boasts of about two hundred and fifty ethnic groups with cultural and in recent times religious variances. Traditionally some of these cultures are matrilineal, while the majority are patrilineal. In simple patrilineal Igbo society, for instance, there is long established male dominance of all the arts, belief and social institutions. Ogba (ibid.:93) noted that this is why the Ibo's address their wives as "Oriaku" or Ndi Oriaku which translated to mean "consumer" or the "consumer of wealth." In the average African and Nigerian society, man is the head of every family. The wife/wives and children are completely dependent on him for socioeconomic upkeep.Oduyoye (1986:34) comments on this, and posits that

> The man is usually the head of the family and the breadwinner. He has the responsibility for the welfare of his members. In order to achieve this goal, he is expected to exercise complete control over such members. He has the final say on their movements and actions. Women and young people are not expected to participate in activities outside the home without the knowledge and permission of the head of the family. (ibid.)

Cultural inhibitions in the traditional Igbo society presents kolanut (an important spiritual and cultural object) to the man, even if the male present is younger than all the female. The male pours libation, breaks the kola and picks his own before any female, after allowing all present males the choice to pick. The woman is even offered her piece without being allowed to dip her hand in the "sacred plate" (ibid.:97). The Yoruba conception of the woman's opinion is faulty. It is often said,

Oro obirin ni
A woman's word

which is to say it cannot be considered important or it is inconsequential. A yoruba superstition also opines that if one meets a woman on his way out, his engagement or activity for that day would be a failure. In Igbo culture an adage states, "But for women and children, every Igbo word would have been spoken in proverb" (ibid.).

This is to show the inability of the woman to do constructive reasoning. It is no wonder that women's opinions are not sought in decision making. In historical records of achievement, there is a ratio of about one hundred to one record women of repute, such as queen Amina of Zaria, Efunsetan of the Yoruba mythology (a prominent Ibadan trader), madam Tinubu of Lagos, Moremi of Ile-Ife, the Yeye oba and Aremo-birin in the palace organization, Princess Daurana of the Bayajjida legend in northern Nigeria, Princess Inkpi of Igala, Queen Kambasen of Ijaw and Queen Qari of Ilesha (Ilesanmi, 1998:29)

The colonial period removed the little traditional paraphernalia of power that women had in the traditional culture, Ilesanmi insisted (ibid.). Colonialism concentrated on ensuring peaceful governance of the white man. Such social structures met on arrival were not recognised, new structures considered available options such as teachers, clerks, cooks, mission workers, a male purview were introduced. At independence therefore the new set of educated Nigerians were almost a hundred percent male. With the spread of feminist movements from Europe, educated women like Oyinkan Abayomi led social movements in campaigns for social reformation. Mrs. Charlotte Obasa formed Lagos Women League in 1923. Mrs. Funmilayo Ransome Kuti and her Elite Ladies Club was a woman activist who promoted the Egba women's interest in political participation in the colonial period. The Aba womens riots and Onitsha women uprising were all attempts to prevent the relegation of women to the background of society.

To Akintunde and Fola Ighodalo (Centre for Democratic Studies, 39), the greatest impact of the British colonial legacy was women marginalisation. Post-colonial attempts to resolve this crisis were with pockets of leadership of women like Mrs. Kuti who formed the Federation of Nigerian Women Societies in 1953 to encourage women participation in socio cultural, economic and political life of the state and encourage women's education. By 1958 the National Council of Women Societies was formed with nationwide branches. The National Commission for Women and Mrs. Marian Babangidda's Better Life for Rural Women were later attempts to better the lot of women. Military regimes did not promote gender balance and there has barely been any female participant in the Nigerian military regimes since independence. Because of religion the northern women were disenfrachised till 1929. The 1999 constitution gave adult suffrage to all Nigerians. By 1991,the situation improved and we had two female deputy governors, more female director generals and two heads of service, an improvement from the 1979 situation.

The National Commission for Women had a mandate to look after the welfare of women and assist them to get integrated into the development process. There have been emphasis on education and the formation of female professional associations to protect their interest. There is the W.I.N (Women in Nigeria), a radical organisation designed to hasten the integration of women into development. Despite all these it can be concluded that much success has not been achieved especially in decision making, mass enlightenment and removal of cultural and traditional practices that militate against them.

Scholars such as Seidman (1974), Renninger (1982, 1979), and Akinrinade and Berlin (1989) agree that development must be a matter of fusing social and economic objectives, not only for an increase in production but in order to ensure considerable structural and social transformations as well as reinforce redistribution, resulting in improvement that will benefit the entire community while ensuring a process of continuity.

Masculinity as expressed within the confine of culture, and social traditions, legal, religious and economic structures as well as exploitative and dependency relations at various levels of social interactions have conbined to limit the role of women and their benefits from the development process. This without doubt is also despite international organisations and development agencies diversion of human and material resources to the need to ensure that the benefits of economic growth and development are spread more widely and equitably to the marginalised womenfolk. The amount of studies available testify to the contribution of women to the national income and the national economy.

National and international development cannnot be discussed with any pretence of isolating the role of women in development. The problem of poverty, lack of access to resources and how to improve the productive capacity and the ability to determine their own needs and goals within the confine of exploitative economic and sexual relations persist as barrier to a just world in which women, as well as men, will share equally in the available resources. The United Nations in several fora has taken verbal and practical lead in underwriting the need for women to achieve full equity and participation in the challenges and benefits of societal development.

The problem of women participation is reflected in their growing poverty, inferior status in society and family and unequal access to legal rights, social welfare, education, property, political participation, and access to information and communication. There is therefore a need to remove long standing prejudices. A design to change the overall pattern of beliefs and perceptions of women in the society and the involvement of men in this laudable project is important.

THE WAY FORWARD

Despite inequalities women in Africa and Nigeria have struggled to exert their influence by playing active roles in the affairs of their societies. Tamuno (1983:184) noted

> The women of Ete in Nsukka division had a reputation for restoring peace by coming between combatants. (Onuoha, 1995:1)

Yolah (1996:5) also noted that our culture informs us on how we view and orient ourselves, act our social norms, attitudes and values to issues of development, emphasising that a dynamic culture must have the ability to jettison antiquity, outdated and negative practices and even laws, while encouraging the positive aspects which in fact are abundant in African society.

The African social interactive process has historical roots in courtship. Proposals and marriage rights give men the mandate to "own" their women. There is a lack of freedom in the interactive process, so much so that a woman is labeled negative if she tries to assert freedom (in after work meetings). A beautiful woman is considered free access if she is self assertive to achieve her goals. The biblical "woman is the crown of her husband," she is expected to promote and support him always. And a reversal of roles does not ensure a similar support for the woman. Women are expected to be noncontroversial peacemakers. Female docility is reinforced by societal attitudes of suppport through stereotype. At the United Nations Geneva conference in 1989, Nhiwatiwa insisted,

> they are supposed to be peacemakers, especially in public. It is usually not expected of a woman to pick a quarrel with people or engage in an argument in public . . . she loses her public esteem and self respect. Society do not readily accept her even though her argument may have been right. This perception by society of a woman as docile being has been encouraged and reinforced into such endearing term as "what a sweet lady," "the better half," the "weaker sex," etc. These stereotyped image of women can hinder them from expressing their views in controversial debates, even though their views could lead to an answer to the problem under debate. (Konez, 1989:15 in Ogba 2006:16)

A woman that maintains her argument is judged tough. Even media coverage in such situations are negative. Further in her argument, Ogba (ibid.) insists evolution of roles, sets and attitudes place a psychological effect born out of the biological difference between men and women and the manner in which society has responded to the variables. The sense of accomplishment and identity of individual depended on the success of their roles as husband, wife, mother or father. Fusi Cagicavanus (1989:90–91) emphasised that:

> Sexual segregation of activities does not permit the development of potentials as it exists in an individual.

Traditionally, family finances are managed by men. This is a limiting factor to enter into politics. History and tradition delimit political participation. The concept of divide and rule applies in the application of masculinity to belittle gender. Women should be aware that men's attitudes set them against each other. This could be intentional. A husband would make small talks about women politicians and socialites, in an attempt to dissuade his wife from pursuing such goals. A competitive spirit between women promote conflict; it is often the claim that women are quarrelsome. When women are in position, the societal expectations of failure ensures a do or die attitude. An extra mile of stress is added reducing the success in other areas such as family life.

It is important to lobby for abolition of customs and practices which are unfair to women and impede their participation with other women's groups both locally and internationally. In Nigeria there are no laws which ban women fron actively participating in the political, socioeconomic life of the country, but the cultural perception of women as inferior to men and other hidden discriminatory attitudes have been the barrier to the progress of women. There is a need to change these negative focal processes, policy formulation and implementation on women issues should improve. For women to achieve empowerment, they need training access to power and male allies. Elements within the society such as language, values, habits, and traditions which influence gender perception should be redressed for value reorientation.

CONCLUSION

Masculinity has for centuries given a positive advantage to men. The challenge faced by women is having to compete in the same marketplace with men. There is need for coping srategies. Adaptability and perseverance is very important with high emotional maturity to handle uncertainty. The adage "it is not a woman's job" should be replaced with "I can do it." As Palmer (1985) noted, "no project that attempts to increase production or enhance benefits can afford to ignore the economic potential and needs of one half of the population." Men and women have their own natural and peculiar qualities which complement each other, there is no opposition but complementarity, within a positive milieu for cultural changes. A programme of sustained reorientation and education, reverse discriminatory policies, and role modeling activities to encourage female participation is necessary. The solution should begin within the family where both sexes should be taught how to be equally relevant in the home and society. Religion should not be a hinderance to equity of participation.

REFERENCES

Afonja, S., and B. Aina (ed) (1995) *Nigerian Women in Social Change*. Ile-Ife, OAU Programme in Women Studies.

Akinrinade, O., and J. K. Barling (ed) (1989) *Economic Development in Africa*. London: London Printer Publishers Ltd.

Ako, R. T. (2003) Theoretical Issues and the New Definition of Development, in F. E. Iyoha et al.

Ako-Nai, R. I. (2004) *Organising for Change: Global Initiatives and the Growth of Women Interest Groups in Nigeria*, paper presented at the National Conference on Social Problems and Development and the Challenges of Globalisation. Organised by Department of Sociology and Anthropology, Obafemi Awolowo University Ile–Ife, Osun State.

Ann, S. (1974) *Planning for Development in Sub-saharan Africa*. New York: Praeger Publishers.

Charlton, E., and M. Sue (1984) *Women in Third World Development*. Boulder CO: Westview, Press Inc.

Deborah, S. D., and B. Robert (ed) (1976) *The Forty Nine Percent Majority: The Male Sex Role*. Reading, PA: Addison Wesley.

Ezeaku, I. et al. (1990) *Socio Philosophical Perspective of African Traditional Religion*. Enugu: New Age Publishers.

Gender Empowerment and Sustainable Development in Africa'Iroko, Vol. 2, No. 3. August, 1997. A Networking Publication of the Atlass Project.

Honsby, A. S. (2001) *Oxford Advanced Learners Dictionary*, 6th Edition. New York: Oxford University Press.

Ilesanmi, T. M. (1998) The Significance of the Myth of Women Socio-Political Role Sharing among Yoruba People. In M. E. M. Kolawole (ed) *Gender Perception and Development in Africa: A Socio Cultural Approach*. Ibadan: Patmag.

Kauffman, L. (ed) (1989) *Gender and Theory: Dialogues on Feminist Criticism*. Oxford, UK: Basil Blackwell Limited.

Nhiwatiwa, P. N. (1989) Keynote Report at the Inter-parliamentary Symposium on the Participation of Women in the Political and Parliamentary Decision-making Process. Reports and Conclusion Series, Report and Documents No. 16, Geneva.

Oduyoye, M. (1986) *The State of Christian Theology in Nigeria, 1980–81*. Ibadan: Daystar Press.

Ogba, O. (2006) *Women for Ordination: An Analytical Look*. Ibadan: Daystar Press.

Olusi, O. J. (undated) Socio Cultural, Economic and Environmental Determinants of African Women's Poverty and Disempowerment: The Nigerian Example. International Fund for Agricultural Development.

Omoleke, I. I., and L. A. Bisiriyu (2004) *Discrimination Against Women: An Overview of the Problem of Gender Inequality in the Public Service in Nigeria*. A paper presented at the National Conference on Social Problems Development and the Challenges of Globalisation. Organised by Department of Sociology and Anthropology, Obafemi Awolowo University Ile-Ife, June 16–17.

Onuoha, A. (1995) *Women and Children in Traditional African Societies*. Aba, Nigeria: Frontier Publications, Ltd.

Oquaye, M. (1996) Discrimination Against Women in Africa: An Agenda for Public Policy Reform, paper presented at Conference on Women and Development, United Nations, Institute de Formation et de Rechenche Demographiques (IFORD) University of Yaounde 11, February 5–7.

Palmer, I. (1985), *The Impact of Agrarian Reform on Women*. West Hartford: Kumarian Press.

Paper presented at the Workshop on Practical Strategies for Enhancing the Participation of Women in the Political Decision Making Process. Center for Democratic Studies. Abuja. May 6–8, 1991.

Pereira, C. (2001) *Feminist Theories*, presentation prepared for the Gender Institute, Social Science Academy of Nigeria, held at Ogun-Osun River Basin Development Authority Guest House, May 22, Alabata' Abeokuta.

Project Paper, Center for Democratic Studies, Abuja. Undated.

Renninger, J. P. (1982) The Future of Economic Cooperation Schemes in Africa with Special Reference to ECOWAS, in T. Shaw (ed), *Alternative Futures for Africa*. Boulder, CO: Westview Press; see also J. P Renninger (1979) *Multinational Cooperation for Development in West Africa*. New York: Pergamon Press for UNITAR.

Seidman, A. (1994) *Planning for Development in Sub-saharan Africa*. New York: Praeger Publishers.

Serageldin, I. (1993) Making Development Sustainable. *Finance and Development* Washington Vol. 30, No. 4.

Shaw, M. S., and J. Lee (2001) *Women's Voices, Feminist Visions: Classic and Contemporary Readings*. New York: McGraw-Hill Higher Education Publishers.

Tadesse, M. (1992) *The Role of African Women in the Informal Secto: Problems and Prospects*. Background Document for the AAPAM 12th Roundtable Conference.

Valerie, B. (1992) *Feminist Political Theory: An Introduction*. New York: Macmillan Press.

Yolah, K. H. (1996) *Socio-Cultural Factors Affecting Women's Advancement and Development*. Paper presented at the Women Development Consultative Seminar, at Strategic Management Center, Lekki, Lagos. November 19.

9

Influence of Age, Marital Status, and Environment on Sexism in Nigeria

Ogunleye J. Adedeji (PhD) and
Adebayo O. Sulaiman (PhD)

ABSTRACT

This study attempts to find out the demographic factors for the ingrained sex discrimination in Nigeria. Seven hundred and seventy-nine research participants completed the Ambivalent Sexism Inventory (ASI) developed by Glick and Fiske (1996). The independent t-test statistics was employed for data analysis and results showed that age, marital status and environment of living are significant factors influencing sex discrimination (sexism) in Nigeria. The findings were discussed in light of the available literature.

INTRODUCTION

The social dominance theory, a major integrative framework seeking to understand and explain group-based prejudice and oppression (Pratto, 1999), postulates that every complex society can be characterized by the existence of group based hierarchy in which at least one group is dominant over others and enjoys a disproportionate share of privilege and at least one group occupies a subordinate position. The theory recognizes three basic types of group based social hierarchies which are: an age system, a gender system, and an arbitrary set system. The arbitrary set system consists of hierarchies of socially constructed groups based on any social relevant group distinctions. Such group distinctions may include, among others, marital status, employment or occupational status, etc. These distinctions are environmentally relative and may be different in their effects on social stratification though they basically influence sex discrimination.

The prevalence of sex discrimination (sexism) and its attendant gender role expectation is evident in most social institutions such as: the family, work environment, politics, the military, the church, and even education and the milieu of the street (Connell, 1987).

Although the potential deleterious effects of sex discrimination (sexism) have been well documented in the world over, less is known about the variables that affect the phenomenon (sexism) in Nigeria. Scholars (e.g., Leaper and Tenenbaum, 2002; Akrami, 2005) have classified some of the variables as "person centered characteristics" or as "contextual characteristics." Person centered characteristics, in this context, include attributes as age and marital status while contextual characteristics refer to attributes of the situation or environment.

Glick and Fiske (1996, 2001b) differentiated between hostile and benevolent sexism. According to them, hostile and benevolent sexism are two forms of sex discrimination that originates and often follow from held sexist ideologies. The scholars argued that hostile and benevolent sexism are a predictable product of structural relations between men and women that is common to human societies. Whereas, patriarchy (i.e., the accord of more status and power to men than women) and competitive gender differentiation (i.e., differentiation of men from women in terms of social roles and trait ascriptions) are identified as creating and reinforcing hostile sexism (sexist antipathy toward women), benevolent sexism (i.e., subjectively favorable, yet patronizing beliefs about women) is seen as a subtle form of prejudice in which gender inequality is promoted through the appreciation of women as valuable resources in the areas of child bearing, nurturance, and provision of sexual and intimacy needs.

Social psychologists generally regard sexism as a social psychological problem resulting from prejudice. According to them, the building of a healthy environment devoid of crime, hatred, violence, disorderliness, war, and genocide, among others, is resilient in the understanding of behaviors of organisms within the environment. Behavior (B), according to Lewin (1936), is a function of the environment (E) and the personality predispositions of individual organisms (P) in the environment [B = f(P,E)].

Building upon this formulation, Kelly, Holmes, Werr, Reis, Rusbult, and van-Lange (2002) posited that socialization starts from a dyad, and if social psychology studies relationships between people within a social context, then to develop a truly social psychology will require attempts at understanding that interactions between persons is mediated by needs, thoughts and motives in relation to one another and in the context of the specific social situations in which their interactions transpire. Thus, where motives, needs and thoughts are colored and blurred by sociocultural learnings to the extent that persons feeling for, and perceptions of one another within a social context become rather negative, most especially as a result of belonging to an opposite sex, then it spells sexism (sex discrimination) and disrupts the peaceful coexistence of people within the social context as much as it is detrimental to society.

Upon this backdrop therefore, the present sets out to find out the influence(s) of age, marital status and environment on sexism in Nigeria. Specifically, the study is set to find out whether:

i. Younger people (aged between 15 and 35 years) will be more sexist in their ideologies and behavior than older people (above 35 years).
ii. People who are single will be more sexist in their ideologies and behavior than their married counterparts.
iii. That there will be a significant difference in the sexist ideologies and behaviors of rural and urban dwellers.

It is hoped that findings from this study will contribute appreciably to available literature on sex discrimination (sexism).

METHOD

Participants

The study was conducted in Ekiti State, Nigeria, using a total of 779 research participants drawn from among the residents of the three senatorial districts in Ekiti State. The multistage random sampling technique was used to select sample localities and research participants.

Specifically, 290 research participants were drawn from Ekiti Central Senatorial District comprising of Ado, Efon, Ijero, Ekiti West and Irepodun/Ifelodun Local Government Areas. The 284 research participants were drawn from Ekiti North Senatorial District Comprising of Ikole, Ilejemeje, Moba, Oye and Ido/Osi Local Government Areas while a total of 205 participants were drawn from Ekiti South Senatorial District comprising of Ikere, Ise/Orun, Gbonyin, Emure, Ekiti South-West and Ekiti-East Local Government Areas of Ekiti State.

Sample selection for this study is based on parameter of population distribution figures where total figures were 461, 686, 553, 257 and 614, 219, respectively, for Ekiti South, Ekiti North and Ekiti Central Senatorial Districts (NPC, 1991).

Altogether, 427 (54.9 percent) of the research participants were males while 352 (45.1 percent) were females. Three hundred ninety-three (50.5

percent) were single and 386 (49.5 percent) were married. A total of 512 (65.8 percent) of the participants lived in the urban places in Ekiti State while 267 (34.2 percent) were rural dwellers.

Urban centers in this study are the state capital and local government area headquarters in the state. These places are classified as urban because of the presence of basic amenities and infrastructures that may, in themselves, be educative to dwellers in the towns. A total of 426 (54.74 percent) of the research participants are young (i.e., below 35 years old) while 353 were old (i.e., above 35 years). Participants' mean age was 31.91 years with a range between 15 and 69 years.

Variables

Independent Variables

The independent variables are age, marital status and environment. The influences of these variables were considered on sexism (sex discrimination).

Dependent Variables

Sexism (the exhibition of sexist ideologies and behavior) constitutes the dependent variable of this study. Glick and Fiske (2001) in their ambivalent alliance postulated two dimensions of sexism as being hostile and benevolent. Therefore, the effect of each of the independent variables on each of the dimensions of sexism was considered in this study.

Research Design

The survey research design was employed to investigate the influence of age, marital status and environment of living on the acquisition of sexist ideologies and behavior. The overall design of the research incorporates the two independent groups' design in order to achieve the objectives of the study. Thus, it was possible to compare research participants on their sexist ideologies and behavior along the lines of their age (young/old), marital status (married/single) and environment of living (rural/urban) using the two independent groups' design.

Research Instruments

A questionnaire tapping research participants' biographic information was used to determine participants' age (in complete years), marital status and environment of living. Standardized psychological measure was also used to measure sexism (the dependent variable). The psychological measure of sexism is the Ambivalent Sexism Inventory (ASI). This measure is a 22 item self report measure developed by Glick and Fiske (1996) to measure sexist ideologies and attitudes of men and women and their relationships in contemporary society. ASI is a likert measure with separate eleven items each for hostile and benevolent sexism scales.

Procedure

Copies of questionnaire containing ASI together with biographic information eliciting items were given to 960 respondents to complete. Of these 960 distributed copies, 779 were properly filled and these were analyzed for this study.

RESULTS

From Table 9.1, it is clear that rural and urban dwellers differ significant in hostile sexism [t (777) = 3.21, P < 0.01]. However, no significant differences exist between the rural and urban dwellers in benevolent sexism. A comparison of the mean ( ) scores revealed that rural dwellers are more sexist in their ideologies and behavior (= 36.75 and 39.58, respectively, for hostile and benevolent sexism) than their urban dwelling counterparts.

Also, it can be seen from the table below that although the married individuals are more hostile in their sexist ideologies and behaviors (x = 36.09) than their single counterparts [t (744) = -2.23, P < 0.05], no significant difference exists between the two categories in their benevolent sexism [t (744) = -1.39, P > 0.05].

It is shown, however, that the married individuals are more sexist in their ideologies and behavior than their single counterparts (x =36.09 and 39.69, respectively).

Results from the table also shows that young and old people differ significantly in their hostile sexist ideologies and behavior [t (777) = -3.24, P < 0.01]. From a comparison of mean scores, it is shown that older people (i.e., aged above 35 years) are more hostile in their sexist ideologies and behavior than their younger (i.e., below 35 years) counterparts whose mean scores is 34.33.

No significant difference exists, however, between young and old people in benevolent sexism [t (777) = -1.53, P > 0.05].

CONCLUSION

Klonoff and Landrine (1995) alluded to the fact that age, marital status, ethnicity, etc. could predict sexist events and Lott (1987) submitted that

Table 9.1

Variables		*N*	*X*	*SD*	*SE*	*df*	*t*	*P*
Hostile Sexism	Urban	512	34.54	9.12	0.40	777	3.21	<0.01
	Rural	267	36.75	9.15	0.56			
Benevolent Sexism	Urban	512	38.89	8.46	0.37	777	1.07	NS
	Rural	267	39.58	8.90	0.53			
Hostile Sexism	Single	361	34.59	8.71	0.46	744	-2.23	<0.05
	Married	385	36.09	9.65	0.49			
Benevolent Sexism	Single	361	38.82	8.09	0.43	744	-1.39	NS
	Married	385	39.69	8.94	0.46			
Hostile Sexism	35yrs & below	427	34.33	8.78	0.43	777	-3.24	<0.1
	Above 35yrs	352	36.47	9.53	0.51			
Benevolent Sexism	35yrs & above	427	38.70	8.29	0.40	777	-1.53	NS
	Above 35yrs	352	39.65	8.99	0.48			

single women may behave in an assertive and independent manner that elicit gender discrimination.

Results of this study, however, showed that married people are more hostile in their sexist ideologies and behavior (x = 36.09) than their single counterparts (x = 34.59). This result suggests that the married people, while trying to assert their gender identities and ascribe gender roles will tend to be hostile to forestall a sudden usurpation of powers by the opposite sex; most especially in marriages. That the singles are less sexist may be due to changes that are continually occurring in the society in which case the unmarried people marry more lately nowadays than it was before. These singles may have learned to be less sexist in order that they could readily get partners to marry and settle down with. After all Elder (1995) argued that adaptations change with time, changing life circumstances and role expectations.

Leaper (1994) and Tenenbaum and Leaper (2002) argued that rural-urban living affects the process and acquisition of gender stereotypes. These scholars posited that children in the urban centers become more increasingly influenced by extra familiar factors (e.g., the media) and as such they do not adopt traditional beliefs but are largely egalitarian in their beliefs and orientation. Findings from this study confirm the positions of Leaper (1994) and Tenenbaum and Leaper (2002) with regard to hostile sexism because results of the study revealed that rural dwellers are more hostile in their sexist ideologies (x = 36.75) than their urban dwelling counterparts (x = 35.54).

With regard to benevolent sexism, however, no significant differences were found between the rural and their urban dwelling counterparts. These results suggest that irrespective of the environment of living, women, for example, are regarded as nurturers and are expected to perform integrative, expressive and emotional roles while men are expected to be task oriented, dominant and concerned with status and independence. This position was alluded to by Aries (1996) in her reconsideration of the differences between men and women in interactions.

On the whole, both as posited by Leaper (1994) and Tenenbaum and Leaper (2002) and as is evident in the comparisons of mean scores (x) of the two groups in this study, where the rural dwellers' scores on hostile and benevolent sexism are 36.75 and 39.58, respectively, as against mean scores of 35.54 and 38.89, respectively, for urban dwellers' hostile and benevolent sexism, rural dwellers are more sexist in their ideologies and behavior than their urban dwelling counterparts.

That the rural dwellers were more sexist can be understood on the basis of the possibility that they are more traditionalist in terms of gender roles and they are most likely to jealously guard and guide against the occurrence of role reversals as may be occasioned by Western education and modernization.

That younger people (i.e., aged between 15 and 35 years) will be more sexist in their ideologies and behavior was not confirmed in this study. Results from this study showed a significant difference in hostile sexist ideologies of young and old respondents; and no significant difference in the benevolent sexist ideologies of the groups.

A comparison of mean scores of both the old and young respondents showed that with regard to hostile sexism, older respondents (i.e., aged above 35 years old) are more sexist (x = 36.43) than their younger (i.e., below 35 years old) counterparts (x = 34.33).

This finding suggests that as one grows older, he acquires more knowledge and understanding of relationships between sexes. Such understanding may be more male chauvinistic and therefore tend to aggravate hostile sexism the more. One may be right to reason that sexist ideologies that were acquired in early adolescence may have become highly internalized and unchangeable at adulthood when peer influence becomes rather minimal if there were no structural changes to dissuade sexist ideologies and behavior acquisition from adolescence.

Conclusively, results from this study have showed that age, marital status and environment of living significantly influence the process of acquisition of sexist ideologies and behavior. It therefore becomes imperative that the Nigeria government should make concerted efforts at ensuring the provision of an environment that will promote psychologically well-adjusted individuals who will be good examples to upcoming generations in terms of value judgments and moral rectitude.

REFERENCES

Akrami, N. (2005) Prejudice: The interplay of personality, cognition and social psychology. Doctoral dissertation from the faculty of the social sciences, Uppsala University, Sweden.

Aries, E. (1996) *Men and Women in Interactions: Reconsidering the Differences.* New York: Oxford University Press.

Connell, R. W. (1987) *Gender and Power.* Stanford, CA: Stanford University Press.

Elder, G. H., Jr. (1995) The life course paradigm: Social change and individual development. In P. Moen, G. H. Elder, Jr., and K. Luscher (Eds.) *Examining Lives in Context* (pp. 101–139). Washington, D.C.: American Psychological Association.

Glick, P., and S. J. Fiske (1996) The ambivalent sexism inventory: Differentiating hostile and benevolent belief about men. *Psychology of Women Quarterly*, 23, 519–536.

Glick, P., and S. T. Fiske (2001b) An ambivalent alliance: Hostile and benevolent sexism as complementary justifications for gender inequality. *American Psychologist*, 35(2), 109–118.

Kelley, H. H., J. G. Holmes, N. L. Kerr, C. E. Rusbult, and P. A. M. van-Lange (2002) *An Atlas of Interpersonal Situations.* New York: Cambridge University Press.

Klonoff, E. A., and H. Landrine (1995) A measure of life and recent sexist discriminations in women lives. *Psychology of Women Quarterly*, 28, 430–472.

Leaper, C. (1994) Exploring the consequences of gender segregation on social relationships. In C. Leaper (Ed.), *Childhood Gender Segregation: Causes and Consequences, New Directions for Child Development* (pp. 67–86). San Francisco: Jossey-Bass.

Leaper, C., and H. R. Tenenbaum (2002) Are parents gender schema related to their children's gender-related cognitions? A meta-analysis. *Developmental Psychology*, 38 (4), 615–630.

Lewin, K. (1936) *Principles of Topological Psychology*. New York: McGraw-Hill.

Lott, B. (1987) Sexist discrimination as distancing behaviour 1: A laboratory demonstration. *Psychology of Women Quarterly*, II (1), 47–58.

National Population Commission (1991) 1991 Population Census Figures. Abuja: NPC.

Pratto, F. (1996) Gender politics: The gender gap in the bedroom, cupboard, and the cabinet. In D. M. Buss and N. M. Malamuth (Eds.), *Sex, Power and Conflict: Evolutionary and Feminist Perspectives* (pp. 179–230). New York: Oxford University Press.

10

Sex, Sex-Role Orientation, Personality, and Sexism in Nigeria

Adedeji J. Ogunleye (PhD)

ABSTRACT

This study was designed to investigate the influences of sex, sex role orientation and personality variables on sexism in Nigeria. With the aid of a set of questionnaires comprising Bem's Sex Role Inventory (BSRI) developed by Bem (1974), Ambivalent Sexism Inventory (ASI) developed by Glick and Fiske (1996) and the Big Five (Personality) Inventory (BFI) developed by John, Donahue and Kentle (1991), data were collected from 780 research participants drawn from among Nigerians resident in South Western Nigeria. Participants' age range is 15–69 with a mean age of 31.91 years. Using a 4 x 2 x 2 analysis of variance (ANOVA) and regression analysis, it was found out that sex and sex role orientation have main and interaction effects on sexism. It was also revealed that sexism is significantly jointly predicted by personality variables. However, the dominant personality trait of an individual was found to determine the type of sexist ideological leanings and behaviors displayed by the person. These findings were discussed in the light of available literature and recommendations were made.

INTRODUCTION

Bandura (1977, 1986) in his social learning theory asserts that through observations, identifications and internalizations, behaviors are learnt. Unlearning (undesirable) behaviors and changing the society toward more sustainability, however, requires behavior modifications by various actors and in many domains through a clear understanding of the characteristics of target groups, and of the mechanisms and motives that underlay behaviors.

Societies, generally, thrive and are stable and orderly when conditions and situations that threaten a group's values are effectively and efficiently managed.

Sexism, a social problem, undermines the rights and potentials of women in societies. Since 1975, when the world conference of the International Women's Year was held in Mexico City, the discourse on women's advancement process has evolved.

Sexism, around the world, focuses on the prejudice (negative attitudes) and discrimination (negative actions) that males direct at females. This is because many societies of the world are patriarchal (i.e., the social organization is such that males dominate females) (Harris, 1991). Corroborating Harris' submission, United Nations Report (1998) posits that men typically rule, dominating the highest status roles in government, academics, and business across the globe.

The phenomenon of sexism (sex discrimination) in Nigeria, as in most parts of the world, is skewed against women (Adebayo, 1992; Akumadu, 1998; Olaoye, 2004) and it objectively permits or promotes the social and economic exploitations of women and their political marginalization (Enemuo, 1999).

Rosenberg and Alaya (1977), for example, reported that Mrs. Horace Tremlitt, who accompanied her husband to Nigeria during the colonial era, remarked that sex discrimination (sexism) was pervasive and prevalent in Nigeria. According to these scholars, Mrs. Tremlitt said:

> I found myself reflecting rather bitterly on the insignificant position of a woman in what is practically a man's country. . . . If there is one spot on earth where a woman feels no importance whatsoever, it is in Nigeria.

Even after the colonial era, and up till this day in Nigeria, there is the problem of the old chauvinistic prejudice and discrimination against women. They seem to be limited by their description as the "weaker sex"; a phrase coined to weaken their meaningful participation in the scheme of things. Omede (2004) observed, for example, that only about 2 percent of the population of females in Nigeria is politically involved despite the 1991 population census figures which put the number of females in Nigeria at about 50 percent of the total population. WIN (2001) also reported that in the 1999 elections in Nigeria where there were 11,107 elective positions, women got a paltry 178. This feat was also repeated in the 2007 elections in Nigeria with only a slight change. It is worthy of note too that the first female speaker of Nigeria lower parliamentary house (House of

Representatives) was consumed and sacked from office by attritional war from her male colleagues. This is evident because her male successor has been involved in the much heavier scandal of purchase of Peugeot cars involving several millions of Naira, yet he is, till this day, holding forth as the speaker of the house because, perhaps, he is a male candidate.

Olaoye (2004) remarked that females' participation in Nigerian politics at the gladiatorial level in the modern era has been somewhat negligible in terms of decision making. He observed that the bulk of their political participations are at the spectatorial and apathetic levels and he blamed these on value-related and social structural factors. According to him, the fact that Nigeria is patriarchal and hence male dominated infringes on the freedom and free will of females to actively participate in politics and decision makings; hence, their marginalization in policy formulations. It must be noted however that social structural factors alone are not accountable for sexism. Leaper and Tenenbaum (2002) and Akrami, (2005) have classified some of the variables of sexism as person centered characteristics or as contextual characteristics. Thus, it is expedient that the person centered characteristics be explored in addition to the social structural factors that had been indicted.

Researches (e.g., Kirk, 1982; Aina, 1998) have demonstrated that the impediments on the part of women in their quest to assert and distinguish themselves in various spheres of life throughout the world have resulted in their ignorance and tenacious hold onto, and teaching of, traditional sexist ideologies and behavior to their off springs.

Adewumi (2003) remarked that either overtly or covertly, women are discriminated against in Nigeria. He argued that customs in many places in the North and some areas in the South prevent women from owning and inheriting landed properties. As such, many women do not have collateral for accessing credit facilities and hence operate their business on a low scale. This exacerbates their impoverishments and infringes on the national development process because women are not empowered to initiate, mould, and execute public policies and legislations; most especially as they include discriminatory laws, policies, programmes, and oppressive cultural practices; mass poverty and low social status.

The world's bias against women calls for a change in behaviors and attitudes toward them for equality, economic prosperity, social advancement, and political emancipation to engender mutual coexistence and more sustainability. This study, thus, attempts to find out the effects of sex, sex-role orientation and personality on sexism (sex discrimination).

It is hoped that findings from this study will constitute an addition to existing literature on the phenomenon of sexism and give an insight to understanding the causes of sex discrimination with a view to devising a mechanism for its combat to engender sustainable development and economic growth.

This study therefore seeks to ascertain whether:

i. Males and females will differ in their sexist ideologies and behavior.
ii. That sex role orientation will significantly influence sexism.
iii. That there will be a significant interaction effects of sex-role orientation and sex on sexism.
iv. That the personality dimensions of extraversion, neuroticism, agreeableness, openness to experience and conscientiousness will independently and jointly influence sexism.

METHOD

Research Participants

Seven hundred and eighty research participants were used for the study. They comprised 428 males and 352 females drawn from among the residents of Ekiti State, Nigeria. Participants mean age is 31.91 with a range between 15 and 69 years.

Variables

The influence of personality, sex and sex-role orientations on sexism were considered. Thus, the independent variables are:

- personality,
- sex, and
- sex-role orientation.

The dependent variable, therefore, is sexism. Glick and Fiske (2001) in their ambivalent alliance postulated two dimensions of sexism as being hostile and benevolent. According to them, hostile sexism combines dominative paternalism (the belief that men ought to have more power than women), competitive power differentiation (the belief that, as a group, women are inferior to men on competence related attributes), and hostile heterosexuality (the belief that women's sexuality is dangerous to men's higher status and power); while benevolent sexism comprises protective paternalism (the belief that men should protect and provide for the women on whom they depend), complementary gender differentiation (the belief that women are the better gender, but only in ways that suit conventional gender roles), and intimate heterosexuality (the belief that men can achieve true happiness in life only when involved in romantic relationships with women). Therefore the effect of each of the independent variables on each of the dimensions of sexism was considered in this study.

Research Design

A 4 x 2 x 2 Analysis of Variance (ANOVA) design was used for the study. This made it possible to answer questions regarding the main and interaction effects of sex role orientation (masculinity, femininity, androgyny and undifferentiated) and sex (male and female) on sexism (hostile and benevolent).

The correlation design was also employed and it made it possible to test for the relationships between the personality dimensions (openness to experience, extraversion, agreeableness, conscientiousness and neuroticism) and sexism.

Research Instruments

A questionnaire tapping research participants' biographic information was used to determine participants' sex while standardized psychological measures were used to measure personality variables, sex-role orientation (independent variable) and sexism (dependent variable).

Sex Role Orientation

Shaffer (1994) defined sex role orientation as sex typed behavior which individuals learn in interpersonal relationships as they are socialized into their environment. According to Bem (1974), sex typed behaviors are masculinity and femininity characteristics which are biologically associated with male and female gender, respectively. They are learned in interpersonal relationships and they usually include: masculine, feminine, androgyny and undifferentiated sex role orientations. For the purpose of this study, sex role orientation is measured as a respondent's masculinity and femininity, which are higher than norm as set using Bem's Sex Role Inventory (BSRI). The norms for this study are 47.22 (masculinity) and 53.73 (femininity) ($n = 780$).

BSRI is a 40 item inventory containing a list of adjectives that describes an individual person developed by Bem (1974). It measures individual's sex typed behaviors in interpersonal relationships which includes: masculine, feminine, androgyny and undifferentiated. Whereas androgyny is characterized with high masculinity and high femininity, undifferentiated is characterized with low masculinity and low femininity.

Personality, according to Burger (1997) refers to consistent behavior patterns and intrapersonal processes originating within an individual. It is a person's unique pattern of traits (Guilford, 1959). In the present study, this variable is measured as a respondent's scores on the Big Five Inventory. The Big Five Inventory (BFI) is a psychological test developed by John, Donahue and Kentle (1991). BFI is a 44 item inventory that assesses personality from five dimensions. The dimensions are:

i. extraversion
ii. agreeableness
iii. conscientiousness
iv. neuroticism
v. openness to experience

A respondent's score that is higher than the mean score for a personality dimension indicates that the respondent is high on the particular personality dimension and a lower score than the mean score indicates that the participant is low on the particular personality dimension.

Sexism

Sexism refers to individuals' prejudice toward, and discrimination against, members of the opposite sex on the basis of sex difference. An individual is sexist in the case of this study when his average scores on the sexism scale (Ambivalent Sexism Inventory) are above 54.8. Such individuals have the trait of both hostile and benevolent sexism (Ambivalent Sexism Inventory subscales) and tend to have polarized or extreme reaction to women depending on which aspects of their attitudes is activated. Ambivalent Sexism Inventory (ASI) is a 22 item self report measure developed by Glick and Fiske (1996) to measure sexist ideologies, behavior and attitudes of men and women and their relationships in contemporary society. ASI is a likert type measure with separate eleven items each for hostile and benevolent sexism scales.

RESULTS

The results presented in Tables 10.1 and 10.2, which show that sex has a significant main effect on hostile sexism [$F (1,771) = 6.414, P < 0.05$] and on benevolent sexism [$F(1,771) = 26.660, P < 0.01$].

Similarly, sex role orientation has significant main effect on hostile sexism [$F (3,771) = 12.983, P < 0.01$] and on benevolent sexism [$F (3,771) = 43.713, P < 0.01$].

Sex and Sex Role Orientation also have significant interaction effect on hostile sexism [$F (3.771) = 3.456, P < 0.05$] and on benevolent sexism $F(3,771) = 3.203, P < 0.05$]. Post hoc comparison of the mean scores (x) using the least significant differences' test (LSD) are shown in Tables 10.3 and 10.4.

As shown in Table 10.2 above, sex role orientation significantly influenced hostile sexism [$F(3,771) = 12.98, P < 0.01$] and benevolent sexism [$F (3,771) = 43.71, P < 0.01$].

Table 10.1 Descriptive Statistics Table Showing the Mean and Standard Deviation Scores of Male and Female Participants along Sex Role Orientation on Sexism

	Sex	*Sex Role Behavior*	*Mean*	*Standard Deviation*	*N*
Hostile	Male	Masculine	37.0750	7.67171	80
		Feminine	35.9275	7.60286	69
		Androgyny	39.4088	8.08954	159
		Undifferentiated	32.4417	8.09481	120
		Total	36.4579	8.69066	428
	Female	Masculine	36.9063	10.53828	32
		Feminine	33.6024	8.97278	83
		Androgyny	34.7130	10.98225	115
		Undifferentiated	32.4793	8.00010	121
		Total	33.8808	9.57541	351
	Total	Masculine	37.0268	8.53869	112
		Feminine	34.6579	8.43212	152
		Androgyny	37.4380	10.07726	274
		Undifferentiated	32.4606	8.03064	241
		Total	35.2965	9.18410	779
Benevolent	Male	Masculine	38.2125	7.90881	80
		Feminine	37.4638	7.18777	69
		Androgyny	40.7421	8.33037	159
		Undifferentiated	34.4417	8.34628	120
		Total	37.97.43	8.44416	428
	Female	Masculine	41.6563	8.29539	32
		Feminine	42.4870	7.61182	83
		Androgyny	44.4870	6.61652	115
		Undifferentiated	34.9835	8.27948	121
		Total	40.5328	8.62875	351
	Total	Masculine	39.1964	8.13494	112
		Feminine	40.3289	7.84855	152
		Androgyny	42.3139	7.86586	274
		Undifferentiated	34.7137	8.29991	241
		Total	39.1271	8.61699	779

A comparison of the mean scores, as shown in Table 10.3 based on the post hoc test (least significance difference test performed) showed that respondents with masculine sex role orientation were more hostile (x = 37.03) in their sexist ideologies than their feminine (x = 34.66) counterpart. In the same way, respondents with feminine sex role orientation were less hostile (x = 34.66) in their sexist ideologies than the androgynous respondent (x = 37.44).

With regard to benevolent sexism, it can be seen from Table 10.4 based on post hoc test that the mean scores of the masculine respondents (x = 39.20) is less than the mean scores of their feminine (x = 40.33) and

Table 10.2. Summary of 4 x 2 ANOVA Showing the Main and Interaction Effects of Sex Role Orientation and Sex on Sexism

Dependent Variable	*Source*	*SS*	*df*	*MS*	*F*	*P*
Hostile	Sex	502.098	1	502.098	6.414	<0.05
	Sex Role Orientation	1049.026	3	1016.342	12.983	<0.01
	Sex *sex Role Orientation	811.716	3	270.572	3.456	<0.05
	Error	60354.534	771	78.281		
	Total	1036136.000	779			
Benevolent	Sex	1653.116	1	1653.116	26.660	<0.01
	Sex Role Orientation	9131.859	3	2710.620	43.713	<0.01
	Sex *sex Role Orientation	595.768	3	198.589	3.203	<0.05
	Error	47809.543	771	62.010		
	Total	1250362.000	779			

Table10.3 Summary of Least Significant Difference (Post Hoc) Test Showing Difference in Hostile Sexism Based on Sex Role Orientation

S/No	Sex Role Orientation	N	Mean	2	3	4
1	Masculine	112	37.03	2.37*	-0.41	4.57*
2	Feminine	152	34.66	---	-2.78*	2.20*
3	Androgynous	274	37.44	---	---	4.98*
4	Undifferentiated	241	32.46	---	---	---

Table 10.4 Summary of Least Significant Difference (Post Hoc) Test Showing Difference in Benevolent Sexism Based on Sex Role Orientation

Sex Role Orientation	*N*	*Mean*	*2*	*3*	*4*
Masculine	112	39.20	-1.13	-3.11*	4.48*
Feminine	152	40.33	---	-1.98*	5.62*
Androgynous	274	42.31	---	---	7.60*
Undifferentiated	241	34.71	---	---	---

androgynous (x = 42.31) counterparts, depicting that respondents with feminine or androgynous sex role orientation are more benevolent in their sexist ideologies than their masculine (x = 39.20) and undifferentiated (x = 34.71) counterparts.

Table 10.1 above also reveals that the male respondents who are androgynous in their sex role orientation are more hostile (x = 39.41) in their sexist ideologies than their counterparts who are masculine (x = 37.08), or undifferentiated (x = 32.44). In a similar vein, female respondents who are masculine in their sex role orientation are more hostile in their sexist ideologies (x = 36.91) than their feminine (x = 33.60), androgynous (x = 34.71), or their undifferentiated (x = 32.48) counterparts.

Also, regarding benevolent sexism, mean score comparisons based on least significant differences test (post hoc test) reveal that the male respondents who are androgynous in their sex role orientation are more benevolent in their sexist ideologies (x = 40.74) than either masculine (x = 38.21), feminine (x = 37.46), or undifferentiated (x = 34.44) counterparts. In all, the undifferentiated respondents (irrespective of sex) are generally less sexist in their ideologies than their masculine, feminine, and or androgynous counterparts.

From this matrix, all personality dimensions are related to both hostile and benevolent sexism. However, neuroticism is negatively related to both hostile and benevolent sexism.

Table 10.6 shows that the personality dimensions jointly predict hostile sexism [F (5,773) = 12.52, < 0.01]. Moreover, extraversion (B = 0.116) and openness to experience (B = 0.179) independently predict hostile sexism.

Table 10.5 Correlation Matrix Showing Relationships between Personality Dimensions and Sexism

		Masculinity	*Feminity*	*Extraversion*	*Agreeableness*	*Consnto*	*Neurotic*	*Openness*	*Hostile*	*Benevolent*
Masculinity	Pearson									
	Correlation									
	Sig. (1-tailed)									
	N									
Feminity	Pearson	.467**								
	Correlation	.000								
	Sig. (1-tailed)	780								
	N									
Extraversion	Pearson	.373**	.432**							
	Correlation	.000	.000							
	Sig. (1-tailed)	780	780							
	N									
Agreeableness	Pearson	.338**	489**	.456**						
	Correlation	.000	.000	.000						
	Sig. (1-tailed)	780	780	780						
	N									
Consntos	Pearson	.450**	.457**	.405**	.653**					
	Correlation	.000	.000	.000	.000					
	Sig. (1-tailed)	780	780	780	780					
	N									
Neurotic	Pearson	-.289**	-323**	-.263**	-.439**	-.501**				
	Correlation	.000	.000	.000	.000	.000				
	Sig. (1-tailed)	780	780	780	780	780				
	N									
Openness	Pearson	.448**	.421**	435**	.444**	.455**	-.312**			
	Correlation	.000	.000	.000	.000	.000	.000			
	Sig. (1-tailed)	780	780	780	780	780	780			
	N									

		Masculinity	*Feminity*	*Extraversion*	*Agreeableness*	*Consnto*	*Neurotic*	*Openness*	*Hostile*	*Benevolent*
Hostile	Pearson	.262**	.200**	.261**	-.152**	.186**	-.158**	.300**		
	Correlation	.000	.000	.000	.000	.000	.000	.000		
	Sig. (1-tailed)	779	779	779	779	779	779	779		
	N									
Benevolent	Pearson	.285**	.417**	.294**	.342**	.317**	-.256**	374**	422**	
	Correlation	.000	.000	.000	.000	.000	.000	.000	.000	
	Sig. (1-tailed)	779	779	779	779	779	779	779	779	
	N									

*Correlation is significant at the 0.05 level.
**Correlation is significant at the 0.01 level.

Table 10.6 Regression Table Showing the Independent and Joint Predictions of the Personality Dimensions on Hostile Sexism

Variables	*R*	*R2*	*F*	*p*	*B*	*t*	*p*
Constant	0.274	0.069	12.52	0.01			
Extraversion					0.116	3.01	0.01
Agreeableness					-0.005	-0.18	NS
Conscientiousness					0.052	1.19	NS
Neuroticism					-0.023	-0.61	NS
Openness to Experience					0.179	4.70	0.01

Table 10.7 Regression Table Showing the Independent and Joint Predictions of the Personality Dimensions on Benevolent Sexism

Variables	*R*	*R2*	*F*	*P*	*B*	*t*	*p*
Constant	0.40	0.16	29.47	0.01			
Extraversion					0.059	1.61	NS
Agreeableness					0.118	2.93	0.01
Conscientiousness					0.051	1.22	NS
Neuroticism					-0.125	-3.43	0.01
Openness to Experience					0.221	6.10	0.01

Table 10.7 shows that the personality dimensions jointly predict benevolent sexism [F(5,773) = 29.47, P < 0.01]. Nonetheless, extraversion (B = 0.059) and conscientiousness (B = 0.051) do not significantly contribute to benevolent sexism.

CONCLUSION

In looking at the effects of sex role orientation and sex on sexism, it was expected that sex role orientation and sex would significantly independently and jointly influence sexism. This expectation, which informed the formulation of hypotheses 1, 2, and 3, was informed by the following:

a. Lytton and Romney's (1991) thesis that parents treat their sons and daughters differently in accordance with the children's sexes.
b. Goldner's (1991) submission that on the basis of parental treatment, children are forced to disown thoughts, acts and self conception that are not congruent with their gender; having been socialized into differential gender roles and experience of division of labour that allocates different work and responsibilities to male and female.
c. Tenenbaum and Leaper's (2002) observation that parents gender schema is related to the offspring's gender related cognition.
d. Grusec and Kuezynski's (1997) position that parent–child concordance in values may be moderated by the quality of the parent–child relationship as influenced by the local cultural community.
e. Williams and Best's (1990) submission that males are more positively evaluated than females.
f. Bem's (1993) submission that children evaluate behaviors in terms of whether they are gender appropriate according to cultural definition and will reject behaviors that are inappropriate for their own gender.

The result of the test of main and interaction effects of sex role orientation and sex on sexism showed that sex had significant main effect on sexism (hostile and benevolent) with males being more hostile (x = 36.46) in their sexist orientation while the females were significantly highly benevolent in their ideologies (x = 40.53).

Similarly sex role orientation had significant main effect on sexism. And sex role orientation had significant interaction effect on sexism. A comparison of the mean scores of the four sex role orientation based on post hoc test (least significant different test performed) showed that respondents with masculine sex role orientation were more hostile in their sexist ideologies than their feminine counterparts. With regard to benevolent sexism, a comparison of mean scores (x) based on post hoc test showed that respondents with feminine or androgynous sex role orientation were more benevolent in their sexist ideologies than their masculine or undifferentiated counterparts.

These findings suggest that once an individual identifies himself/herself as a male or female, there comes a tendency to internalize gender appropriate behavior as spelt out by his/her social environment while socializing so that a "deviance" label can be avoided and ostracism escaped. The internalization interpretation is also consistent with Pence's (1985) argument that society teaches men to love and trivialize women while the women are taught to love and resent men. Thus males internalize assertiveness, dominance, competitiveness, and leadership behaviors while their female counterparts internalize expressiveness, sensitivity, compassion, cooperation and yielding behaviors.

Gray's (1992) position that men are task-oriented, dominant and concerned with status and independence, whereas women are expressive, responsive, supportive and concerned with intimacy and connection seems to be justified by this study. Also the gender schema theory's argument that children learn to judge themselves according to the traits or construct considered to be relevant to their gender and thus have their self concepts blended with the gender schema of their culture is most relevant to the findings of this study.

The results of this study, moreover, revealed that the personality dimensions of extraversion, agreeableness, conscientiousness, neuroticism, and openness to experience jointly predict sexism (hostile and benevolent). However, it is only extraversion and openness to experience that independently significantly predict hostile sexism. Also, extraversion and conscientiousness do not significantly predict benevolent sexism.

These findings suggest that individuals who are highly dominant, sociable, and aesthetical in orientation are more amenable to learning hostile sexist ideologies than their counterparts who are tender-minded and highly irritable. A naturally dominant character might be authoritarian and traditional (rather than egalitarian); and thus be more hostile in his sexist ideologies than his pro-social and modest counterpart. These findings are consistent with the submission of Pratto et al. (1994). These scholars submitted that high SDO (social dominance orientation) people tend to rank social group in superior-inferior hierarchy.

Furthermore, from the correlation matrix computed in this study, it is evident that all the personality dimensions are related to both hostile and benevolent sexism. However, neuroticism has a negative relationship to both hostile and benevolent sexism while agreeableness has a negative relationship with hostile sexism. This depicts that neuroticism (i.e., anxiety or nervous tension characteristic) decreases as one become more sexist; and hostile sexist ideologies decreases as one gets more pro-social, altruistic, modest and tender-minded owing, perhaps, to enlightenment and expositions from interpersonal relationships. All other personality characteristics increase with increasing sexist ideologies and behavior acquisition. This suggests that as one socializes within the environment, more things are learned and more experiences garnered to help in the navigation through the world. Such experience may include the acquisition of sexist ideologies and behaviors, which inadvertently may impact on the individual's later life profligacy with regards to sex role orientations given to younger generations.

IMPLICATIONS OF FINDINGS

Findings from this study corroborates the postulations of earlier scholars, e.g., Bem (1974, 1993), Kohlberg (1966), Pratto et al. (1994, 1996) with regard to the process of acquisition of sexist ideologies and behavior. Personologists and personality psychologists are therefore needed to help in the processes of enlightenment, exposition and change of people's perception, personality and structure of the mind for the appreciation of value judgments.

It is, however, suggested that further studies be conducted on equality, equity, fair play and justice between sexes for integration and sustainable national development, most especially as these have to do with people, their perception and their behaviors toward one another.

REFERENCES

Adebayo, C. O. (1992) Female circumcision and other dangerous practices to women's health. In N. K Mere (Ed.), *Women's Heath Issues in Nigeria.* Zaria: Tanaza Publishing Coy.

Adewunmi, F. (2003) Chief (Mrs.) Bisi Ogunleye (Mama COWAN): A leadership profile. Centre for Social Science Research and Development, *Positive Leadership Monograph series,* No. 5.

Aina, O. L. (1998) Women, culture and society. In Amadu Sesay and Adetanwa Odebiyi (Eds.), *Nigeria Women in Society and Development.* Ibadan: Dokun Publishing House.

Akrami, N. (2005) Prejudice: The Inter-play of Personality, Cognition and Social Psychology. A doctoral dissertation from the faculty of the social sciences, Uppsala University, Sweden.

Akumadu, T. U. (1998) *Beast of Burden. A Study of Women's Legal Status and Reproductive Health Rights in Nigeria.* Lagos: Civil Liberty Organization.

Bem, S. L. (1993) *The Lenses of Gender: Transforming the Debate on Sexual Inequality.* New Haven, CT: Yale University Press.

Bem, S. L. (1974) Measurement of psychological androgyny. *Journal of Consulting Clinical Psychology,* 42, 55–62.

Bem, S. L. (1981) Gender schema theory: A cognitive account of sex-typing. *Psychology Review,* 88, 324–354.

Enemuo, F. C. (1999) Gender and women empowerment. In R. Anifowoshe and F. C. Enemuo (Eds.) *Elements of Politics.* Lagos: Malt-House Press Ltd.

Foundation for Population and Development (2005). Abuja: AFPODEV.

Glick, P., and S. T. Fiske (1996) The ambivalent sexism inventory: Differentiating hostile and benevolent beliefs about men. *Psychology of Women Quarterly,* 23, 519–536.

Glick, P., and S. T. Fiske (2001) An ambivalent alliance: Hostile and benevolent sexism as complementary justifications for gender inequality. *American Psychologists,* 36 (2), 109–118.

Goldberg, S., and M. Lewis (1999) Play behavior in the year old infant: Early sex differences. *Child Development,* 40, 21–23.

Goldner, V. (1991) Towards a critical relational theory. *Psychoanalytic Dialogues,* 1(3), 249–272.

Gray, J. (1992) *Men Are from Mars, Women Are from Venus.* New York: Harper Collins.

Grusec, J. E., and Kueczynski (1997) *Parenting and Children's Internationalization of Values: A Handbook of Contemporary Theory.* New York: Wiley.

John, O. P. (1990) The "Big Five" factor taxonomy: Dimensions of personality in natural language and in questionnaire. In L. A. Dervein (Ed.) *Handbook of Personality Theory and Research.* New York: Guilford.

Kirk, K. W. (1982) Women in male-dominated professions. *AMJ Hosp. Pharm.,* 39, 12–17.

Kohlberg, L. (1966) A cognitive development analysis of children's sex role concept and attitudes. In E. E. Maccoby (Ed.) *Human Development.* Stanford, CA: Stanford University Press.

Lytton, H., and D. M. Romney (1991) Parents' differential socialization of boys and girls: A meta-analysis. *Psychology Bulletin,* 109, 267–296.

National Population Commission (1991) 1991 *Population Census Figures.* Abuja: NPC.

National Population Commission (2006) *Provisional Population Census Figures.* Abuja: NPC.

Olaoye, E. O. (2004) The Nigeria State and women's participation in politics: Challenges and options. *Nigeria Journal of Counseling and Applied Psychology,* 2(1), 236–250.

Omede, O. J (2004) Women and the 2003 general elections: Observable trends. *Nigeria Journal of the Social Sciences,* 3(1) 63–80.

Pence, E. (1985) *Coordinated Community Response to Domestic Assault Cases: A Guide for Policy Development.* Duluth, MN: DAIP.

Pratto, F. (1996) Gender politics: The gender gap in the bedroom, cupboard, and the cabinet. In D. M. Buss and N. M. Malamuth (Eds.) *Sex, Power and Conflict: An Evolutionary and Feminist Perspectives* (pp. 179–230). New York: Oxford University Press.

Pratto, F. J. Sidanius, L. Stallworth, and B. Malle (1994) Social dominance orientation: A personality variable predicting social and political attitudes. *Journal of Personality and Social Psychology*, 67, 741–763.
Roseberg, A., and S. Araya (1977) Women in men's country. *Sociological Bulletin*, 2, 8–13.
Tenenbaum, H. R., and C. Leaper (2002) Are parents gender schema related to their children's gender related cognition? A meta-analysis. *Development Psychology*, 38(4), 615–630.
Willams, J. E., and D. L. Best, (1990) *Measuring Sex Stereotypes: A Multi-National Study*. Newbury Park, CA: Sage Publications.
Win, (2001) *Women and Politics in Nigeria: Agenda for Political Participation*. Kaduna: Women-in-Nigeria (Win).

Part III

POLITICS AND GENDER PARTICIPATION

11

Gender and Peace Building in Nigeria's Delta Region

Stephen A. Faleti (PhD)

ABSTRACT

The use of the word "gender" is often erroneously taken as being synonymous with references to women. Women's activists have been the traditional champions of gender issues, which are often presented as social inclusion advocacies that are targeted at empowering women and encouraging their participation at multiple levels of society in a way that will ensure equality of opportunities for both males and females. This form of advocacy itself flowed from the premise that the rights of women and their social conflict management role have been downplayed for far too long and to their detriment.

INTRODUCTION

The use of the word "gender" is often erroneously taken as being synonymous with references to women. Women's activists have been the traditional champions of gender issues, which are often presented as social inclusion advocacies that are targeted at empowering women and encouraging their participation at multiple levels of society in a way that will ensure equality of opportunities for both males and females. This form of advocacy itself flowed from the premise that the rights of women and their social conflict management role have been downplayed for far too long and to their detriment.

In proper usage, "gender" refers mainly to socially assigned roles of the sexes; especially the relationships, experiences, and expectations that are attributed to social categories on the basis of their sex and denotes all the qualities of what it is to be a man or a woman which are socially and culturally, rather than biologically, determined. This differentiation has multiple forms of conflict-generating implications for social relationships and one of its outcomes—gender inequality reflects power imbalances in social structures that exist in pre-conflict periods and are exacerbated by armed conflict and its aftermath (El Jack, 2003).

According to Pankhurst (2000), gender approaches offer insights into and address questions of power, control, competition, and models of development in economic, cultural, and political terms. Further, he goes on to note that gender analyses operate at three main levels: the more common theoretical approach of identifying gender differences; the practical focus on specific forms of gender imbalance and ways of righting them; and the strategic transformation of gender relations to provide a basis for justice and equity, not just between men and women but between different groups within society.

Apart from the fact that extant analyses of violence against women have focused more on the physical rather than the cultural, psychological or structural dimensions, it is seldom acknowledged that exclusion of women from active participation in decision-making processes in the search for peace only promote negative peace that promotes the forms of inequalities and social exclusion that gender advocates seek to redress. For example, when policies that are focused on socioeconomic development such as macro-economic reform are being considered, it may be necessary to examine the extent to which such policy will deepen or reduce existing cleavages, inequalities and tensions among social categories. For this reason, efforts geared toward gender equality are focused on attainment of 'positive peace', a critical component of peace building.

Conceptually, peace building involves a number of long-term activities that are focused on building stable communities and peaceful societies where individuals and groups do not live under the grind of cultural, physical, psychological, and structural violence by building societies on a solid foundation of justice and reconciliation and concerted efforts to transform unjust practices and sociopolitical policies that may directly or indirectly hinder people from attaining their highest possible potential. It therefore focuses on all social factors that could constitute ingredients of negative peace that in most cases incinerate social justice and fair play among social actors.

Various definitions that have been offered by peace scholars suggest among others, that peace building involves: attempts to overcome structural relationship and cultural contradictions which lie at the root of conflict (Miall, 1999); the building and strengthening of social structures for constructive transformation of conflict and promotion of values such as benevolence, compassion, cooperation and justice among persons and groups (Ehsan, 2000); and the provision of support for social, political and institutional structures and processes which strengthen the prospect for peaceful co-existence (Goodhand and Hulme, 1999).

According to Arne (2004), peace may be built "from above" or "from below." While the former focuses on restoring normalcy during periods of acute crises and violence, the latter focuses on developing trust and building confidence among communities and relationships at the local level. In essence, building "from below" emphasizes conscious activation and retention of mutually beneficial relationships between different categories of stakeholders that makes it easy for them to commit and pool their resources and talents for securing peace in their communities. In terms of typology, peace building could be "political" (restoring peace after conflict outbreaks); "structural" (increasing people's awareness of their capabilities, rights and responsibilities); "social" (attitudinal and behavioral changes that promote peaceful outcomes); and "community-based" (strengthening the role of local people and their social and political institutions).

According to Ball (1996), the crucial tasks that are incorporated in peace building include ensuring access to the basic means of survival; supporting reconciliation and confidence-building at the local level by focusing on bringing people together out of common interest; promoting rural and urban economic revitalization; job creation; addressing the needs of uprooted and disaffected persons; strengthening civil society for effective engagement of decision-making processes; creating or strengthening mechanisms for resolving disputes and strengthening the rule of law; initiation and pursuit of crucial reforms; insistence on protection of human rights; contributing to ways in which victims of violence and the accompanying trauma can lead normal lives again; and development of mechanisms for dealing with conflict outcomes as a whole.

GENDER AND PEACE BUILDING: A GROWING DEBATE

The history of intra-state conflicts in the last two centuries show that women sometimes constitute more than half of the combatants recruited by non-state armed groups at some point or the other. In such situations, the chances are that their participation as combatants, nurses, cooks, or "sex slaves" is either voluntary or forced. Although some women have served in more recent times as suicide bombers and terrorists, it is still commonly believed that violence and war is an affair for men while women and children constitute the bulk of victims. The reality, however, is that while women experience considerable disadvantage in the course of armed conflict, it does not necessarily mean that men are always the perpetrators and women the losers (see Jacobs, Jacobson and Marchbank 2000; Moser and Clark, 2001).

As the first witnesses to atrocities during periods of violence, they are more impacted by conflicts and crises outcomes when compared with their male counterparts—as mothers, wives, sisters, and kinsfolk of male casualties. In the recently ended conflicts in Kosovo, the Great Lakes and the Mano River regions of West Africa, women were subjected to horrid forms of violence such as sexual slavery and "systematic rape" used as weapons of war (Vandenberg, 2000). The same is true of the raging conflicts in northern Uganda and the Democratic Republic of Congo.

Flowing directly from the above, the role of women in peace-building processes is an issue that became more and more pronounced in discourses on conflict management and transformation from the 1970s when the OHCHR Declaration on the Protection of Women in Emergency and Armed Conflict (1974) and the Convention on the Elimination of All Forms of Discrimination Against Women (CEDAW) were enacted in 1979. Identification of the interface between women and armed conflict was one of the critical areas of concern at the 1995 Fourth World Conference on Women in Beijing. After Beijing came the landmark decision in 1998 to recognize rape and other sexual violence as crimes against humanity when committed within the ambit of war.

The need to increase women's representation in managing and resolving conflicts has been the subject of proceedings at several forums of the United Nations and regional organisations, the G8 Summit, and the European Parliament. The UN Security Council proclamation on the International Women's Day in March 2000 recognized that gender equality is an integral component of peace. On 31 October 2000, it passed Resolution 1325, which called on member states, their governments and other multilateral agencies and mediators to include women in negotiations and settlements that have to do with conflict resolution and peace building.

Other laws and conventions that have been developed with the specific purpose of lifting women above the current morass of insensitivity to the role they can and do play in peace building include the Nairobi Forward-looking Strategies for the Advancement of Women (1985); the Office of the United Nations High Commissioner for Refugees (UNHCR) Policy on Refugee Women (1990); UN Vienna Declaration and Programme of Action (1993); UN Declaration on the Elimination of Violence Against Women (1993); Beijing Declaration & Platform for Action (1995); Optional Protocol to CEDAW (1999); Windhoek Declaration: The Namibia Plan of Action on "Mainstreaming a Gender Perspective in Multidimensional Peace Support Operations" (2000); and the European Parliament Resolution on Gender Aspects of Conflict Resolution and Peacebuilding (2000).

Resolution 1325 recommended, among others, the integration of a gender perspective into peacekeeping missions; active support for women's grassroots organizations peace initiatives; the involvement of women as participants in peace negotiations and agreements; integration of a gender perspective into disarmament, demobilization, and reintegration of former combatants in post-war situations; and the protection of women and girls from gender-based violence. The underlying assumption that prompted both the proclamation and the resolution that came later is that since violent conflict results in conditions which consign vulnerable social categories (such as women and children) to the mercy of unpredictable challenges that stretch their coping abilities, conflict of any intensity could not be transformed without their active involvement and full integration (Upadhyayam, 2003).

Given their status as marginalized categories in decision-making processes at community governance level, women have had negligible participation in conflict resolution processes after de-escalation of most violent crises, and the social reconstruction that often follow. In spite of the fact that such forms of marginalisation and neglect have been consistently criticized for more than a decade, women remain sidelined in peace-building projects; receive less attention than men in peace-building policies; and gender analysis rarely informs peace-building strategies (Pankhurst, 2000).

There is no doubt that women are victims of gender-specific violence and have the capability to contribute to conflict transformation and reconciliation in several ways, yet they are usually excluded from high level negotiations and the decision-making processes leading to peace. In the few instances where they have been involved, their input was fractional and is invited mainly to "fulfill all righteousness." In any case, many women find it intimidating to become immersed in formal peacemaking processes and participate actively in a process that is often clearly geared to masculine mien and temperament, or to look beyond the culture of "hegemonic masculinity" that promotes male dominance of post-conflict processes.

TEST CASE: NIGERIA'S NIGER DELTA

The Niger Delta, Nigeria's oil and gas belt, is home to over 28.9 million Nigerians (UNDP, 2006). Nigeria grossed over N84 trillion in 45 years from oil and made N8.7 trillion in 2008 alone (Chukwu, 2009). Despite its strategic importance as purveyor of the nation's oil wealth that contributes 95 percent of export revenues, 76 percent of government revenues, and about a third of Gross Domestic Product (GDP) (IBRD, April 2006), it is plagued by frequent schisms within community groups and between them and multinational oil companies working in the region over the impacts of their operations. Instead of making the region the standard bearer of development in Nigeria, oil presence appears to have deepened the marginalization of the region; and enriched only a tiny fraction of the population while the rest have become further impoverished.

Apart from the direct, wasting nature of large-scale mineral extraction activities, there are extensive social and environmental impacts including community displacement, extensive pollution leading to land and water contamination, which further impoverish vulnerable local communities by disempowering those who rely on land and water resources for their livelihood (Aladesuwa, 2000; Ojo, 2002). Other active triggers of intermittent conflicts relate to the absence of infrastructural development and the resultant high level of poverty. This confirms the argument of Klare (1999) who argued that a sizeable number of future conflicts would be over the availability and accessibility of fresh water, and that of Basedau (2005) that oil production impacts the domestic, political and social environments of places where it takes place.

Conflict theorists have for long argued that disparity in access to resources, insecurity, as well as a high level of inequality are structural conditions that increase the threat of destructive conflict (Williams and Timberlake, 1984). It is arguable that the Niger Delta suffered from sources of insecurities that included low income level, unclean water, illiteracy, lack of food, lack of housing, and preventable death. It is the case that the absence of such political freedoms, economic facilities, social opportunities, transparency guarantees, and protective security all of which facilitate conflict avoidance or prevention within communities are key ingredients of social upheavals across the ages. For Watts, Okonta and von-Kemedi (2007), large numbers of the conflicts at the local level in the Niger Delta emerged from challenges to customary forms of community governance, precipitated by the presence and activities of oil operations, and expressed through struggles among groups over land rights, and access to oil company rents, leases and patronage.

The contradiction of poverty in the midst of plenty, continuing ecological devastation of the oil-producing communities, the economic and political exclusion of the people, the complete underdevelopment of communities, and prolonged neglect by all levels of government prompted local communities to adopt "pressure tactics" (picketing, blockage of access to flow-stations, internationalization of agitation, etc.) against oil companies. Unemployment occasioned "youth bulge" and created a mass of unemployed and unemployable young people who are easily mobilised by crime syndicates and armed non-State actors for militancy and other acts of violence. Career criminals also took advantage of the situation to engage in illegal oil bunkering, pipeline vandalization and use of "terror tactics" (hostage taking, abduction of oil workers, security racketing, and so on). The delta became a combustible nexus of third world militancy, deprivation and government corruption (Nossiter, 2009).

In August 1990, the Movement for the Survival of the Ogoni (MOSOP) drew up "the Ogoni Bill of Rights," which emphasized peaceful and sustained resistance to oil exploration activities in the Ogoni area. Other bills, charters and declarations that emerged after, such as the Izon People's Charter (1992), the Charter of Demands of the Ogbia People (MORETO) (1992), and the Kaiama Declaration (1998) all justified the use of confrontational strategies that transformed the Niger Delta region into a swamp of insurgency and violence.

The Kaiama Declaration in October 1998 activated widespread resistance and militancy that culminated in occupation of oil installations, hostage taking, the kidnapping of oil workers (especially expatriates) for ransom, pipeline vandalisation and violent confrontations within or between communities, and between militant formations and Nigerian security forces that led to thousands of deaths; many of them in the confused crossfire between militants and soldiers (*The New York Times*, November 29, 2009).

During the Warri crisis, oil companies were forced to embark on forced shut-downs, which culminated in deferments of 13,425,000 barrels per month and 120,825,000 barrels over active phase of the conflict. Calculated at the rate of $19 per barrel, Nigeria lost about $2.3 billion (Nkoro, 2005). Within 2007 alone, there were more than 18 attacks against oil facilities, and about 70 foreigners were abducted (Knight, 2007). In June 2009, militants destroyed Shell's Cawthorne Channel 1, 2 and 3 flow stations feeding the Bonny export terminal and the Forcados offshore platform killing 23 soldiers in the process. The International Crisis Group reported that more than 1,000 people had been killed within the first nine months of 2009 (ICG, October 2009).

CORPORATE AND STATE RESPONSE

In response, while oil companies developed myriads of engagement programmes that were expected to deflect the hostility of communities and militant formations, the Nigerian government has used a combination of ameliorative and strong arm tactics. On the one hand, it cracked down viciously on protesting communities, imprisoned outspoken community leaders and activists, including nine leaders of the Movement for the Survival of Ogoni People (MOSOP) who were sentenced to death by hanging in November 1995.

Government also deployed military contingents that sacked entire communities (e.g., Odi, Opia, Ikiyan, Odioma), and laid siege on the region by deploying the Joint Task Force (JTF), an internal security operation code-named Operation Restore Hope. On February 21, 2005, about 17 people were killed when the JTF personnel raided the town of Odioma. Their mission was ostensibly to arrest members of an armed vigilante group suspected of killing 12 people, including four local councilors. The suspects escaped but approximately 80 percent of homes in Odioma were razed. Similarly, when the JTF bombed Kurutie, Kokodiagbene, Kunukunuma, Oporoaza and Okerenkoko communities in Gbaramatu kingdom of Delta State on May 13, 2009, the majority of the casualties were women, the aged, and children.

On the other hand, ameliorative strategies involved the establishment of of the Niger Delta Development Board; Oil Mineral Producing Area Development Commission (OMPADEC) in 1989, and the Niger Delta Development Commission (NDDC) in year 2000 the Consolidated Council on Socio-Economic Development of the Coastal States of the Niger Delta, and lately, the establishment of the Ministry of the Niger Delta in 2007. Most of these initiatives failed to kick start development in the region.

Immediately after his inauguration on May 29, 2009, President Yar Adua made the Niger Delta crisis one of the priority projects encapsulated in his government's "7-Point Agenda." Subsequently, he appointed a 45-person technical committee with a mandate to harmonise all existing reports on the Niger Delta from the Sir Henry Willinks Commission's report (1957) to the Ogomudia Panel report (2002), and the Niger Delta Peace and Conflict Resolution Committee report (2007).

In contrast, current engagement programmes by oil companies in the Niger Delta include sponsorship of job training for youths, community development projects covering infrastructure, health, education, power, water, as well as economic empowerment programs targeted at women and youths in host communities. Oil-company funded women empowerment programmes aimed to involve women in local development by addressing inadequacy in access to education, training and skills acquisition. It was also designed for economic empowerment that would strengthen women's role in their family and communities; improve their health; and build capacity in local democracy and governance.

ENGENDERED ACTIVISM

In the Niger Delta, women's economic activities include the gathering of sea foods, fuel woods, gin distillation from raffia palm trees, collection of African mango seeds ("Ogbono"), weaving of mats and other objects/items from screw pine, raffia palms and bulrushes, subsistence farming, collection of snails and other non-timber products, tapping of rubber trees, and pottery. Because it is woven around land and water resources, women's livelihoods are most impacted whenever pollution leading to land and water contamination occurs. Apart from this, acquisition of land for exploration activities also means that the amount of such resources available to women shrinks on a continual basis.

One key problem that have dogged oil companies' community engagement programmes concerns how to mainstream communities' participation in the planning and implementation of programmes and projects that are meant for the benefit of whole communities. Oil companies' interface with communities is usually limited to community chiefs, elders and leaders who, given the patriarchal structure of Niger Delta communities, are mostly male because even though women do most of the peasant farming, land is controlled by men. When cash payments for "homage," security contracts, compensation for spillages and ground rent are made, women are usually not in the picture. In cases where confrontations and protest occur, ensuing negotiations and settlements are often limited to community elders and leaders. This culture of exclusion probably explains why women sometimes take matters in hand by insisting on direct negotiation with government agencies and oil company officials.

Women-only activism both in their own interests, and in the corporate interests of their communities against the oil industry in the Niger Delta started as far back as the colonial period. At that time, they took the form of struggles against colonial exploitation, tax riots, market closures and cocoa holdups, the unseating of kings, the kidnapping of colonial officials and warring against menfolk who subvert the interests of their community. Turner and Oshare (1993) chronicled episodes in both eras: the Aba women's riot of 1928–1929 and the Egba women's movement of the early 1930s to the 1950s; as well as the earliest and most notable in the post-independent period—the Ogharefe women's uprising of 1984, the Ughelli women's anti-tax protests of 1985–1986 and the Ekpan women's uprising in 1986 all of which took place in Warri. In the 1990s, MOSOP organised protests against Shell and had over 100,000 Ogoni women and men mobilised for day-long demonstrations (*Newswatch*, 25 January 1993).

On July 8, 2002, one hundred and fifty women of Ugborodo community invaded and occupied Chevron's Escravos terminal and tank farm in protest over what they described as the negative impact of its exploration activities on local livelihoods and insensitivity to the plight of the community. By July 17, they had successfully negotiated and obtained a commitment from Chevron to address a number of their demands. The incident marked the first time women were protesting as a group in the Niger Delta. Hundreds of other women from neighboring villages followed their lead by invading and shutting down other oil facilities operated by Chevron Texaco. They also made claims and demands similar to those made by their counterparts at Escravos.

After the company reneged on its agreement with the women, claiming the 7-page Memorandum of Understanding that was brokered by the State government was signed under duress, the women mobilized for a larger protest involving a combination of Itsekiri, Ilaje and Ijaw women outside the premises of two oil companies in Warri, Delta State. Their peaceful protest was broken up violently by soldiers. In the process, five women were shot, one died, and several others were badly injured. It is on record that soldiers and policemen sent to protect the interest of multinational oil companies killed more than two thousand people in host communities between 1992 and 2002 (Olukoya, 2002).

Sometimes, women lose scarce resources in the course of agitating for a better deal. This was the case in Abiteye community, host to Chevron Texaco Abiteye flow station from where the company has operated for about 30 years. According to the people of Abiteye, the only positive role played by the company is the occasional privilege they have to travel in the company's speedboats. When the oil company revealed its plan to withdraw its speedboats in June 2002, community women expressed their displeasure by using their canoes to block a creek that lead to the company's premises in the hope that the company would rescind its decision. Instead, the company responded by sending two military gunboats which sank two of the canoes by ramming into them. With their boat sunk in this way, the women had to swim to safety. On July 16, barely a month after the incident, Ijaw women of Gbaramatu and Egbema clans defied the heavy security presence around the same facility and occupied the flow station, bringing its exploration and production operations to a halt.

The women's action which culminated in the effective occupation of four other facilities ended after about ten days after agreements were reached between the women and senior Chevron officials to provide employment and provide of social amenities in Abiteye. It achieved a remarkable result without the loss of lives that is usually associated with similar actions by community youths.

THE EXCLUSION GAME

While women have initiated positive change in livelihoods, attitudes and conflict outcomes in several instances, they have experienced and continue to experience multiple forms of direct and indirect violence in the Niger Delta. They have been victims of collateral damage during reprisal action by coercive apparatus of the State and suffer loss of livelihood each time spillage occur due either to defective exploration equipment occasioning ruptures and blowouts, or deliberate sabotage by aggrieved youths. Despite this, their interests seldom appear on priority listings whenever and wherever the State, oil companies and international development agencies decide to carry out interventions.

While indeed a number of empowerment programmes especially by oil companies and development actors target women, these hardly go far enough and barely penetrate the deep-rooted indigence that confront the women in the region. The focus of most of such activities are on how to win over restive youths and by so doing, neutralize their wrecking power.

During interventions, women rarely receive recognition for their contributions as providers and care givers, or reward for their roles as social and political organisers. A few examples will suffice here.

Oil companies usually offer a number of incentives that help them to deflect the anger of militant youths and powerful groups within communities involve commissioning community youth groups to secure their facilities and facilitate uninterrupted passage for personnel. One of such carrots is what they often refer to as "security" or "surveillance" contracts. They also make substantial payments for allowing oil work to continue by hiring youth as "ghost workers." In engaging the youths in this way, they hope to enlist their cooperation by pay-rolling them. "Homage" payments usually go to community chiefs and elders council, who in most cases, are males. Although female community members sometimes win contract awards (mostly for cleaning and catering), the value often pales in significance when compared to what their male counterparts access from time to time when oil companies hire barges and other equipment, and award contracts for clearing of work sites and casual labour.

Interventions by the State have followed the same pattern. For example, since the Niger Delta Development Commission (NDDC) was formed in year 2000, its senior management cadre has remained male-dominated. Most of the interventions it undertook, especially in the area of empowerment left women at a disadvantage. For instance, the stupendous sums it spent on thousands of mass transit buses directly empowered only males (as drivers). Membership of road transport unions who leased such vehicles is also exclusively male. The same is also true of speedboats and ferries that were acquired by NDDC and by oil companies at different times.

After the Nigerian President offered unconditional pardon to all Niger Delta militants who were willing to lay down their weapons in June 2009, the false assumption of the government that guided other actions from that point was that all militants were male. This assumption propelled it to completely overlook the vital support roles that young women played as members, lovers and key intelligence providers to members of militant formations, and the fact that as daughters, sisters, wives and mothers, women had a big stake in the eventual outcome of the process.

In the post-amnesty phase, the Nigerian State has made provisions to assist and reintegrate only male ex-militants with little thought for the daughters, sisters, wives and mothers who bore the brunt of personal and material losses during the active phase of protest and militancy in the Niger Delta. There has been little or no acknowledgement of the impact of the immediate past crisis on women or of the significance of their inclusion in the peace-building processes and post-amnesty social transformation. In essence, gender discrimination continues through economic marginalization and political exclusion.

Clearly, violence experienced by women is not usually limited to periods of "hot" or high-intensity conflicts. Apart from physical insecurity, challenges that women confront even in the post-conflict phase include extreme poverty, the destruction of extant social networks and coping mechanisms, limited options for employment and livelihood-generation, and the more excruciating pain of exclusion from political and decision-making processes of post-conflict peace building. On reasons why women's contributions in both the crisis and post-conflict phases of peace building are devalued, Strickland and Duvvury (2003) are of the view that this happens because such contributions take unconventional forms, occur outside formal peace processes, or are seen as extensions of women's existing gender roles.

CONCLUSION

Peace-building strategies focus on the attitudes and socioeconomic status of ordinary persons especially those that will facilitate greater inter-group contact. They also tend to focus on relationships rather than the issues that precipitate conflicts between people. Such contact improves attitudes when it is intimate, pleasant, between equals, socially supported, and in pursuit of common goals (Ryan, 1995).

The involvement of women in peace building is noticeable at both the formal and informal levels of peacemaking in the Delta (Eno, 2000). Such involvement include initiatives that seek to dissuade their kith and kinfolk from resort to self-help and violence through person-to-person suasion, provision of early warning information to appropriate responders on imminent conflict outbreaks at both the macro (community) and the micro (family) level, and facilitation of community cohesion through collaborative support for indigent members and victims of violence (see Turshen and Twagiramariya, 1998; Bouta and Frerks, 2002).

Despite depressing culture-bound and violence-induced outcomes that result in gendered loss of voice and exclusion, women continue to build peace by striving to improve their household and community livelihoods through cooperative ventures that assist their members to ride the waves of repeated economic and social setbacks that they routinely experience as a result of the crises in the Niger Delta region. By providing small scale credit that often attracts little or no interest payment; they build peace by enabling social cohesion and preventing poverty-induced family disintegration. In coalescing in small groups, they provide critical support to whole communities in seasons of intense distress.

Women opposition to conflict-generating actions and practices by community leaders and youths prevented potential intra and inter-community conflict outbreaks in many instances and their resilience where such early warning is ignored help most communities to cohere thereafter. Whenever their activism for improvement of community livelihoods succeed, they have helped to avert potentially costly face-offs and violence, loss of income due to production deferments, and continued discord from problematic community engagement policies and practices by oil companies and development agencies of the Nigerian State. It is a paradox, however, that the response that women's peace-building activism triggers in most of these instances have not resulted in maximal benefits to them as a group. Even where compensation for loss of livelihood is sought and paid, male-only community leaderships routinely annex and expropriate such payments.

Women are not just victims of the conflict in the Delta; they were components of the protest and militancy, survivors, caregivers, leaders and potential peacemakers. During periods of crises involving violence within their communities, their responsibilities increased as they became the main breadwinners and primary caregivers when spouses and male relatives are absent or incapacitated due to incarceration, death or injury. They are also compelled to minister to the needs of children and aged members of the family during seasons of anomie.

Peace building involves entrenching democratic governance, human rights, rule of law, sustainable development, equitable access to resources, and environmental security. It may involve conflict prevention, conflict resolution and other activities that help to consolidate peacefulness in post-conflict environments. Despite the negative impact of violent conflicts and crises on their persons, Niger Delta women are resisting the general tendency to see them only in the mold of victims. Instead, they strive to be acknowledged as legitimate and active participants in the process of restoring normalcy to the Niger Delta.

In view of their exclusion, women groups have repeatedly demanded for the right to be at the negotiating table where key decisions and policies relating to restoration of normalcy will be hammered out. Instead of focusing only on their brothers, sons, husbands and fathers, they want their experience, abilities and particular needs to be taken into account by the Nigerian State and development actors who are involved in the current efforts to entrench sustainable peace in the Delta. This tendency is well captured in Upadhyayam's observation that "they (women) ask not for charity, but for recognition of their right to participate fully in processes that will shape the future of their communities" (p. 8).

REFERENCES

Ball, N. (1996) *Priority Tasks for Rebuilding War-torn Societies*. Washington, DC: International Development Research Centre.

Bouta, T., and G. Frerks (2002) *Women's Roles in Conflict Prevention, Conflict Resolution and Post-Conflict Reconstruction: Literature Review and Institutional Analysis*. The

Hague: Netherlands Institute of International Relations, www.clingendael.nl/cru/publications/publications_occ_papers.htm

Brume, F., (n.d.) Oil-pipeline vandalization in the Niger Delta: The way out. Urhobo Historical Society, www.waado.org

Byrne, B. (1996) *Gender, Conflict and Development*, Vol. I: Overview, BRIDGE Report 34. Brighton: BRIDGE/Institute of Development Studies.

Cockburn, C. (1998) *The Space Between Us: Negotiating Gender and National Identities in Conflict*. London: Zed Books.

El Jack, A., *Gender and Armed Conflict*: Overview Report

Eno, J. (2000) Women's strategies for peace: Gains and losses in Sierra Leone, in *Report on the Workshop on Conflict Transformation in Africa: African Women's Perspectives*. London: International Alert and African Women for Research and Development (AAWORD), www.international-alert.org/pdf/pubgl/workshop.pdf

Fentiman, A. (1996) The anthropology of oil: The impact of the oil industry on a fishing community in the Niger Delta. *Social Justice* Vol. 23, Issue 4. Crime & Social Justice Associates.

Ferris, E. (1993) *Women, War and Peace*. Life and Peace Research Report 14. Uppsala: PRIO.

Galtung, J. (1995) Twenty-five years of peace research: Ten challenges and responses. *Journal of Peace Research*, 22.

Giles, W., and J. Hyndman (2003) *Sites of Violence: Gender and Conflict Zones*. Berkeley: University of California Press.

Human Rights Watch (May 1999) *Crackdown in the Niger Delta*. HRW, Vol. 11, No. 2 (A).

Jacobs, S., R. Jacobson, and J. Marchbank (eds) (2000) *States of Conflict: Gender, Violence and Resistance*. London: Zed Books.

Moser, C., and F. Clark (eds) (2001) *Victims, Perpetrators or Actors? Gender, Armed Conflict and Political Violence*. London: Zed Books.

Pankhurst, D. (2000) *Women, Gender and Peacebuilding*. Centre for Conflict Resolution Working Paper 5, Department of Peace Studies, University of Bradford, August.

Ryan, S. (1995) *Peace-Building and Conflict Transformation in Ethnic Conflict and International Relations*. Dartmouth, NH: Dartmouth Publishing.

Strickland, R., and N. Duvvury (2003) *Gender Equity and Peacebuilding (From Rhetoric to Reality: Finding the Way)*. Washington, DC: International Centre for Research on Women.

Turshen, M., and C. Twagiramariya (eds) (1998) *What Women Do in Wartime: Gender and Conflict in Africa*. London: Zed Books.

UN/OCHA (2000) Nigerian Women Occupy Oil Facility. UN Office for the Coordination of Humanitarian Affairs (June); www.un.org/womenwatch/daw/public/eWPS.pdf

United Nations (UN) (2002) *Women, Peace and Security*. Geneva: United Nations.

Upadhyayam, A. S. (2003) Gender and Conflict Transformation: Focus on South Asia. Paper delivered at the workshop organized by the Canadian Committee on Women, Peace and Security and South Asia on October 20.

Vandenberg, M. (2000) *Kosovo: Rape as a Weapon of "Ethnic Cleansing."* New York: Human Rights Watch, www.hrw.org/reports/2000/fry/index.htm

12

Women in Yoruba Indigenous Politics in Nigeria

I. O. Aransi (PhD)

ABSTRACT

This chapter examines the role of women in Yoruba indigenous politics in Nigeria. It x-rays the women's contributions in the field of politics beginning from the pre-colonial, through colonial and the contemporary period. The chapter also highlights the various factors responsible for unimpressive performance of women in indigenous Yoruba politics. Furthermore, it discusses the way forward for women's contribution in politics in contemporary Nigeria.

INTRODUCTION

In any democratic dispensation anywhere in the world, women are vital stakeholders. All over the world, studies have demonstrated the importance of women in all spheres of life: social, economic and political. In Nigeria, for example, the role of women in politics cannot be underestimated. Women constitute a greater percentage of voters in elections in Nigeria thereby making them active participants in democratic dispensation. Although pre-colonial or indigenous Nigeria was a largely patriarchal society, women were able to make their mark in the area of political leadership with historical figures like Queen Amina of Zaria, Moremi of Ife, among others leading the pack. There is no longer any doubt that nowadays, political power is tilted in favour of men. For long, women have made efforts to break the stronghold. It has, however, not been a huge success so far. But then, the minimal success recorded could be attributed to the awareness, doggedness and, of course, changing circumstances on the part of women. The prominent role played by indigenous Yoruba women in politics in Nigeria cannot be underestimated.

All over the world, the traditional roles of women are those of nurturers of families and those who engage in domestic work. In fact, in the olden days, women's home was, undoubtedly, confined to the kitchen. Indigenous women were supposed to be seen and not heard. It is pertinent to note that very few women have had the opportunity of being part of the decision-making processes of their societies while politics was regarded as an exclusive preserve of men (Pogoson, 2003). The African woman also bears the overwhelming burden of providing food for the family, in addition to being the hewer of wood and fetcher of water. Statistics show that in sub-Saharan Africa women process the food, 80 percent of the work to transport and store the food, 60 percent of the work to market the food and provide 90 percent of the water, wood and fuel. This they do using rudimentary handheld tools and without appropriate modern technology. Indeed, women meet the basic survival needs of the continent, despite the fact that they own only 1 percent of the land, receive less than 7 percent of farm extension services, receive less than 10 percent of the credit given to small-scale farmers. The rural African female farmers are undernourished, illiterate and lack voice in the decisions affecting their lives (Chikwe, 2003).

It is no gainsaying the fact that under the current democratic dispensation in Nigeria especially under the leadership of the former president, Chief Olusegun Obasanjo, women have a better deal, which the current president is trying to improve upon.

Prior to the current democratic experiment, particularly in the First Republic, the number of women who participated in active politics was near zero and consequently, none of them made it to the corridors of power to engineer a favourable atmosphere for women in politics. Chief (Mrs.) Wuraola Esan and Hajiya Gambo Sawaba of the Northern Elements Progressive Union (NEPU) were about the only women in partisan politics of that generation. The likes of Chief (Mrs.) Funmilayo Ransome-Kuti and Chief (Mrs.) Margaret Ekpo were very influential women who demonstrated outstanding leadership qualities during the struggle for independence, and after, but they did not initially engage in partisan politics. The dearth of women occupying leadership position in politics could be traced to their non-representation in political parties; the indigenous Yoruba women inclusive.

CONCEPTUAL ELUCIDATION AND CLARIFICATION

To facilitate their usage in this chapter, three concepts are worthy of elucidation and clarification. These are "women," "indigenous," and "politics."

"Women" can simply be described as "fully grown human female" or "female persons with female nature or qualities, such as caring for weak creatures, personal attractiveness, and interest in people" (Procter, 1978). "Women are honoured for their womanhood as mothers, particularly in Yorubaland. All human beings, male and female pass through the mothers who had (and culturally still have) total control over the person from the womb foetus to the grave." Homage is always due to women. Purity, virginity, the secret of the dark dye, and the power of the bird (witches) are all associated with women. It is believed that women are in a vantage position (based on their privileged knowledge about life) to control the world, especially at the cultic and mysterious levels, much more than men are privileged to do. It is, therefore, not surprising that many traditional artists shower homage on women at the inception of their public performances (Ilesanmi, 1998).

By the concept "indigenous," this chapter refers to "native," or belonging to a place" (Procter, 1978). Indigenous Yoruba women are therefore women of Yoruba origin who belonged to the Southwestern part of Nigeria.

Many scholars and authors have conceptualized "politics" as a term, severally. To Edelman (1972), politics in its simplest form is the "power to allocate powers between individuals, communities and nations." Ayoade (1997) elucidates this conceptualization by considering politics as "any collectivity, which is bound together, must regulate its affairs, define its boundaries, assign roles, rights and obligations. The dynamics of such decision-making is politics. Ideally, all people come under the ambiance of such decisions. It is the desire to maximize benefits that necessitates participation in politics. When participation is low and restricted, benefits are concentrated in a few hands, and the quality of benefit to the majority of the people is low. Active participation in politics limits the powers of those who form the government because the electoral vigilance of the people is the surest guarantee of a limited government; on the other hand, electoral apathy is invitation to bad governance. But the attempt by the government to obstruct legitimate participation of people in politics is more likely to increase participation. Bad governance inadvertently and paradoxically results in high political mobilization of a radical kind. Politics is like a rubber ball kept under water. It remains potent and active and will jump to the surface at the slightest opportunity. Political instincts are irrepressible. It is politics that defines the government, which in turn defines the lives of the citizens, who in the final analysis define politics of the state. Politics is also a public act and the natural instinct of the people. It is an inclusive, public participatory act, which produces government." Politics, to Harold Lasswell, is the "authoritative allocation of values, who gets what, when, and how." Ranney (1958:4) posits that politics consists of conflict among human groups whose values—the things their members collectively desire and the common ends they wish to achieve—to some extent differ from and are incompatible with each other. Hence, if some groups' values are satisfied, the values of other groups go unsatisfied; and it is impossible to satisfy equally the values of all groups. Each group, to some extent and in some manner acts to satisfy its values as fully as possible; and this inevitably brings it into conflict with some other group or groups holding contrary values. In international as in domestic politics, in short, conflict among human groups is no unfortunate but temporary and avoidable aberration from the political norm; it is the very essence of politics and human life itself—and international no less than domestic politics is a perpetual struggle over "who gets what, when, and how." The next section focuses attention on women in politics during pre-colonial and colonial periods.

WOMEN IN POLITICS DURING PRE-COLONIAL AND COLONIAL PERIODS

Faseke (1998), reviewing the role of women in traditional Yoruba society, opines that one aspect of women's activities, which has attracted an exciting study, is their role in politics. Ile-Ife traditions speak of female Ooni in earlier times (Law, 1973). In the early period of Oyo kingdom, long regency followed the death of Agunaju who reigned in the fifteenth century when his wife, Iyayun ruled the kingdom in the name of his posthumous son, Kuri. Iyayun, according to Samuel Johnson (1921), wore the crown and put on the royal robes and was invested with the Ejigba, the Opa Ileke and other royal insignia. She ruled the kingdom as a man until her son was of age. Ilesa tradition recalls many female Owa while Ondo traditional history recounts that a woman (Babayemi 1987) founded the town. Faseke (1998) contends that, although the authenticity of these traditions have not been proved, they are plausible. It is, therefore, not very wise to dismiss the stories as "mere fabrication." The Yoruba traditional society is not the only society that attributes great political power to women in the distant past.

It would appear that not many women Alaafins ruled in Oyo. The ones remembered were Iyayun and Orompoto. However, women played important roles in the elaborate administration and palace organization. Babayemi (1987) discusses the prominent role of the "Ayaba," the Alaafin's wives in the politics of Oyo. All the men and women in the palace were dominated by the Ayaba. Members of the Oyomesi should be with the Alaafin. In addition, the Ayaba swere matrons to the provincial rulers like the Okere, Onigbanna, Onikoyi and Onjo. Thus, the Ayaba wielded the power of the Alaafin both in the capital and in the provinces.

Fadipe (1970) discusses women's political associations such as Egbe-Iyalode among the Oyo-Yoruba. The Egbe-Iyalode, comprising craftswomen and traders, could make representations to the political authorities in respect of trade and general political issues. Some times, as in Ibadan, the Iyalode in the council of state represented the association. In Ibadan, Iyalode was a kind of queen. She was the first lady of the state. The office of Iyalode was very powerful in Abeokuta and Ibadan. The office gave women an opportunity to participate directly in the decision-making process through their representatives. Two renowned Iyalode about whom much has been written are Tinubu of Lagos and Egba and Efunsetan of Ibadan. Although both of them were Egba, they did not make their career in Egbaland except for Tinubu who in her late years settled in Abeokuta where she played a major role in the defence of the Egba state against Dahomey and was rewarded with the title of Iyalode. Before settling down in Abeokuta she had earlier meddled in Lagos politics (Biobaku, 1960). Efunsetan made her debut in Ibadan where she rubbed shoulders with powerful warriors. Perhaps the point to stress from the foregoing is that women could attain the position of first lady not by birth or marriage but by hard work (Faseke 1998).

It is pertinent to note that indigenous Yoruba women played some kind of role in politics in the indigenous Yoruba society. However, women were not adequately represented in the decision-making process. Legendary women Obas apart, there is not much evidence to show that women were crowned in traditional Yoruba society. Generally, women were not prominent in political organization. This is not surprising since Yorubaland was essentially partrilineal (Faseke, 1998).

Indigenous Yoruba women have come a long way in their search for emancipation of the womenfolk and relevance in political participation. Activities of women like Queen Amina of Zaria who fought wars in the northern part of Nigeria, Moremi of Ife who is reputed to have saved her people from the attacks of enemies and Queen Idia of Benin who sacrificed herself to save the throne of her husband showed the strength of women in politics of their communities in Nigeria.

The vigour and strength of purpose were further exhibited in Eastern Nigeria politics where the people were republicans and had their means of selecting their heads. The women here had their market and village groups through which their representatives tabled their concerns at the village meetings. Their protests were more powerfully exemplified in the Aba Women's Riot of 1929. The women staged a revolt against the policies of the colonial government and in particular, that of taxation which later culminated in changes in administrative policies of the colonial government.

In Yorubaland, the indigenous women's acumen in business culminated in the formation of powerful associations led by their leader Alimotu Pelewura. In her capacity as the leader, she was encouraged by the nationalist, Herbert Macaulay to form a pressure group to make it possible for them to present one united front. With such a force, the women were able to confront the colonial government at different times. Some of these confrontations include the rejection of taxation of women between 1914 and 1946, their perceived arbitrary arrests of underaged children seen hawking, the imposition and the control of prices which was introduced to check food prices especially, staple foods like "garri" and cassava during the second world war.

Indigenous Yoruba women, among others, were not left out of the struggle for the country's independence. These include the likes of Mrs. Funmilayo Ransome-Kuti, Mrs. Adunni Oluwole, Mrs. Janet Mokelu and Chief (Mrs.) Wuraola Esan. They all stood unwavering in fighting discrimination and oppression of women.

Mrs. Funmilayo Ransome-Kuti, a teacher and later politician, bestrode the economic and political scenes gallantly; gaining mention as the only woman that was in the delegation that went to London in 1947 for the Constitutional Conference. Being a party activist, she was entrusted with responsible positions at both the local and national levels. She was elected as the treasurer of the NCNC in Egba Division and also became a member of the National Executive. At that time, the political terrain was not a ground considered favourable for women. But Mrs. Ransome-Kuti stood resolutely by her conviction that the many constraints facing her as a woman needed to be done away with for a better future for women. Speaking later about her membership of NCNC and what she wanted to do for women, Mrs. Ransome-Kuti said that she joined the party because it was thought to be in the interest of the common man. She said: "I joined NCNC because I wanted to see what I could do for the common man rather than think of myself alone." She added that her status as a woman made her "unwanted in the political circle then largely dominated by men and this made her unhappy and decided that she would fight to force a change of attitude towards women" (*Sunday Tribune Magazine*, 2002:9–11). She was also the figure behind a series of public demonstrations by Egba women that rocked Abeokuta and which led a notable Oba to temporarily abandon his throne and flee.

The Northern Nigeria women were not left out in the political arena. The role of woman like Hajia Gambo Sawaba demands a quick exposition. Hajia Gambo Sawaba was a woman who sacrificed a lot in the field of politics at a time Islam had become entrenched in Northern Nigeria. She resisted the stinging policies of the authorities in the North and got harsh treatment for her intransigence. She was defiant to the colonial authorities to their consternation. Despite being imprisoned several times for her stubbornness, she remained unbowed.

Mrs. Remi Aiyedun, a member of the Action Group (AG), became the first Yoruba woman in West Africa to be appointed to a regional legislature in 1953. Mrs. Margaret Ekpo was nominated to the region's House of Assembly. Despite the exploits of women toward securing independence, no woman held any ministerial post in the First Republic. Among the women activists, there were four legislators in the persons of Wuraola Esan, Bernice Kerry, Margaret Ekpo, and Janet Mokelu.

The Second Republic produced only one woman as a senator, Chief Franca Afegbua. Three emerged in the Federal House of Representatives, including Mrs. Biola Babatope and Mrs. Kande Balarabe. Ministerial positions went to Mrs. Ebun Oyagbola, Mrs. Janet Akinrinade and Dr. (Mrs.) Simi Johnson. By the time the Second Republic was ushered in, women had taken the resolve to take a flight from being pigeonholed into the traditional roles of mother and wife. More women started shuttling between the kitchen and the soapbox and a considerable number took the bull by the horns by coming out to seek elective posts.

Prominent among women who took active parts in the Second Republic politics were Hajiya Gambo Sawaba who was a stalwart of Waziri Ibrahim's Great Nigeria People's Party (GNPP), Dr. (Mrs.) Tokunbo Awolowo Dosunmu, in Papa Awo's cap, was a gubernatorial aspirant in Lagos State, under the Social Democratic Party (SDP), while Chief (Mrs.) Oluremi Adikuwu vied for the same ticket in the National Republican Convention (NRC). Others include Chief (Mrs.) Janet Akinrinade, Chief (Mrs.) Ebun Oyagbola, Chief Franca Afegbua, Chief (Mrs.) Titilayo Ajanaku. Chief (Mrs.) Akinrinade's ambition to rule Oyo State under NPP, then, crumbled like a pack of cards, as she lost to Chief Bola Ige of UPN. But, being a woman of steel, she did not waver in her struggle to contribute meaningfully to the society and she eventually landed in the cabinet of President Shehu Shagari as junior minister under Alhaji Bello Maitama Yusuf who was the Internal Affairs Minister.

For Mrs. Adenike Ebun Oyagbola (NPN), who mounted the rostrum and campaigned vigorously, for many weeks, her failure to clinch the House of Representatives seat in her Ogun State base, definitely did not take the steam away from her political struggle, as she got the plum post of Minister of National Planning in the Shagari cabinet.

The Special Adviser to President Olusegun Obasanjo on Women Affairs, Chief (Mrs.) Ajanaku became the first woman Local Government boss in Ogun State when she held sway in Abeokuta North in the Second Republic. During the aborted Third Republic, she made an attempt to rule the state but lost to Governor Olusegun Osoba in the hot race.

In 1987, only two women were elected as Local Government Chairmen on non-party basis, one each in Ogun and Katsina States. Of the 567 members of the Constituent Assembly, only 14 were women, out of which five (5) were elected with nine (9) appointed. In 1991, all the State Houses of Assembly had a total of 1172 members with only 27 being women. Of the 300 persons that contested for the seat of governor that year, only eight were women. But none of them was elected.

FACTORS RESPONSIBLE FOR UNIMPRESSIVE PERFORMANCE OF WOMEN IN POLITICS

Several factors have been pointed out as being responsible for the unimpressive performance of women in indigenous politics. One of the factors is the burden of culture and tradition, especially in developing African countries, including Nigeria, that have all connived to restrict women from engaging in activities that go beyond their roles as housewives and mothers. As such, women find out that when they go out to take part in politics, the men dictate the pace and space of events. In other words, cultural factors, among others, influence women's underrepresentation in politics.

Many of them have pointed to the problem of lack of funds to carry on their campaigns in a terrain dominated by men who have the financial power to fight their way through. This has given concern to women activists who do not think that women should continue to be relegated to the background in political matters. Among them are various women working under various groups including Professor Jadesọla Akande of the Women Law Development Centre, Mrs. Bisi Olateru-Olagbegi of the Women's Consortium, Mrs. Nkechi Nwankwo of the Women Leadership Group, Mrs. Nkoyo Toyo of Gender and Development Action and several others. Other factors include: low level of development in Nigeria, mass media, religion, economy, low education of women, type of politics played in Nigeria and lack of party support and magnetization of politics.

For instance, the low level of development in Nigeria has brought about the unprecedented relegation of women to the background. In fact, when women show their interest in politics, the men, who consider themselves as husbands and heads of the family, discourage them. Men always want to be at the forefront where women want to assert their independence and interest in political activities. This situation points to the fact that the low level of development in Nigeria is responsible for this relegation for women. This is contrary to what obtains in the advanced countries of the world where women are given the latitude to participate in politics as much as they can. To this extent, many countries of the world have witnessed women leaders such as Mrs. Indira Ghandi of India, Queen Elizabeth of England among others.

Another major factor responsible for the unimpressive performance of women in politics in Nigeria is the role of the mass media. The mass media in Nigeria has not encouraged nor assisted women in their various reports concerning women in politics. The picture painted for women in Nigeria is that of a weaker sex who does not possess enough independence and latitude to be able to participate actively in politics. For women to be able to measure up to men in the political arena in Nigeria, the role of the mass media (both print and electronic), cannot be underestimated.

Religion is, undoubtedly, another factor responsible for the unimpressive performance of women in politics in Nigeria. Religious inclinations and beliefs, particularly, Islamic religion, does not give room for women to show themselves in the public, never mind addressing the public in campaigns. The role of women as far as Islamic religion is concerned does not include politics. To the adherents of this religion, politics should be the exclusive preserve of men. Unfortunately, women outnumber men in population in Nigeria. To deny the greater number of the womenfolk from participating in politics may not augur well for political development and attainment of full-blown democracy and participatory governance in Nigeria.

The Nigerian economy is largely dominated, currently, by a mono-product namely, oil. Quite unlike what obtains in the pre-colonial and colonial as well as the early independence period when Nigeria was renowned for agriculture, the mainstay of the economy; women, being a weaker sex, cannot participate actively in the exploitation of the oil which constitutes about 90 percent of the export earnings for Nigeria. This factor is also responsible for the low economic position of women in Nigeria. Politics in Nigeria is not for the poor as moneybags have hijacked the scene constituting themselves to godfathers for the political aspirants and incumbents in power. This is a major factor responsible for the unimpressive performance of women in Nigerian politics.

Another major factor is the low level of education of women in Nigeria. In some localities in Nigeria, particularly in the northern states, women are not given the opportunity to go to school. So, a large percentage of women in the north of the country are illiterate. What political activities can illiterate women participate in? Although Nigeria is trying to redress this imbalance in the educational level of women particularly in the North by introducing the quota system or the federal character principle into the Nigerian constitution, this gesture is still far from meeting the target.

The type of politics played in Nigeria, lack of party support and magnetization of politics, constitute another factor responsible for the unimpressive performance of women in politics in Nigeria. The problem of militarization of politics, arising from long years of military incursion into the Nigerian politics, can be said to be responsible for the absence of democratic principles to percolate the Nigerian polity. In fact, in some cases, the people are not given the chance to discuss issues and participate in decision making on matters affecting them. Among the set of people under consideration are women who constitute the majority in terms of population in Nigeria. Undoubtedly, women are not given the necessary moral and financial support needed to participate actively in politics.

The above factors are rather exhaustive. Suffice this to say that the following are the strategies for improving women representation in politics in Nigeria.

STRATEGIES FOR IMPROVING WOMEN REPRESENTATION IN POLITICS IN NIGERIA

There is the need for strategies and plans to be put in place on how to achieve adequate women representation in politics in Nigeria. For example, there is a need for a road map on how to mainstream gender issues particularly in the field of politics.

Furthermore, there is the need for affirmative action and quotas that would allocate certain percentage of positions to be occupied by women in governance. That is to say, there is the fundamental need for practical intervention to address the various ingrained prejudices and discriminations that women face in politics on a daily basis, which have implications on the willingness of women to participate in the political process.

Moreover, to ensure a better representation of women in politics, there is the need to ensure that the future constitutional exercises must create an atmosphere in which women would be encouraged to participate, so as to project their interest and shape their future.

It is pertinent to note that Nigeria's consolidation of democracy cannot be complete or meaningful without the participation of women and the protection of their interests; a protection which can only be assured and sustained when they are able to access power through holding political offices and utilizing, same in ensuring their general welfare. This may not come to fruition unless women political leaders become determined enough to achieve this by articulating their interests and projecting it to the political arena.

Women in Africa, and indeed Nigeria particularly, Yoruba women deserve commendation for their determination to attain self-actualization in various professions, including politics despite prevalent sociocultural inhibitions in their various communities and countries. The Non-Governmental Organizations (NGOs) and various women pressure groups, as well as individual female activists have done well in gradually and steadily creating the awareness required for combating and correcting those retrogressive practices that have retarded womenfolk in the continent of Africa, in the country of Nigeria and, more specifically, in the Yoruba community.

The declaration of the United Nations Decade for Women added enormous impetus to the campaign for women empowerment on a global scale. And today we are happy that although some work still needs to be done, considerable progress has been achieved in creating the enabling environment for gender parity. Fortunately, Nigeria and indeed most other African countries have joined other nations of the world to adopt the United Nations Convention on the Elimination of All Forms of Discrimination Against Women (CEDAW). The right of every child to have access to good basic education, irrespective of gender, is now entrenched in the constitution of African countries. Gender parity is being entrenched in the national constitutions. Nigeria is in the forefront in this regard. The 1999 Constitution of the Federal Republic of Nigeria clearly states: "Every citizen shall have equality of rights, obligations and opportunities before the law." This Constitution goes further to guarantee equal rights for all citizens regardless of gender, stipulating that: "All citizens, without discrimination on any group whatsoever, have the opportunity for securing adequate means of livelihood, as well as adequate opportunity to secure employment" (see pages 892–893 of the Nigeria Constitution, 1999). Consequently, any woman who is interested in participating in active politics should be given the opportunity to do so without any discrimination.

THE FUTURE OF YORUBA WOMEN IN NIGERIAN POLITICS

Yoruba women are not relenting in their efforts to be more involved in Nigerian politics. So many of them stood for and won elective positions in the elections that ushered in the Third Republic. For example, the Governorship elections held in April 2003 saw two women emerging as Deputy Governors. They are Alhaja Salimot Badru, who ran alongside Otunba Gbenga Daniel of the Peoples Democratic Party (PDP) in Ogun State and Erelu Olusola Obada who ran with Olagunsoye Oyinlola also of the PDP in Osun State. This is an improvement over what happened in the Second Republic where only Mrs. Kofoworola Bucknor Akerele, former Deputy Governor of Lagos State, was the only woman who emerged as Deputy Governor. She did not complete her tenure as she was kicked out over disagreements with Governor Bola Tinubu.

Three women won senatorial seats. The three are all freshers, as the three incumbent women senators did not make it. The senators are Daisey Danjuma, wife of Minister for Defence, Theophilus Yakubu Danjuma. She represented Edo Central Senatorial District. Mrs. Iyabo Anisulowo represented Ogun West Senatorial District, and Mrs Gbemisola Fawora Saraki who formerly represented Ilorin/Asa in the Federal House of Assembly but later represented Kwara South Senatorial District. They all won on the platform of the PDP.

The former women senators are Mrs. Stella Omu, who represented Delta South Senatorial District, Khairat Abdul-Razak Gwadabe, who represented FCT Abuja Senatorial District and Mrs. Florence Ita-Giwa, who represented Cross-River South Senatorial District. In the Federal House of Represrntatives are the likes of Regina Nwaogu, who represented Osisioma/Ugwunagbo among others.

When General Olusegun Obasanjo was elected as the president in 1999, he assured Nigerian women that he would fulfill his campaign promises to them. He promised the women they would have 30 percent participation in his administration. Former Deputy Governor of Lagos State, Alhaja Sinatu Ojikutu had so much belief in the president that, after her visit to him at Ota, she demanded for more than 30 percent participation for women in governance saying: "We are up to the task. There are Ministries men had dominated all along, like the Mineral sector, Telecommunications, Petroleum etc. A woman can be Minister of Economic Planning; some of us are economists by training. There are many fields in which women can excel" (*Sunday Tribune Magazine*, 2002).

Where the inclusion of women in governance is concerned, President Olusegun Obasanjo has indeed set records when compared with President Shehu Shagari's administration. For example, in fulfilling his campaign promises to women, President Obasanjo, in his inaugural cabinet of 44 ministers (first and second), invited five women to manage the affairs in sensitive areas like health (Dr. (Mrs.) Amina Ndalolo from Kwara State, Minister of State; defence (Mrs. Dupe Adelaja, AD Ogun State, Minister of State; science and technology (Mrs. Pauline Tallen, Plateau, Minister of State; solid minerals (Mrs. Bekky Kelebu Igwe, Bayelsa, Minister of State and Dr. (Mrs.) Kema Chikwe from Imo State as Minister of Transport).

In that first outing, President Obasanjo seemed to be testing ground as he placed four of the five female ministers under senior ministers. However, by 2001, when there was need for a cabinet reshuffle, the president not only retained all his female ministers, except one—Mrs. Bekky Kelebu Igwe, former Minister of State, solid minerals; he appointed one more female minister and gave the Kelebu slot to another woman.

Thus, the 49-member cabinet proudly displayed six (6) women ministers: Dr. (Mrs.) Kema Chikwe, who was the Aviation Minister; Mrs. Dupe Adelaja who retained her portfolio in the Defence Ministry, in charge of Navy, before becoming a full-fledged Minister of Solid Minerals in March 2002; Dr. (Mrs.) Amina Ndalolo maintained her status quo, while new faces on the block were Hajiya Aishat Ismail, Minister of Women Affairs and Development, and the amiable Ms. Boma Bromillow Jack, Culture and Tourism Minister. Mrs. Joy Emodi, APP candidate from Anambra State and Mrs. Salome Audu, also in APP, Taraba State, were the women in the ministerial nominee list, but who failed to bag appointments.

In some countries like Sweden, Denmark, Finland, Norway, the Netherlands and Iceland, they embrace the gender quota system and women occupy at least a third in their houses of legislature, while a 1993 constitutional amendment reserving 33 percent of seats for women in local councils injected about one million women into India's politics. In South Africa, women have secured nearly 30 percent of cabinet positions following the introduction of proportional representation and the adoption, by the African National Congress (ANC), of a 30 percent women quota for its party list.

Likewise, in France, a 1999 constitutional amendment voted 50 percent representation for women in the country's party lists, while parties that neglected this equal ratio in their lists faced sanctions. Uganda, Tanzania, Bangladesh and some ten Latin American countries have also joined the trend in pursuit of a good platform for the womenfolk to contribute meaningfully to their own upliftment.

Although President Obasanjo is already a pacesetter where the gender-friendly initiative is concerned in governance, there is a need to endeavour to inject more women into key positions in the current and future administrations in order to engender foresight, skill and purposeful leadership.

Many political observers thought that women's massive turn-out and active participation in politics will yield them electoral fortunes through elective offices in particular and appointments in general. What they saw was a kind of retrogressive politics, as they usually go back into their shells to do what they know how to do best—"clapping and dancing."

Yoruba women should endeavour to participate actively in politics to enhance their status. All hindrances and impediments that may militate against the achievement of this objective should be removed. The government of Nigeria should formulate policies aimed at raising the standards of women. Women should be encouraged to attain top positions in any career, politics inclusive. Government should encourage equal access to education and skill acquisition programmes for women in order to increase the demand for their labour at all levels, but particularly at the managerial and executive levels. Government should remove all constraints militating against women's attainment of social justice and equity. Also, government should eliminate all forms of discrimination against women and empower them through enhanced strategic human resource development.

CONCLUSION

This chapter examines the role of women in Yoruba indigenous politics in Nigeria. It x-rays the women's contributions in the field of politics beginning from the pre-colonial, through colonial and the contemporary period. This chapter also highlights the various factors responsible for unimpressive performance of women in indigenous Yoruba politics. Furthermore, it discusses the way forward for women's contribution in politics. The time to allow women to take leadership position in the political arena is now if their contribution and participation in politics since time immemorial is to be given the pride of place it deserves. Undoubtedly, African women and Nigerian women in particular can contribute meaningfully to African politics if they are given the opportunity to proof their mettle. It is my belief that they can amazingly perform wonderfully well in political leadership as they have proved so in

Europe and Middle East. In fact, African should borrow a leaf from the countries of the world where women have demonstrated a high degree of patriotism and political leadership, their biological composition notwithstanding. The time is now when Africa and Nigeria in particular should allow women to take leadership position in the political arena.

REFERENCES

Ayoade, J. A. A. (1997) *Nigeria and the Squandering of Hope*. An inaugural lecture delivered at the University of Ibadan. Ibadan: Vantage Publishers Limited, pp. 2–3.

Babayemi, S. O. (1987) The Role of Women in Politics and Religion in Oyo. Paper presented at the Institute of African Studies, University of Ibadan on Seminar on Women's Studies, The State of the Arts Now in Nigeria, November 5.

Chikwe, K. (2003) Prospects of women in meteorology, in *This Day Newspaper*, Saturday, May 24, p. 32.

Edelman, M. (1972) *The Symbolic Uses of Politics*. Urbana: University of Illinois Press, pp. 1–201.

Fadipe, N. (1970) *The Sociology of the Yoruba*. London: Oxford University Press, p. 253.

Faseke, M. (1998) The Role of Women in Traditional Yoruba Society: A Review, in Deji Ogunremi and Adediran 'Biodun (eds.) *Culture and Society in Yorubalan*. Ibadan: Rex Charles Publication in association with Connel Publications, pp.149–151.

Federal Republic of Nigeria (1999) *The Constitution of the Federal Republic of Nigeria*. Lagos: Federal Government Printer, pp. 892–893.

Ilesanmi, T. M. (1998) The significance of the myths of women in socio-political role sharing among Yoruba people, in Kolawole E. Modupe (ed.) *Gender Perceptions and Development in Africa: A Socio-Cultural Approach*. Lagos: Arrabon Academic Publishers, p. 32.

Johnson, S. (1921) *The History of the Yorubas from the Earlier Times to the Beginning of the British Protectorate*. London, 1921 (reprinted 1956).

Law, R. C. C. (1973) Traditional History, in S. O. Biobaku (ed.) *Sources of Yoruba History*. London: Oxford University Press, p. 38.

Pogoson, A. I. (2003) Redefining the Role of Women in Power and Decision-Making. Paper presented at a seminar paper at the Department of Political Science, University of Ibadan, Ibadan, p. 2.

Procter, P. (1978) *Longman Dictionary of Contemporary English: International Student Edition*. London: Longman Group Limited, p.1266.

Ranney, A. (1958) *The Governing of Men*. New York: Henry Holt and Company, p. 4.

Sunday Tribune Magazine (2002) Women in power. Cover choice of the *Sunday Tribune*, June 30, pp. 9-11.

The Guardian, Sunday, October 13, p. 18.

Ugbodaga, K. (2003) Women political leadership: Overcoming the barriers, in *Daily Times on Saturday*, August 2, p. 7.

Uzoanya, E. P. (2002) Women taking the political centre stage, in *The Guardian Newspaper on Sunday*, October 13, pp. 20–21.

13

Democracy and Gender Participation in Nigeria

A Case for Gender Mainstreaming in Politics

I. D. David

ABSTRACT

The wave of democratization that swept across the globe in the 1990s did not leave Nigeria behind as it experienced two democratic adventures during this period after a series of intermittent military interventions in politics and more than a decade of military subjugation, since 1983. Within this short democratic history, Nigeria has established for itself a history of marginalization of the female gender, a section of the population that has been argued to account for about 50 percent of the electorate and entire population of the country, in the democratic process and policy. Overall, the Nigerian woman continued to be under-represented in politics and their level of participation in policy under the newly earned democracy continued to fall short of the 30 percent requirement recommended by the Beijing Platform for Action, in 1995. In view of this, this chapter argues for gender mainstreaming of politics in Nigeria as a way of facilitating direct participation of women. Adopting an alternative theoretical perspective, the study situates the poor participation of women in politics in the neoliberal nature of the Nigerian democracy, which, in addition to reducing democracy to government through periodic electioneering, has commoditized it to the level of a "government of the highest bidder." The study identifies corruption and ethno-religious divisions as two features of the democratic process in Nigeria that are essentially bound to this neoliberal ideal, and which present serious challenge not only to gender participation but to democracy itself in Nigeria. It is in line with this position that we argue that the biggest threat to democracy and gender participation in Nigeria is the neoliberal nature of the Nigerian democracy itself. In view of this, the study calls for a rethink of the democratic ideology and process in Nigeria. This will not only enhance gender participation, it will also strengthen democracy and democratization in Nigeria.

INTRODUCTION

Hitherto, politics in Nigeria has been characterized by intermittent military interventions that started with the coup d' etat of January 15, 1966, which terminated the First Republic. The nature and character of the execution of the coup and the counter-coup that attended it gave expression to the deep division and dissatisfaction that existed in the young Nigerian state, a situation that threw the country into a civil war between 1967 and 1970.

After endless promises of a transition to civil rule that never saw the light of day, the regime of General Gowon was overthrown by the dynamic regime of Murtala/Obasanjo on July 29, 1975. Apart from re-posturing Nigeria on the map of Africa and the world in general through a proactive foreign policy, the Obasanjo regime, which was actually an extension of the Murtala regime, successfully midwifed Nigeria into another democratic dispensation. This was a landmark achievement at the time, as it was the first time that a military regime willingly handed over power to a civil rule.

Unfortunately, partly as a result of the election crisis that trailed the attempted civilian-to-civilian transition under Shagari in 1983, the military took over the mantle of power again under the leadership of Major General Mohammadu Buhari on December 31, 1983. Before this regime could set any democratic agenda for the nation, it was overthrown through a palace coup led by General Babangida. The Babangida administration set up an endless transition program that was to culminate with the annulment of the June 12, 1993, presidential election, acclaimed by many to be the freest and fairest in the history of Nigeria.

Subsequently, an Interim National Government (ING) was instituted under the leadership of Ernest Shonekan, who was brushed aside by the Abacha junta in November 1993. The Abacha junta epitomized the height of misrule, mismanagement, suppression, and subjugation of the voices and aspirations of the general masses. Nigeria was ostracized from the comity of nations and declared a pariah during the Abacha regime. There was large scale violation of fundamental human rights and politically motivated and sponsored killings and assassinations. The country was gradually moving toward economic suicide as it could not attract the needed foreign investment and international funding and aid assistance due partly to the prevailing political instability and partly due to various international sanctions imposed on it. The hostile environment of the Abacha era gave birth to civil crisis and disturbances. There were mass protests by the people and the civil societies. However, the sudden death of Abacha in 1998 brought an end to his self-succession bid of transition to a civilian regime and opened a new chapter of democratization in Nigeria.

May 29, 1999, ushered in a new democratic dispensation in Nigeria with the swearing-in of Olusegun Obasanjo, an ex-military Head of State, by the transition government of General Abdul Salami Abubakar. This marked a culmination of the democratization process that started in the early 1990s under Babangida after two previous failed attempts of the First and Second Republics. To Nigerians, the new democracy meant hope after several years of military misrule and suppression, which was epitomized by the "Iron Fist" regime of the late General Sani Abacha.

However, with the attainment of democracy came new problems and challenges. Of particular interest and importance are those challenges that pertain to the very nature of the Nigerian democracy itself, and of special interest in this study are those problems that have to do with the issue of participation, especially gender participation. Interest in the issue of gender participation in politics and governance in Nigeria since the attainment of democracy is spurred by the continual marginalization of women in politics and policy in Nigeria by successive regimes. Whether civilian or military, the Nigerian woman has been severely marginalized in the political scheme of things right from the earliest history of the political enclave called the Federal Republic of Nigeria, a fact that is yet to see any significant change since the attainment of the new democratic dispensation in 1999. Consequently, upon this reality, it could be argued that women have been generally disempowered and denied the basic necessity for self-actualization and sustainable development, since they cannot actively and fully take part in policies and decisions affecting them. The low participation of women in politics in Nigeria does not just impact negatively on women and their fundamental human rights, it also jeopardizes and compromises the national quest for sustainable development and democratic governance.

It is instructive to note that after 12 years of the latest democratic experiment Nigeria is yet to produce any female political executive (president or state governor). This unequal gender power relation is a reality that underscores the marginalization of the female gender in the political center of power in Nigeria. It is indicative of the conscripted political space, especially for gender participation in the country. We argue in this study that the low participation of women in politics in Nigeria puts the Nigerian democracy to question in a way similar to Ake's postulation on democracy in crisis. This therefore calls for a critical reflection on the Nigerian democracy to determine its nature and the implications of this nature for participation, especially gender participation.

THEORETICAL FRAMEWORK AND CONCEPTUAL CLARIFICATIONS

Theoretical Framework

Participatory Democracy

The word democracy has its origin in the Greek words: *demos* meaning "people" and *kratos* meaning "rule." It is in this sense that democracy is conceived as "rule by the people." Ake (2000), in conceptualizing democracy, took his point of departure from this ancient Athenian perspective of direct democracy. He conceptualizes democracy as popular power, where popular power is conceived as the rule by the people (ibid.). For Athenians, as indicated by Ake, democracy meant strict adherence to the principle of equality and rule of law. With this position, Ake suggests that democracy was not merely an ideology; it is a practice that must be operationalized at great pains. It was not a political convenience. He argues that Athenians held that a life devoid of direct participation or involvement in rulership is without merit, for the citizen's involvement in the exercise of sovereignty is the major business of life (ibid.). In view of this, Ake was able to demonstrate that Athenians were just as precise about what the rule of the people means as they were about who the people are. The outcome of this clarification is that he was able to eliminate any suggestion of confusion regarding the meaning of democracy, at least from the Athenian sense. He contends that ancient Athens stuck uncompromisingly to the direct rule by the people, shunning notions of consultation, consent, and representation (ibid.).

Trivialization of democracy is a central theme in Ake. He argues that democracy is in crisis everywhere since it has been trivialized everywhere (ibid.). He contends that democracy has been trivialized everywhere to the point that it is no longer threatening to elites around the world, a fact that has made it globally attractive and that is also responsible to a good extent for its globalization (ibid.). This trivialization has been justified on the need to operationalize or clarify the concept of democracy, which has been argued to be complex and confusing. However, Ake opines that there is nothing complex or confusing about the concept of democracy as indicated in ancient Athens where it precisely meant popular power. He maintains that the trivialization was done as a matter of political convenience that allows ruling elites to enjoy democratic legitimacy without adherence to democratic practices and principles (ibid.).

Ake traces the emergence of this democracy of convenience or "politics of the belly" to the French Revolution where its ideals of popular sovereignty were incompatible with the rising European Bourgeoisies' aspirations for private ownership of property. Ake notes that, although the revolution was received by the bourgeoisies with open arms because of its hostility to institutions and feudalism, they were however disenchanted by the implications of its ideals of popular sovereignty and political participation for private ownership of property. So while democracy served their interest in that it dislodged monarchy and feudalism, it also threatened their existence on the other hand. Democracy therefore created for itself an enemy in the rising capitalists, thus marking the beginning of the journey to replace popular democracy with liberal democracy. The emergence of liberal democracy can therefore be seen as deliberate efforts or conscious desire of a class to preserve itself.

According to Ake, there is a marked difference between liberal democracy and democracy even though they share significant affinities. Significantly, liberal democracy replaces the collectivity with the individual; government by the people with government by the consent of the people; sovereignty of the people with sovereignty of the law (ibid.). Ake sums up liberal democracy as a repudiation of popular power, a political convenience, which is the political correlate of the market.

This study draws extensively from Ake in its conceptualization of democracy. In view of this, democracy is seen first and foremost as popular power or the rule of the people, and popular power is conceived in terms of participation, an essential feature of democracy. Essentially, democracy in this study is conceived as participatory democracy, a democracy that contends that direct participation on the part of the citizens is the best approach to democracy. Citizen involvement is thus the essence of participatory democracy.

Fundamentally, participatory democracy argues for direct democracy in place of representative democracy (Pateman, 1970; Barber, 1984). In addition to asserting that a more participatory democracy can work, advocates of this position contend that only with greater participation can the other principles of democracy be fulfilled. The wisdom in this argument is that people will never be equal or free until they become active and involved citizens. Lyman (2009) notes that while most advocates of participatory democracy are not in opposition to representative democracy, they however do contend that voters must be more directly consulted and involved in decision making and that representatives should be kept on a shorter leash.

While this study recognizes the need for representative democracy, in the case of political space for women in politics in Nigeria, we argue for representation through participation. We contend that until women are adequately represented in politics in Nigeria through direct participation, the concept of representative democracy will remain meaningless. The concept of representative democracy in relation to Nigeria raises the question: who best represents the female voice in politics other than their kind? This question suggests the need for gender representation through gender participation. For as long as the political space for women participation in politics is constrained and restricted, they will continue to be underrepresented as the present condition in Nigeria indicates. Gender participation in politics is necessary for the empowerment of women in Nigeria. To limit the political space for gender participation is to disempower women. Underrepresentation of women in politics through direct participation is not just a denial of their fundamental human rights, it also limits their potential and the overall potential for sustainable development in Nigeria. This is because an essential part of the population has been exempted from the development process, which is supposed to be an all embracing and inclusive process.

It is in view of the above argument that this study makes a case for participatory democracy, not necessarily as an alternative to representative democracy but as a complement. Direct participation of women in politics in Nigeria will strengthen and reinforce the present representative democratic arrangement, since it will give a voice to the needs and aspirations of Nigerian women by ensuring that they are adequately represented in the democratization process in the body polity.

Conceptual Clarifications

Gender

A common denomination that runs through various attempts to conceptualize gender in literature is that it is socially constructed. Roles are ascribed to different sexes not because of biological make-up, but because of societal sentiments. Accordingly, Omotola avers that:

> the concept of gender typifies not women or men per se, but the ideological and material relation between them, which historically has been an unequal relationship. It connotes a kind of "socially constructed inequality between women and men." It also relates to the political, economic and cultural contexts of relations between men and women, where the latter are most often subordinated to the former. (Omotola, 2007)

Gender, as conceptualized by the UN World Survey on the Role of Women in Development (1999b), refers to "the social meanings given to biological sex differences" as well as "ideological and cultural construct" that is also reflected in influencing material practices. On this ground, gender is seen as a social stratifier that is similar to other stratifiers such as race, class, ethnicity, sexuality, and age (UN, 1999a). It also "refers to socially constructed roles of women and men ascribed to them on the basis of their sex, whereas the term sex refers to biological and physical characteristics."

Amadiume (1995) conceives gender in terms of biological determinism and ideological determinism and thus related the former to Western European societies and the latter is identified with African societies. A similar view was expressed by Omololu (1997), who suggests that gender is not far from ideological construct that is susceptible to manipulation by both men and women, since its biological determination becomes analytically less substantial in present-day society. Snyder and Tadesse (1995:14) conceived "gender" as "a social construct that asserts that the expectations and responsibilities of men and women are not always biologically determined." They therefore aver that gender is a social construct that emphasizes the roles and responsibilities of men and women in development process are not always determined by biology but also by cultural principles and practices (ibid.).

Pietila (2002) sees gender as a social problem, and posits that the perception of gender as a social problem, especially among women is provoked by a widespread discriminatory philosophies and practices that the majority of the female population is exposed to in patriarchal social structure globally. In the light of this, the political marginalization (Toyo, 2003), economic disempowerment (Garba, 1997), educational deprivation (Isiugo-Abanihe, 1997), sociocultural deficit (Olojede, 2000) and religious subservience being suffered by women portrayed them as a sidelined sect; a minority group (Wirth, in Haralambos, 2000) in Nigeria.

Gleaning from Omotola (2007), gender is defined in this study as a socially constructed inequality between men and women. Within the context of development and democratization in Nigeria, it is a social construct that often places women at the disadvantaged end compared to their male counterparts.

Gender Mainstreaming

In a Report of the Fourth World Conference on Women, gender mainstreaming has been conceptualized as:

> Mainstreaming a gender perspective is the process of assessing the implications for women and men of any planned action, including legislation, policies or programs, in all areas and at all levels. It is a strategy for making women's as well as men's concerns and experiences an integral dimension of the design, implementation, monitoring and evaluation of policies and programs in all political, economic and societal spheres so that women and men benefit equally and inequality is not perpetuated. The ultimate goal is to achieve gender equality. (UN, 1997)

Equality between male and female at all levels is the ultimate goal of gender mainstreaming as spelt out in this report. Within a state, community or household, gender mainstreaming could be expressed in terms of men and women, boys and girls having equal access to public or common good without discrimination. Within the framework of participation in a democratic process or governance it will imply as equal access to political representation and participation whether in terms of voting or being voted for.

The Report (UN, 1997) went further to spell out certain principles that will enhance gender mainstreaming as it recommends that in relation to gender:

i. Issues across all areas of activity should be defined in such a manner that gender differences can be diagnosed—that is, an assumption of gender-neutrality should not be made.
ii. Responsibility for translating gender mainstreaming into practice is system-wide and rests at the highest levels. Accountability for outcomes needs to be monitored constantly.
iii. Gender mainstreaming also requires that every effort be made to broaden women's participation at all levels of decision making.
iv. Gender mainstreaming must be institutionalized through concrete steps, mechanisms and processes in all parts of the United Nations system.
v. Gender mainstreaming does not replace the need for targeted, women-specific policies and programs or positive legislation, nor does it substitute for gender units or focal points.
vi. Clear political will and the allocation of adequate and, if need be, additional human and financial resources for gender mainstreaming from all available funding sources are important for the successful translation of the concept into practice.

Participation

Fundamentally, participation is conceived in this study as empowerment and direct involvement in policy and decisions. It is seen within the framework of power relations between men and women in politics. Within the context of democracy and gender involvement in Nigeria, it is conceived as political empowerment and involvement of women in politics and decisions. More specifically, it refers to women having access to political and elective offices without discrimination. It is women occupying positions of authority and decision in politics as recommended by the Beijing Platform for Action, 1995.

Wright (1990) has linked participation to empowerment by indicating that participation as empowerment is an approach in which supposed beneficiaries of a program hold complete power over and are fully in control of the program or institutions set up for the purpose of the program. This is similar to Tjondronegoro (1992), who conceives it as the involvement of target groups at program or project level in the development context, and the kind of involvement whereby target groups are motivated and activated, and even willing to make sacrifices for improvement of the groups in achieving specific and agreed objectives stipulated in the program or project.

Gleaning from the above, gender participation in politics in Nigeria can be rightly conceived as occupation of power posts by women or holding of political power by women. The conceptualizations above also lend credence to our idea of gender representation through direct participation of women in politics. Further, they give expression to the view that women should best represent women on issues affecting women. They should be in control of programs targeted at their gender. Participation is therefore essential for their development and empowerment. This much was asserted by Wright (1990) by the proposition that the aim (of participation) is to achieve human potential by people becoming subjects in their own world rather than objects in other people's worlds. Perhaps it is for this reason that Ford (1985) as cited by Cruz (1992) advocates that a broad-based people's participation at the local level is the key to articulating the aspirations and mobilizing people's energies.

Further, within the context of democracy in Nigeria and power relations between men and women, we can view participation as opportunities available for active involvement. This conception bears some semblance to Midgley's (1983) definition of participation as "the creation of opportunities to enable all members of a community and the larger society to actively contribute and influence the development process and to share equitably in fruits of development." In line with our conception of democracy and gender participation in Nigeria, Selener (1997) hypothesizes two types of participation, namely, technical and political. Selener then goes further to postulate that on the one hand participation of technical nature may not promote empowerment or social change, as it can be manipulated by power holders to fulfill their own needs. However, on the other hand, participation of a political nature means acquiring power and taking greater control of a situation. This position makes a case for gender mainstreaming in Nigerian politics, especially in the present democratic setting.

Krishna and Lovell (1985) make a strong case for the injection of elements of participation in development programs. In the first instance, they argue that participation improves the development plans in general and specific priorities and projects in particular. Second, they observe that programs and projects cannot be implemented if they do not suit the people or are not properly conceived. The third case they make has to do with sustainability of developmental projects. The last case they make for participation is premised on the need for equity. In relations to gender participation in politics in Nigeria, the issue of equity raises a fundamental question of women's rights, an essential aspect of human rights. A major argument in this study is that the low level of women participation in politics in Nigeria is a violation of fundamental human rights that impacts negatively on their potential for self-actualization. It is on this ground that we argue in this study that the Nigerian democracy is exclusive and a mere political convenience, in that it ignores the issue of participation, particularly gender participation.

POLITICS AND GENDER SPACE IN NIGERIA

Globally, democracy is viewed as the best system of governance as it promotes virtues such as rule of law, democratic participation, probity, integrity, and transparency. On the general acceptance of democracy, Yusuf (1994:113) observes that it is also preferred because it posits and insists that power springs from, and therefore belongs to the people. And that those who exercise power should use it in the interest of the people or at least, the majority of the people (ibid.). This however does not imply that the interest of the minority can or should be overlooked.

In fact, it demands unequivocally that while the majority should rule and even in most cases, have its way, the minority must be able to have its say, and its say must be listened to while its rights must be respected and protected. In other words, democracy is against marginalization of all kinds. Yusuf expresses this sentiment as he further observes that preference for democracy also springs from the fact that it demands that people should be availed equal opportunities to participate in the administrative and decision-making machinery of the state (ibid.). He also contends that democracy embodies a free, fair and independent judiciary; equality of all before the law; supremacy of the law; and fundamental human rights for the people (ibid.). It is in this regard that most scholars agree that democracy implies a national political regime based on free elections and broad political representation (Huntington, 1991; Potter et al., 1997; Diamond, 1999).

From what we can see from the above, representativeness and participation are two essential aspects of democracy, at least from the neo-liberal perspective. Democracy is a representative form of government in which the people, encompassing majority and minority, choose their leaders. Even if the majority must have their way, the minority too must at least be heard. While the female gender can rarely be regarded as minority in the Nigerian context, since they make up almost half of the Nigerian population and 56 percent of voters (World Bank Report, 1996:13), they have continued to suffer marginalization and poor representation in government.

Politics offer little opportunities for women in Nigeria. Nwankwo (1996) points out that women have continued to be poorly represented in politics and public decision making. Unlike elsewhere where women have a high participation in politics, the return of democracy to Nigeria has not translated into increased representation for women in politics and public decision. Nwnakwo further observes that while Nigeria had a mere 5 percent women representation at parliament between 1990 and 1999, Norway and Sweden had a female representation of between 35 percent and 60 percent. O 'Barr (1984) reinforces the position that women are politically marginalized in Africa generally and by extension Nigeria. He posits that after a global survey of women in politics, most African countries registered 5 percent or less of women at every level, in every sphere of government (ibid:154). A similar indication was given by the World Bank which states that a review of Nigeria's attempt at contemporary government and civil rule shows a 4 percent average of women involvement in power, although women constitute about 56 percent of voters (World Bank Report, 1996:13).

This low participation of women in politics in Nigeria is against the recommendation of the Beijing declaration that there should be a minimum of 30 percent representation for women in politics. Table 13.1 provides evidence of marginalization of women in politics. The table shows female representation in politics in Nigeria between 2003 and 2007, using the 2003 and 2007 general elections as pointers. The table shows that there was only a marginal increase in female representation in elected offices in Nigeria between 2003 and 2007. Between the aforementioned periods, Nigeria has neither been able to produce a female Head of State nor a Vice President (Table 13.1). In 2003, of the 109 seats at the Senate, women only occupied three seats corresponding to 2.27 percent (Table 13.1). This merely increased to 9 seats corresponding to 8.26 percent of the total available seats. The table also shows that the country has been unable to produce an elected female governor till date. Similarly, at the Federal House of Representatives, there were only 21 female members out of a total membership size of 360. This corresponds to a mere 5.83 percent of the total number of available seats. In 2007, it increases to a negligible 6.98 percent. The table indicates that the condition at States Houses of Assembly is nothing better. Overall, the table shows a large scale marginalization of women in politics in the country. This condition does not enhance sustainable development

Table 13.1 Gender Representation in Politics in Nigeria

SN	*Position*	*Number of Available Seats*	*Number of Women Elected and % Total in 2003*	*Number of Women Elected and % Total in 2007*
1	Presidency	1	0	0
2	Senate	109	3 (2.27)	9(8.26)
3	House of Representatives	360	21(5.83)	25(6.98)
4	Governorship	36	0	0
5	State House of Assembly	990	38(3.84)	54(5.45)

Source: Gender Audit and IPU PARLINE database (2003 and 2008).

as it excludes an important aspect of the population from policy and decision making.

In terms of direct participation in government, the condition of the Nigerian woman has not improved, even with the just concluded 2011 general elections. If anything, it has deteriorated significantly from the 2007 position. For instance, out of the 109 senators who emerged winners at the 2011 polls, only 7 (6.4 percent) were women compared to 8.26 percent in the 2007 general elections. Similarly, the 2011 general elections only succeeded at producing just one female deputy governor compared to the 2007 elections, which produced six female deputy governors (Nwankwo, 2011:13).

This state of gender marginalization in politics negates not just the concept of participatory democracy it also runs contrary to the tenet of participation through representation as advocated in this study. Investigating the causal factors of marginalization of women in political life in Nigeria is therefore a first and necessary step toward finding lasting solutions to the problem. We contend that gender marginalization in politics is a problem because it hinders not just the development of women and their capability for actualization of potentials, but it also presents a challenge to the overall sustainable development of the Nigerian state. This is simply because gender marginalization translates into exclusion from developmental processes. But development is not exclusive, rather it is inclusive and all-embracing, that is if it is to be sustainable. If therefore it is taken for granted that sustainable development is all-embracing, then any exclusive process, like the present democratic system in Nigeria, represents a challenge to sustainable development.

It is in light of the above that we shall examine the essential features of democracy in Nigeria and the challenges and disincentives they present to gender participation in politics.

FEATURES OF DEMOCRACY IN NIGERIA

Attempt is made in this section of the study to identify and discuss some of the salient features of the democratization process in Nigeria. This is done with the intention to draw out the bearing they may have on gender participation in the political life of the country. In view of this, two broad areas have been identified, and they are discussed below.

Corruption and Electoral Malpractices

A common trend runs through the literature on the conceptualization of corruption, according to which it is conceived as using of public position, resources, and power for private gain (Nye, 1967; Dobel, 1978; Amuwo,

2005; Obayelu, 2007; Fjeldstad and Isaksen, 2008; Ogundiya, 2009). In spite of the various attempts to place corruption in the right conceptual perspectives, there seems to be a consensus in literature that corruption poses a serious threat to democracy (Osaghae, 1995; Johnston, 1991; Obayelu, 2007; HRW, 2007; Fjeldstad and Isaksen, 2008). In view of this, corruption is defined as "the betrayal of public trust for individual or group gain" (Dobel (1978) cited in Ogundiya, 2010:233). In this study, within the context of democracy and acquisition of power through democratic means, we see corruption as "efforts to secure wealth or power through illegal means for private gain at public expense; or a misuse of public power for private benefit" (Obayelu, 2007).

Ogundiya (2010:235) seeks to supply the link between democracy and corruption in Nigeria. Consequently, he opines that democracy has remained grossly unstable and the future seems to be very bleak because of rampant systemic bureaucratic and political corruption. He goes further to assert that corruption has reached a high crescendo such that an average Nigerian now possibly associates democracy with corruption, thereby showing the general public disenchantment and disillusionment with the Nigerian democratic process.

Ogundiya identifies some of the negative manifestations of corruption in Nigeria as:

> cyclical crisis of legitimacy, fragile party structure, institutional decay, chronic economic problem and underdevelopment and, above all, general democratic volatility. (ibid.)

From this, he established a link between corruption, economic development and democratic stability by contending that:

> the effects of corruption on a nation's economy are damaging. Indeed a nation inundated with corruption cannot be viable economically neither can the system generate enough support/affection required for the survival of democratic system. This is the situation in Nigeria where corruption has become part and parcel of the political culture. Corruption has indeed robbed Nigerians the benefit of economic development because scarce available resources that should have been deployed to execute developmental projects have gone into private foreign accounts. (Ogundiya, 2010: 235–236)

Ogundiya (2010:236) avers that the democratic process and the fortunes of the economy have a cybernetic feedback interaction, such that democracy facilitates economic development, while economic backwardness and decline impedes democratization. This he argues is the case in Nigeria, where the level of corruption has adversely affected the performance of the economy, thereby making the ground unsuitable for democracy to thrive.

Corruption is a cankerworm that has eaten deep into the fabric of Nigeria. It is a hydra that rears its head at every developmental level in the country. With regards to Nigeria, it is plausible to argue that corruption is a clog on the wheel of national progress. It is a menace that manifests in almost every aspect of national life. Even the political scene and the process of democratization have not been spared from the negative impacts of corruption. A very good indicator of the impact of corruption on the democratic process in Nigeria is the widespread electoral malpractices that have come to characterize electioneering in Nigeria. Vote buying is not an uncommon phenomenon in Nigerian democracy. In addition to this, electioneering in Nigeria is characterized with ballot boxes hijacking, rigging of results, stuffing of ballot boxes, double or even multiple voting, etc.

Just as politicians are the main culprit in these malpractices, they find ready accomplices in the masses whose mentality have been battered by years of marginalization and abject poverty foisted on the society by the neoliberal democracy that is operational in Nigeria. One distinctive feature of democracy in Nigeria is the continued widening of the gap between the ruling elites and the masses, a fact that cannot be divorced from corruption. Poverty is rife in Nigeria, and this pervading poverty is one of the adverse effects of the corruption that has come to characterize the Nigerian system. With 70.8 percent of Nigerians living below the poverty line of $1 a day and up to 92.4 percent living below $2 a day at year 2003 (The United Nations International Children's Fund, 2003; World Bank, 2006), it is plausible and logical to categorize Nigeria as a poverty stricken country. However, it has been argued in this study that the poverty in Nigeria is self-inflicted, majorly a consequence of widespread and deep-rooted systemic corruption. This, in addition to a teeming population of unemployed youths, provides a fertile breeding ground for electoral malpractices and violence.

The failure of neoliberal democracy to alleviate poverty in Nigeria makes the masses vulnerable to the manipulations of politicians during elections. This partly explains why some members of the masses willingly sell their votes to the highest bidders. So, besides reducing democracy to a periodic electioneering process, neoliberal democracy has also commoditized democracy and democratization in Nigeria, such that it has become a commodity for the highest bidders, who are majorly owners of capital.

A major implication of the commoditization of democracy in Nigeria is the further shrinking of the already narrow political space, since it has become a good for owners of capital rather than a public good. This conscription of the political space has a special implication for gender participation in politics in Nigeria, since women are the most marginalized within the marginalized sections of the country. With fewer resources in their hands relative to their male counterparts, women are disadvantaged in the democratic process of the highest bidder that characterizes the Nigerian system.

A good indication of this is the poor gender participation in politics characteristic of past and present democratic regimes in Nigeria.

Ethno-Religious Politics and Electoral Violence

Ethnicity and religion are two important determinant of identity formation in Nigeria. There is a general division of the entire population along ethno-religious lines. Campbell (2010:1) notes the level of divisions in Nigeria:

> Nigeria is a country of overlapping regional, religious, and ethnic divisions. Rifts between the North and the South of the country, ethnic groups, and Islam and Christianity often coincide and have sometimes resulted in sectarian violence.

There have been several attempts in literature to locate the root of ethnic politics in Nigeria, and the common approach is to situate it in the colonial history of the country. For instance, Ibeanu (2000:54) notes that:

> from the early 1980s, a near consensus was emerging that ethnicity is a historically contingent, fluid and flexible social form, which was "manufactured" or invented by colonial administrators and constantly reinvented by the post-colonial African elite to serve political purposes. (Hobsbawm and Ranger, 1983; Ranger, 1994; Doombos, 1982)

He went further to assert that:

> specifically, writers on the left of the ideological spectrum saw ethnicity as the creature of the exploitative project of colonialism and the manipulative politics of the petty bourgeoisie.

Moreover, based on this observation, Ibeanu (2000:54) maintains that in both cases, ethnicity served a class project (Nnoli, 1978; 1995b; Mafeje, 1995). Citing Nnoli (1978), Ibeanu opines that it is this class purpose that assures the persistent politicization of ethnicity in Nigeria.

Ibeanu sees a need to contextualize the link between ethnicity and democracy besides drawing the general link between politics and ethnicity. He identifies two theoretical perspectives in literature (Ibeanu, 2000:55). First there are those who argue that multi-party democracy reinforces ethnicity; and therefore there is a negative impact of multi-partism on ethnicity (Wolfinger, 1965; Parenti, 1967). He also points to those that contend that ethnicity has a positive link with multi-party democracy, and that democracy offers an auspicious context for the management of ethnicity, particularly through a policy of equalitarian pluralism (Marger, 1992; Osaghae, 1986; Schwarz, 1979). However, in spite of this theoretical divergence, Ibeanu, citing Nnoli (1992:7–18), opines that these differences point to divergences in theoretical foundations. He went further to maintain that these theoretical debates point to the need to study the link between ethnicity and democracy concretely, based on the historical experiences of multiethnic societies. This position is premised on the argument that:

> it is by so doing that we can understand the seeming Janiform association between democracy and ethnicity, whereby their reciprocal impact is sometimes complementary, and at other times opposing. (Ibeanu, 2000:55)

It is within the context of this observation by Ibeanu (2000), which stresses the need to contextualize the link between ethnicity and politics that we shall examine the historical experiences of the Nigerian political and democratic architecture with ethno-religious divisions and the inevitable impacts.

With regard to ethnicity, the country is made up of three major ethnic groups living alongside several ethnic minorities of up to 250 or even more. From the religious perspective, there are two major religious groups, Christians and Muslims. This ethno-religious divide has serious implications for politics and democracy as power, the core objective of politics, has been keenly contested along ethnic lines right from independence. This is a fact that is underlined by the regional orientation of the various post independence parties. These parties were regionally based, and even those that had national spread maintained a strong regional root. For instance, the NPC had the North as its base, while the Action Group (AG) was strongly rooted in the Western Region.

More than 50 years after independence, political parties in Nigeria are still struggling to break loose from the tentacles of regionalism. While one may be tempted to argue that party politics in Nigeria has transcended the realm of regionalism, empirical evidence suggests the contrary on critical reflection. Rather than transcending the realm of regionalism, what we have in the Nigerian polity is a modification of the regional-orientation of party politics. This position is underscored by rhetoric such as zoning, rotational presidency, federal character, quota system, which are common features of intra-party politics and structure in Nigeria. The People's Democratic Party (PDP) fits into the description above. While it enjoys a considerable national spread, it is internally divided along ethnic lines. This explains why it had to adopt various zoning arrangements in order to maintain internal cohesion, a point well captured and anticipated by Campbell:

> since the end of military rule eleven years ago, Nigeria's elites have largely cordoned off national presidential elections from sectarian divisions by predetermining presidential and vice presidential victors. Their People's Democratic Party (PDP) nominates one southern Christian and one northern Muslim for the presidency and vice presidency and rigs these candidates into office.

> Every eight years the party rotates the office for which it nominates Christian and Muslim candidates. Excluded as it is from this process of political horse trading, known as zoning, Nigeria's ethnically and religiously fractured public has become increasingly indifferent to the country's national electoral politics. (ibid., 2011:1)

Similarly, on another level, the spate of violence in Northern Nigeria that greeted the emergence of Goodluck Jonathan, a southern Christian, as the elected president in the May 29th, general elections speaks volume to the ethno-religious orientation of politics in Nigeria. Campbell (2011) rightly captures the ethno-religious division in Nigeria in his post election analysis of the 2011 general elections:

> with the country's political elites divided, candidates may be tempted to use ethnic and religious identities to form local coalitions, mobilize their supporters, and smear their opponents. This process is already under way at the local and state levels in Plateau state, where politicians are using their common Christian identity to build multiethnic coalitions against the Muslim Hausa-Fulani. (ibid.:2)

He then sums up the likely outcome of an election conducted along ethno-religious divisions thus:

> supporters of candidates illegitimately denied the presidency would thus be more inclined to protest election irregularities violently, as happened following some of the 2007 gubernatorial elections or the 2008 Jos local elections, which left seven hundred dead. Even in the unlikely event that the elections are broadly credible, some losing candidates will almost certainly have sufficient grounds to convince their supporters that victory has been stolen, especially if the winner has a different ethnic or religious identity. (ibid.)

This position summarizes the nature of the post election violence that was unleashed in the Northern part of the country, where the supporters of Muhammadu Buhari strongly felt or were made to believe that their candidate was rigged out of the elections. Targets and victims of the violence, which were churches and members of the National Youth Service Corp, mainly from the South, serving in the North depict the ethno-religious coloration of this post election violence.

Electoral violence is a common feature of democracy in Nigeria. This again cannot be separated from the neoliberal commoditization of democracy that has made democracy an investment that must yield returns. It is plausible to argue that this monetization of democracy raises the stake to a competitive zero-sum game of survival of the fittest in which winner takes all. This neoliberal do-or-die "politics of the belly" provides a fertile thriving ground for electoral violence. This explains why there have hardly been any elections in Nigeria that was not attended with violence. The spate of electoral violence that attended the May 29, 2011, general elections in Nigeria is still very fresh in the memory. This violent nature of electoral democracy in Nigeria provides further disincentives for gender participation in politics.

A CASE FOR GENDER PARTICIPATION: SUSTAINABLE DEVELOPMENT

From the point of view of sustainable development, we can make a case for equal gender participation in politics in Nigeria. World Commission on Environment and Development (WCED) defines sustainable development as "development that meets the needs of the present without compromising the ability of the future generations to meet their own needs" (WCED, 1987:43). It further states that "sustainable development requires meeting the basic needs of all and extending to all the opportunity to satisfy their aspirations for a better life."

We conceive gender participation as essential to a sustainable development in Nigeria. This is because we believe that for women to actualize their fullest potentialities, they must be actively involved and engaged in shaping their own destinies through direct participation or representation by their gender. After all, it is only the person that the shoe pinches that knows the source of the pain. In other words, things affecting women are better handled by women. The condition of women in Nigeria is instructive of political marginalization and powerlessness, and indicates that Nigeria is far from the road to sustainable development.

From a gender perspective, there are both qualitative and quantitative data to show that poverty has a feminine face in Nigeria (CEDAW Shadow Reports, 2008). Although poverty affects men and women in different ways, women are predominantly in the affected groups. Analysis has shown that poor women outnumber poor men. As at 2006, statistics show that women constitute over 65 percent of the 70 percent Nigerians who are estimated to live in abject poverty, that is, on less than $1 per day (National Gender Policy, 2006). In view of this, we subscribe to the view that poverty has a feminine face in Nigeria.

We must point out at this stage that gender marginalization is a global issue. This was rightly pointed out by the UNDP (1997:39), as it asserts that "no society treats its women as well as its men." This much is underscored by the fact that the "Gender-related Development Index value of every country is lower than its Human Development Index value" (UNDP, 1997:39). This statement is also typical and symptomatic of the Nigerian situation where disparity still exists in literacy rates between men and women, for example. While male adult literacy is 70.1 percent, female adult literacy is 54.6 percent (CEDAW Shadow Report, 2008).

CEDAW reports that despite the existence of the National Gender Policy, patriarchy, gender roles and stereotypes still dominate all aspect of women's lives and have impeded economic productivity, resulting in an unequal access to and unfair distribution of resources. It went further to contend that the methods of socialization and cultural practices are highly skewed in favor of men (CEDAW Shadow Reports, 2008). For example, the boy to girl enrollment in primary schools for 2003, 2004 and 2005 shows the ratio of 56:44 percent, 55.02:44.89 percent, and 55.12:44.88 percent, respectively (National Gender Policy, 2006).

CONCLUSION

We can link the poor representation of women in policy and decision making, and politics in Nigeria to a high rate of poverty among women, since they have limited access to power and resources compared to their male counterparts. In the sense, one may observe a two-way relationship between poverty and political marginalization, such that they are mutually reinforcing. In other words, just as political marginalization can induce poverty, poverty can also induce political marginalization.

The political marginalization for women has implications beyond the realm of politics; it extends to other spheres of national life. It is a state of powerlessness with economic and sociocultural implications. The high prevalence of poverty among Nigerian women is indicative of this state of powerlessness in Nigerian politics, where money speaks. In addition, to this, the low literacy among women and preference for boy-child education are instructive of the sociocultural marginalization of women that springs from political powerlessness. It must however be stated that the underlying cause of gender marginalization in the political scheme of things, and by extension economic and sociocultural, is the neoliberal orientation of the Nigerian democracy.

An ideological re-orientation of democracy and the democratization process is inevitably essential for a way out of this quagmire. It is important that the people, rather than capital, be situated at the heart of the democratization process through popular participation and equal opportunities. The result is that democracy will become a public good rather than a commodity for the highest bidder in a zero-sum game of survival of the fittest as presently obtains. This will go a long way in opening the already frozen space for an inclusive democracy, gender participation in particular.

REFERENCES

Ake, C. (2000). *Feasibility of Democracy in Africa.* Council for the Development of Social Science Research in Africa (CODESRIA), Dakar, Senegal.

Amadiume, I. (1995). Gender, political systems and social movements: A West African experience (pp. 78–89) in M. Mamdani and E. Wamba-dua-Wamba (Eds.), *African Studies Movements and Democracy.* Dakar Senegal: CODESRIA.

Amuwo, K. (2005). The peripheral state: Critical perspectives on the structure and role of the public bureaucracy. *Journal of Development and Alternative Area of Studies,* 24(3–4): 119–130.

Barber, B. R. (1984). *Strong Democracy: Participatory Politics for a New Age.* Berkeley: University of California Press.

Campbell, J. (2010). *Electoral Violence in Nigeria.* Council on Foreign Relations, Center for Preventive Action, Contingency Panning Memorandum No. 9.

Convention on the Elimination of All Forms of Violence Against Women (CEDAW) (2008) and Accountability to Gender Equality in Nigeria: A Shadow Report.

Cruz, F. A. (1992). *New Perspective of Community Development.* Discussion paper presented in Department of Agricultural Extension and Rural Studies (DAERS) Research, Extension, and Curriculum Planning. Workshop held on December 20, 1992. University of the Philippines Los Baños (UPLB), Philippines.

Dobel, J. P. (1978). The corruption of a state. *American Political Science Review,* 72(3): 958–973.

Doornbos, M. (1982). Ugandan Society and Politics: A Background, in G. N. Uzoigwe (Ed.), *Uganda: The Dilemma of Nationhood.* New York: NOK.

Fjeldstad, O., and J. Isaksen (2008). Anti-corruption Reforms: Challenges, Effects and Limits of World Bank Support. Background Paper to Public Sector Reform: What Works and Why? An IEG Evaluation of World Bank Support.

Garba, P. K. (1997). A strategy for empowering women: Application to trade union activities (pp. 244–276) in P. K. Garba, B. Akanji, and I. Isiugo-Abanihe (Eds.), *Women and Economic Reforms in Nigeria.* Ibadan: WORDOC.

GENDER ISSUES. An Occasional newsletter of National Coalition on Affirmative Acton (NCAA), an umbrella organization of over 100 NGOs across Nigeria working on women's rights and affirmative action. Vol 1, No. 2, p. 10.

Hobsbawn, E., and T. Ranger (Eds.). (1983). *The Invention of Tradition.* Cambridge, UK: Cambridge University Press.

Human Rights Watch (HRW) (2007). Criminal Politics: Violence, "Godfathers" and Corruption in Nigeria. 19: 16(A), October.

Ibeanu, O. (2000). Ethnicity and transition to democracy in Nigeria: Explaining the passing of authoritarian rule in a multi-ethnic society. *African Journal of Political Science,* Vol. 5, No. 2, pp. 45–65.

Isiugo-Abanihe, I. M. (1997). Women's education and structural adjustment in Nigeria (pp. 156-174) in P. K. Garba, B. Akanji, and I. Isiugo-Abanihe (Eds.), *Women and Economic Reforms in Nigeria.* Ibadan: WORDOC.

Johnston, M. (1991). Political corruption: Historical conflict and the rise of standards. *Journal of Democracy,* 2(4): 60.

Krishna, R., and C. Lovell (1985). *Rural Development in Asia and the Pacific.* The Synopsis of ADB Regional Seminar in Asia and the Pacific. October 15–23, 1985. Asian Development Bank. Manila: Philippines.

Lyman, T. S. (2009). *Contemporary Political Ideologies: A Comparative Analysis*. Belmont, CA: Wadsworth.
Mafeje, A. (1995). *Demographic and Ethnic Variations: A Source of Instability in Modern African States*. Paper presented at the 8th General Assembly of CODESRIA, Dakar (June).
Marger, M. (1992). Ethnic policy, in M. Hawkesworth and M. Kogan (Eds.), *Encyclopaedia of Government and Politics*, Vol. 2. London: Routledge.
Midgley, J. (1986). Community participation: History, concepts, and controversies, in J. Midgley (Ed.), *Community Participation, Social Development and the State*. London.
Nigeria (2006), National Gender Policy.
Nnoli, O. (1978). Ethnic Politics in Nigeria. Enugu: Fourth Dimension Publishers.
Nnoli, O. (1992). *Reflections on Ethnicity and Multiparty Democracy in Africa*. Paper presented at the Bellagio Conference of Fellows of the Rockefeller Reflections Programme (September 21–26).
Nnoli, O. (1995). *Ethnicity and Development in Nigeria*. Aldershot, UK: UNRISD and Avebury.
Nwankwo, O. (2011). *Reviewing the 50+ Years of Women's Participation in Politics in Nigeria*. WACSERIES Vol. 2, No. 1.
Nye, J. S. (1967). Corruption and political development: A cost-benefit analysis. *American Political Science Review*, 51(2): 417–427.
Obayelu, A. E. (2007). Effects of Corruption and Economic Reforms on Economic Growth and Development: Lessons from Nigeria. Paper prepared for 2007 African Economic Conference, Retrieved from:www.adb_admin_pg/documents/AEC.org. Accessed July 20.
Ogundiya, I.S. (2010). Corruption: The Bane of Democratic Stability in Nigeria. *Current Research Journal of Social Sciences* 2(4): 233–241.
Ogundiya, I. S. (2009). Political corruption in Nigeria: Theoretical perspectives and some explanations. *The Anthropologist*, 11(4): 281–292.
Olojede, I. (2000). *Women's Interest Organisations: Encounters with the State on Issues of Good Governance*. Ibadan: Simlad Press.
Omololu, F. O. (1997). Women's movements in the context of economic adjustment: A critique (pp. 66–82) in P. K. Garba, B. Akanji, and I. Isiugo-Abanihe (Eds.), *Women and Economic Reforms in Nigeria*. Ibadan: WORDOC.
Osaghae, E. (1986). Do ethnic minorities still exist in Nigeria? *The Journal of Commonwealth and Comparative Politics*, 24 (2).
Osaghae, E. E. (1995). Amoral politics and democratic instability in Africa: A theoretical exploration. *Nordic Journal of African Studies*, 4(1): 62–78.
Parenti, M. (1967). Ethnic politics and persistence of ethnic identification. *American Political Science Review*, 61 (4).
Pateman, C. (1970). *Participation and Democratic Theory*. Cambridge, UK: Cambridge University Press.
Pietila, K. (2002). *Engendering the Global Agenda: The Story of Women and the United Nations*. Geneva: UNCTAD/UG, LS/191.
Ranger, T. (1994). The invention of tradition revisited: The case of colonial Africa, in P. Kaarsholm and J. Hultin (Eds), *Inventions and Boundaries: Historical and Anthropological Approaches to the Study of Ethnicity and Nationalism*. Occasional Paper No. 11, International Development Studies, Roskilde University.

Report of the Fourth World Conference on Women, Beijing, September 4–15, 1997 (United Nations publication, Sales No.E.96.IV.13), chap. I, resolution 1, annex II.

Schwarz, H. (1979). Ethnic minorities and ethnic politics in China, in W. Peterson (Ed.), *The Background to Ethnic Conflict*. Leiden: E. J. Brill.

Selener, D. (1997). *Participatory Action Research and Social Change*. Ithaca, NY: Cornell University.

Snyder, M. C., and M. Tedasse. (1995). *African Women and Development: A History*. Johannesburg: Witwatersrand University Press.

Tjondronegoro, S. M. P. (1992). *A Sociological Evaluation of Participatory Approaches in Planned Rural Development: Some Experiences from Selected Third World Countries*, Mimbar Sosek Nomor 4, Juni 1992. Bogor: Institut Pertanian Bogor.

Toyo, N. (1997). *Women Organisations and Political Development*. Paper presented at the Center for Research Documentation Workshop on Women's Rights, Politics and Democratisation, Kano, November 26–28, 1997.

United Nations for Children Education Fund (UNICEF) (2003). *Girls, Education and Development*. Geneva.

Wirth, L. (2000). *Sociology: Themes and Perspectives* (in M. Haralambos and R. Holborn). London: Collins Publishers.

Wolfinger, R. (1965). The development and persistence of ethnic voting. *American Political Science Review*, 59 (4).

World Bank (2006).*World Development Report 2006: Equity and Development*. Oxford, UK: Oxford University Press.

World Commission on Environment and Development (WCED, 1987). *Our Common Future* (Brundlandt Report). Oxford, UK: Oxford University Press.

Wright, S. (1990). Development theory and community development practice. In H. Buller and S. Wright (Eds.). *Rural Development: Problems and Practices*. Newcastle upon Tyne, UK: Atheneum Press Ltd.

14

Gender Equality for a Better Quality of Life for All

(Mrs.) A. O. Ologunde

ABSTRACT

This chapter examines gender equality as a precondition for sustainable people-centered, social and economic development. The objectives of this study included highlighting the key principles for the promotion of gender equality and identifying the steps to be taken in gender planning. Using secondary data obtained through review of relevant literature, the study revealed that some of the key principles for the promotion of gender equality are: that achieving gender equality is the responsibility of all in the society and not of women alone; that gender-specific measures are needed to advance the status of women in a society; that promoting gender equality will benefit all in the society, and that gender equality needs to be addressed in all development programmes. The study further showed that steps to be taken in gender planning include: carrying out a gender analysis, giving equal chances to men and women, giving women a voice as well as addressing gender inequality. The chapter concluded that equality for everyone is a basic fundamental right that must be encouraged by changing personal attitudes and practices, values and norms in the society and that investment in both men and women is crucial for sustainable socioeconomic development.

INTRODUCTION

Equality between women and men, or gender equality, refers to the equal rights, responsibilities and opportunities of men and women, girls and boys. Gender equality is not a "women's issue," it concerns men as well. Equality in rights means that women and men have the same rights as human beings and workers. All people have a right to fulfill their basic needs, to be treated with respect, not to be exposed to violence in whatever form and to be given chances for development. Equality in responsibilities and opportunities does not mean that women and men need to become the same, but that the division of labour and distribution of resources, benefits and decision-making power is fair and just, i.e., women's and men's responsibilities and opportunities will not depend on whether they are born male or female. For example, there will be inequality if two people are equally hungry, but one is given enough food while the other is given only half of the portion.

Lessons from experience indicate that women and men both contribute to economic growth and human development. However, the experience worldwide is that there are inequalities in that women share a major proportion of work but their work is invisible and less rewarded, women's workload is larger, women have less access to education and training, women are underrepresented in leadership and management. As a result women's views, interests and needs are often not met. Equality between women and men is both a human rights issue and a precondition for sustainable people-centered, social and economic development. Thus, promotion of gender equality is not only the right thing to do but also the smart thing to do, because it leads to a better quality of life for everybody.

DEFINING KEY CONCEPTS

Sex refers to biological differences between men and women that are universal.

Gender refers to social differences between men and women that are learned, change over time, and vary widely within and between societies. Gender refers to the opportunities associated with being born as a man or a woman, and to the relations between women and men, boys and girls, as well as the relations between women and those between men in any given social context. In most societies, there are differences and inequalities between women and men in the responsibilities they are given, the activities they do, the workload they have and in access to and control over resources and in decision-making opportunities. Gender is a socioeconomic variable to analyze: roles and responsibilities, constraints and opportunities, and needs of men and women. Gender is an important variable (or classifier) in society. Gender is affected by other variables such as age, class or caste, race and ethnicity, and by the geographical, economical, political and cultural environment.

Gender equality or equality between women and men refers to the equal rights, responsibilities, opportunities, treatment and valuation of women and men: in employment, in the relation between work and life. Gender equality does not mean that women and men need to become identical, but that women's and men's rights, responsibilities and opportunities, the way they are treated and their work is valued and does not depend on whether they are born male or female. Gender equality includes: the same human and workers' rights, equal value and fair distribution of responsibilities and opportunities, workload, decision making and income. Equality between women and men leads to a better quality of life for all. It is both a human rights issue and a pre-condition for sustainable people-centered, social and economic development.

Gender issue, concern or bias is any aspect of gender relations that relates to inequalities or imbalances between the position of men and women.

Gender roles are the different activities that men and women actually do (e.g., women do housework, men are leaders). Gender roles often illustrate and are reinforced by gender values and stereotypes but they can and do change, often faster than stereotypes and values. Changes in gender roles often occur in response to changing economic, natural or political circumstances, including development efforts, economic restructuring or other nationally or internationally based forces. The gender roles of men and women within a given social context may be flexible or rigid, similar or different, and complementary or conflicting.

Gender values and norms are the ideas that people have on what women and men should be like and what activities they should do (e.g., women should be charming, men should be brave).

Gender stereotypes are beliefs that people have on what men and women are capable of and what they can do (e.g., women are better housekeepers, men are better leaders).

The gender gap is the extent of inequality between men and women, for example, in workload, access to or control over resources or benefits and education.

Practical gender needs arise from the actual conditions which women and men experience because of their sex and the gender roles assigned to them in society. These are often related to women as mothers, homemakers and providers of basic needs, and are concerned with inadequacies in living and working conditions, such as food, water, shelter, income, health care and employment. For women and men with low income, these needs are often linked to *survival strategies*. Addressing them only perpetuates the disadvantaged position of women or men in their societies. It does not promote gender equality.

Strategic gender needs of women refer to the subordinate position of women to men in society, and relate to the empowerment of women. They vary according to the particular social, economic and political context in which they are formulated. Usually they concern *equality issues* such as enabling women to have equal access to job opportunities and training, sharing of family responsibilities, equal pay for work of equal value, equal rights to land and other assets, prevention of sexual harassment at work and domestic violence, and freedom of choice over childbearing. Men usually also have strategic gender needs. Boys and men in many societies are taught to be dominant, take the lead in most spheres of life and repress their feelings. In combination with lack of good role models, this can lead to the wrong channeling of energy in the form of aggressive, pushy behaviour and violence toward children, women or other men. The strategic gender needs of many men relate to stimulating their "caring" role. Addressing these needs involves a slow and gradual process of changing attitudes and practices in societies.

KEY PRINCIPLES FOR THE PROMOTION OF GENDER EQUALITY

Achieving gender equality is not a "women's concern" but the responsibility of all in society.

In the past most advocates for the promotion of gender equality were women. It is, therefore, sometimes thought that this subject only concerns women and not men. However, this idea is now fast disappearing. There is increasing consensus that gender equality is the responsibility of all in society and requires contributions and inputs from both women and men.

In case of pronounced imbalances, gender-specific measures are needed to address inequalities and advance the status of women in society.

The relation between the promotion of gender equality and the advancement of women is not always well understood and sometimes it is thought that these are two different issues.

This is not the case. The advancement of women is a necessary strategy whenever they are in a disadvantaged position compared to men. As current inequalities are often quite large, equal treatment of men and women from now on is usually not sufficient, as existing inequalities could remain or might even become larger. Gender-specific measures are usually needed to redress existing imbalances between the position of men and women until women can participate in, and benefit from, development on an equal footing with men. Gender-specific measures usually involve both women and men.

Promoting Gender Equality Will Benefit All in Society

Sometimes a fear exists that advancing the position of women means that something is taken away from men. However, the promotion of gender equality does not imply giving more power to women and taking away power from men. The promotion of equality between women and men is empowering for both sexes and leads to a win-win situation for both. "Power-over" which refers to a situation of subordination on the one hand and domination on the other, is unjust and detrimental to development because of the unequal exchange it entails. A win-win situation is created by advocating:

- power to be: creative and enabling type of power, people's empowerment
- power with: group power, the whole is greater than the sum of its parts
- power within: spiritual strength, self-confidence

Gender equality needs to be "mainstreamed," for instance, addressed in all development programmes and at all stages of the programming cycle

It is sometimes thought that the promotion of equality between men and women is only relevant in soft sectors, such as education, health and welfare, and not in hard sectors, such as macro-economics. In other instances, it is considered that gender equality will be achieved if something small and extra is done especially for women. These ideas do not lead to progress in practice, because gender inequalities are deeply ingrained in the social, economic, cultural and political fabric of societies. Gender equality is an issue which needs to be addressed in all development fields and at all stages of the programming cycle, i.e., at the planning and design, implementation, monitoring and evaluation stages.

In other words, the main strategy for the promotion of gender equality is gender mainstreaming. The following definition was adopted by the UN in 1997:

- The ultimate goal of mainstreaming is to achieve gender equality.
- Mainstreaming a gender perspective is the process of assessing the implications for women and men of any planned action, including legislation, policies or programmes, in any area and at all levels.
- It is a strategy for making the concerns and experiences of women as well as of men an integral part of the design, implementation, monitoring and evaluation of policies and programmes in all political, economic and societal spheres, so that women and men benefit equally, and inequality is not perpetuated.

Address Practical and Strategic Gender Needs

The roles of men and women in families, workplaces, organizations and institutions are generally different. Therefore, their needs may also vary.

Two types of needs are usually identified to develop strategies that promote equality between men and women.

Practical needs arise from the actual conditions which women and men experience because of the gender roles assigned to them in society. These are often related to women as mothers, homemakers and providers of basic needs, and are concerned with inadequacies in living and working conditions, such as food, water, shelter, income, health care and employment. For women and men in the low-income levels, these needs are often linked to *survival strategies*. Addressing them alone only perpetuates the disadvantaged position of women or men in their societies. It does not promote gender equality.

Strategic needs of women refer to the subordinate position of women to men in society, and relate to the empowerment of women. They vary according to the particular social, economic and political context in which they are formulated. Usually they concern *equality issues* such as enabling women to have equal access to job opportunities and training, sharing of family responsibilities, equal pay for work of equal value, equal rights to land and other assets, prevention of sexual harassment at work and domestic violence, and freedom of choice over childbearing. Strategic gender needs of men relate to increasing their "caring" role in their family and society. Addressing these needs involves a slow and gradual process of changing attitudes and practices in societies.

GENDER PLANNING: STEPS FOR ACTION

Step 1: Carry out a gender analysis

- what are the roles and activities of men and women and what is the division of work between them
- how are resources and benefits distributed among men and women
- what are the needs of men and women
- are there imbalances or inequalities between men and women, if yes, what are these

Step 2: Give equal chances to men and women

- respect for the human dignity of children, women and men
- equal opportunities to education, information, knowledge and services
- equal sharing of duties (in the household and voluntary work for the community)
- deciding together, not alone: involvement of both men and women in decision making

Step 3: Give women a voice

- listen to women in the family and in meetings
- organize meetings in a place and at a time that women can attend
- setting up of women's committees is good, if women are not allowed to speak in mixed gatherings or meetings. This enables them to gain confidence, for example, in public speaking
- ensure women's representation in mixed committees. Keep in mind that only one or a few women is not enough. Generally, the male/female ratio of representation should range between 40 percent and 60 percent. A handy ground rule is to ensure a representation rate of around 30 percent of each sex as a minimum; otherwise it becomes difficult for those in the minority to effectively have a voice. When the aim is to increase women's role in decision making, for example, in project steering committees, or in training of trainers' activities: allocate two-thirds of the available positions for women and one-third for men.

Step 4: Address gender inequalities

- set targets for girls' and women's, boys' and men's participation, for example, in education and training
- organize gender awareness training in communities to enable men and women to share duties and responsibilities more equally in the family and community
- develop special measures and activities for women to advance their position (literacy training, confidence building, and provision of credit)

GENDER EQUALITY AND BETTER QUALITY OF LIFE FOR ALL

Equality for everyone is a basic fundamental right that must be encouraged by changing personal attitudes and practices, values and norms in the society. Until recently the contribution of women to the well-being and development of families and societies has been overlooked. Women often face a double or triple burden, taking care of the family and the home, earning income and contributing to community welfare. They have limited access to resources and do not participate equally in decision making. To make policies and regulations in which such problems of inequality are properly addressed, gender equality training is needed at all levels. Such training will enable people to know that:

- Gender roles and relations shape the entire world of work and life in both paid and unpaid work, decision making about resources and benefits, and the relation between work and life.
- Working toward more equality involves, first of all, an analysis of the roles and relations between men and women. When inequality is found this needs to be addressed. Usually it involves giving more opportunities and chances to women and empowering them to play a greater role in decision making.
- Consensus needs to be built in families and societies on the desired balance between gender roles and responsibilities between men and women and they need to come to an agreement on how to achieve gender equality at home, in the workplace and in the community.
- Sometimes a fear exists that advancing the position of women means that something is taken away from men. However, the promotion of gender equality does not imply giving more power to women and taking away power from men. The promotion of equality between women and men is empowering for both sexes and leads to a win-win situation for both.

Gender equality is not supposed to be a "women-only" topic. It is vital to raise awareness among men about gender equality issues, because gender equality is a matter of both sexes, and the only way to change the existing structure is to involve both women and men. The recent increase in women participation in the labour force has brought about important changes in their lives and families, they cease to be economically dependent and become economic supporters with dependants, leading to the expansion of economic opportunities associated with the opening up to the global economy. With gender equality, when everyone that works is seen as a worker, whether they work as civil servant, informal sector worker, casual worker, home worker or as a housewife or houseman. Then, the most vulnerable groups like informal sector workers, home workers and domestic workers will no longer be excluded from policies and workers' rights.

Development goals are effectively advanced only when gender equality is advanced; that is, development occurs when women's rights are fully respected and guaranteed, when agreements for environmental sustainability are implemented and when human rights are given the opportunity to flourish. It is generally believed that there is ample evidence that as long as half of the population is not in a position—due to gender discrimination—to develop and use its capacities and participate in social, economic and political life, both society as a whole and economic development suffer from the resulting inefficiency.

Development, is a social phenomenon, its central goals are: the elimination of poverty, unemployment and inequality. The Millennium Development Goals aim to cut poverty in half by 2015. We know that poverty is a feminized phenomenon, with poor women bearing the brunt of inequality. Firm political will is required to make gender equality a priority as one of the central goals of development; without that commitment, no aid mechanism can be effective in delivering sustained poverty reduction. According to Valentine Moghadam (2005) the vast majority of people living in poverty are women (around 70 percent, based on UNDP data) and the three main dimensions of this phenomenon are: the expansion of female-headed households, the persistence of intra household inequalities and bias against women and girls, and the implementation of neoliberal economic policies around the world.

The feminization of labour markets resulting from gender equality reflects a variety of interrelated factors. Rising levels of education, declining family size, falling fertility rates and changing aspirations for themselves and their families together make it both possible and desirable for women to take up paid work. In addition, women have been "pushed" into the labour market by the decline in agricultural production and growing levels of landlessness, the rising costs of living associated with the privatization of public welfare services and withdrawal of subsidies and declining levels of male employment and male wages as a result of the retrenchments associated with Structural Adjustment Programmes and the dismantling of state owned enterprises (UNRISD 2005; Chen et al., 2004). The feminization of paid work has also been driven by the rising levels of female migration, internal as well as international (UNFPA, 2006), which in earlier decades was male dominated has added to the flexibility of labour markets, acting as a global reserve army for receiving countries.

Stress at work affects both men and women. However, women are often faced with the additional burden of combining family and work responsibilities. Due to occupational segregation, women often find themselves in jobs where there is a heavy workload combined with little decision-making autonomy or participation. These two factors result in women often having to deal with more stressful situations than men. While some stress is normal and necessary, negative stress activates a variety of physical and emotional symptoms that can lead to more serious diseases such as burnout, emotional exhaustion or even suicide, if the situation lasts. *At work*: Stress may result in poor quality of work, low productivity, high turnover and absenteeism. It also negatively affects creativity, innovation, learning and knowledge. *In the community*: Stress may eventually result in unemployment, psychological and physical problems that strongly influence an individual's social position. Stress and violence together cost the community between 1 percent to 3.5 percent of gross domestic product.

What Measures Can be Taken?

To reduce stress, the causes of stress at work should be first examined. Attention should be paid to the following main stressors: combination of workload and time pressure; capacity of the individual to respond to the demands; and social support in the working environment

CONCLUSION

This chapter concluded that gender equality is a fundamental human right and an essential condition for achieving effective democracy, social justice and that all human beings, irrespective of race, creed or sex, have the right to pursue both their material well-being and their spiritual development in conditions of freedom and dignity, of economic security and equal opportunity. This fundamental principle of equality of opportunity and treatment between women and men is also seen as a matter of sustainable development, by promoting the participation of women in decision making and their involvement in shaping development and labour policies and practices that adequately respond to equality objectives. Investment in both men and women is crucial for sustainable socioeconomic development. It gives high returns in families, and the whole society.

REFERENCES

Cecilia Alemany, Nerea Craviotto, Fernanda Hopenhaym, Ana Lidia Fernández-Layos,

Clark, Cindy, and Sarah Rosenhek (2008), Implementing the Paris declaration: Implications for the promotion of women's rights and gender equality. Commissioned by the Canadian Council for International Cooperation (CCIC) and developed by AWID and WIDE.

Chen, M. A., J. Vanek, and M. Carr (2004), *Mainstreaming Informal Employment and Gender in Poverty Reduction.* London: Commonwealth Secretariat.

Equality@work an information base on Equal Employment Opportunities for Women and Men. ILO Geneva, 2001

Gender Issues in the World of Work, ILO Gender Training for ILO Staff and Constituents for the Promotion of Equality for Women Workers, INT/93/MO9/NET, 1995, Geneva.

Handbook on Women's Empowerment through Legal Awareness, Gender and Development for Cambodia (GAD/C), 2002, Phnom Penh, Cambodia.

ILO Geneva (2000), A partnership of equals, Bureau for Gender Equality.

Kabeer, N. (2003), *Mainstreaming Gender and Poverty Eradication in the Millennium Development Goals.* London: Commonwealth Secretariat.

Kabeer, N. (2007), Marriage, Motherhood and Masculinity in the Global Economy: Reconfigurations of personal and economic life. Institute of Development Studies, (IDS) working paper 290, www.ids.ac.uk/ids/bookshop

Modular Training Package—Women Workers' Rights, ILO Geneva, 1994.

Moghadam, Valentine (2005), *The Feminization of Poverty and Women's Human Rights*. SHS papers in women's studies/gender research No. 2, UNESCO, July 2005.

Nelien Haspels, and Rosalinda Terhorst (2004), Women Workers Rights and Gender Equality: Easy Steps for Workers in Cambodia Bangkok, ILO, 2004.

Nelien Haspels, (2001–2003), Gender Equality at Work, Various Briefing Notes, BAO/EASMAT, ILO Bangkok.

Nelien Haspels, Zaitun Mohamed Kasim, Constance Thomas, and Deidre McCann (2001), Action Against Sexual Harassment at Work in Asia and the Pacific, International Labour Office, Bangkok.

Nelien Haspels (2001), Training of trainers' (TOT) *Manual on Gender Equality at Work in Viet Nam*. Briefing Notes for Participants, ILO Bangkok, 2001.

Nelien Haspels, (2001), *Report of Workshop on Participation of Indigenous Men and Women in Development* (11-13 December 2000, Chiangmai, Thailand), ILO/EASMAT, 2001.

Organisation for Economic Co-operation and Development's Development Assistance Committee (OECD DAC) (2007), Workshop on development effectiveness in practice: Applying the Paris Declaration to advancing gender equality, environmental sustainability and human rights, Dublin, Ireland, April 26–27, 2007.

Promotion of Equality for Women Workers, INT/93/MO9/NET, 1995, Geneva.

Report on National Seminar on Action Against Sexual Harassment at Work, Malaysia, (2001), jointly organized by Department of Labour, Ministry of Human Resources, Malaysia and International Labour Organization, Bangkok and Geneva Offices.

Rosalinda Terhorst (1999), Training Package for Awareness Raising about Legal Rights, Workers' Rights and Gender Equality. Trainers' Manual, ILO Kathmandu.

The Oxfam Gender Training Manual, p. 183, Oxfam, UK and Ireland, 1994.

UNFPA (2006) *A Passage to Hope: Women and International Migration*. New York.

United Nations Economic and Social Council (UNESCO): Agreed Conclusions E/1997/L.30, p. 2); www.undp_povertycentre.org.

UNRISD (2005), *Gender Equality, Striving for Justice in an Unequal World*, Geneva.

15

The Place of Women in Nigerian Public Service

A Sublime Feminist Analysis

Anthony M. Oladoyin

ABSTRACT

The position of women in the Nigerian Public Service is just emerging. The service is proportionally occupied by more men than women. This chapter x-rays the placements of women in major federal ministries and discusses the reasons accounting for the disadvantages position of the female gender in the public service. The analysis reveals that in spite of legislative intervention and campaigns for women empowerment, there have been minimal improvement in the political and senior/management positions in the public service. Where the number of women is high is in the non-management positions such as typists, clerks and secretaries. This chapter concludes that the efforts of government and other national and international bodies have only yielded marginal improvement in the position of women in the political and civil service landscape of Nigeria.

INTRODUCTION

Most discussions about women in the intellectual parlance usually revolve around gender inequality or differences, which constitute the cornerstone of feminist ideology. Feminist ideology in the radical sense does not only seek to minimize the differences between men and women (Haralambos and Holborn, 2008:100) but is concerned with the belief that there is a "Female nature that has been concealed and/or distorted throughout history; one that needs to be liberated and revealed" (Pamela Abbott, Claire

Wallace and Melissa Tylor (2005:33). They are not particularly interested in gender equality but are primarily concerned with the issue of women's rights (ibid.). This group of people is usually criticized for gynocentricism. On the other hand, it is important to clarify from this outset that the subject of this chapter is not in line with radical feminism but liberal, which is herein refined as sublime feminist analysis. Haralambos and Holborn (2008:102) summarises the liberal feminist position as follows:

> Liberal feminists aim for gradual change in political, economic and social systems of Western societies. To the liberal feminists, nobody benefits from existing gender inequalities; both men and women are harmed because the potential of females and males alike is suppressed. For example, many women with the potential to be successful and skilled members of the workforce do not get the opportunity to develop their talents to the full, while men are denied some of the pleasures of having a close relationship with their children. The explanation of this situation, according to liberal feminists lies not so much in the structures and institutions of society, but in its culture and the attitudes of individuals.

Following from the above excerpt, it follows that this chapter objectively presents a descriptive scenario, which is naturally produced, given the existing power relations, ecological and inevitable historical circumstances in which women find themselves in Nigerian society.

OBJECTIVE OF THE STUDY

For the purpose of this chapter, attention will be focused on the position of women in Nigerian public service.

OUTLAY OF THE CHAPTER

The following outline will be followed in the ensuring presentation and analysis of the position of women in the Nigerian public service.

(1) The Nigerian public service.
(2) The question of gender equality in the Nigerian public service.
(3) Concrete instantiations of the position of women in selected Nigerian public sector organizations.
(4) Analysis of factors affecting the position of women.
(5) The affirmative action principle and women empowerment: any effect?

(6) General assessment of the contribution of women to the development of the Nigerian public service.
(7) Challenges facing women in public service.
(8) Recommendation and conclusions.

The Nigerian Public Service

The public service is a body of career officers employed by the three tiers of government in Nigeria in the ministries, departments and agencies and the parastatals in which these governments have majority shares (Orewa, 1997:44). The public service covers virtually all spheres of life in a given society, for instance, it includes the military, the police, ministries, agencies, extra-ministerial departments, boards, commissions, parastatals, the governors office, the presidency and any such office where administrative activities relating to government business take place whether at local or state or federal government level. Persons that work in any of the public service units are called public servants. Those at the state level are called civil servants. Irrespective of the nomenclature, they are expected to render honest, efficient and loyal service to the public. The source of their salaries is public funds, which come from taxes, royalties and proceeds from government investments.

The public servants' job is usually a career job with the advantage of permanence of tenure. Impliedly, they are free to terminate the contract as of free will once confirmed. At retirement, they are entitled to retirement benefits and pension. While in service, they are only to be seen and not heard. They are expected to be loyal to their political boss, who enjoys electorates' mandate. The public servant is not expected to use his public office/position selfishly but selflessly because he is presumed to be holding the position in trust for the public. Hence, a public servant is expected to be accountable, diligent, loyal, transparent, politically neutral, honest, prudent, courteous and polite in the conduct of his/her official duties. A public servant must also maintain a high level of discipline, integrity and confidentiality, in the performance of his/her roles.

The Question of Gender Equality in the Nigerian Public Service

The clamor and struggle have always been on to ensure gender equality in the Nigerian public service particularly at the senior staff and management levels. Since independence in Nigeria, the position of women vis-à-vis their men's counterpart has been dismally disproportionate. Even though it was not a deliberate ploy by men but the traditional beliefs, customs, and cultural environment have indeed marginalized women from being active participants in the public service. Not until the 1980s, the situation has been really bad. However, there has been steady progress in the rate of women representation and participation in public work and civil service placements.

Before now the feminist struggle has been intense and many conventions have held on issues of women's rights and need for economic-cum-political empowerment.

Concrete Institutions of the Position of Women in Selected Nigerian Public Sector Organizations

An x-ray of the position occupied by women relative to their men's counterpart is expedient at this juncture. This exercise will be done by selectively analyzing the gender factor in public service recruitment and placements.

Olojede's and Robert's works have been the most ground-breaking gender analysis in the Nigerian public service as far as positions occupied by women in the public service positions are concerned. Olojede's research findings showed that men dominated key decision-making positions in federal civil service between 1988 and 1991. In her submission, male dominated the service with 88.6 percent (4,243) compared to women's position with 11.34 percent (480) for the number of top managers in the federal civil service (Olojede, 1990). According to Amadel (1996), women are in large number in some professions or industries, which are analogous to extensions of domestic work, for example, nursing, teaching, secretarial work, fashion industry, hairdressing and such other related works.

Between 2001 and 2004, the percentage difference between men and women in the federal civil service is very low. Although the table indicates steady growth over the years the growth rate is very slow. The performance (in terms of the position held) of women in selected ministries as presented in table 15.2 is equally relatively low.

Even in the Ministry of Women Affairs that one naturally expects that women will be dominant, Table 15.2 indicates that women's percentage is 40.6 to men's, which is 59.4 percent.

Analysis of Factors Affecting the Position of Women

The following factors have been identified and considered worthy of explanation as reasons accounting for why women are disadvantageously placed vis-à-vis their men counterpart as far as position of leadership in the Nigerian public services are concerned.

a. Gender-cum-development gap. Over time, women have indeed lagged behind. It is only until recently when sensitization and campaigns as well as concrete empowerment program were stepped up and put in

Table 15.1 Percentage of Men and Women in Federal Service

Year	Percentage of Men	Percentage of Women
2001	71.5	28.5
2002	71.3	28.7
2003	69.3	30.7
2004	70.5	29.5

Source: Robert (2004:2009) Analysis and survey conducted in Nigeria 2000.

Table 15.2 Percentage of Men and Women in Selected Ministries

Ministry	Percentage of Men	Percentage of Women
Presidency	69.9	30.1
Defence	60.3	30.7
Justice	81.3	18.7
Labour	61.7	38.3
Power	68.5	31.5
Women	59.4	40.6
Works	72.1	27.9

Source: Robert (2004:2009) Analysis and survey conducted in Nigeria 2000.

place, respectively, that a good number of women are now getting economically and politically empowered. In those periods when women were lagging behind, it was expected that a gap, which would be difficult to cover, would have been created. The gap would of course put men at an advantage in times of political, social and economic competition.

b. Inability to favorably compete in risk taking as men would do. Following from a long gap, which had created a wide range of social, economic and political inequality, it becomes hard for women to possess the necessary wherewithal to take the kind of risk men would effortlessly take particularly in politics.
c. General cultural influence. Undoubtedly, culture in the Nigeria context has reinforced the male gender as a more valuable gender endowed with leadership traits and qualities. Men thus see themselves in that light. It is not the case that men naturally dishonor their female counterpart but they see them as a weaker vessel to be cared for. This by implication predisposes women to situations that may not allow many of them in top management positions in the Nigerian public service.
d. Religion. Just as culture is a limiting factor on women's developmental potentials, religion constitutes another surrogate limitation. Religion

consists of different doctrines that relegate the female gender to the background in the policy making. The Islamic and Christian religions do not expect a woman's voice to be heard. They are expected to be subject to their husbands and take permission from their husbands before they could be permitted to speak in the presence of a male gathering. This will no doubt affect their collective chances of getting to the top of the state or federal civil service.

e. Male chauvinistic tendencies. Following from the influence of religion and culture, men do feel superior in their social interaction with women. With the chauvinistic tendencies reinforced by economic advantage fostered by a long period of gender gap, the female gender do suffer setbacks in gaining a competitive edge in positions in the Nigerian public service.
f. Patriarchal society. The Nigerian society is built on patriarchal authority, where the men claim titles over the women and the children. Women at marriage lose their parents' names and start answering to the name of their husband. In equal vein, the children answer to their father's name; not the mother's. Situations like this further reinforce the ego of the man. In the civil service, it is not therefore unlikely that women may be given very stiff competition for crucial positions in the Nigerian public service. (Igbuzon, 2005:46–55)
g. Limitation by domestic work in the home. This is a major limitation. Before the woman attends to all the domestic chores in the home: cooking, washing, sewing, cleaning, mending, etc, she would have been seriously fagged out, with little time left for administrative responsibilities or political issues and contestations.

The Affirmative Action Principle and Women Empowerment

It was not until the turn of the twenty-first century that the empowerment of women started occupying a priority position in the scheme of things in the "mind" of government (Bello-Imam, 2010:459). Feminist agenda have been on the rise across Africa with women recording varying degree of success in the manner in which they participate in the public work force, politics and social activities (Amina Mama, 1997:77–98; NPC 2001:1–6)

The crux of the affirmative action as a principle majorly emphasizes the subject of equal opportunity. It requires that since it may not be naturally forthcoming, it must therefore be induced through legislation such that at all times, a fair representation of the womenfolk is guaranteed in public service employment, politics, education and everything going on in the society.

According to Rosenbloom and Goldman (1999), affirmative action entails the establishment of goals and time table for the hiring, promotion

Table 15.3 Summary of Seats Held by Women and Men in National Assembly by Year and Gender

Legislators	*1999*		*2003*		*2007*	
Senate	*Number*	*%*	*Number*	*%*	*Number*	*%*
Male	106	97.25	105	96.33	100	91.74
Female	3	2.75	4	3.67	9	8.26
Total	109	100.0	1091	100.0	109	100.0
House of Reps. Male	348	96.67	339	94.17	334	92.78
Female both Houses	12	3.33	21	5.83	26	7.22
Male	454	96.8	444	94.7	434	92.5
Female	15	3.2	25	5.3	35	7.5
Total	469	100.0	469	100.0	469	100.0

Source: FRN, National Bureau of statistics (2008:26).

and/or job training of members of certain minority groups and women. It strives to remove all forms of gender, religion, race, ethnicity, color, religion or citizenship problems. Affirmative action supports proportional representation of various social groups, in public administrative posts at all levels (ibid.).

In Nigeria, affirmative action has not been finally passed as law in the National Assembly but it has been operated as an implicit policy. Regarding its impact, it is apposite to commend the sensitivity of government even though it has not fully yielded the full dividend of democracy.

Affirmative action is practiced more in the public service. Tables 15.4, 15.5 and 15.6 show a broad analysis of the improvement of women in their level of representation in political offices.

Table 15.4 Political Positions: 1999

Position	*Women*	*Men*	*Total*	*% Women*
Minister/Special Adviser	9	35	44	20.5
Speakers	1	35	36	2.5
Governors	0	36	36	0
Deputy Governors	1	35	36	2.7
Total	11	141	152	6.5

Source: FRN, National Bureau of Statistics (2008:28).

Table 15.5 Political Positions: 2003

Position	*Women*	*Men*	*Total*	*% Women*
Minister/Special Adviser	12	32	44	27.3
Speakers	0	36	36	0
Governors	0	36	36	0
Deputy Governors	2	34	36	5.5
Total	14	138	152	8.13

Source: FRN, National Bureau of Statistics (2008:30).

Table 15.6 Women as Proportion of Federal Civil Service Staff in Nigeria (end period)

Period	*Percentage (%)*
1991	24.6
1992	24.0
1993	24.1
1994	22.0
1995	24.0

Source: FOS (1999) Annual Abstract of Statistics.

General Assessment of the Contribution of Women to the Development of the Nigerian Public Service

Like any other sector, women do contribute their quota to the development of the public service in qualitative terms because women are equally educated, imaginative, and diligent like men. In most cases, they are even more stable than men. Empirical evidence shows that more women are found in the intermediate category in the public service. Many women are also found in the clerical positions.

"Women are less mobile than men in the labor market" (Awopeba, 2004:485). Hence women tend to stabilize the civil service. Awopeba (ibid.) is also of the view that "available data show that the rate of participation of women declined between 1991 and 1995 ranging between 22.0 percent (1994) and 24.6 percent (1991)." Table 15.6 shows and confirms this position.

Analyzing the higher public servants, government appointments and elective posts, the women have been greatly discriminated against (Onwuekwe, 2000). It is against the backdrop of both real and perceived discrimination suffered by women that makes the issues of gender a critical intellectual and political matter all over the world. An example of women in public service is shown in the case of Power Holding Company of Nigeria, Osogbo Business Unit below.

More importantly, women have contributed to development in the public service by creating social capital. In the area of some basic public services such as health care, education and water services, women's contribution is high and notable. Tables 15.5 and 15.6 show a broad view of the performance. Notable also is the performance of women in such sectors as banking, communication and hotels, restaurants and tourism.

Table 15.8 shows clearly that women are trying to catch up. However, their representation in some sectors like agriculture, mining and quarrying and transport is very low.

Tables 15.9 to 15.16 on the whole confirm that areas where appreciable progress is being recorded and the areas where women still need much to be done. The relative summary point to the fact that much is still left to be desired in the representation of women in most public sector organizations.

Challenges Facing Women in the Nigerian Public Service

In the public service, women face a number of challenges that usually affect them in gaining access to top positions in the Nigerian public service

First, the carryover effect of household chores affect the concentration of women in their place of work, which eventually affect their productivity and access to top management positions in the public service.

Table 15.7 Staff Distribution by Gender in Osogbo PHCN Business Unit (2011)

Stations	*Senior Male*	*Staff Female*	*Total Number*	*Junior Male*	*Staff Female*	*Total*	*Total A&B*
Osogbo District Office	76	28	104	11	1	12	116
Osogbo Undertaking	31	13	44	4	0	4	48
Aytoro Undertaking	11	10	21	6	0	6	27
Okefia	12	6	18	0	1	1	19
Ikirun	34	2	36	6	1	7	45
Ilaorangun	16	0	16	0	0	0	1
Computer center	0	9	9	0	1	1	10
Total	180	68	248	27	4	31	279

Source: Osogbo Business Unit as at February, 2011.

Table 15.8 Percentage Distribution of Employment by National Economic Activity and Gender (2001–2005)

Sector	*2001*	*2002*	*2003*	*2004*	*2005*	*National Econ. Act.*
Agriculture	Female 17.71	15.66	18.98	18.9	21.76	17.51
Manufac. & Processing	10.4	9.99	12.34	12.1	12.3	11.31
Hotels, restaurants & tourism	35.52	35.66	35.92	35.45	34.87	34.81
Transport	9.17	11.7	11.58	12.08	14.85	11.62
Communications	31.05	31.29	27.04	29.08	28.69	25.53
Education services	41.29	41.21	39.99	34.11	37.65	42.26
Mining and quarrying	0.2	2.44	1.99	1.66	2.5	1.29
Banking	37.38	42.96	47.9	48.8	44.28	41.31
Health	62.69	64.59	64.16	64.55	62.57	63.11

Source: FRN, National Bureau of Statistics 2008: 23.

Table 15.9 Women as Percentage of Employed Persons in Selected Metropolitan Area, 1998

Sector	*Aba*	*Abuja*	*Ibadan*	*Jos*	*Kano*	*Lagos*	*Maiduguri*	*Port Harcourt*	*All Areas*
Agric, forestry and hunting	40.4	38.5	15.4	42.0	-	34.6	8.3	45.9	30.6
Mining and quarrying	-	50.0	50.0	21.4	-	35.3	60.0	25.0	30.8
Manufacturing and processing	26.4	48.4	42.3	29.7	7.7	26.5	27.3	32.1	30.6
Electricity, gas and water	11.1	28.6	17.6	28.6	16.7	17.5	-	-	16.5
Building and construction	10.0	8.7	8.6	16.7	-	8.4	9.1	-	6.8
Wholesale and retail trade	56.1	59.6	76.6	47.1	15.4	65.3	24.3	57.0	57.8
Transport and storage	6.2	10.0	6.7	8.4	-	11.9	16.7	15.8	9.5
Finance and insurance	21.4	14.6	35.1	27.8	-	28.8	14.4	68.7	27.2
Community, social and persona services	52.6	41.8	45.8	31.8	21.5	47.4	25.7	46.0	43.0
Total	43.6	37.1	48.7	34.2	13.0	43.0	19.8	40.5	39.6

Notes: The figures are based on a simple survey of selected metropolitan areas in Nigeria. Source: National Manpower Board (1998).

Table 15.10 Number and Proportion of Nigerian Women Employed in Various Manpower Categories in Nigeria, 2002

Manpower Category	*Number of Nigerian Women Employed*	*Women as % of Total Nigerians Employed*
Administrative and managerial manpower	19, 160	19.85
Senior level	18, 042	22.72
Junior level	163,202	26.28
Technical, scientific and allied manpower		
Senior level	3, 439	6.42
Intermediate level	4,880	4.31
Other professionals	30, 649	7.02
Senior level	55,453	12.32
Intermediate level	22,813	9.61
Junior level	172,991	15.44
Agricultural manpower		
Senior level	31,225	12.02
Intermediate level	7,691	17.01
Junior level	105	7.82
Health manpower		
Senior level	26, 318	15.83
Intermediate level	81,504	45.83
Junior level	66,004	48.73
Grand total (all categories)	733,642	17.72

Source: National Manpower Board, stakeholder forum in Manpower Development in Nigeria in Abuja, August 28, 2003.

Table 15.11 Economically Active Population (10+) and Labour Force

Nigeria	*Economically Active Population 10+*	*%*	*Population in Labour Force*	*%*
Both sexes	60,147,873	100	27,936,529	100
Male	29,810,840	49.6	17,562,642	62.9
Female	30,337,033	50.4	10,373,887	37.1

Source: Nigeria 1991 population census.

Table 15.12 Women as Proportion of Medical Practitioners in Nigeria

Year	*%*
1984	14.6
1985	14.8
1986	15.4
1987	15.4
1988	15.7
1989	16.0
1990	16.4
1991	17.0
1992	17.5
1993	17.5

Source: FOS (1999) Annual Abstract of Statistics. Note: Figures exclude non-Nigerians.

Table 15.13 Gender, Labor Force and Major Occupations

Occupation in Major Groups	*Both Sexes*		*Male*		*Female*	
	Number	*%*	*Number*	*%*	*Number*	*%*
Professional/technical	1,806,333	6.8	1,207,100	7.2	599,332	6.1
Administrative/ managerial	654,066	2.5	508,299	3.0	145,767	1.5
Clerical and related work	831,819	3.1	599,99	3.3	271,820	2.8
Sales worker	5,934,503	22.2	2,066,470	12.3	3,868,033	39.4
Service worker	857,813	3.2	535,603	3.2	3,22,210	3.3
Agriculture and related work	11,976,451	45.0	8,484,722	50.5	3,491,679	5.5
Production and related work	3,687,598	13.9	2,804,029	16.7	883,569	9.0
Occupation not stated	876,343	3.3	636,650	3.8	239,693	2.4
Total	26,624,926	100.0	16,802,823	100.0	9,822,103	100.0

Source: Nigeria 1991 Population Census.

Table 15.14 Women as Proportion of Academic Staff in Nigerian Universities

Grade/Year	*1990–1991*	*1992–1993*	*1991–1997*
Professors, association professors, readers	5.0	5.7	5.6
Senior lecturers, senior research fellows	11.2	11.9	12.8
Asst. lecturers and junior research fellows	17.5	16.8	17.2
Others	8.5	19.2	15.2
All grades	9.7	13.5	14.2

Source: FOS (1999) annual Abstract of Statistics.

Table 15.15 Females as Proportion of Primary and Post Primary School Teachers in Nigeria

	1992	*1993*	*1994*	*1995*	*1996*	*1997*
Percent of primary school teachers	n.a	44.8	46.4	47.1	47.6	47.0
Percent of post primary school teachers	33.5	34.5	36.0	36.2	35.5	n.a

Source: FOS (1999) Annual Abstract Statistics.

Table 15.16 Profile of Gender in Federal and State Government in Nigeria

Position Title in Ministry	*Male*	*Female*	*Missing Variables*	*Total*
Directors	3	3	-	6
Asst. directors	9	5	1	15
Managers	24	8	1	33
Asst. managers	14	28	-	19
Supervisors	44	-	-	73
Professors	5	-	-	42
Others	8	-	-	44
Missing variables	2	1	3	6

Source: Robert (2004:2009) Analysis and survey conducted in Nigeria 2000.

Second, the challenge of relative poverty is a serious factor. Most women are poor because they do not occupy strategic positions that can connect them to opportunities that can provide the necessary contact to make them as wealthy as most men. Moreover, many women are in lower and middle-level positions that do not attract much money.

Third, women do not possess the gregariousness to struggle for position and challenges that may be of much pecuniary reward.

Fourth, women are not as mobile as their male counterparts, who usually change jobs at random with associated monetary benefit. Worse, women abandon their jobs to follow their husbands and are often forced to take lower-paid jobs in order to save their marriage. The dire economic implication further put women in a disadvantaged position vis-à-vis their male counterparts.

Fifth, women are not given equal opportunities due to cultural limitations. For instance, women are supposed to be seen but not heard. As such, they are not usually involved in policy formulations.

Sixth, which is a derivative from the foregoing is the issue of discrimination in relation to leadership positions. Most men still hold the cultural notion in public places in their interaction with women even when women are found competent for some positions. The mere feeling or argument in a male dominated system against a woman will automatically put the woman at a disadvantage.

Seventh is the challenge of sexual harassment. This is common in the public service. It affects recruitment, advancement (promotion), discipline and motivation of women. This automatically affects women's chances in accessing top level positions in the Nigerian public service.

CONCLUSION

The need to empower women cannot be overemphasized particularly in a democratic society which recognizes the challenges faced by women in the public service. In suggesting a broad recipe for redressing gender bias in human resources planning in the public service, remedial action must be drawn from both the internal and external environments. The government should institute a quota system in appointments. This will enable women to overcome the issue of tokenism as they become part of a critical mass and are thus able to act as centre of power to influence change. Women should be given equal opportunities to contribute in decision making for national development.

Government should put in place sufficient mechanisms in the public service for the advancement of women. They should be encouraged to take up hard challenges. Working women should be adequately rewarded and praised.

Adequate day care facilities should be provided for nursing mothers so that their babies can be taken care of while they perform their duties in their offices and they should not be made to stay beyond the close of work.

The present cultural limitations should be revisited; they should be understood that we are now in a globalizing/industrialized world where women can no longer be relegated to the background. Women should be given equal opportunities with their male counterpart to contest favorably in politics and for public offices.

A major step forward in correcting the gender imbalances has been the recognition that not only do females have the right to improved status, but that it is the interest of everyone in the society. It is hope that efforts will go beyond recognition of the problems to concrete actions to further correct the gender imbalances in the public sector. This makes it necessary for all stakeholders to develop sensitivity to gender issues and actively promote the empowerment of women in all spheres of endeavors.

In Nigeria and the world at large, the crucial role of women must be acknowledged and appreciated. This can only become a reality if gender issues are given appropriate recognition and attention in human resource management in the public sector/service.

REFERENCES

Federal Government of Nigeria (2004), *National Economic Empowerment Development Strategy.*

Federal Republic of Nigeria (2008), *National Gender Policy: Strategic Implementation Framework and Plan*, Abuja.

Federal Republic of Nigeria, National Bureau of Statistics (2008), Women and Men in Nigeria, Facts and Figures 2001–2006, Vol. 2, September.

Haralambos and Holborn (2008), *Sociology: Themes and Perspective.*

Igbuzor O. (2005), *Perspective on Demcoracy and Development.* Lagos Abuja: Joe Tolani and Associates.

Mama A. (1997), Feminism or Democracy? State Feminist and Democratization, in Ibrahim J. (Ed) *Expanding Democratic Space in Nigeria.* Daka, Senegal: CODESRIA National Studies Service.

National Population Commission (NPC), United Nation's Population Fund (UNPF) 2001, Gender and Sustainable Development. Nigeria Population Census 1991 analysis NPC Abuja, May.

Olojede I. (2009), Women: The Neglected Force in Public Administration. An inaugural lecture delivered at Lagos State University, Lagos, May 5.

Olojede, I. (2009), *Women: The Neglected Force in Public Administration.* Lagos: Fortune News Publication.

Orewa G. O. (1997), *We Are All Guilty.* Ibadan: Spectrum Books Ltd.

Robert D. (2004), Public Administration Politics and Change in the Principle of Government in Nigeria, Lagos. Mbeyi & Associates (Nig) Ltd.

Rosenbloom D. H., and D. D. Goldman (1999), *Public Administration: Understanding Management, Politics & Law in Public Sector.* Singapore: McGraw-Hill.

16

African Women and the Changing Notion of Security

Funso Adesola

ABSTRACT

The female gender has, arguably, been a culturally and historically subdued category in many parts of Africa. This standpoint is no longer sustainable in view of the changes that the contemporary international system has undergone. This study, therefore, posits that fixed meaning of security in international politics is now undergoing a change process. Thus, African women are appraised in the context of the changing security debate. It concludes that extant definition of security is turgid and its expanded definition should take care of women, feminist and African peculiarities.

INTRODUCTION

This study argues that change is an engaging and a dynamic term. Its employment in this study speaks to the unsustainability of a fixed meaning of security in today's international politics. It is within this prism that it attempts a gendered perspective on the notion of security. It further argues that the orthodox definition of security is not only inelastic and weak; but it is also desirous of a nuanced and an expansive treatment. It draws from myriad of scholars, both African and Western, who have made submissions on a shift away from the extant and over-flogged notion of security.

Part of the conclusion that it has drawn, using a gendered template, is the convergence of the notion of human and national security. *Inter-alia*, a nation is deemed to be secured to the extent that its women and children (citizens) are empowered, catered for and developed. It also concludes, however, with a hint that in today's increasing clamor for an elaborate security's catchment areas, we should be cautious not to consider all threats to human beings as threats to security.

The study is divided into four parts. Following this introduction is a section on theoretical framework for analysis. The third part is an appraisal of African women in a changing or more diffused security environment and the fourth is the concluding remarks.

THEORETICAL BACKGROUND TO THE CHANGING NOTION OF SECURITY

> Peace and security is an idealized or hypothetical image of what human society should be, has never been and might never be. So peace and security is a never-ending process. . . . It sets the stage for improvements at the societal and collective psychological levels . . . and the socialization of less imperfect human beings, on the basis of the implementation of social policies consistent with its core theoretical principles and ideas. (Jinadu, 2000:9)

The above quotation emphasizes the inherent continuity, social and theoretical relevance as well as the transformation which the twin issues of peace and security have undergone. For the purpose of this study, the theoretical basis and analysis of the changes in the meaning and scope of security, especially as it affects Africa and women, is hereby attempted.

For a start, change is one of the variables that distinguish one school of thought from the other in international relations. In the contemporary international system, international relations is in the throes of a major theoretical re-organization because change (in itself) in the field seems to be noticed everywhere. The change also speaks to different perspectives on the human condition, especially as it affects different continents and men/women alike all over the world. To the realists, the change in international relations is limited to the narrow parameters of alteration of power, the poles of power, or the cast of great power characters. But most of the tools of these realists would not be effective in explaining military and diplomatic life of the whole world today, even though they are useful in explaining the eighteenth and nineteenth century Europe. The liberals, constructivists and post-modernists are of the view that sovereignty and anarchy—which are the main conceptual tools of the realist tradition, are no longer consistent with the observed facts of life (Holsti, 1998:1–2).

Susan Strange thus argued that: "Social Scientists . . . in politics and economics cling to obsolete concepts and inappropriate theories. These theories belong to a more stable and orderly world than the one we live in (Strange, 1996:3) now. This was corroborated by James. N. Rosenau when he remarked that we are living in an era of profound change, yet our ways of perceiving the world have not changed and as such, an attempt should be made toward what he called "an intellectual jailbreak" in order to move beyond ritual invocations of concepts that once had theoretical and descriptive uses, but are no longer able to capture those things that are truly new and novel in the world (Rosenau, 1990). Arising from this, there is the need to reconfigure our conceptual tools (Deibert, 1997:167–192). Therefore, an attempt is made in this study to examine what has fundamentally changed in the conception of security and what has not profoundly changed. It also explains, with the aid of some illustrations, what makes the changing events in Africa, theoretically significant.

Traditionally, security has been a subject of various interpretations by scholars and analysts. Arnold Wolfers posits that "security rises and falls with the ability of a nation to deter an attack or to defeat it" (Wolfers, 1962:150). Morton Berkowitz and P. G. Bock see it as ". . . the ability of a nation to protect its internal values from external threats" (Berkowitz and Bock, 1968:40). To Mohammed Ayoob, the term security is "that which threatens or have the potential to bring down or weaken state structures, both territorial and institutional and governing regimes" (Ayoob, 1991:257–283). So in the Third World, especially in Africa, state security is also synonymous with regime survival; because any threat that can hamper state's and regime's effective performance of its duties, both at the domestic level and at the level of international politics, is considered to be a national security risk. Ayoob is also of the opinion that security must impact mainly and firmly within the realm of political consequences, though other societal variables may filter into it (Ayoob, 1995:9–16).

What we can deduce from these orthodox definitions or conceptualizations of security is that they are state-centric and speak mainly of a military capability to ward-off external aggression or subdue an aggressor. It can also be said that anything that undermines regime survival and hinders diligent performance of a state's functions, as it were, is a critical national security issue.

However, the meaning and scope of security, as employed in this study, transcends the traditional usage. To be sure, security occupies a predominant position as a concept within international relations and is central to the understanding of interstate relations. Security was used as an instrument by the superpowers in the Cold War rivalry. It was used as either rolling back communism or as containing domino and emulating effects of capitalism. In a way, the French involvement in Africa during the Cold War era was actually complementary to the larger North Atlantic Treaty Organization's (NATO's) design—which was salient during the rivalry between the East and the West.[1] In fact, the United States (US)—the leading NATO power—has cultivated the habit of deferring to metropolitan initiatives in the African continent, except in critical cases such as Zaire (Shaba), Southern Africa and an important state like Nigeria. This is borne out of the fact that it is cost effective for NATO, and colonial ties between the imperial powers and their colonies make it possible to utilize specialist experience (of the colonialists) in working with Africans. It is this same design that made the US condone France to use its limited military resources for interventionist endeavors in Africa because it is not antithetical to NATO's/West's strategic design in that continent (Ate, 1992:17–20). France through this means had legitimized its (and NATO's) involvement in Africa. The US and Britain could not freely do this without provoking or risking a series of reactions from African countries and without risking some kind of counter-action by the Soviet Union and its allies. But in the guise of bilateral agreement or a pretext of legitimate invitation, France had dispatched troops to many of its erstwhile colonies.

Again, in the traditional sense, security as seen by the realists and idealists is pre-occupied with a particular type of state and how it is to be peacefully maintained. For example, Barry Buzan sees security as that which mainly concerns the great powers. While saying this, he employed the realist tools—that eventually dominates security debate in international relations (Buzan, 1991:216). This development was what led to strategic studies because superpowers rivalry requires that they keep abreast of the latest developments in weaponry, early warning systems and other related issues. So, the need to change the concept of security became unnecessary and dangerous in order not to rupture the delicate balance that had prevented nuclear conflict. Obviously, in this realist template, the Third World, and as such African security, hardly features.

Going by Lloyd Pettiford's account, this realist paradigm makes regime survival the essence of Third World/African security. Governments' preoccupation was to mainly keep "minimum values" which they use to justify keeping internal order at any cost. This in turn led to repression and increased military expenditure to satisfy certain narrow interests. Therefore, as defined by the realists school, it could be said that security is negligent of the imperatives of many people in the world's poorer states—especially the plights of women and children as we have in the continent of Africa. It is only the pluralists and structuralists paradigms of security that challenged the realists paradigm. While the realists use a "billiard ball" model of international relations, the pluralists see the world as a "cobweb"—where many actors are in interactive sessions. To the pluralists, security is less about self-help, but more on the idea of well-being. They emphasize wars, but glorify international stability. The structuralists too are of the dependency school. They have "Marxian" persuasion—where copious explanation of international relations and mode of production and contradictions generated therefrom is attributed to "class struggle" (Pettiford, 1996:289).

According to K. Booth, in view of the contemporary development in interstate interactions, security is no longer on military matters alone, because many Third World and particularly African problems could no longer be understood using only the traditional doctrine of security (Booth, 1990). In line with Booth, Tony Blair—the then British Prime Minister—appropriately remarked on the occasion of NATO's 50th anniversary, that:

> We cannot ignore new political ideas in other countries if we want to innovate, we cannot turn our backs on conflicts and the violation of human rights in other countries if we still want to be secure. (Blair, 1999:19)

K. Booth and Tony Blair are not alone; Lloyd Pettiford and Melissa Curley, Sola Akinrinade, J. A. Tickner and Caroline Thomas also strongly believe on the need for reconceptualization or re-examination of security. Pettiford and Curley are of the view that security has a fixed meaning in international relations, but this meaning is undergoing some modifications in recent years (Pettiford and Curley, 1999). J. A. Tickner pointed out that since 1983 when Barry Buzan's book—*People, States and Fear*—came out, the concept has been redefined, re-theorized, reconceptualised or refigured (Tickner, 1995:175). Barry Buzan himself has this to say: "Security, in its prevailing usage, the concept is so weakly developed as to be inadequate" (Buzan, 1991:1); this is what dominated his thought and analysis in the above mentioned book.

In the same vein, Sola Akinrinade argued that the concept and issues of security, as contained in extant literature, are largely of Western origin and cannot be automatically applied to Africa and Third World situations. Citing Mohammed Ayoob, Arnold Wolfers and Walter Lippman, Akinrinade pointed out that security is based on the notion that most threats are externally generated and that these threats are military in nature, which require military response, if the security of the state is to be preserved (Akinrinade, 1999:219).

Akinrinade further mentioned that one interesting development after the recession of nuclear threat and perceived decline of military power, an enlargement of broader concepts of security in Western discourse emerged—as threats of terrorism, drugs and environment began to appear. So in Africa, various threats of secession, irredentism, and border dispute as well as legitimacy crisis have continued to perturb the security of regimes—hence using the orthodox definition of security for Africa is problematic and inadequate. We should, therefore, be speaking of endogenous African security concerns rather than the ones that are externally conditioned.

Caroline Thomas' seminal work on expanding the definition of security to suit the Third World countries situations is apposite for reference here:

> Security does not simply refer to the military dimension, as it is often assumed in Western discussions of the concept, but to the whole range of dimensions of a state's existence which are already taken care of in the more developed states. (Thomas, C. 1987)

Horace Campbell aligns with the position of Pettiford, Curley, Akinrinade, Tickner and Thomas on the need to expand the definition of security. He employs Afrocentric intellectual tools, in the tradition of Amilcar Cabral, Cheikh Anta Diop and Frantz Fanon in challenging the unsuitability of the conventional Eurocentric notion of peace and security, which, according to him, is either ahistorical or selectively historical and ideologizes the African situations. He concluded that this conventional notion is not only peripheral in treating the African situation, but also could not wholly explain the main issues surrounding conflicts in Africa (Campbell, 2000).

Also, on expansion or reconceptualization of security, Mary Kaldor is of the view that after the Cold War, hopes are that the global security concept will expand and encompass a wider range of other issues, which are meant to supplant the narrow, defense-oriented concepts aimed only on security of nations and blocs. Military spending was expected to drop dramatically and thus many wars prevented. But these hopes were dashed even after over ten years post Cold War when rhetoric pervaded the globe on the need for respect and promotion of human rights, democratization and activation of the civil society. This rhetoric is at odds with continuing violence, insecurity and militarism, coupled with the fact that there are more wars and the attendant refugees' crisis and displaced persons (Kaldor, 2000:1–2).

Kaldor further noted that military spending has only dropped with respect to the defunct Soviet Union, but not with Western Europe and the US. To her, all these are a product of misdiagnosis of the sources of insecurity and are meant to allow the fantasies of technologists, military industrial institutions, military planners, the spin of instant television coverage and traditional assumptions of diplomats to dominate our definitions of security issues. By extension, this explains the unwillingness of advanced countries to engage their armed forces to take responsibility in enforcing global security in areas outside 'home' as the need arises, no matter how imperative and expedient such could be. To these advanced countries and their security planners, new wars are merely described as "military operations other than war" or "low intensity conflicts" or "internal conflicts." Retired military officers, unemployed military specialists, mercenary groups and unpaid or spatially paid regular armies are the major characters in the new wars. They make light weapons available or sell them on the black market. They are the ones that contribute to the unending series of new wars (Kaldor, op. cit., 3–15), especially in Africa.

In order to properly locate Africa within the context of the contemporary change in the meaning and scope of security, it is fruitful to refer to D. Deudney and S. Watt whose submission is that: today, security encompasses numerous actors and issues. Furthermore, it could not be gainsaid that the security of many of the actors in the international system is closely linked; hence, it is not profitable to study any type of actor in isolation (atomistically), but rather as a part of a whole (holistically). But we must be careful not to consider all threats to human well-being as threats to security (Deudney, 1990:211). What is clear now is that, there is a change in paradigm. This paradigm shift should not be seen as if the world is on a cutting-edge of profound historical change. Again, there is no doubting the fact that expansion or reconceptualization of security is desirable and justifiable, but the rapidity of this change does not guarantee or readily present a finished theory.

Evidently, strategic studies leapfrog the realists paradigm of focusing security debate only on state actors and military affairs alone. But the end of the Cold War and the threat of nuclear war (on which strategic studies were based) did not mean the disappearance of threats of nuclear war, but gave way to other actors and issues that impact on security debate. It is within this new process that the security needs and realities of the Third World and *ipso facto* African countries are appreciated and given vent. This explains why Mohammed Ayoob said that:

> The orthodox definition of security is ethnocentric and statist. It was not value neutral and perhaps a Western ahistorical and acultural generalization. (Then), its redefinition or reconceptualization, expansion or re-theorization is somewhat more historical and culturally specific. (Ayoob, op. cit., 59)

It is, therefore, from the foregoing perspectives that we would be able to locate African women in the security debate. It should be added also that, to the detriment of human security, most Third World/African leaders' making and implementing foreign and domestic policies are preoccupied (if not obsessed), by state and regime security and they shape their policies accordingly. This explains why security vote accounts for about 19 percent of most Third World countries total annual budget (USACDA, 1990). This has increased in many parts of Africa from 1990 up till 2010.[2] Many African governments have justified swollen defence spending on the altar of maintaining peace in view of rising citizens' agitations and demonstrations (against misrule); resurgence of separatist movements and other anomie groups. Indeed, governments spend more on defense and less on health and education if there has been a recent conflict. Small arms and light weapons (SALW) are mainly used in such conflicts and France and the United Kingdom appear to be the two main suppliers of SALW to sub-Saharan Africa. Thus, there is a connection between recent conflict and higher rates of mortality, malnutrition and maternal mortality for those under age of 5 (O'Hare and Southall, 2007:564). In fact, some states in Africa and the Third World in general, normally understate military expenditures and hide security expenditures under different budget headings; hence, the actual percentage of it in the national budget is often higher than those presented to the public (Ball, 1988:388). Regime security in Africa and the Third World are mostly guaranteed by the armed forces (military and paramilitary alike); hence, defence, security and/or military budgetary allocations are heavy. It is on the strength of the paradigm shift, as that which has been elaborated in our earlier discussions, that we seek to correct the anomaly evident in the focus and coverage of the term security, doing so especially by appraising African women.

AFRICAN WOMEN AND THE EXPANDED NOTION OF SECURITY

Women are an important segment of African society. Demographically, the female sex outnumbers its male counterpart.[3] However, there have been ample cases of women's marginalization—because most of their ordeals go unreported. Indeed, many of them are disadvantaged either by virtue of culture or natural phenomenon. In their category, though not exclusively, are the unemployed, illiterates, "half-educated," physically challenged, single parents, divorcees, unmarried, singles and "professional housewives" as well as widows. All of these pose their own kind of unconventional/cultural-specific security challenges. The following are the observable outcomes of the changing notion of security with respect to African women:

- an increased demand for women's access to material resources;
- an expansion of political space to ensure women's wider participation in the economy. This is otherwise known as women empowerment;
- an incorporation of women's rights law into national/international/institutional law book/statutes;
- a propelling of multilayered/multidisciplinary research and *ipso facto*;
- a groundswell of gender-sensitive policies by public and private institutions and foreign agencies began to emerge (Jaquette and Summerfield, 2006:2).

It has also been observed that both customary and civil laws tend to favor men but impoverish women. Gendered issues on property rights which were hitherto undermined have now come to the fore today in the world of a changing notion of security. More than ever before, causes have also emerged to challenge certain traditions and praxis that make it difficult for women to assert their legal rights. In many parts of Africa, inheritance of land and home are integral parts of human security issues. In the same genre, the world of a changing notion of security has also criminalized and accentuated discourse on trafficking in persons (ibid., 7), mainly women or girls.

Central to the foregoing is also a spirited effort to support women to survive or compete in a marketised and highly integrated/competitive world—in ways that will make them benefit from the somewhat peace—dividend of the post-Cold War international system. Furthermore, gender-sensitive appointments into high administrative positions in many parts of Africa as well as effective gendered local action stoked by women's movements within and outside Africa are the other dividend of the world of a changing notion of security for the hitherto "neglected" and "silenced" or "gagged" African women (ibid., 12).

Overall, many cultural and ethical constraints especially those imposed on women in the areas of marriage; pregnancies; sexual harassment; housing; women in politics; maternity leave; work ethics; and general issues on resource control and livelihood have not only been in the front burner of discourses today, but they have also been "re-conditioned" in a world of a changing notion of security (Merry, 2009:39–88).

We further discovered that extant male-dominated discourses underlining a notion of international politics being peopled by (elite) men alone has now been mixed with an openly expressed gendered/feminist analysis. In such events, for instance, social workers now pay attention to a gendered-standpoint on poverty; trade union leaders/economists have had to reflect on considered feminist explanation on wage inequalities (because women are in the disproportionate segment of the economically disadvantaged); male chauvinists have had to yield ground to non-masculine discourses/analyses; international policy makers have also had to factor-in women's/feminist's experiences (Manchanda, 2001:4100).

What we have further seen today in the world of a changing notion of security is the tapping of new perspectives from women experience of what day-to-day human security connotes. This, therefore, generates a holistic notion of what actually constitutes security (ibid., 4101).

In the world of a changing notion of security and with feminists' scholars and peace studies on the increase, alternative insights into male dominated narrative, theories and experiences have emerged to challenge the ungendered aspects of our social and political life. Part of this reminds us that women are the greatest victims of the militarized security regime—as studies on KwaZulu-Natal, other parts of Southern Africa, Nigeria, Eritrea and Uganda have revealed.[4]

Also germane to the issue of paradigm shift in the security agenda especially as it affects African women is the continent's world fastest rate of population growth. The continent's population has doubled since 1970 to nearly 900 million and it is expected to rise to 1.2 billion by 2020.[5] This will be greater than the populations of North America and Europe combined (Carafano and Gardiner, 2003:2). It is striking that the continent has "the world's fastest rate of population growth," in it, however, lies the paradox of a continent blighted by poverty, disease, misrule, corruption, inter-tribal rivalry and so forth. Indeed, sub-Sahara Africa remains the world's poorest region with gross domestic product (GDP) per capital income of just $575 in 2002 (World Bank, 2003). By 2010, the region had the highest incidence of multidimensional poverty—ranging from 3 percent in South Africa to 93 percent in the Niger Republic.[6]

In order to further situate the plight of the African women, it is instructive to review the 2010 human development index (hdi) based on life expectancy, mean/expected years of schooling and gross national income per capital. Out of a total of 169 countries ranked, no African country appeared in the "very high human development" category (out of the 42 countries listed there). Only Libya, Mauritius and Algeria appeared in the 'high human development' category—ranking 53rd, 72nd and 84th positions, respectively, in the global hdi ranking. Again, 10 African countries are in the "medium human development" category (out of 42 countries listed there); while African countries inundate (32 out of 42 countries listed there) the "low human development" category. This latter category showcased important African countries like Ghana, Nigeria, Senegal and Ethiopia—ranking 130th, 142nd, 144th and 147th positions, respectively, in the global hdi ranking.[7] Thus, the chunk of the African population, that of the female sex,[8] becomes the main object of indignity arising from their vulnerability to all sorts of unwholesome socioeconomic conditions. Ways by which such conditions could be accommodated and addressed in today's security agenda become imperative.

More pertinent is the fact that the world's population is expected to grow from 5.3 billion in 1990 to 6.2 billion in 2000 and to 8.5 billion in 2025 (Solomon, 1995:43). This presents grave environmental economic, sociocultural and political consequences. One that readily comes to mind is the problem of resource distribution in an overcrowded land. For instance, the crisis in Rwanda is attributable to the fact that it has one of the highest levels of population density in Africa (Solomon and Cilliers, 1996). In addition to this, population explosion is also accountable for two-third of the increase in carbon dioxide that is entering the atmosphere.[9] Worrisome is the fact that little of the projected population growth will take place in the North. The developed industrialized states' share of the world population is 22 percent in 1950, 15 percent in 1985 and it is projected to be 5 percent by 2085 ((Solomon, op. cit). On the reverse, the projected population growth will be in the South, for example, in Nigeria the population is expected to increase from 132 million in 1990 to 301 million by 2025, and Ethiopia from 47 million in 1990 to 112 million by 2025 (ibid.). Feeding this growing population with increasing dependence on foreign food becomes worrisome. The bloated population, mainly of the female category—as established elsewhere in this study—places greater stress on the infrastructural facilities, as it exacerbates housing shortages and unemployment.

In addition to the problem of massive African population growth, there is an estimated 30 million Africans that are infected with human immunodeficiency virus/acquired immuno deficiency syndrome (HIV/AIDS).[10] In effect, HIV/AIDS have:

- overwhelmed the continent's health services;
- created millions of orphans;
- decimated health workers and teachers;
- caused socioeconomic crises by weakening the work forces, sapped economic strength and deprived many of education and has the tendency of destroying the very fabric of complete societies. Coupled with that, it has frustrated hopes and aspirations for a decent life.[11]

Deplorably, out of eleven million orphans so far left by the global AIDS epidemic, 90 percent were African children.[12]

In one international forum organized by the Security Council of the United Nations, Mr. Kofi Annan, the former Secretary General of the Organization, is of the opinion that AIDS in Africa was no less destructive than that of warfare itself. For instance, in 1999, AIDS has killed about ten times more people in Africa than had armed conflicts. Borders could not keep it out.[13] Zambia has the fifth highest HIV prevalence in the 2010 Human Development Report.[14] This pandemic further puts a lot of strain on public services, dignity and the fate of several hundreds of thousands of African womenfolks. We can then see the need that a focus on security today (especially as it affects Africa) should be on issues that address these women/children-dominated challenges.

Apart from the rapidity of African population growth and AIDS on the need for a paradigm shift on security, is the issue of migration in Africa. For instance, one in almost one hundred and fourteen people is displaced worldwide (Solomon, 1999:3) and it is estimated that there are twenty million internally displaced people worldwide (Loescher, 1999:8). African examples on those displaced as a result of ethnic/civil strife, economic decline and environmental disasters abound in Liberia, Ethiopia, Somalia, Burundi, Sierra Leone, Mozambique, Sudan etc. These sorts of migrations not only gave rise to humanitarian problems, but also create domestic instability, generate interstate tension and threaten international security—which adversely affect women and children mainly.

CONCLUDING REMARKS

In this study, we maintain that older generalizations about the fundamental characteristics of international politics are outdated. The enormous non-military sources of insecurity have challenged the traditional Clausewitzian conception of security. Nonetheless, there is an urgent need for concerted efforts to address the challenge of poverty and underdevelopment especially if specific examples of Sudan, Ethiopia, Angola, Sierra Leone, Liberia, Burundi, Nigeria and so forth are anything to go by. It is obvious that many African countries today have become ever more impotent in dealing on their own, through national legislations and institutions, with material and political realities that are increasingly threatening the safety and well-being of their citizens (Brown, op. cit., 3).

More than ever before, a devotion to the security concern of the ordinary man on the street should now be the preoccupation of the state's functionaries. This could be translated to opening opportunities up to all and sundry—for them to benefit from the "commonwealth"—namely, creating ample opportunities for sustainable employment, good health services and other forms of social services. This will form the benchmark for security in Africa, seemingly unending agitation for gender equity and reduce the threat of state collapse and implosion in the continent. We should also not forget that rebuilding war-torn societies is much more expensive and time consuming than fighting a war. Therefore, changes in the global security agenda require a multi-faceted approach and a blending of "hard" and "soft" security instruments.

Certainly, there are traditional and nontraditional threats to world peace and stability and obviously the type of threats that dominate Africa's (world's) security today are nontraditional. In fact, issues of gender, arm proliferation, ethnic warfare, criminal violence, human migrations and all sorts of social dislocations, dearth of infrastructures and attendant social problems, failed states and climate change, to mention but a few are likely to figure most in the continent's/global discourse on international peace and security.[15] A major fallout of these new security concerns is a recurrence of theses and actions on cultural and ethical constraints on women—such as prenatal sex determination, sex-selective abortion, sex-specific abortion, women and childlessness, women's property rights, sexual harassment; women in politics; maternity leave; women and work ethics, women and marriages; and women and migration during warfare and general issues on resource control.

It is, therefore, pertinent to close with Goran Hyden's observation:

> Politics is dynamic. For Political Scientists therefore it is natural to accept that our theories are not for ever. The explanatory power of a particular theory shifts

with changes in the empirical realm over which neither the theory nor the theorist has much, if any, control. As researchers we invest not only reason but also values in what we do. When history moves only gently forward, reigning paradigm continue to dominate our minds, however, when significant events occur, new paradigm and theoretical perspectives arise. (Hyden, 1992:12)

NOTES

1. *The Financial Times*, June 2, 1978; also Sean Gervase (1976), "South Africa under the NATO Umbrella," Africa Report, September–October, pp. 12–15.

2. *Human Development Report* (2010) (20th Anniversary Edition), "The Real Wealth of Nations: Pathways to Human Development," United Nations Development Programme, pp. 32–36.

3. http://ucatlas.edu/gender/gratio.html (date accessed 07-02-2012); CIA World Factbook, www.cia.gov/library/publications/the-world-factbook/goes/xx.html (date accessed July 2, 2012; A. Klasen and R. Wink (2003), Missing Women: Revisiting the Debate, *Feminist Economics*, Vol. 9, Nos. 2 & 3, pp. 263–299; A. Sen (2001), Many Faces of Gender Inequality, *The Frontline*, October 27.

4. Debby Bonnin (2000), Claiming Spaces, Changing Spaces: Political Violence and Women's Protests in KwaZulu-Natal, *Journal of Southern African Studies*, Vol. 26, No. 2, pp. 301–316; Lindiwe Zulu (1998), Role of Women in the Reconstruction and Development of the New Democratic South Africa, Feminist *Studies*, Vol. 24, No. 1, pp. 147–157; Donna Pankhurst (2003), The "Sex-War" and Other Wars: Towards a Feminist Approach to Peace Building, *Development in Practice*, Vol. 13, Nos. 2/3, pp. 154–177; Doris Burgess (1989), Women and War: Eritrea, *Review of Political Economy*, Nos. 45/46, pp. 126–132; Akin Iwilade (2011), Women and Peace Talks in Africa, *Journal of International Women Studies*, Vol. 12, No. 1, pp. 22–36; Sally Engel Merry (2001), Rights, Religions and Community: Approaches to Violence against Women in the Context of Globalization, *Law and Society Review*, Vol. 35, No. 1, pp. 39–88; Zillah Eisenstein (1997), Women's Publics and the Search for New Democracies, *Feminist Review*, No. 57, pp. 140–167; Annie Marie Goetz (1998), Women in Politics and Gender Equity in Policy: South Africa and Uganda, *Review of Political Economy*, Vol. 25, No. 76, pp. 241–262.

5. United Nations Population Division (2003), World Population Prospects, The 2002 Report, Population Database (available at: http://esa.un.org/unpp/).

6. *Human Development Report* (2010), op. cit., p. 8.

7. Ibid., pp. 143–146.

8. http://ucatlas; CIA World Factbook; Klasen and Wink and Sen, op. cit.

9. *New Scientists* (1990) Too much Life on Earth? May, 19.

10. BBC News Online (2002), HIV Infections Top 40 million (No. 26).

11. Press Release, SC 6781, (2000), Security Council Holds Debates on Impact AIDS on Peace and Security in Africa. January 10, p. 1.

12. Kofi Annan, The UN Secretary General said at the beginning of the Millennium.

13. Press release, op. cit., p. 3.

14. *Human Development Report* (2010), op. cit., p. 30.

15. For more, see Michael T. Klare and Yogesh Chandrani (Eds.) (1998), *World Security: Challenges for a New Century*. New York: St. Martins Press, p. vii.

REFERENCES

Akinrinade, Sola (1999), Democracy and Security in Africa: Towards a Framework of Understanding, *Journal of Contemporary African Studies*, Vol. 17, (July), p. 219.

Ate, Bassey (1992), The Presence of France in West-Central Africa as a Fundamental Problem to Nigeria, in Bassey E. Ate and Bola Akinterinwa (Eds.), *Nigeria and Its Immediate Neighbours: Constraints and Prospects of Sub-Regional Security in the 1990s*. Lagos, Nigerian Institute of International Affairs (NIIA) in co-operation with Pumark Nigeria Ltd., pp. 17–20.

Ayoob, Mohammed (1991), The Security Problematic of the Third World, *World Politics*, Vol. 43, No. 2 (January), pp. 257–283.

Ayoob, Mohammed (1995), *The Third World Security Predicament*, op. cit., p. 59.

Ayoob, Mohammed (1995), *The Third World Security Predicament: State Making, Regional Conflict and International System*. Boulder, CO: Lynne Rienner, pp. 9–16.

Ball, Nicole (1988), *Security and Economy in the Third World*. Princeton, NJ: Princeton University Press, p. 388.

Berkowitz, Morton, and P. G. Bock (1968), National Security, in David L. Sills (Ed.), *International Encyclopedia of the Social Sciences*. New York: Macmillan, p. 40.

Blair, Tony (1999), Doctrine of the International Community, excerpt of speech at the Hilton Hotel, Chicago, April 22, p. 19.

Booth, K. (Ed.) (1990), *New Thinking about Strategy and International Security*. London: Unwin Hyman.

Brown, Seyom(1998), World Interests and the Changing Dimensions of Security, in Klare and Chandrani (Eds.), *World Security: Challenges for a New Century*, op. cit., p. 3.

Buzan, Barry (1991), *People, States and Fear—An Agenda for Security Studies in the Post-Cold War Era*. London: Harvester Wheatsheaf, p. 216.

Buzan, Barry (1991), *People, States and Fear: An Agenda for International Security Studies in the Post-Cold War Era*, 2nd ed. Hemel Hempstead, UK: Harvester Wheatsheaf, p. 1.

Campbell, Horace (2000), Peace Narrative and Education for Peace in Africa, in Adele Jinadu (Ed.), *The Political Economy*, op. cit.

Carafano, James Jay, and Nile Gardiner (2003), US Military Assistance for Africa, *Heritage Foundation*, October 15, p. 2.

Deudney, D. (1990), Environment and Security: Muddled Thinking, *Bulletin of Atomic Scientists*, Vol. 47, No. 3, pp. 22–28; and S. Watt (1991), The Renaissance of Security Studies, *International Studies Quarterly*, Vol. 35, No. 2, pp. 211–237.

Deibert, Ronald J. (1997), Exorcismus Theoriae: Pragmatism, Metaphors and the Return of the Medieval in International Relations Theory, *European Journal of International Relations*, Vol. 3. No. 2 (June), pp. 167–192.

Holsti, K. J. (1998), *The Problem of Change in International Relations Theory*. Institute of International Relations, The University of British Columbia, Working Paper No. 26, December, pp. 1–2.

Hyden, Goran (1992), Governance and the Study of Politics, in Goran Hyden and Michael Bratton (Eds.), *Governance and Politics in Africa*. Boulder, CO: Lynne Reinner Publishers, p. 12.

Jaquette, Jane S., and Gale Summerfield (2006), *Introduction*, in Jane S. Jaquette and Gale Summerfield (Eds.), *Women and Gender Equity in Development Theory and Practice: Institutions, Resources and Mobilization*. Durham, NC: Duke University Press, p. 2.

Jinadu, L. Adele (2000), Introduction: The Dialectics of Democracy, Development, Peace and Security in Africa, in L. Adele Jinadu (Ed.), *The Political Economy of Peace and Security in Afric-Ethno-Cultural and Economic Perspectives*, Harare. Africa Association of Political Scientists (AAPS) Books, p. 9.

Kaldor, Mary (Ed.) (2000), *Global Insecurity: Restructuring the Global Military Sector*, Vol. III. London: Pinter Publishers, pp. 1–2.

Loescher, G. (1999), Refugee Movements and International Security, *Adelphi Papers 268, Brasseys*, London, p. 8.

Manchanda, Rita (2001), Redefining & Feminizing Security: Making a Difference in Security Policies, *Economist and Political Weekly*, Vol. 36, No. 43. October 27–November 2, p. 4100.

Merry, Sally Engel (2009), Rights, Religions and Community: Approaches to Violence against Women in the Context of Globalization, *Law and Society*, Vol. 35, No. 1, pp. 39–88.

Pettiford, Lloyd (1996), Changing Concepts of Security in the Third World, *Third World Quarterly*, Vol. 17, No. 2, pp. 289–304.

Pettiford, Lloyd, and Melissa Curley (1999), *Changing Security Agendas and the Third World*. London: Pinter Publishers.

O'Hare, Bernadette A. M., and David P. Southall (2007), First Do No Harm: The Impact of Recent Armed Conflict on Maternal and Child Health in Sub-Saharan Africa, *The Royal Society of Medicine*, Vol. 100, No. 12. (December), pp. 564–570.

Rosenau, James (1990), *Turbulence in World Politics*. Princeton, NJ: Princeton University Press, Chapter 2.

Solomon, Hussein (1995), The Challenges of Global Change to International Relations Theory, *Politeia*, Vol. 14, No. 1, p. 43.

Solomon, Hussein (1999), Population Movements into South Africa: Trends, Outlook, Policies, Occasional Paper Series No. 2, Foundation for Global Dialogue, Braamfontein, p. 3.

Solomon, Hussein, and John Cilliers (1996), Sources of Southern African Insecurity and the Quest for Regional Integration, in H. Solomon and J. Cilliers (Eds.) *People, Poverty and Peace: Human Security in Southern Africa*. IDP Monograph Series, No. 4 (June).

Strange, Susan (1996), *The Retreat of the State: The Diffusion of Power in the World Economy*. Cambridge, UK: Cambridge University Press, p. 3.

Thomas, Caroline (1987), *In Search of Security: The Third World in International Relations*. Brighton, UK: Wheatsheaf Publishing House.

Tickner, J. A. (1995), Re-visioning Security, in K. Booth and S. Smith (Eds.), *International Relations Theory Today*. Cambridge, UK: Polity Press, pp. 175–197.
US Arms Control and Disarmament Agency (USACDA) (1990), World Military Expenditures and Arms Transfers, Washington, D.C.
Wolfers, Arnold (1962), *Discord and Collaboration: Essays on International Politics*. Baltimore, MD: Johns Hopkins University Press, p. 150.
World Bank (2003), World Development Indicators (available at www.worldbank.org/data).

ACKNOWLEDGMENT

The author hereby acknowledges that this study benefited immensely from the grant he received from the Council for Development of Social Science Research in Africa (CODESRIA) that is based in Dakar (Senegal).

Part IV

FEMINISM AND SOCIAL MOVEMENT

17

"Unknown Soldier"

Women's Radicalism, Activism, and State Violence in Twentieth-Century Nigeria

Mojúbàolú Olúfúnké Okome (PhD)

ABSTRACT

In "unknown soldier," Fela Anikulapo Kuti in 1979 eulogized his mother, Olufunmilayo Ransome Kuti, through his protest music. Most Fela fans first met his mother through this eulogy. Fela, like his mother, remained unbowed by the crushing repression of the Nigerian military regime under General Olusegun Obasanjo, which deployed armed forces to Kalakuta Republic, Fela's multi-story residence where he lived with his mother and entourage in Yaba, Lagos. In the melee, mayhem and arson that ensued, Fela's mother was thrown out of a window, which eventually led to her death. She was a Marxist who opposed injustice, abuse of power and racism, colonialism, imperialism and neo-colonialism. In her heyday, Olufunmilayo Ransome Kuti led Abeokuta (a town in South Western Nigeria) women to oust the Alake (King/traditional ruler) from power for being a colonial stooge. She spearheaded the founding of a nationwide women's organization and participated in negotiations preceding Nigeria's independence from British colonialism. Instead of being treated as a national treasure, she was mostly ignored in her older years and was finally murdered by the state. Nigerian women's activism has historically occurred within a political system where the checks and balances against absolutism in the precolonial era were already being significantly eroded in the nineteenth century—a period of flux marked by wars in Yorubaland, slave raids in both Yoruba and Igboland, and the transition from trade to colonial monopolies. Historically, the deployment of naked state violence was the norm, and fighting state repression could unleash the "unknown soldier" against non-conformists, demonstrators, and protesters. Thus, more conciliatory measures, including willingness to be coopted have been more popular than radicalism. It remains to be seen whether the embrace of liberal democracy since the latter years of the twentieth century would make a difference.

INTRODUCTION

The 1920s Igbo Women's War in South Eastern Nigeria did not have one leader. It was a popular uprising that could have become a political movement. Nonetheless, it manifested the "unknown soldier" phenomenon, since state-deployed soldiers shot and killed numerous women demonstrating against colonial repression. Through their indigenous organizations, Igbo women spread the word from hamlets to villages and towns to organize an uprising against this injustice in a well organized resistance in which they attacked all symbols of British colonialism. Prior to this, Efunsetan Aniwura and Madam Tinubu fought against local and international states in the 19th century in the interest of women and the nation (from the title of Odim-Johnson and Mba's biography of Funmilayo Ransome Kuti). Contending that these women's actions were radical in the sense that they fought against male dominant colonial, local and national state projects, this chapter would argue that the lack of a radical women's movement in Nigeria is due to the responses to state repression and its "unkown soldier."

"You may have been born but you were not bred! Would you speak to your mother like that?" Mrs. Funmilayo Ransome-Kuti's response to the British District Officer who told Abeokuta women demonstrators, "Shut up, you women!" (Soyinka, 1989). "There is no satisfying Mrs. Ransome-Kuti. Right now, she is up to another devilry. She is opposed to women of Abeokuta paying water-rate. I am sure that if she would devote as much time to agitating for progressive measures as she does to everything that is conducive to disorder, she would become the greatest woman in Abeokuta, nay, in Nigeria." Alake of Abeokuta, Sir Ladapo Ademola in a 1959 interview with *Drum Magazine* (Ottah, 1998). "So we gave a hell of a time to the chiefs, the government, to all those who were responsible for the systematic pauperisation of the mass of the people," said Mrs. Funmilayo Ransome-Kuti in a March 1959 interview with *Drum Magazine* (Ottah, 1998). "This assembly shall be known as the Federation of Nigerian Women's Societies [FNWS], where the voice of all Nigerian women will be heard and known."

In "unknown soldier," Fela Anikulapo Kuti in 1979 eulogized his mother, Olufunmilayo Ransome Kuti, through his protest music in 31 minutes of his classical Afrobeat. To state his displeasure with the dictatorial military regime of the day that had set in motion the events leading to his mother's death, Fela also led a protest that laid a coffin at the doorstep of General Olusegun Obasanjo. Most Fela fans first met his mother through this eulogy.

UNKNOWN SOLDIER PHENOMENON VERSUS WOMEN RADICALISM

Fela followed his mother's lead in many regards. Like his mother, he remained unbowed by the crushing repression of the Nigerian military regime under General Olusegun Obasanjo, which deployed armed forces to Kalakuta Republic, Fela's multi-story residence where he lived with his mother and entourage in Yaba, Lagos. In the melee, mayhem and arson that ensued, Fela's mother was thrown out of a window. In the precolonial era, Efunsetan Aniwura, the Iyalode of Ibadan led the way by standing against another military state, this time, an indigenous one led by Are Latosa. She was assassinated in circumstances that could be incorporated under the heading of "unknown soldier." Leading the charge of radical women in the colonial era, Madam Tinubu, Iyalode of all the Egba also fought against male dominated indigenous and colonial states in Abeokuta and Lagos. Aba market women who were relatively autonomous from the men were also able to wage the Women's War of 1929, against colonial monopoly trading companies and their practice of imposing prices on agricultural commodities manufactured goods under the protection of an undemocratic regime, which planned to levy taxes on women's income from trade. About twenty years later, Mrs. Funmilayo Ransome-Kuti led Abeokuta women in a powerful challenge of Alake Ademola, widely perceived to be a colonial stooge who spearheaded the imposition of undemocratic laws and administrative policies and refused to curtail his officials abuse of power including "stripping young girls naked on the pretext of assessing them for taxation" (Agozino and Anyanike, 2007).

Bolanle Awe does not deal explicitly with the unknown soldier phenomenon, but alludes to the underlying circumstances that make for the operation of the unknown soldier in Nigeria's political history. For her, the latent divergence and variance between the formal structure of the Nigerian state and people are primary causal factors for the crisis it faced from the colonial to postcolonial periods. She contends that although the exercise of political power in the precolonial period mostly guaranteed the involvement and the inclusion of the general interest and welfare, and women and the youth were not left out, from the colonial to the postcolonial era, the state became hostile and draconian in its relations with the people and the interest of the majority was sacrificed to serve those of the ruling elite. The extended military era amplified this estrangement, as did ethnic and religious conflict, the oil boom and the corruption it generated. The challenge to state excesses from civil society dates from the colonial era, and while it waned in the years immediately following independence, it was harassed and barraged almost to non-existence during the military era (Awe, 1999).

Fela's music is only one of the indications that while government suppression and violence was alive and well, civil society was not dead. The murder of Olufunmilayo Ransome Kuti was indicative of the military regime's fear that left unchecked, pockets of opposition could grow into waves of resistance. Using the vehicle of the unknown soldier, General Olusegun Obasanjo inflicted extra-judicial force on citizens, spreading chaos, mayhem, wanton destruction of property and death in its wake. Fela, as one of the survivors of this war against its people by the government of Nigeria, made sure that he gave us a lasting memorial to his illustrious mother and documented as best he could some of her contributions to Nigerian political development. He also made sure that we will never forget who was responsible—the unknown soldier.

Olufunmilayo Ransome Kuti died following the Unknown Soldier attack and so did several Aba women participants in the Igbo women's war. Funmilayo Ransome Kuti was a Marxist. She shared with the Aba women, Efunsetan Aniwura and Madam Tinubu, opposition to injustice, abuse of power and racism, colonialism, imperialism and neo-colonialism. In her heyday, Olufunmilayo Ransome Kuti led Abeokuta (a town in South Western Nigeria) women to oust the Alake-(King/traditional ruler) from power. She also spearheaded the founding of a nationwide women's organization and participated in negotiations preceding Nigeria's independence from British colonialism. Instead of being treated as a national treasure, she was mostly ignored in her older years and was finally murdered by the state.

Funmilayo Ransome Kuti, the Aba and Abeokuta women engaged in group action against colonial government both to defend community interests and the interests of women as a corporate group. At both sites in Southern Nigeria, women's traditional associations were organized, mobilized and deployed using modes of resistance that "express their disapproval and secure their demands by collective public demonstrations, including ridicule, satirical singing and dancing, and group strikes" (Forde and Jones, 1959:21). The women also exercised collective associational power that gave women political influence in precolonial, colonial, and postcolonial society, as explicated in the Nigerian experience of the popular Aba Women's War of 1929. Mba (1982) noted that it was the mass movement of Abeokuta Women's Union (AWU) and demonstrations against a flat rate tax of the Egba women that led to Alake of Abeokuta's abdication on 3 January 1949.

Nigerian women's explicit involvement in politics has an illustrious history that embraces the contributions of Queen Amina of Zauzzau, Efunsetan Aniwura, Iyalode of Ibadan, Madam Tinubu, Iyalode of all the Egba, Queen Emotan of Benin, Mrs. Fumilayo Ransome-Kuti, Lady Oyinkan Abayomi of Lagos, the participants in the Igbo Women's War, and in the Abeokuta Great Weep of 1943, as well as Madam Magaret Ekpo. This contribution is documented from the precolonial era to the present, in struggles and campaigns for sociopolitical and economic changes as well as changes in gender relations. According to Mrs. Ransome-Kuti, Nigerian women suffered from diminished economic and political power due to colonialism, and ordinary women could and should use indigenous methods, mechanisms and strategies of organizing social, political and economic action (Mba, 1987). Funmilayo Ransome Kuti took her own advice and mobilized Abeokuta and Nigerian women to resist corrupt, abusive and draconian state policies.

Nigeria manifests the paradox of plenitude of women's social, economic, and political participation combined with profound loss of visibility and prominence particularly in the public political sphere, where there are gross deficits in women's political power, both quantitatively and qualitatively, i.e., in terms of numbers and effectiveness, inequitable distribution of power and persistence of male dominance, systematic and systemic disenfranchisement of women, danger of cynical acceptance of male dominance as the norm, strong perception that women who succeed in politics are mere tokens, and the general subversion of democracy. Women have had to engage in radical politics to bring attention to their cause. Given the dangers faced by such radical women, their action has been necessarily sporadic and strategic, with women fighting and running away, so that they could live to fight another day. Some scholars contend that women's political leadership is relatively new in Africa. Aili Mari Tripp is a good example. For her, there was only a trickle and active participation, a late twentieth-century phenomenon that occurred in the 1990s, which was the first time in the post-colonial era for more women to strive for national and local public elected office. Refusing to be deterred by the low impact and visibility of their initiatives, there was even more insistence on women's political representation and participation. New women's parties were formed to address challenges like non-sensitivity and lack of responsiveness to women's issues and to encompass women's political aspirations, which were either absent or excluded from the male dominated parties. The female political parties were also better able than the male dominated ones to attract multi-dimensional coalitions that transcend religious and ethnic lines.

Tripp paints an encouraging picture that gives much cause for optimism for anyone interested in women's empowerment, but does not capture the experiences of African women either accurately or completely. It is well-documented, for instance, that women were equal participants in the nationalist and liberation struggles in most African countries, and that while colonialism eroded a significant amount of women's formal political power, drawing upon their precolonial bases of power, women in most African countries asserted their rights, sometimes even succeeding in extending such rights, even in the weakened indigenous political structures and institutions. Multi-religious constituencies then were possible with existing parties. Nigerian women formed Western-style political pressure groups early in the 1900s. However, Indigenous women's groups such as the Lagos Women's Market Association, led by Madam Alimotu Pelewura, and other indigenous originated women's corporate organizations preceded these Western-style institutions.

The Lagos Women's League, which was founded in 1901, and led by Mrs. Charlotte Obasa, was an example of the modern pressure groups. Trailblazing efforts were developed in the 1940s when under the leadership of Mrs. Kofoworola Abayomi, the Nigerian Women's Party was formed (on May 11, 1944) as a reaction to women's marginalization in the male dominated political parties, which for Mrs. Oyinkan Abayomi and others, had demonstrated that they were not interested in women's issues and allowed for no women in their leadership. Similarly, Mrs. Funmilayo Ransome Kuti founded the Abeokuta Women's Union (AWU) in 1949, and the organization became the Nigerian Women's Union (NWU) later that year. Both the AWU and NWU involved a combination of Western educated women with women traders. The AWU used this coalition to challenge the combined powers of Alake Ademola and the British colonial government for compelling women to pay taxes. The AWU mobilized, supported, and joined the women in public disobedience campaigns that culminated in the temporary abdication of the Alake.

Between 1948 and 1949, branches of the Union were formed in Ijebu Ode, Ijebu Remo, Ilaro, Egbado area, Benin, Ibadan, Calabar, and Aba. Mrs. Margaret Ekpo had founded the Aba Women's Association earlier, and was inspired to join the NWU after Funmilayo Ransome Kuti's visit in 1949. Similarly, Janet Okala, G. I. Okoye, and Madam Peter Okoye had founded the Enugu Women's Association in 1945. The organization's name was changed to the Nigerian Women's Union, Enugu branch in honor of Funmilayo Ransome Kuti's visit on December 18, 1949, in the aftermath of a fatal violent attack by colonial police against striking miners in Enugu. By 1950, there were branches of the Union in Enugu, Aba, Ijebu Ode, Ikare, and Onitsha. Between 1950 and 1953, there were branches in Zaria, Kaduna, Jos, Kano, Jebba, Kafanchan, Funtua, Ilorin, Ekiti, Ilesha, Ado Ekiti, Asaba, and Abakaliki. The organization was conceived as a federation with autonomous branches. Funmilayo Ransome Kuti was the national President as well as the President of the Abeokuta branch. Mrs. Ekpo was National Secretary and she presided over the Aba branch. The political objectives of the Union were:

(1) Achievement of the franchise for women.
(2) The abolition of electoral colleges.
(3) The allocation of a definite proportion of representation to women with women being allowed to nominate their own representatives on the local council, which should not be headed by traditional rulers.

In 1952, Elizabeth Adekogbe founded the Women's Movement in Ibadan. Nigerian women also participated in most of the indigenous pressure groups and political parties formed in the nationalist era: the Nigerian National Democratic Party (NNDP), Action Group, National Council of Nigeria and the Cameroons (NCNC), the Nigerian Youth Movement (NYM). All these instances of Nigerian women's political participation and activism preceded the illustrious actions of the women detailed by Aili Mari Tripp.

Nkoyo Toyo, President of Gender and Development Action (GADA), makes a somewhat different point: "Nigerian men have always dominated the political space with women playing inconsequential political roles at all levels of decision-making. Even the women who were actively involved in the independence struggles soon found out that when it came to sharing the spoils they were dispensable." However, she goes on to distinguish between conditions now and the precolonial situation when there were women founders and rulers of kingdoms such as Ebele Ejaumu, founder of the Igala kingdom. A woman is reputed to have founded Ondo, and Ilesa had five women Owas (monarchs). In addition, there were a variety of women's associations. Orompoto, who succeeded her brother, Egungunoju was one of Òyó's precolonial Aláàfins (monarchs) who were women. Queen Amina of Zauzzau is renowned for her leadership in war and peacetime, and several institutions existed that gave formal political power to women.

WOMEN'S RADICALISM AND ACTIVISM

"What have we women done to warrant our being taxed? We women are like trees which bear fruit. You should tell us the reason why women who bear seeds should be counted." Enyidia of Oloko (one of the protagonists of the Aba Women's War) Women's activism in the anticolonial struggle in Southern Nigeria reveals how the form of rule shapes the form of revolt against it, and how indirect rule both "reinforced ethnically bound institutions of control, and led to explosions from within." By considering the struggle of women in Southern Nigeria, it is possible to evaluate the limits of citizenship for women under a system that in postcolonial Nigeria still maintains the essential characteristics that originally marginalized and excluded them. Three different types of administration were imposed on Southern Nigeria as part of the indirect rule system—the Sole Native Authority system in the South-Western Provinces, the Warrant Chief System in the South-Eastern Provinces, and the Local Township government system in the Colony of Lagos.

In each case, women were consciously excluded. (While the traditional power of chiefs, priests, king makers and other titleholders to provide checks and balances against abuse of power and arbitrary rule was eradicated, women did not reap the benefits. Male titleholders could be appointed to the native authority councils, and men were appointed as warrant chiefs. In Lagos, however, women could participate in the traditional political system that was allowed to coexist with the colonial administration but the Lagos Town Council (LTC) was created as a counter-force to traditional authority. This allowed for women's participation, albeit in a limited way, given the constraints of a colonially imposed political order. In the South-Eastern and South-Western provinces women's prior access to political power was eliminated and avenues for them to exercise authority prevented. Women chiefs like the Iyalode were stripped of their power and the avenues for their exercise of autonomy cut off.

In spite of being entirely circumscribed by the oppressive colonial state, women activists in Southern Nigeria engaged in vigorous struggles against the infringement on their interests and those of their communities. State imposition of unfair and unjust taxation galvanized women into political action in both the South-Western and South-Eastern provinces. Education for girls, equal pay for equal work, increased employment opportunities and political representation for women were issues that were identified as crucial. Women's organizations were formed which built on the precolonial pressure groups and associations organized and controlled by women in rejection of their status as oppressed subjects under colonial rule. With the development of anticolonial nationalism, political organizations that were led by men welcomed and encouraged the involvement of women only to the extent that they would be foot soldiers in the struggle to deracialize power.

To the extent that women's organizations were agreeable to joining nationalist organizations as members of their adjunct women's wings, there were grounds for the cooperative struggle against colonialism and for nation building. When women refused to be subsumed under male-controlled party rule, they were marginalized in a manner akin to the treatment meted out to women by the colonial state. The struggles of women in the South-Western and South-Eastern provinces and the colony of Lagos from 1914 to 1966 are indicative of the imposition of the citizen-subject dichotomy on Nigerians under British colonization. It also indicates a rejection of subjection by women activists, the demand for citizenship not just for women, but for poor men as well. This potentially democratizing move toward the decentralization of the power of the native authorities and warrant chief system, and for the extension of civil and political rights to Nigerians in the colony, was nipped in the bud.

As self-government and independence approached, the emphasis shifted from a combination of deracialization and democratization to an admixture of deracialization and despotism. Traditional checks and balances against despotic rule had been eliminated under colonial rule. It is a hallmark of postcolonial Nigerian politics that the struggle for federal resources has taken on a "no holds barred" nature that pits community against community and generates the riotous politics for which Nigeria is renowned.

There were several indicators of women's rejection of the status of subject under colonial rule. By resisting government encroachment against their sphere of influence, women in the protectorate of South-Eastern Nigeria used their tradition of collective sex solidarity to push for influence in society. This, in spite of colonial constraints against the visibility, representation, and participation of women in the public sphere. While some of the early women's movements and associations called for a return to traditional society and social mores, later groups sought active participation in politics during the nationalist era.

Although traditional symbols (mass dancing while singing derisive songs to send distinct messages on women's displeasure) were used to express women's displeasure during the Nwaobiala movement in the mid 1920s, colonial standards of justice were questioned. The legitimacy of a system that was externally imposed was also rejected. The Ogu Umunwanye, the Women's War, which started in 1929, went even further to challenge colonial policies that were abhorrent economically, morally, psychologically, and politically. Taxation without consultation and representation was rejected. The women's puzzlement was expressed eloquently during the collective punishment inquiry for the Oloko native court area that was conducted by the colonial government. Enyidia of Oloko, for instance, said in an interview, "What have we women done to warrant our being taxed? We women are like trees which bear fruit. You should tell us the reason why women who bear seeds should be counted." This, according to Afigbo, is a challenge to the ethical and philosophical basis of taxation. It is also a critique of governance through imposition, without explanation of the rationale for the government's action. Ogu Umunwanye was also indicative of a rejection of the warrant chief system, which victimized women, and excluded the legitimate traditional rulers.

In the event that the colonial government was loathe to eliminate the warrant chief system, some women proposed the election of chiefs in a process where men and women participated by suggesting that "If a new man is appointed, then all the women should be present and all the men should be present and both should approve his appointment." Some women, believing that white women got superior treatment, asked for the same treatment that white men gave to their womenfolk. A case in point was Mary Onumaere, a leader in Nguru, who said: "We have not been treated well. We wish to be treated just as Europeans treat their women in their own country. We don't want to be oppressed by our menfolk." The tenacity and breadth of organization involved in the women's war is indicated in the continuation of the agitation in other areas of the protectorate, such as the Owerri province. Protests did not stop until it was certain that women were not to be taxed and courts were reorganized to allow for limited terms, people's participation, and the inclusion of some traditional rulers (the ezeala) and "younger, enlightened men" The women's war was significant as a catalyst for women's organized mass protest against the injustices of colonial administration.

Protest against taxation continued into the 1950s. With self-government came an imposition of taxation on women in the Eastern Region. Women in Aba and Onitsha resisted through mass demonstration; Aba women formed a new organization, the Aba Women's Association, which passed a vote of no confidence against Mrs. J. N. Egbutchay, president of the Aba branch of the National Council of Nigeria and the Cameroons (NCNC), and the sole woman councillor in the Aba District Council for supporting the government's finance law. Onitsha women's market association issued a press release which threatened to support an independent candidate against the NCNC in the next elections. In response, the Eastern House of Assembly raised the minimum taxable income for women. In debates of the finance bill in the Eastern House of Assembly, at least one member, Eyo Ita, argued that if women were to be taxed, they should also have representation in the local councils and House of Assembly.

FROM LADINES TO WOMEN: MASS MOBILIZATION IN DEFENSE OF WOMEN'S RIGHTS IN THE WESTERN REGION

The more women sought active participation in politics during the nationalist era, the more the emergent bourgeoisie sought their incorporation as subaltern support groups. The political activism of the Abeokuta Women's Union (AWU) was an example of Egba women's struggle against the despotism and exclusionary politics of the Sole Native Authority (SNA) system. The SNAs had sweeping, far-reaching powers. All previous checks and balances on the power of the traditional ruler, the Oba, were cast away under the indirect rule system. King makers, chiefs, and priests who previously could act to limit the abuse of power and arbitrary rule of Obas were now dependent on the SNA for their appointment to advisory councils. In essence, they were rendered ineffectual. For women chiefs such as the Iyalode and Erelu, the limited entree that allowed the male chiefs to participate in the Native Authority System was nonexistent. A few women's titles such as Iyalode and Erelu remained but they were devoid of power.

Under the leadership of Mrs. Olufunmilayo Ransome Kuti, a mass movement was organized, which built on the existing organizations of Egba women. Through it, they resisted the status of subject under the SNA. The objectives pursued included resistance against the poll tax, against the harsh enforcement of sanitation regulations, and the payment of the water rate, as well as the removal of the Alake of Abeokuta, Oba Ademola from office. Resistance against colonial taxes and against the imposition of the SNA in Ijemo in 1914, and Adubi in 1918 were met with violence from the colonial state. By 1946, Egba women were not only protesting against the imposition of direct taxation, they opposed price controls and the negative ramifications of its policies on their group interests. The well-organized Egba Women Dyers and Adire Trading Union were able to oppose the Alake's prohibition of the use of imported dyed and caustic soda as damaging to their trade, and were able to mount a sophisticated campaign of petitions and memorializing to the Alake, the ENA council, District Officer, Resident, and the members of the Legislative Council representing Abeokuta and Lagos.

The organizations hired a Lagos-based lawyer, WNA Greary, to defend them. They engaged in press campaigns and mobilized so much pressure against the Alake that he was forced to establish a Commission of Inquiry in 1936 which found the SNA's contention that the women's use of caustic soda and imported dyes was damaging adire cloth (tie-dye and batik) baseless. Based on the commission's recommendations, the Alake-concocted restrictions were lifted. Other women traders were not as well organized to combat the SNA's incursion on their autonomy by imposing price controls on food. However, the cooperative mobilization of Western educated and non-Western educated women traders under the leadership of Olufunmilayo Ransome-Kuti moved women's activism to a higher level of radicalism. Initially, Mrs. Ransome Kuti's focus was on social welfare. Together with other educated women, she was the founder of the Abeokuta Ladies Club (ALC)—a group of Christian-educated women teachers and traders who engaged in good works, sewing, and catering, and who were actively supported by the wives of British officials in Abeokuta.

The organization aimed among other things, "To help in encouraging learning among adults, and thereby, wipe out illiteracy . . . and to help in raising the standard of womanhood in Abeokuta." The literacy campaign combined with teaching and sewing to market women directly involved the ALC in market women's struggles against colonial government seizure of their goods without compensation (on behalf of the rice sellers association). Complaints to the Assistant District Officer, the District Officer, and the Resident yielded no relief. Attempts to lobby the members of the ENA council were stymied by the Alake who refused to allow the council to discuss the matter. The ALC publicized their campaign in the press thus: "We the members of the ALC, on behalf of all Egba women, appeal to the press of Nigeria to help bring the seriousness of the position to the attention of the authorities before it is too late." Six days later, rice control was eliminated in Abeokuta.

The ALC followed up its success by drawing up resolutions demanding improvements in sanitation, water supply, provision of clinics and playgrounds in schools, and financial support for adult education. These resolutions were circulated widely to the holders of power—the Alake, ENA council, Resident, and 20 prominent chiefs. Part of the resolution was: That there should be no increase on the taxation paid by women, as the majority of women in Abeokuta are very poor and can hardly afford what they are now paying. That there should be free trade between Egba people and all other provinces, and that there should be no restrictions as to what should be taken from one place to another except such restrictions as dictated by national necessities which must be determined by the judgement of the majority. The ALC was absorbed into the Abeokuta Women's Union (AWU) in 1946, with its leadership assuming leadership in the new organization. While continuing its interest in social welfare, it became radicalized in its goal of "eliminating the causes of hardship."

Guided by Olufunmilayo Ransome Kuti's vision of non-violent struggle, socialist orientation, and anticolonial ideology, the AWU was motivated to consider Nigerian women as oppressed under colonial rule, as having lost more than men (due to the loss of their traditional economic and political power) as a result of the decentralized despotism of the SNA system. In addition, women were denied suffrage, forced to pay taxes, and denied basic social services. To combat the gross exploitation of women, radical mobilization was necessary. Women had to organize to gain political power, demand suffrage and participation in government, and if necessary, changes in the system. Accordingly, the Aims and Objects of the AWU Constitution were directed toward defending, protecting, preserving, and promoting the social, economic, cultural, and political rights of women in Egbaland and cooperating with all organisations seeking and fighting genuinely and selflessly for economic and political freedom and independence of the people.

The achievement of women's rights, interests, and freedom from the SNA was considered impossible without the abdication of Alake Ademola and the eradication of the SNA system. The Alake was vigorously criticized, since he was considered the personification and symbol of the SNA to the detriment of his people's well-being. Although ultimately the colonial government was the source of real power, the AWU attacked its agents, the SNA and Alake. For Nina Mba, this was an indication of the lack of understanding of the real source of power. Mamdani however presents an alternative way of considering the revolt against native authority. For him, native authority was a site of struggle for those chafing under colonial oppression, particularly because the subject population had been incorporated into the arena of colonial power through the despotic organization of power under the native authority. The AWU's struggle against the native authority can then be seen as a struggle for bottom-up democratization, which, if it succeeded, strikes at the heart of the decentralized despotism of colonially imposed domination. The rationale for resisting despotism at the local level arose from considering the despotism of foreigners as unacceptable, but still as paling in significance to one's own kinfolk's collaboration with the oppressor. If collaborators can be curtailed and disabused from selling out, the basis on which despotic rule is based is challenged, political participation can be broadened and principles of consultation and representation respected.

The AWU challenged the Alake's abuses of food and price controls, his interference in trade, particularly the attempt to establish monopolies by obtaining special privileges from European firms, interference in court matters, particularly the abuses of dowry payments, and of the dipomu system (that enabled women who sought refuge from their abusive spouses to take refuge in the Alake's palace. Once they grabbed hold of a support column on the premises, they were traditionally guaranteed refuge). It was alleged that the Alake was profiteering from the system by charging women for accommodation, and that he also demanded sex from some of them. In addition, the Alake was charged with exploitative and corrupt practices in the leasing of land and the enforcement of building regulations. For the AWU, the documentation and publicization of its grievances were a crucial element in the struggle against the inequities and injustices of the despotic SNA administration. In a memo to the Resident's Commission of Inquiry on May 31, 1948, the AWU said: "The system of SNA system had been a great source of the oppression and suppression to the Egba people."

Even most of the members of the council were not free to express their minds. The Alake always posed as "Mr. Know All." The complaints of the union also included grievances about the abuse of power by the native authority police and the SNA's disinterest in checking them, the demand of taxation from women without any commensurate benefits, and the failure to provide social services for women and children. In essence, the AWU demanded guaranteed rights of citizenship. To redress some of the inequities and injustices under the SNA system, the AWU hired an accountant to audit the SNA treasury in order to document unnecessary expenditures. The AWU argued that women did not have to pay taxes if the SNA husbanded its resources properly and took alternative measures instead of direct taxation to raise revenue. Ultimately, the AWU challenged the poll tax by arguing that there should be "no taxation without representation," thus, it called for the representation of women on all bodies that administered Egba affairs by members of the union. The AWU's rationale was that since men had not protected women's rights, women's representatives are needed to do so.

Using mechanisms including mass demonstrations, which involved the singing of derisive songs and abuse directed against the Alake; pressure group tactics, including petitions and propaganda; legal processes; press campaigns, including letters to the editor, articles, and press conferences, the AWU achieved one of its primary objectives when Alake Ademola abdicated on January 3, 1949. Other objectives were achieved to a limited extent. These included the abolition of women's taxation and increase in the flat rate for men in 1948 and the appointment of four women to the Egba Central Council that replaced the SNA. Egba women gained political participation on an unequal footing vis-a-vis men (as construed by the ideals of liberal democracy), but they were only able to generate a limited degree of change in the colonial policy of excluding women.

The limited gains made by women did not translate into participation in decision making. Men dominated in the first political parties while actively depending on material and mobilizational support from women. The Nigerian National Democratic Party (NNDP), National Council of Nigeria and the Cameroons (NCNC), and Nigerian Youth Movement (NYM) garnered varying levels of support from women's groups. However, women did not feature prominently in the leadership of these and other parties during the nationalist era and after independence. The few parties formed by women either died quick deaths or were absorbed into the male-dominated parties.

THE POSTCOLONIAL PERIOD

Increasingly, women were incorporated into the political system as subordinate, ineffectual adjuncts to men. Thus, the nature of their incorporation reveals the persistence of male dominance and gender bias over time. Some women were elected into local government councils in the South. In 1961, three women were elected into the Eastern House of Assembly. From 1960 to 1966, two women were appointed to the federal senate. There were no female ministers at either federal or regional levels. Women did not feature prominently during the preparations made by the Obasanjo/Yar'Adua regime for returning power to civilians. No woman was appointed to the fifty-member Constitutional Drafting Committee, very few women were elected into the local government councils during the 1976 elections, and only Mrs. Janet Akinrinade was elected to the Constituent Assembly. Four other women were appointed to the 250 member assembly. This limited the potential influence and participation of women in bringing issues that favored them to the forefront. The design of mechanisms for enforcing existing constitutional protections for women was also unaddressed. The administration appointed Mrs. Womiloju Idowu as head of the Ogun State government during the final stage of the transition to civilian rule. She was the only woman so appointed. 51.3 percent of the registered electorate were women, five of the 52 associations formed were led by women, but none was registered by the Federal Electoral Commission (FEDECO).

The National Council of Women's Societies, formed in 1959 as an umbrella group for all women's associations in Nigeria, formed the League of Women Voters for the purposes of educating women voters on the exercise of their civil rights, identifying candidates and parties that would promote the interests of women, and working toward involving more women in policymaking. The League was later disbanded. Many of its prominent members had entered politics, and the FEDECO required that it should be registered as a political association. The nature of women's involvement in the political process has remained constant over time. During the transition to the second republic, there was a resurgence of women's wings in all the registered political parties. The women's wings had representation in the parties' national executive, but did not participate in the policymaking caucuses.

The positions that women held in the parties did not go beyond that of one out of the many vice chairpersons. As happened during the prelude to independence, and during the first republic, parties nominated women as candidates for elections in constituencies where they had little chance of being elected. No woman was nominated as presidential or gubernatorial candidates. Some women were drafted as gubernatorial running mates, and the People's Redemption Party nominated Bola Ogunbo as Aminu Kano's running mate. Four women contested for the 95-seat Senate, all lost. Seventeen of the 2,000 candidates for the 450-seat Federal House of Representatives were women. Three won. Forty-two out of the 5,000 candidates for State Houses of Assembly were women. Five won. Only two of the five registered political parties had any provisions that related to women. The National Party of Nigeria promised to involve women fully in public life, and the Great Nigeria People's Party that day care centers would be provided.

Women gained more prominence during the second republic, but their political presence in decision making remained highly circumscribed. The Shagari regime appointed three women as federal ministers, more women than ever before won elections into the national and state assemblies, and the policy of having one female member in each state cabinet, instituted by the Mohammed/Obasanjo regime, continued. Although these gains were made, there were no concomitant improvements in the quality of life of the majority of Nigerians. Infringements on the rights and liberties of citizens increased, with the government using the police and military forces to terrorize its opponents. Women's groups demanded and got a National Committee on Women and Development, but it was made a unit of the child and family welfare section of the Directorate of Social Development in the Ministry of Social Development, Youth and Sports. Its functions were advisory, and the government resisted all demands to upgrade it to departmental level and to grant it executive status, as required by the OAU and UN.

After the coup d'etat that catapulted it to power, the Buhari regime continued with the Obasanjo/Yar'Adua policy of token representation for women in federal and state cabinets. The Babangida palace coup in 1985 ushered in a regime that had no women in the federal cabinet, but proclaimed a policy of equal opportunity, and the emancipation of women. Thus, one out of every four nominated local government councillors was a woman, there was a woman on every government board and parastatal, two women were appointed Vice Chancellors, and the Better Life Program was inaugurated ostensibly to "fully integrate women into the production process."

As part of the process of designing Nigeria's future political system, a Political Bureau was created. Although the bureau was charged with making recommendations on the role of women, only two women were appointed to the Political Bureau in 1986. Several women's associations were commissioned by the bureau to present Nigerian women's ideas. It is instructive to consider the recommendations made by Women in Nigeria (WIN), one of these associations. WIN consulted with ninety-seven women's associations in seven zones. It did not only consider the role of women in politics, but the gendered nature of the structure of government and forms of representation, family relations, the socioeconomic and legal systems. Legal and constitutional rights were not only sought in the public sphere, but in the family, work place, and society. WIN's recommendations broadened the concept of democratization to include all spheres of life. As with the women's war, there were instances where women's rights as mothers and qualities attributed to women were used to push, argue for, and promote the superiority of women as leaders.

In general, women's associations demanded 30 to 50 percent representation in legislatures and cabinets. The NCWS demanded the revival of the League of Women's voters, and that all administrative and legal impediments to women's equality be removed. The Political Bureau recommended that 5 percent of legislative seats at all levels be reserved for women. However, the government rejected this recommendation, maintaining that reverse discrimination would constitute an infringement on equal opportunity for all. This is in spite of the existence of a quota system in Nigeria and the use of the principle of "federal character" to ensure balanced geographical spread in employment, admissions, the location of projects, and recruitment into the armed forces. The regime was later to appoint six women to serve in the Constitution Review Committee (CRC), a forty-six member body. Nine women were appointed, and five elected to the 567 member Constituent Assembly.

Within the Constituent Assembly (CA), the identification of some issues as "no go areas" by the Babangida regime ensured that the jurisdiction of Sharia courts and the structure of Nigerian federalism would not be discussed. Sharia courts operate only in the Northern states, and they make decisions on all aspects of a Muslim's life, particularly in the area of personal law. Laws of inheritance, divorce, property rights, and custody of children are some areas where women have traditionally been discriminated against. Some women's groups that made representations to the Political Bureau demanded legal reforms in these areas. The government, however, foreclosed any opportunities of discussions and possible reforms. The operation of the federal structure in Nigeria has also had discriminatory ramifications for women who marry and live outside their state of origin. Such women may be discriminated against in employment, promotion, admission to schools, and other entitlements. When women asked for a redefinition of the federal structure, they wanted these issues to be discussed and resolved. Again, this was not done.

Although not formally allowed yet, most of the parties that were formed in preparation for the third republic were formed in the CA. Since women were in the minority, it stands to reason that there would be few formed by them. In addition, only the very affluent could afford to meet the conditions established for party formation—an office, paid officials, at least 200 members in all 499 local government areas. It was also required that twenty copies of the names, photographs, and other information on the members be submitted to the NEC within three months of lifting the ban on partisan politics. The Nigeria Labour Party was formed in large part, due to the efforts of the Nigeria Labour Congress Women's Wing. Unfortunately, the party was one of the thirty that applied for registration and was rejected by the NEC. Most of its members later joined the Social Democratic Party (SDP). When the National Republican Congress (NRC) and SDP were created by government fiat and registered, the National Electoral Commission ruled against women's wings, thus ending the institutionalized formalization of Nigerian women's subordination to male politicians. While this could well be interpreted as ending the treatment of women as second class citizens, it did not provide institutionalized amelioration of their subordinate position in the political arena. In response, the National Commission for Women (NCW) and NCWS demanded that both parties outline their platforms for women but the political parties only made a cursory reference to women's issues, barely stating a commitment to their full emancipation, participation, and involvement in all areas of life.

Paradoxically, the very measures that were introduced to ensure that women had more prominence and visibility only reinforced the predominant tendency toward the tokenism and co-optation of prominent women. As part of the Babangida regime's commitment to a dual transition, while the political transition was underway, the Structural Adjustment Program was also adopted against the wishes of the overwhelming majority of Nigerians. The pains of the program were much deeper than the meager gains yielded. On the one hand, the Babangida regime engaged in convincing

Nigerians that there were some gains to SAP, and upon failing to convince them, provided some vestigial measures that were woefully inadequate to assuage labor and other anti-SAP critics. On the other hand, the first lady, Maryam Babangida consulted with an ad hoc committee composed of professional women to develop the Better Life for Rural Women Program (BLP). According to its architects, the program was to have empowered women politically and economically, but it institutionalized a system where the first lady became the national chairperson. Governors' wives became the state chairpersons, and wives of local government chairmen, the local government chairpersons. Women were thus co-opted into the state as was done previously—as a subordinate but ineffectual part of the power structure.

There is no doubt that Mrs. Babangida wielded a great deal of power when compared with previous first ladies. There also is no doubt that the highest levels of decision making were devoid of women. Much money was spent on the BLP. Several programs were established, and mobilizational campaigns undertaken to register women voters. More women than men voted in the elections. Pressure from women's organizations led to a decree establishing NCW in 1989. The commission had an advisory board composed of one chairperson and ten members, all appointed by the president. Its secretariat was headed by an executive secretary. It was charged with implementing the board's recommendations. The commission was part of the executive branch, and since it was located in the presidency, it was hoped that it would bring women's issues into the forefront, and institutionalize women's participation in decision making.

The BLP was incorporated into the NCW as one of its three departments, and eventually, Mrs. Babangida replaced Professor Bolanle Awe as the chairperson of the Advisory Board. This shifted the focus of the commission in favor of BLP programs. The BLP succeeded in having a presence in every local government area, but its tangible achievements were very limited. In general, women's participation in decision making was highly circumscribed, but within the bureaucracy, as is customary in post-independent Nigeria, some women who rose to prominence successfully pushed for better conditions of service, including an end to discrimination in salaries, wages and taxation, as well as tax relief for women with children. In spite of these gains, the Babangida regime remained essentially authoritarian. Government opponents and critics were harassed and detained. The spouse, and female relatives of coup suspects were detained and held hostage until the suspects surrendered. Some state assemblies passed laws that targeted and penalized women. Within the NRC, there were two state chairpersons, Bosede Oshinowo in Lagos, and Helen Gomwalk in Plateau State.

Within the SDP, more women had positions of authority at the local government and ward levels. Compared with 1,091 men who were chairpersons, deputy chairpersons, and secretary in both parties, there were only twenty-nine women in similar positions. A total of 209 women were party executives, but 31 percent of them were ex-officio members. There were 159 women members of local government councils, which included 6.9 percent as chairpersons, 31.5 percent as deputy chairpersons, and 61.6 as councillors. A total of twenty-seven women out of 1,172 members of state houses of assembly were women (2.3 percent), one woman out of ninety senators, and ten women out of 593 members of the Federal House of Representatives. There were seven women out of 293 gubernatorial candidates, none was elected, although there were two deputy governors. Only one woman ran during the 1992 presidential elections, which was later canceled. One woman participated in the presidential primaries in 1993. Although there are, no de jure barriers against women's participation in decision making, there are in fact, few opportunities to participate on an equal footing with men. The process is dominated by the wealthy and most of these are men.

As the Babangida regime became more dictatorial and authoritarian, and as the ramifications of the combined effect of Nigeria's economic crisis and the Structural Adjustment Program led to deepened poverty among majority of Nigerians, it also became clear that the regime was unwilling to leave power. Critiques and protests increased exponentially. These included demands for economic as well as human and civil rights. Such demands were mobilized by workers' pro-democracy and women's associations. When the regime scuttled the transition, there were women among its critics and also women among those calling for its perpetuation in power. The same was true for conditions under the Abacha regime, which unceremoniously threw out the transitional government put in place by Babangida after he was forced out of office. The regime created the Ministry for Women, and the Family Support Program to replace the National Commission for Women and the Better Life Program. The Family Support Program further subsumed women's issues under those directed at protecting family integrity.

During the transition to civilian rule, women were again, relegated into the background. Many news media reports attest to the marginalization of women in contemporary Nigeria's political economy. Do reports like these indicate that women are perpetually marginalized, and that this is a condition that derives from traditional mores? To properly answer this question, it is clear that gender analyses have to be more rigorous. If as Nigerian women, we claim that our marginalization is an integral part of our tradition, we have to indicate in what manner such marginalization has occurred, we have to be specific about what forms of marginalization were manifested, and moreover, we have to indicate what women we refer to in our analyses. Is every female a woman in each and every case of social, economic, and political interaction? Is each woman equal to the other? Do all women suffer in the same manner from the heavy weight of patriarchy, and thus, become automatic lifetime card-carrying members of a global sisterhood of the oppressed? Is the observed marginalization of women in contemporary Nigerian politics a legacy of our precolonial past, our unchanging culture, and our primitivity? Luckily, there are now new and different voices that approach these questions from a more informed, balanced perspective.

Funmi Iyanda's article in Tempo, titled "An Opinionated Female" is just one example of a more accurate rendition of history, a clearer vision in representing women's history and the role of women among the Yoruba in Nigerian society. The contention that I make is that despite the gross diminution of women's power and presence in the public sphere that attended the colonial project that, despite postcolonial governments' relegation of women into the background, there is still evidence of women's power. Such evidence largely go unrecorded because most of our work replicates those that study us precisely to dominate us. It is clear that there is a hegemony in the production of knowledge that favors the West and Westerners, whether they are men or women, friends or critics of Africans. This hegemonic system produces or signs off on most of the knowledge on Africans, including Nigerian women. Thus, scholarship on all things African reveals a great deal of homogeneity. The concluding section will address these questions in the context of Nigerian federalism.

STATE VIOLENCE IN 20TH-CENTURY NIGERIA

Scholars and analysts differ over whether or not Nigerian women have always participated actively in the country's politics. For some, despite the difficulties encountered during the colonial era, women's political activism was directed at recovering some of the administrative and political powers that were denied them (Mba, 1982). Historically, Nigerian women have been shown to participate in governance since the precolonial period. Some were rulers; others were public officials with institutionalized offices and powers in their communities and realms. The position of women in society was clear. Ibibio women, for example, had the Iban Isong organization, which protected and extended women's political, economic, and social privileges. Many women's organizations continued to thrive under colonialism. However, political rights were denied both men and women, and as incremental rights were granted to men, women became increasingly excluded and marginalized.

The imposition of colonialism and its structural consolidation generated some powerful resistance, some memorable ones spearheaded by women, who resented the erosion of their powers and the imposition of unacceptable draconian measures such as taxation without representation and illegitimate rulers who refused to be responsive to their people's needs. Notable among these was Ogu Umuwanyi, waged by the Igbo and Ibibio women which culminated in the 1929 Aba women's war. Mrs. Funmilayo Ransome Kuti and the Abeokuta Women's Union also confronted an insensitive Alake who was widely believed to be a colonial stooge. In a categorical denial of women's rights, the British left them out as they undertook gradual political reforms such as elections and constitutions. Women could neither vote nor contest elections. Thus, Ityavyar was right in saying: "one would not be far from right to suggest that colonialism is the midwife of the political marginalization of women in Africa."

Nationalist struggles continued during the relaxation of some of the draconian conditions that marked the end of colonialism and the inception of Western forms of democratic governance, but did not yield much gain for women in the higher echelons of public office and political power structure. This tradition continues today and has become the watershed characteristic that is used in most analysis to define Nigerian women's political participation and power. For most others, the marginalization and oppression of Nigerian women in indigenous society continued unabated until the present.

Apologists could well make a claim that there were no women in military or the top echelons of the civil service, but there was neither sensitivity to the need for policies that ensured that women could aspire to rise to these positions through training, mentorship, and sponsorship for requisite higher education. None of the military governors appointed by General Gowon was a woman. The Federal Executive Cabinet was composed of 11 civilians and 14 members of the armed forces and police. Not one was a woman. This blatant disregard for women was most unwarranted because there were numerous Nigerian women professionals in law, medicine, and higher education who had advanced degrees and requisite experience and could have been recruited for the positions seemingly reserved for men. There was a similar absence of women in the cabinets of state military governments, but a few had one token woman.

In his first iteration as the primary decision maker in Nigeria, General Olusegun Obasanjo maintained the male dominant strategies of colonial and previous postcolonial governments in Nigeria. Women were also prevented from participating in determining the rules under which the country would operate in the proposed post-military era. This decision was met with complaints and agitation. The Constitution Drafting Committee (CDC), a body of 50 "wise men" were selected for their qualifications, experience, and on the basis of ensuring equitable representation from the 19 states, in existence at the time. Unfortunately, although it was well past the middle of the twentieth century (1978), not one Nigerian woman was included. While women in Southern Nigeria got the franchise in the 1954, along with all Nigerian men, women in Northern Nigeria were still not allowed to vote or be voted for until Obasanjo's military regime, though a decree approved the universal franchise for women in 1976.

The women in the South had been enfranchised for over 29 years before their sisters in the North. The deliberate denial of the franchise to Northern Nigerian women was not uncontested. One very significant example is the case of Hajia Gambo Sawaba, who was a tireless, tenacious, and relentless champion for the rights of the poor, marginalized, and excluded. She fought valiantly for women's rights, including the franchise. Just because of her participation in politics, government officials labeled Sawaba a prostitute. She was beaten, jailed more that 17 times and was once expelled from the city of Kano by the Emir of Kano. This onerous experience means that she holds the record as the most frequently jailed Nigerian woman, jailed purely because of her involvement in politics.

Idika Ogunye collected and analyzed diachronic (historical) statistics for Nigerian women's participation in politics. She demonstrates that in the democratic transition process of the early 1990s, only 27 (2.3 percent) of 1,172 legislators in the various states' House of Assembly were women, and none of them won. Only one woman was elected senator in the second and third republics. The political executive committees did not fare better; 3.99 percent of the executive committee members of the Social Democratic Party (SDP), and 4.32 percent of those of the National Republican Convention (NRC) were women. Only two to three women were appointed as cabinet members during the period. The trend continued in the 1997 local government elections when less than 1 percent of the elected chairpersons were women. Less than 1 percent of the members of the House of Representatives (in 1998) were women.

In the first term of the Obasanjo civilian administration (1999–2003), women represented only 3 out of 108 senators, 12 out of 360 members of the House of Representatives, 1 out of 774 Local Government Chairpersons, and 1 deputy governor out of 36. This very marginal presence of women in positions of authority is better appreciated if considered against the fact that women constitute about half of Nigeria's population, and more than half of its voters (27 out of 47 million in 1999). Apart from malicious and pernicious myths about women's inferiority, there are also inaccuracies about the impact of high levels of social and economic indicators. For example, it is generally believed that better and higher levels of education and socioeconomic status signal increased levels of women's political participation.

This assumption is questionable, since Nigeria's South-West zone has women who are well educated and affluent, but who have not done significantly better than women in the Northern political zones in producing women who are elected into political office. Even parties that claim to be devoted to women's advancement such as the AD and PDP do not engender policies that support affirmative action and promote women's issues. All the political parties are also beset by factionalization, dissension, clashes among opposing forces, carpet-crossing to bandwagon with the winning coalition, and a benign neglect of any agenda that would propel women into the forefront of Nigerian politics.

During the Abacha years (1994–1998) Nigeria experienced the most brutal dictatorship in its history, and the dictator had plans to succeed himself as an elected civilian head of state. In the same period, the State and Federal Commissions for Women were converted into Federal and State Ministries of Women Affairs. Theoretically, the new policy was designed to enhance the participation of women in decision making. Many women participated in the Abacha transition. After the 1998 elections, which were held before Abacha died, 20 women became members of the 360-strong Federal House of Representatives, while 9 women became senators out of a total of 109. Upon Abacha's death, the elections were revoked. Women were not as successful in the succeeding elections organized by General Abdulsalam Abubakar in 1999.

The elections leading to the fourth republic produced disquieting results. Only 631 women out of 11,881 candidates for elected positions were women. Of these, 12 women made it into the House of Representatives, a minuscule number out of 360 members, and there were only 3 women out of 109 Senators. Twenty-seven million or about 57 percent of the 47 million registered voters in the 1999 general elections were women; however, only 1.6 percent of them won elections. Women's membership in political parties was 5 percent in 1999, only 7 percent of them were party executive members and a mere 8 percent were party delegates.

Today, despite the weight of Nigeria's postcolonial history, one of the encouraging signs in the Nigerian political terrain is the emergence and efflorescence of civil society organizations among which women's organizations, women's activist organizations, and women's studies scholars are in the vanguard. Another encouraging sign is the large number of women candidates relative to past elections. The impediments to women's participation in politics include the lack of consideration for women's issues, violation of party rules and plans for affirmative action, weak political institutions, the use of zoning and other gerrymandering strategies to prevent women from attaining political office, the pervasiveness of an "old boys' club," supported by rich and powerful men dubbed "godfathers," collusion to engage in corrupt practices, the construction of religious and cultural prohibitions against women's public role in governance, lack of financial capacity, power politics, the use of strong arm strategies, intimidation and violence, machinations within political parties, the construction of gender to forbid women's active participation in politics, women's acceptance of the status quo, structural collusion, and smear campaigns that ruin the reputation of women who dare to participate.

As seen above, there is an enduring culture of the marginalization of women in Nigeria's political system. In spite of the clear desire of more women to participate in the political system, the rhetorical pronouncements by Nigerian rulers on the importance of including women in governance on an equal footing with men, the encouragement given by many women's Civil Society Organizations (CSOs), International Non-Governmental Organizations (INGOs) and Multilateral Organizations, and the impetus drawn from the Beijing Conference, are concrete achievements that demonstrate the realization of affirmative action goals are lacking. This informs Nigerian women's activist organizations' response in their demand for participation that is not restricted to voting in elections, but extended also to the process of ensuring the deepening and broadening of democracy in Nigeria. Thus, women's rights organizations demand the entrenchment of respect for constitutionalism in Nigeria by contesting actively the state's wanton neglect and abuse of citizens' and, especially, women's rights.

Clearly, it is more enlightened and accurate to recognize that there was significant reduction in women's political power during colonialism, and this trend continued in the postcolonial era. This is part of Nigerian history and political culture, but should by no means be considered the beginning point. Men gained distinct political and economic advantages during the colonial era that have in the postcolonial period, been parlayed into strengthening the male-dominant and patriarchal elements of formerly fluidly determined social structures. Women's activism, however, only responds to the contemporary power of men as a given, rather than a reconstructed system of advantages that can be challenged through the use of tried and true old and new mechanisms. Thus, the project that is faced by Nigerian women today is less an unqualified embrace of Western feminist ideology and praxis than a welding together of rehabilitated and recovered best practices from indigenous traditions with strategies, mechanisms, and institutions derived from best practices in the global women's and feminist movements.

Simply stated, gender is socially constructed and concerns the manner in which a society conceptualizes the roles that men and women play, and the power capabilities that are attached to these roles. It is impossible to engage in gender analysis without considering the social context in Nigeria, where seniority sometimes trumps gender, and gender roles are not necessarily biologically determined. This fundamental difference between Nigerian and, indeed, many African societies and Western social relations imply that being female does not confer perpetual second class citizenship on an individual, since the same person who may be discriminated against and assigned to a weaker social role in some respects, for example, as a wife, may also exercise significant power as a "husband" in her natal family. In the precolonial era and during the early days of colonialism, some institutions like woman-to-woman marriage also enabled women to acquire other women's labor and children in order to enhance their ability to generate wealth. Applied to social relations in general, gender could empower or marginalize, depending on the existing temporal and material conditions as well as social circumstances.

What is the best way to conceptualize political participation? Most scholars tend to use elections as a gold standard for measuring levels and depth of citizen participation. However, most scholars of democracy are also highly skeptical that elections can generate the deepening of democracy, while activists and the development industry in general vouch for the efficacy of elections as a tool for instantiating and consolidating democracy. A minority, including Staffan I. Lindberg, and Samuel Huntington, present a strong defense of elections as a valuable resource for the deepening of democracy. The scholars distinguish between political competition (as candidates for elections) and political participation (as voters who elect the candidates, and as pressure groups and interest groups in civil society). Pearl T. Robinson in considering transitions from authoritarianism highlights the strong impact of the culture of politics on regime change and democratic transitions. For Robinson, the "culture of politics" is socially legitimated and validated political practices that are derived from a community's historical and contemporary knowledge base. Its mores can be easily apprehended by all, be they elites or ordinary people. They are also not immutable, but are subject to constant change, consequent upon political learning. They permeate the social codes, practices, traditions that regulate relations of "power, authority, participation and representation."

There is no consensus on how to conceptualize or understand women's political participation and the consequent effects on politics and political systems. Some scholars complain that there is much confusion and misunderstanding of what women's political participation entails, and why it is essential. Thus, there is widespread belief that women's participation in politics is only about mainstreaming gender through equitable representation of women in the political system, and thus, that this is an exclusively women's question. Instead, women's participation ought to be seen as crucial to the success and endurance of democracy. It is then imperative that those interested in women's political participation also attend to all matters related to fostering women's power throughout the political system. According to Lovenduski, women's political participation can be conceptualized as crucial to the deepening of democracy, and it involves both descriptive and substantive representation. Descriptive representation concerns the election and appointment of women into office, while substantive representation can flow from descriptive representation, and it relates to the insertion and incorporation of women's issues into policymaking.

Commitment to gender balance in governance and the creation of an agenda and structure that makes this possible are fundamental aspects of required strategies. The persistence of gender inequalities retards both economic development and social well being for all citizens. Research-derived evidence indicates that more impoverishment, less economic growth, lower quality of life and standard of living accompany gender inequality, and tilt the balance in all respects toward countries that work assiduously toward gender equality. In countries desirous of equal participation in the global agenda setting, gender equality is a matter of national security. There is a belief on the part of Nigerian women's organizations that there is rampant discrimination and gross marginalization of women in Nigerian politics. The need for increased and more effective women's participation is widely acknowledged. Consequently, these organizations decry the incremental nature of changes but acknowledge there are some noteworthy gains. The most significant to date is that a woman has been speaker of the House of Representatives. However, the percentage of women in the national and state legislatures, as well as in the executive branch, and in local government councils remains woefully inadequate. For these organizations therefore, the struggle continues, at least until the 30 percent Beijing and Millennium Development Goals recommended threshold be reached.

There is still a great deal of misperception of women's political participation. Since most attempts to enhance women's participation in politics focus on achieving gender equality, this issue still tends to be perceived as limited to pushing women's interest and not as a human right that is also vital to the survival of democracy. What ought to be done is to concentrate on the initiatives that would give women more powerful roles and make their participation worthwhile. For this to be accomplished in Nigeria, it is crucial that the political system be structurally re-designed to accomplish gender balance in governance issues. Awé, Johnson-Odim and Mba give us examples of women who have taken leadership roles in their societies. From these studies, it is clear that when we speak of women, we ought to specify that there are class differences among them which imply that some women are granted social, political, and economic privileges that are not open to others.

CONCLUSION

The majority of Nigerian citizens remain subjects in the colonial tradition. The rights of citizenship are extended to the few. The only meaningful difference between colonial and postcolonial governments in Nigeria is the deracialization of state power without the concomitant decentralization of power. Thus, in de facto terms, most Nigerians stand in relation to the state, as subjects, not citizens. During the colonial era, citizenship, defined as the ability to explicitly and actively participate in government as a vigilant member of civil society, was extended to the few Nigerians that "qualified." The postcolonial state maintained that situation. Until the rights of citizenship are extended to all Nigerians, particularly women, through decentralization that allows full participation in the political process, the state will remain remote from the people. It will also not reach its full potential. By continuing to exclude women, the state and the Nigerian federation remain incomplete.

From its inception, the state in Africa has excluded categories of people—all the "natives," and particularly, their women. When very few Africans were redeemed from "nativeness," to citizenship, women were deliberately and consciously excluded and so were the poor. Nigerian governments continue to do this, whether military or civilian. The problem with Nigerian federalism is the fusion of power at local, state, and federal levels. This is clearest under, but it is not limited to, military regimes. Military regimes have only narrowed the political arena by abrogating the rights of participation through voting. This chapter addressed questions of the meaning of political power, the capacity to exercise that power, and the extent to which women can participate in the political system as full citizens. It considered issues related to the meaning and the implications of the unequal access that is built into the state structure.

REFERENCES

Agozino, Biko and Anyanike, Ike (2007) IMY AHIA: Traditional Igbo Business School and Global Commerce Culture. *Dialectical Anthropology* Vol. 31, No. 1–3, pp. 233–252.

Awé, Bólánlé (1977) The Iyalode in the Traditional Yoruba Political System, in Alice Schlegel (ed.), *Sexual Stratification: A Cross-Cultural View*, chap. 7, pp. 144–60. New York: Columbia University Press.

Awé, Bólánlé, ed. (1992) *Nigerian Women in Historical Perspective*. Lagos: Sankore/Bookcraft.

Awe, Bolanle (1992) Saviours of their Societies, in *Nigerian Women in Historical Perspective*, Bolanle Awe (ed.), Lagos: Sankore Publishers Ltd., 1–10.

Ayandele, E. A. (1966) *Missionary Influence on Modern Nigeria, 1842–1914. A Political and Social Analysis*. London: Longman.

Coquery-Vidrovitch, Catherine (1996) *African Women: A Modern History*. Boulder, CO: Westview Press.

Drewal, Margaret Thompson (1992) *Yoruba Ritual: Performers, Play, Agency*. Bloomington: Indiana University Press.

Forde, Daryll, and G. I. Jones (1950) *The Ibo- and Ibiobio-speaking peoples of South-Eastern Nigeria*. London.

Johnson-Odim, Cheryl, and Nina Emma Mba (1997). *For Women and Nation: Funmilayo Ransome-Kuti of Nigeria*. Urbana: University of Illinois Press.

Lawal, Babatunde (1996) *The Gèèlèèdéé Spectacle: Art, Gender, and Social Harmony in an African Culture*. Seattle: University of Washington Press.

Matory, James Lorand (1994) *Sex and the Empire That Is No More: Gender and the Politics of Metaphor in Oyo Yoruba Religion*. Minneapolis: University of Minnesota Press.

Mba, Nina (1982) *Nigerian Women Mobilized*. Berkeley: Institute of International Studies, University of California.

Okome, Mojúbàolú Olúfúnké (2001) African Women and Power: Reflections on the Perils of Unwarranted Cosmopolitanism, *Jenda: Journal of African Culture and Women Studies*, 1(1).

Oyewùmí, Oyerónké (1998) *The Invention of Women: Making an African Sense of Western Gender Discourse*. Minneapolis: University of Minnesota.

Oyewumi, Oyerónké (1997) *The Invention of Women: Making an African Sense of Western Gender Discourses*. Minneapolis: University of Minnesota Press.

Wescott, Joan, and Morton-Williams, Peter (1962) The Symbolism and Ritual Context of the Yoruba Laba Shango," *Journal of the Royal Anthropological Institute of Great Britain and Ireland*, 92(1): 23–37.

18

Women, Grass Roots Movements, and Democratization in Nigeria

Iwebunor Okwechime and Akin Iwilade

ABSTRACT

This chapter examines the role of women in grass roots movements in Nigeria. It argues that while grass roots movements are central to the ferment of democratic values in the country, they have been generally excluded from the organized civil society and that this undermines their ability to impact on the democratic process. The chapter situates the exclusion of grass roots movements from the broader agenda of civil society within the continued dominance of liberal political ideals that privilege corporate monopoly organizations with the resources to engage the state and transnational NGOs. These organizations are increasingly able to frame the democratic discourse in ways that exclude grass roots movements and their typical radical views about the nature of wealth creation and distribution. The chapter argues that women's organizations have been particularly active in this radicalization of grass roots politics. This is because the peculiar gendered impact of economic crisis on the grass roots makes women particularly vulnerable and thus forces them to define local resistance in the context of relations of power and its implications for economic reproduction. Women are thus victims of not only economic crisis but also of social structures that marginalize them. In this analysis, however, the role of women organizations within grass roots movements is located largely in the struggle against exploitation by hegemonic forces rather than a struggle against male power. This is critical to draw attention to the practical utility of women's involvement in local resistance rather than to abstract feminist ideals. In the analysis, we examine two women organizations: the Federation of Ogoni Women Associations (FOWA) and the Niger Delta Women for Justice (NDWJ). These two movements demonstrate both the successes and challenges of women groups within the context of grass roots movements and situate their exclusion from civil society. They also highlight the importance of economic conditions in inducing the participation of women in local resistance movements and demonstrate the imperative of their incorporation for democratization. In concluding, the chapter looks at the impact of exclusion on the democratization process and makes a case for not only the inclusion of grass roots movements within the architecture of civil society, but also the incorporation of gender sensitivities within grass roots movements themselves.

INTRODUCTION

At the core of this chapter is an interrogation of the role of women organizations in grass roots movements in Nigeria. It examines this role within the context of global discourses of disempowerment and resistance and of the widespread economic crisis that has deepened the radicalization of the grass roots. It also examines it within the context of feminine identity and its practical utility in social mobilization and resistance. This is unlike orthodox Western constructs of gender that tend to place emphasis on abstract rights rather than on concrete benefits.

The chapter also places women's involvement in grass roots movements within the democratic discourse. By looking at the democratic deficit that is a consequence of the tendency to exclude grass roots movements from mainstream civil society and therefore from peaceful engagement with the state, the chapter highlights the salience of grass roots movements in the democratization process and makes a case for their incorporation.

In setting out its arguments, the chapter is divided into seven closely linked sections, the first of which is this introduction. In the next three sections, we engage conceptual issues like democracy, civil society, and grass roots movements. This places our analysis within firm conceptual boundaries and highlight the context within which we use the terms. In the next two sections, we look at the relationship and linkages between the terms. We then go on to examine the specific experiences of two women organizations (Federation of Ogoni Women Associations (FOWA) and Niger Delta Women for Justice (NDWJ). After this, we examine in a broader context the experience of grass roots organizations within civil society. We then go on to situate this problematic within the democratic movement. The seventh section sums up our arguments and concludes.

CONCEPTUALIZING DEMOCRACY

Even though many Western democracies consider the liberal version as most appropriate for the provision of public goods and for promoting sustainability in the development process, this view may not necessarily capture the specific conditions of the developing world. Political theory offers a rich variety of approaches to democracy that more accurately reflect the differences in history and social formation that have framed international politics. While Sen and Dreze (Sen, 1981; Sen and Dreze, 1989) argue, for instance, that democratic systems are more likely to prevent absolute disasters such as famines, a natural throwback to Immanuel Kant's democratic peace theory, public choice theorists contend that it may in fact compromise economic development. They therefore call for strong states with the "political will" to push through required economic reforms. This perception of the role of the state in the economic system underpinned the adjustment interventions of the World Bank and IMF and largely spurned authoritarianism all over Africa (Gibbon, Bangura, and Ofstad, 1992). Although scholars like Francis Fukuyama (1992) consider liberal democracy as the highest possible political achievement possible, others call for caution at establishing a hasty "end of history." Hawthorn (1993), for instance, argues that the particular history of democratic development in the United States had been unduly used as the singular prism through which democracy was viewed. This ignores the specific histories of many states in the developing world whose experience with democracy has been far less than rewarding. To those states, therefore, the notion of what constitutes an optimal political system may vary immensely. This perspective indicates that to be relevant in the developing world, political inquiry must grapple with the very different social conditions and must recognize the salience of this dynamic to the emergence of specific political systems.

Ake (1993) argues that, for Africa, democracy has no meaning if it does not involve concrete economic gains. His approach questions the prevailing orthodoxy in the global democracy movement which has reduced popular participation in the democratic process to the mere election of representatives. In his opinion, the African conception of democratic participation is "quite unlike the Western notion of the occasional opportunity to choose, affirm or dissent. It is rather the active involvement in a process, that of setting goals and making decisions" (Ake, 1993:243).

Tracing the origin of the capitalist state and the form of government built to sustain it, Ake notes that the need to protect private property was the principal reason the state was instituted and that the political processes of the state would inevitably exclude the property less class except to the extent that it keeps them from threatening the rights of the propertied (Ake, 2000:7–32). This assertion agrees fundamentally with Marx and Engels that the state arose out of irreconcilable class antagonisms.

Perhaps the most significant aspect of Ake's perspective is its attempt at particularizing democracy in Africa and establishing a critical framework from which its peculiarities may be understood. Also important for our purpose here is the re-establishment of the pre-liberalism conception of politics as not the moment of particularity but that of universality, the marriage of the individual to the collective in such a way as to emphasize the common good without necessarily hindering the egoistical advancement of the individual. In the African context, this perspective of rights is of particular importance as Africans view individual social existence as essentially tied to that of the collective and as Ake (1993:243) puts it, they do not regard themselves as self-regarding atomized beings in competitive and potentially conflicting interactions with others.

The emphasis on concrete economic benefits for the largest possible percentage of the populace as the basis for the legitimating of the democratic or indeed any other system is fundamental to our treatment of Nigeria's democracy and the place of grass roots organizations in it. This becomes particularly significant where disaffection occasioned by the perceived unfair distribution of resources between classes on the one hand and within the privileged class on the other is generating violent resistance and increasingly forces the state to react in kind thereby undermining the democratization process.

The fundamental concern of the democratic system is to align itself in inextricable ways to the central values of the society and to ensure that the people actually govern. This can only be achieved when the opportunities for creative self-expression in both the political and socioeconomic realms are completely decentralized and de-bureaucratized. The democratic state in this sense exists only for the purpose of protecting the polity from tyranny and enlarging the platforms for leadership.

WHAT IS CIVIL SOCIETY?

Identifying the conceptual boundaries of civil society presents complex analytical challenges. Civil society may refer to the realm of organized social life that is open, voluntary, self-generating, at least partially self-supporting, autonomous from the state, and that is bound by a legal order or a shared set of collective rules (Diamond, 1999:221). This definition limits civil society to those groups that accept the primacy of the state and locates it in democratic politics and is accepted by many other scholars (Walzer, 1991; Cohen and Arato, 1992; and Anheir, 2004). Adebayo Olukoshi (1997:474), in contrast however, defined civil society as being made up of associations—voluntary, autonomous, professional or non-professional which have arisen out of the self-organizational efforts of various social forces. While this definition effectively captures the broad outline of civil society groups in much of Africa, it fails to situate them within the overall context of the state. In an attempt to emphasize their autonomy, the significance of state action or inaction is largely lost. It however allows the conceptualization of organizations that compete, at times violently, with the state as a part of that space called civil society.

In a much broader perspective however, civil society has been articulated as differentiated from both the economy and the state. In this version of a threefold society, culture plays an important role in providing societal cohesion and continuity in the event of societal chaos triggered by the failure of both an undemocratic state and a totalitarian economy.[1] This theory explains civil society from the perspective of state hegemony. The state is not to be understood in the narrow sense of the government; instead, it is made up of "political society," which is the arena of political institutions and legal constitutional control, and "civil society," which is commonly seen as the "private" or "non-state" sphere, including the economy. The former is the realm of force and the latter of consent. One important feature of this conceptualization of civil society is that it highlights the relevance of state action and notes that the space referred to as civil society may indeed, in reality, often overlap with that described as political society. Another important feature of this conceptualization of civil society is that it demonstrates the ability of alternative hegemony, albeit that of consent, to develop within the civil space to challenge the arbitrary exercise of state power.

Implicit in this conception of civil society is its functional purpose as an alternative center of power. The idea of civil society as the realm of consent does not necessarily imply consent to state authority. That consent mentioned by Gramsci refers to the nature of power relations *within* the alternative social forces. Its relations with the state are hardly that of consent. Civil society in fact, particularly in the context of a state that fails to provide answers to developmental questions, thrives on its ability to confront, at times violently, the state. Civil society is thus legitimated less for its normative value and more for its functional value as a competitor for popular support and a challenge to state authority.

Indeed, rather than civil society operating within the realm of consent with the state, it often operates indifferently to it. This thesis is at the heart of Peter Ekeh's work on the "two publics" in Africa (Ekeh, 1975). Viewing civil society from this perspective, one may easily draw the conclusion that state action or inaction is crucial to the direction and texture of civil advocacy. It largely defines the type of contact that will characterize the fault line of contestation between the state and society. It therefore precludes the exclusion of violent organizations like the Movement for the Emancipation of the Niger Delta (MEND) from the broad space referred to as civil within society.

As Fatton (1995:71) explains it, civil society can be quite uncivil; being replete with antinomies. Acute social problems created by the existence of a shadow economy indicate that "civil society can be a source of great inequalities and coercions." This implies that civil society need not be "civil" in its agenda and *modus operandi* to qualify for that appellation. It also implies the understanding that it would be naïve, indeed false, to expect civil society to be divorced or abstracted from its social base. It will inevitably reflect the patterns of social relations and the class structures of society. Thus, civil society, "by generally reflecting the lopsided balance of class, ethnic and sexual power" tends to "privilege the privileged and marginalize the marginalized" (Fatton, 1995:72).

In the light of this challenge to the "doing good" perception of civil society, it is clear that its character is affected by the political economy of the state. For instance, the pre-industrial nature of African states makes significant shadow economies inevitable. These shadow economies in turn fund and perpetuate linkages that easily connect to the class based patronage system of the state and undermines the value of civil society as that mythical all encompassing movement for popular empowerment and economic change (Bayart, 1986; Chazan, 1992; Diamond, 1988). The political climate also plays a significant role in the texture and character of civil society. It is in this sense that we view civil society in the context of democracy. There are unique features of civil society to be found in a democracy, whether nominal or popular.

WHAT IS A GRASS ROOTS MOVEMENT?

The very idea of democracy depends on the participation of citizens in the political process. The concept of grass roots therefore speaks to the most basic forms of participation. It addresses the depths of society and champions the needs of the most vulnerable. The concept of "grassroots" was once very specific: it meant the basic building blocks of society—small rural communities or urban neighborhoods where the "common people" lived. In some contexts, it was used to signify the poor, labor, or working class, as opposed to dominant social elites; in others, it was usually applied to rural, village-level communities rather than to urban ones (Batliwala, 2002:393–409).

Today, globalization and the emergence of a "global" citizen have changed the way in which the term "grassroots" is used. Consequently, the meaning of grass roots movements is also undergoing profound change. For example, articles,[2] written about both the protests at the World Economic Forum in New York City and the deliberations at the World Social Forum in Porto Allegre are put under the heading "Grassroots Globalization." Both authors make it clear that they consider these very separate activities, attended by very few of the really poor or marginalized, as expressions of grassroots voices. So it would appear that in a national or local context, grassroots means one thing, and in the context of global activism, quite another. This creates conceptual and analytical problems in the attempts to understand grassroots movements at the transnational level.

In the context of developing societies like Nigeria however, grass roots movements cannot but refer to the marginalized class in society. Their social mobilization largely develops out of the failures of the state to fulfill basic elements of its social contract with society and the consequent formation or intensification of other patterns of loyalty that often call to question the very survival of the state. While grass roots organizations in Nigeria are largely defined by ethnic, kinship, and blood loyalties, there is often a decidedly economic motive behind their mobilizations. The need to survive the pressures induced by a failing economy and the collapse of the welfare state is perhaps the most compelling factor that ensures the perpetuation of the grass roots in Nigeria.

It is therefore difficult to assume an active cosmopolitan character for the grass roots without taking into consideration the structures of class, dominance, and power relations that are easily reflected in social mobilization. The salience of economic factors in the texture of social relations is crucial to the understanding of the role grass roots organizations play in defining and/or participating in the agenda of civil society and its consequent role in the democracy project.

WOMEN IN GRASS ROOTS MOVEMENTS: TWO CASE STUDIES IN NIGERIA

This section intends to situate women organizations within grass roots movements in Nigeria. In doing this, it highlights, on the one hand, their exclusion and marginalization by an essentially patriarchal social space and a climate of economic crisis that undermines their chances for economic reproduction. On the other hand, it also demonstrates their resistance to this marginalization and the fruits, however marginal, that this resistance has borne. The two case studies are taken from the oil rich but crisis prone Niger Delta area. This is important because the region provides archetypal samples of the resistance movement in Nigeria. It also places resistance properly within the broad context of the economic pressures and crisis that neoliberal reforms induce and the gendered class interests that often frame the nature of resistance and the distribution of its gains.

The Federation of Ogoni Women Associations (FOWA)

The Federation of Ogoni Women Associations (FOWA) is one of the organizations that make up the Movement for the Survival of Ogoni People (MOSOP); the umbrella organization that champions the resistance of the Ogoni minority to the state-multinational oil company alliance in the Niger Delta. The organization was formed in 1993 along with eight other units that make up MOSOP. According to Barikor-Wiwa (1997:46), this organization had evolved, at a time in its history, to become the strongest of the affiliates of MOSOP and its most vibrant. Along with the National Youth Council of the Ogoni People (NYCOP), FOWA is the arrowhead of the Ogoni struggle against the state-multinational oil company alliance. FOWA can however not be fully contextualized and understood if it is not placed within the broad context of crisis and resistance in the region.

The Ogoni number about 500,000 people and occupy a landmass of about 100,000 square kilometres. This dense population is home to many oil installations. In Naanen's (1995:65–75) words, "Ogoni is host to six oilfields with numerous overland pipes connecting various oil installations, two refineries, a huge fertilizer plant, petrochemical plants and an ocean port." This huge oil complex would appear to make for a highly industrialized and developed region. This is however not the case as Naanen (1995:65–75) makes clear when he refers to Ogoni as representing "the paradox of capitalist accumulation—as the poorest and the most industrialized enclave in Nigeria."

The paradox described by Naanen is at the heart of the crisis that has engulfed Ogoni land since the 1980s and more intensely in the period between 1994 and 1997. The spectre of environmental damage and widespread destruction of livelihoods by activities related to oil exploration and exploitation easily combined with social exclusion and political marginalization to deepen the intense resentment among the Ogoni minority to the very presence of Shell, the major multinational oil company operating in the area, and to the implications of its activities for their capacity for economic reproduction.

This resentment, and the fact that it was generally ignored by the Nigerian state, translated what was essentially a largely peaceful resistance movement into a very violent and tragic one. Before the resistance movement in Ogoni culminated in the execution of Ken Saro-Wiwa and eight others, in November 1995, it had appropriated discourses on the international scene like the declaration of 1993 as a year of indigenous people by the UN and effectively internationalized the struggle. This internationalization added a crucial dimension to the Ogoni struggle that wrested the moral high ground from the state and threatened its very survival. This was to prove very fatal for the Ogoni as the state reacted very brutally, clamping down on MOSOP, arresting and eventually executing its leaders. It was in the context of this highly combustible polity that FOWA emerged. According to Obi (2003:20), FOWA played critical roles in the mobilization, organization, and education of Ogoni women. By its representation in the steering committee of MOSOP, it also made direct inputs into its policies, strategies, and tactics. It was thus an organizational and capacity building platform for Ogoni women. FOWA is unique among the units that constitute MOSOP in that it combined activist roles with cultural and reproductive health issues. This reflected its gendered status and perhaps helped to enhance its relevance within the MOSOP structure and within the Ogoni people itself.

FOWA's participation in the Ogoni struggle had been, from the word go, framed by historical marginalization and vulnerability. Barikor-Wiwa (1997:47) for instance notes that FOWA was to a large extent impelled by the fact that "those who suffered most were the women and children, who, unlike the young men, could not easily migrate to the urban areas." This cultural fixation was at once a liability as it was a critical asset for the Ogoni resistance. In the sense that it magnified the vulnerability of a large part of the society, cultural immobility was a liability for the women of Ogoni and ultimately for the resistance itself. This immobility was however a huge asset for FOWA as it entrenched it within the social formations of the Ogoni and guaranteed that it became the connecting point for other groups. FOWA played this card quite efficiently and grew to become, with NYCOP, the fulcrum around which the resistance revolved.

It should be noted that the success of MOSOP, in spite of brutal state responses, in placing the crisis in Ogoni land and even to a greater extent, the entire Niger Delta region, at the centre of global discourse could not have been possible without the contributions of FOWA. The resource struggle in the Niger Delta was effectively presented within multiple frames by the Ogoni movement. Indeed, the environmental, human rights, gender, security, and developmental implications of oil and capital within the region were highlighted significantly. FOWA was integral to this success.

The role of FOWA within MOSOP reflects the benefits of incorporating women groups in grass roots movements. It also demonstrates the capacity of women to act as agencies of social action rather than subjects or mere victims. With its 126 local branches and international offices in Toronto, St. Louis, Missouri, and Ohio, FOWA demonstrates the capacity of women groups to mobilize, coordinate, and sustain grass roots movements.

FOWA has however not been able to outgrow the crisis bedeviling MOSOP itself, perhaps reflecting a continued dependence of women movements, within the peculiar context of social resistance, to the patriarchal structures of society. As Obi (2003:23) notes, FOWA's fate has been "intimately linked to the fortunes of MOSOP." This raises the question of the overall extent of FOWA's capacity for mobilization outside of the towering image and drive of MOSOP.

THE NIGER DELTA WOMEN FOR JUSTICE (NDWJ)

According to Obi (2003:23), the Niger Delta Women for Justice (NDWJ) emerged from the dialectics of Ijaw resistance against environmental degradation, exploitation, and the marginalization of the Ijaw minority ethnic group. Once again, we see a women organization emerging out of discourses of marginalization and exploitation. Like FOWA, this organization also relied significantly on a close affiliation with a youth group, this time the Ijaw Youth Council. Together, these organizations formed the fulcrum around which the Ijaw grass roots resistance to the state-multinational oil coalition turned.

State attacks on MOSOP had served not only to force its retreat from the resistance but also to underline, for the benefit of other minority groups in the Niger Delta, their precarious position in the Nigerian federation. The Ogoni resistance had a major demonstration effect within the Niger Delta so much so that many other groups promptly picked up the gauntlet following the execution of Ken Saro-Wiwa and the other eight. The Ijaw ethnic group, by far the largest in the Niger Delta region, soon became the poster boy of the resistance movement and the NDWJ played a prominent role in its activities. Formed in December 1998, its birth, according to Obi (2003:24) "coincided with the highpoint of Ijaw youth nationalism and local resistance."

The famous Kaiama Declaration set a radical template for the activities of the NDWJ and inevitably set it on a collision course with the Nigerian state. Even though its involvement in the radical and often violent, local resistance of the Ijaw is what brought it into direct confrontation with the Nigerian state and its allies in the multinational oil industry, the NDWJ was also quite effective, much like FOWA, in promoting social cohesion, cultural survival, and community development within the Ijaw communities. Indeed, in the context of widespread incapacity or even unwillingness of the state to provide the most basic public goods for the region in spite of the huge revenue that was daily being extracted from there, NDWJ appropriated many of the functions of state and further deepening its alienation from the society. The organization, within the limits imposed by its peculiar circumstances, was largely effective in fulfilling its mission statement which was to "facilitate the empowerment of disadvantaged women particularly those in rural areas, through programs of participatory development" (www.ndwj.kabissa.org).

NDWJ also worked with foreign donors like the X-min-Y Solidarity Fund based in the Netherlands and with local NGOs like Environmental Rights Action (ERA) to build coalitions that straddled the critical interface between human rights, environmental governance, gender and political inclusion. In doing this, the NDWJ established its undeniable credentials as an agency of the Ijaw grass roots movement rather than as a pawn in its politics.

It is clear from the above that NDWJ consciously framed its resistance within the broader imperatives of the Ijaw grass roots resistance. It was at the same time able to draw attention to the peculiar gendered interests of women and plug their demands firmly into the global and local discourses of disempowerment and resistance.

The two organizations reviewed briefly above reflect the salience of issues of economic disempowerment and crisis in social mobilization at the grass roots level in Nigeria. The ease with which these women organizations were integrated within the broader grass roots resistance movements also indicate the ability of class identity to transcend or even accommodate gendered interests. What they do not necessarily show however is the relevance of grass roots movements, as distinct and historically peculiar political agents, within the formal organized civil society. Even though the contact of both organizations with civil society organizations like ERA would appear to indicate a coalescing with organized civil society, it should be noted that it does not reflect the dominant trend. In the first place, the Niger Delta region was particularly combustible and its centrality to the survival of the Nigerian state and to the continued solvency of many major oil multinationals makes it a unique analytical space. Grass roots movements have generally been excluded in civil society activities to the extent that their radical claims and demands contradicted that of the much more conservative NGOs. This particular divergence in the perception of the depth of remodeling required for the Nigerian state is at the heart of the tendency to exclude grass roots organizations within the architecture of civil society. It is to this problematic that we now turn.

GRASS ROOTS MOVEMENTS IN CIVIL SOCIETY: THE NIGERIAN EXPERIENCE

Grass roots movements are an important part of the civil society architecture in Nigeria. Even though they remain under researched, they are the kernel of representation of the common people and their priorities are inextricably linked to the developmental challenges faced by the larger population. The question is therefore not whether grass roots movements are a part of civil society, but how well have they been shunted to the mainstream of civil advocacy. To what extent have their priorities connected to the broader developmental issues prioritized by the state? What is the linkage between the largely urban based civil society and the overwhelmingly rural or urban slum grass roots movements? Is the linkage complementary or conflictual? What factors determine the dynamics of that relationship? Is there a specific place for women within this milieu?

In spite of the utility of grass roots organizations in the fermentation of democratic values in Nigeria, there is a tendency to ignore them in research into political processes. This is counterproductive because, in the first instance, these movements represent a broader participatory base than orthodox civil society groups and therefore relate more to the developmental challenges of the common people. In the second place, the common people, whose social formations are, in reality, what is referred to as grass roots movements, run the economic reproduction processes in the informal sectors of the Nigerian economy. This sector is where the larger percentage of the population engages economically. Any development agenda will therefore benefit from putting this at the core of its programs. The participation of grass roots organizations, albeit generally unconsciously, in the broader agenda of civil advocacy can therefore benefit immensely from its examination as a distinct branch of civil society. This is because, unduly broadening the term "grass roots" or subsuming it under "civil society," disguises the very real differences in power, resources, visibility, structure, ideology, and agenda between organizations and prevents the understanding of the peculiar role of grass roots organizations in pushing the development agenda. It is important to note that these imbalances are said to have a direct bearing on who can effectively access advocacy opportunities (Batliwala, 2002) and ultimately on the very texture and success of development interventions. Women groups are particularly vulnerable in this respect. Given the patriarchal nature of the Niger Delta and its peculiar context under the weight of the state-multinational oil company coalition, women groups are the most affected by this situation. Indeed, the very capacity for economic reproduction, not to talk of social mobilization, is adversely affected. In response, women organizations have attempted to reconfigure existing gendered class relations and autonomously organize against the exploitation of oil companies and of course the marginalization by the broader civil society. This much was noted by Turner et al. (2001:21).

The economic context within which grass roots organizations in Nigeria evolve and operate is quite harsh. In a place like the Niger Delta, the challenges are exacerbated by years of conflict and the inevitable social dislocation. These challenges are further intensified by the pressures that oil capital and globalization put on the ability of the most vulnerable parts of society; the poor, women, and children; to reproduce economically. The economic hardship has inevitably put the question of economic survival at the very core of social mobilization in Nigeria. Unlike in the West where groups like People for the Ethical Treatment of Animals (PETA) can focus on "mundane" issues like animal care, a significant percentage of grass roots organizations in the developing world focus almost exclusively on issues directly related to economic survival. The salience of economics in defining the trajectory and dynamics of grass roots organizations in Nigeria can therefore not be over emphasized.

The authoritarian character of the state in Nigeria also plays a major role in defining the texture of grass roots mobilization. In spite of the relative liberalization of the political space since 1999, real competition for power and access to the state remains limited. This situation guarantees that grass roots organizations will mobilize either in competition with or in indifference to the state. The limited possibilities for social mobility, increasing pressures on land and, in the case of conflict-prone areas like the Niger Delta, the dislocation occasioned by conflict, have tended to radicalize grass roots demands for democracy and its dividends.

It will appear that the grass roots are more often than not ignored by the organized civil society in Nigeria. This is largely because the organized civil society, as has been demonstrated above, is a compromised lever for the advancement of the public good. The transnational linkages of these organizations easily set the agenda of engagement and invariably blind them to the priorities of the grass roots. The increasing appropriation of this platform by the local elite also tends to immerse the civil society in the class struggle on the side of the hegemony of state and capital. The implication of this for the participation of grass roots organizations in a "modernizing" political economy is immense. For one, they ultimately may not find class solidarity with the often better organized and more visible civil society, with consequences for the strength and intensity of resistance to the predatory state.

GRASS ROOTS MOVEMENTS, CIVIL SOCIETY, AND THE DEMOCRATIC IMPERATIVE: A CASE FOR INTEGRATION AND SOLIDARITY

In and of themselves, grass roots organizations can only do so much. There are compelling arguments for building networks of solidarity between organizations involved with and of the grass roots. There are also forceful arguments for their incorporation in the democratic agenda. These two planks reflect the need to help grass roots organizations transcend the virtual realm and evolve into the realm of action and existentialism.

For one, there cannot be democracy without grass roots participation. It is clear that grass roots participation and mobilization is the legitimating factor of politics in twenty first century Africa. While electoral democracy and liberal market policies may suffice to legitimate the state in the eyes of the Western dominated international community, these neoliberal contraptions often merely exacerbate the crisis of legitimacy faced by many African states in the eyes of African society. Grass roots participation is thus crucial to the legitimization of the state in Africa.

To understand grass roots involvement, however, one must confront the basis of participation in the first place. The question must be asked, what recruits the African to participation in the political process in the first place? Given the alien nature of the African state, a matter that has been demonstrated by many studies (Ekeh, 1975; Ake, 1981, 1985), what factor(s) were responsible for the initial participation of the common people in the nation building project? And how come that they tend to refrain from participation in the era of supposed "re-democratization" since the 1990s?

The answer to this is both obvious and salient. Democracy is only important to the African to the extent that it resolves the crisis of development. It is a vehicle for the liberation of the common man from hunger, insecurity, and the misery of bare existence. As Nnoli (2000, 182) puts it, "the motive force of the struggle for democracy is the overwhelming power of the state and the possibility of its use for domination, exploitation and oppression. That struggle therefore seeks to control and harness power for the purpose of popular emancipation in the economic, political and social realms." Mafeje (1995) also notes that the common people, unlike the revolutionaries who are often obsessed with capturing state power, are only interested in the "implications of state power for their chances of social reproduction." The point being made is therefore that democracy is a lever for emancipation from a near permanent development crisis. It is not some normative and abstract project to be pursued for itself but rather a platform for popular control of the forces that regulate economic reproduction. If this is true, then popular participation in the democratization process cannot be guaranteed when the authoritarian character of the state precludes the possibility of the political process providing relief from the economic crisis. This crisis is intensified in Africa by the context of criminal patronage systems and corruption.

Participation in the early independence period was a product of widespread, if somewhat misplaced, hope that the end of formal colonization will usher in an age of "freedom for all and life more abundant."[3] The acute failure of the development project created bitter disappointment that was reflected in the retraction of the grass roots from state politics except to the extent that it provided a means to appropriate the state for the benefit of what Ekeh (1975) called the "primordial public." By the 1990s and Huntington's "third wave" of democracy in Africa, Africans had lost faith in the state and the dominating elite so much so that rather than participating in the democratization process for the purpose of state building, they engaged it for the possibilities it offered for primitive accumulation. The political process therefore ended up democratizing tyranny. The disconnection between the popular conception of democracy and the electoral brand that came to be institutionalized (this term is being used quite carefully), signposted the crisis of participation that faced democracy in Africa. In the end, what Africa got was a democracy that had been "rendered meaningless and innocuous without losing its symbolic value" (Ake, 1995) or worse still, "civilian dictatorship in civilian attire, with all the institutions of liberal democracy in place but disemboweled of content" (Gana, 2005).

In light of the foregoing, it may be argued that popular participation cannot come to Nigeria's democratization if the democratic process is not seen, by the common people, as, not only engineered to, but also capable of resolving the acute developmental crisis. It is however difficult for anyone, except perhaps the political elite and the international neoliberal forces that promote electoral democracy, to see this process as either capable of or for that matter engineered to deliver what Nigeria's political elite have come to call the "dividend of democracy."

The above demonstrates that the challenge of incorporating or mainstreaming grass roots movements in the democratic pursuit of Nigeria is indeed inextricably linked to the crisis of development. Grass roots participation flows dialectically from the perception of the system as being capable of or in fact, poised to promote development. Development is in itself tied to the participation of the grass roots; from their taking charge of the agenda setting role. This is the dilemma of democratic participation in Nigeria.

The mainstream civil society is a compromised alternative development platform. Indeed, for all its reproduction of existing power structures and increasing control by "local elites seeking to re-position themselves and consolidate their power in the post-adjustment era" (Sakabe and Eloundou-Enyegue, 2006), it cannot, in the strict sense, be considered an alternative development platform, neither can it be said to be representative of the common people. Grass roots organizations that are, on the other hand, ensconced within Nigeria's social formations in their most basic forms must therefore seize initiative and increasingly define the resistance agenda.

Integration is important so that forces for popular democracy in Nigeria can leverage on their respective strengths to wrest the country away from those who are determined to continue its primitive appropriation and expropriation. Grass roots organizations have agendas that strike at the heart of the development crisis. These often simplistic and narrow agendas tend to be much easier to relate to by a broad spectrum of the masses. The mainstream civil society, as tainted as it is, has capacities in the area of cross ethnic and cross sectoral mobilization that may compensate for the tendency of grass roots organizations to be fixated on narrow and mutually exclusive agendas.

It will appear that the creation of an actual movement out of an otherwise virtual grass roots movement is to emerge out of a coalition of and the integration of the much neglected and isolated grass roots organizations and the discredited mainstream civil society. It is in the merger of these two inherently flawed platforms that the type of social formation required to wrest control of Nigeria from the predatory class can be located.

One cannot be accused of being over concerned about the potential challenges posed by this sought of merger. This is not the focus of this chapter. Research would however benefit immensely from interrogating this issue. For instance, can such merger produce a social formation that will be largely immune from the problem of reproducing existing structures of power? Can it overcome the acute challenge of particularistic ethnicity or indeed is it desirable for it to do so? How will the tensions between the increasingly radical perspectives of the grass roots with regard to resource re-distribution and the neoliberal "property right protecting" conception of resource distribution by the mainstream civil society be resolved? How decisive will this tension be in defining the character of resistance? These are questions that further research may benefit from.

CONCLUSION

What we have done above is to critically examine and demonstrate the salience of grass roots mobilization to the democratic process in Nigeria. In doing this, we have also highlighted the relevance of women organizations, as distinct mobilization and analytical units within grass roots movements, to the architecture of democracy. It is clear that the participation of women in the democratic process necessarily flows from the dialectics of their position of disempowerment and marginalization. By combining, therefore, global discourses of gender equality and the practical imperative of strengthening the capacity of women to reproduce economically, women organizations have demonstrated their relevance to grass roots mobilization, in spite of critical challenges.

The role of dominant neoliberal perspectives of development in the tendency by organized civil society groups to exclude grass roots movements from engagement with the state was also highlighted. This tendency is also driven by the conflicting conceptions of the core essence democratic process. While the grass roots organizations tend to place emphasis on democracy's utility as an agency of economic advancement and resource redistribution, the organized civil society appear to be more interested in its normative ideals of free and fair elections, human rights protection, and civil liberties. These different conceptions of the core essence of democracy creates tensions between grass roots movements and urban based organized civil society that hardly helps the cause of democratization.

Overall, the point must be made that at issue, as the above shows, is the fundamental crisis of broad participation in the political process and how grass roots movements can be brought into the mainstream, their cohesion taken from the virtual to the existential and leveraged to deepen democracy. Women organizations must be encouraged to strengthen within grass roots movements. This is crucial to encourage broad participation in the democratic project and to ensure its eventual legitimation. Women organizations deserve to be fully integrated as active participants genuinely capable of affecting the democratization process because they have unique perceptions of social discrimination, vulnerability, and abuse. Because the socialization process puts women in positions of subservience, they seem to be able to relate to concepts of exploitation in unique ways. The disempowerment bred by the exploitative character of economic reproduction in Africa is enhanced for women by traditional practices that limit their ability to engage outside designated social roles. In the light of this unique position of disempowerment, women groups are capable of bringing strong social justice credentials to grass roots movements. Society will thus benefit from their inclusion. By the very fact of their exclusion from politics, women have less stake in the political positions on which conflict turns. It may therefore be less important for them to display "appropriate" political postures that often make conflict protracted and creates problems for democratization. In clearer terms, "if there is a female propensity for peace, it is perhaps because of the male propensity to exclude women from power" (Smith, 1999).

The ultimate challenge of democracy is the incorporation of the largest possible percentage of citizens. Civil society, as the drivers of the democratic process, can therefore not afford to keep grass roots organizations outside the mainstream. The problem faced by grass roots organizations in Nigeria perhaps mirrors the challenge of marginalization that the entire civil society edifice is confronted with. The patterns of funding that forces African civil society to accept the agenda drawn by donor agencies from the West even when they ignore or even deny the specificities of the African context, reproduces itself in subtle ways on the national scene in Nigeria. The orthodox NGOs who get more media attention and can therefore potentially reach larger numbers tend to ignore the grass roots organizations and their priorities. This has critical implications for the depth of advocacy and its effectiveness. It is important that grass roots organizations be allowed to strengthen and come into the mainstream of civil society. This will increase their visibility and help build broad based coalitions that can effectively confront the authoritarian character of the state and deepen the democratic process.

NOTES

1. These views are largely that of Antonio Gramsci as was captured in *State and Civil Society*.

2. See articles like K. Bruno (February 6, 2002). The whole world was watching: New York stages a peaceful protest against the World Economic Forum. *CorpWatch*. www.corpwatch.org and J. Karliner (February 6, 2002). Porto Allegre: Globalizing hope. *CorpWatch*. www.corpwatch.org

3. This was the motto of one of Nigeria's independence political parties the Action Group. It not only mirrored the optimism with which the elite and of course their followers viewed flag independence but also highlights the salience of economic liberation in making sense of political freedom. Talk of "life more abundant" had deep resonance in that period.

REFERENCES

Ake, Claude (1981), *A Political Economy of Africa*. Essex: Longman.

Ake, Claude (1985), The Future of the State in Africa. *International Political Science Review*, Vol. 6, No.1, pp. 105–114.

Ake, Claude (1993), The Unique Case of African Democracy, *International Affairs*, Vol. 69, No. 2, pp. 239–44.

Ake, Claude (1995), *Democracy and Development in Africa*. New York: Brookings Institute.

Anheir, H. (2004), *Civil Society: Measurement, Evaluation, Policy*. London: Civicus.

Barikor-Wiwa, D. (1997), The Role of Women in the Struggle for Environmental Justice in Ogoni. *Cultural Survival Quarterly*, Fall.

Batliwala, Srilatha (2002), Grassroots Movements as Transnational Actors: Implications for Global Civil Society. *Voluntas: International Journal of Voluntary and Non-Profit Organisations*, Vol. 13, No. 4, pp. 393–409.

Bayart, Jean-Francois (1986), Civil Society in Africa, in Patrick Chabal (ed.), *Political Domination in Africa*. Cambridge, UK: Cambridge University Press, pp. 109–25.

Bermeo, N., and Nord, P. (2000), *Civil Society before Democracy*. New York: Rowman & Littlefield.

Bruno, K. (February 6, 2002), The whole world was watching: New York stages a peaceful protest against the World Economic Forum. CorpWatch.www.corpwatch.org.

Chazan, Naomi (1992), Africa's Democratic Challenge. *World Policy Journal*, Vol. 9, No. 2, pp. 279–307.

Clapham, Christopher (2006), The Political Economy of African Population Change, *Population and Development Review*, Vol. 32, pp. 96–114.

Cohen, J., and Arato, A. (1992), *Civil Society and Political Theory*. Cambridge, MA: MIT Press.

Cooley, A., and J. Ron (2002), The NGO Scramble: Organisational Insecurity and the Political Economy of Transnational Action, *International Security*, Vol. 27, No. 1, pp. 5–39.

Diamond, L. (1999). *Developing Democracy: Toward Consolidation*. Baltimore, MD: Johns Hopkins University Press.

Diamond, Larry (1988), Introduction: Roots of Failure, Seeds of Hope, in Larry Diamond, Juan Linz and Seymour Martin Lipset (eds.), *Democracy in Developing Countries: Africa*. Boulder. CO: Lynne Rienner Publishers, pp. 1–32.

Dreze J., and A. Sen (1989), *Hunger and Public Action*. New York: Oxford University Press.

Easterly, W., and Serven Luis (2003), *The Limits of Stabilization: Infrastructure, Public Deficits and Growth in Latin America*. Stanford, CA: Stanford University Press and the World Bank.

Ekeh, Peter (1975), Colonialism and the Two Publics in Africa: A Theoretical Statement. *Comparative Studies in Society and History*, Vol. 17, No.1, pp. 91–112.

Fatton, Robert (1995), Africa in the Age of Democratization: The Civic Limitations of Civil Society, *African Studies Review*, Vol. 38, No. 2, pp. 67–99.

Federal Office of Statistics (2004), *Report of Nigeria Living Standard Survey 2003/2004*. Abuja: FOS.

Fox, Jonathan (2000), Civil Society and Political Accountability: Propositions for Discussion, Working Paper. Hellen Kelloggs Institute for International Studies, University of Notre Dame.

Fukuyama, F. (1992), *The End of History and the Last Man*. London: Hamish Hamilton.

Gana, A.T (2005), The Democracy-Development Nexus, in A. T. Gana and Y. Omelle (eds.), *Democratic Rebirth in Nigeria*, Vol. 1. Afrigov, NJ: Africanus Multimedia.

Gibbon, P., B. Yusuf, and A. Ofstad (eds) (1992), *Authoritarianism, Democracy and Adjustment: The Politics of Economic Reform in Africa*. Uppsala: Nordic African Institute.

Hawthorn, G. (1993), Liberalization and Modern Liberty: Four Southern States, *World Development*, Vol. 21, No. 1, pp. 1299–1312.

Karliner, J. (February 6, 2002). Porto Allegre: Globalizing hope. CorpWatch.www.corpwatch.org.

Larry, Diamond (1999), *Developing Democracy toward Consolidation*. Baltimore, MD: Johns Hopkins University Press, p. 221.

Love, Roy (2004), HIV/AIDS in Africa: Links, Livelihoods and Legacies, *Review of African Political Economy (ROAPE)*, No. 102, 639–48.

Mafeje, A. (1971), The Ideology of Tribalism, *Journal of Modern African Studies*, Vol. IX, No. 2, pp. 252–62.

Mafeje, A. (1995), Theory of Democracy and the African Discourse: Breaking Bread with My Fellow Travelers, in E. Chole and J. Ibrahim (eds.) *Democracy Processes in Africa*. Dakar: CODESRIA.

Magubane, B. (1969), Pluralism and Conflict Situations in Africa: A New Look, *African Social Research*, Vol. VII, No. 2.

Naanen, B. (1995), Oil Producing Minorities and the Restructuring of the Nigerian Federation: The Case of the Ogoni, *Journal of Commonwealth and Comparative Politics*, Vol. 33, No. 1.

National Bureau of Statistics (2004), *Poverty Profile of Nigeria*. Abuja: NBS.

Nnoli, O. (1980), *Ethnic Politics in Nigeria*. Enugu: Fourth Dimension Publishers.

Nnoli, O. (2000), Globalization and Democracy in Africa, in D. Nabudere (ed.) *Globalization and the Post Colonial African State*. Harare: African Association of Political Science, pp. 173–189.

Obi, C. (2003), Emergent Female Power in Popular Struggles in Nigeria: Women Movements in the Niger Delta. Paper presented at an international workshop on Emergent Actors in African Political Economy, organised by the Institute of Developing Economies, Tokyo, February 14–15, 2003.

Okeke, P. (1998), First Lady Syndrome: The [En] Gendering of Bureaucratic Corruption in Nigeria, *CODESRIA Bulletin*, Nos. 3 and 4.

Olukoshi, A. (1997), Associational Life, in L. Diamond et al. (eds.), *Transition without End*. Ibadan: Vintage.

Putnam, R. (1993), *Making Democracy Work: Civic Traditions in Modern Italy*. Princeton, NJ: Princeton University Press.

Sen, A. (1981), *Poverty and Famines*. Oxford, UK: Clarendon Press.

Sklar, R. (1967), Political Science and Political Integration, *Journal of Modern African Studies*, Vol. V, No. 1.

Smith, Dan (1999), Women, War and Peace, in Ingeborg Breines et al., *Towards a Women's Agenda for a Culture of Peace*. Paris: UNESCO Publishing, pp. 57–74.

Srilatha, Batliwala (2002), Grassroots Movements as Transnational Actors: Implications for Global Civil Society, *Voluntas: International Journal of Voluntary and Non-Profit Organisations*, Vol. 13, No. 4, pp. 393–409.

Tito, Yerpes et al. (2009), Making Sense of Africa's Infrastructure Endowment: A Benchmarking Approach. Policy Research Working Paper 4912. Washington, DC: World Bank.

Tocqueville, A. (1966), *Democracy in America*. New York: Harper & Row [1835].

Turner, T. et al. (2001), Fightback from the Commons: General Class Alliances and Petroleum Struggles in Nigeria's Oil Belt: 1980–2002, *Cambridge Review of International Affairs*, Winter 2001/2, Vol. xiv, No. 3.

United Nations Development Program (2006), *Niger Delta Human Development Report*. Abuja: UNDP.

Walzer, M. (1991), The Idea of Civil Society, *Dissent*, Vol. 38, No. 2, pp. 298–304.

Warren, M. (2001), *Democracy and Association*. Princeton, NJ: Princeton University Press.

Yukako S., and P. Eloundou-Enyegue (2006), The Emergence of African NGO's: Functional or Opportunistic Response? *Africa Notes*, April/May.

Zivtev, L. (1991), *Doing Good: The Australian NGO Community*. North Stanley, New South Wales: Allen and Unwin.

19

Gender and the Niger Delta Crises

The Challenge of Local Feminisms

Mashood Omotosho

ABSTRACT

According to the national population census of 1991, more than half of the Niger Delta population are women yet little attention is paid to the urgent needs of women and the consistent violations of their rights by the government forces and the militants in the region. Both the government forces and the armed militants seriously violated the most basic provisions of core international standards established to protect the rights of women and children. The direct insurgencies of the Joint Task Force (JTF) on women are wide ranging. Human Rights Watch reports that women are seriously brutalised and at times they are subjected to indiscriminate acts of violence, including murder, beatings, rape, enslavement for sexual purposes, and labour. A majority of women are among the most vulnerable populations that suffered psychological trauma during times of violent clashes in the Niger Delta. Countless women and girls have been shot and killed or injured in the region.

This chapter therefore examines Niger Delta crises and its impact on women and the discrimination and subjugation they suffered during confrontation between the government forces and the militants. This chapter proceeds to analyse how conflict in that region has caused severe psychosocial repercussions for women. Many of them exhibit trauma symptoms such as fright and insecurity, thoughts about war, and disturbed sleep. This study indicates that exposure to violence puts women at greater risk of future involvement in violence. Immediate and persistent attention to the needs of Niger Delta women is necessary to end the cycle of humiliation and psychological trauma and move toward a lasting peace. Since very little gender-sensitive research has been done on this problem, the project will aim to expand our knowledge base and also enhance our practical strategies for dealing with the social, cultural, and economic problems that accompany the insurgencies in the Niger Delta. It is our submission that women must be given special attention in efforts to address the impact of conflicts and to create the foundations for a stable and prosperous environment for the women folk.

INTRODUCTION

The United Nations Declaration on the Elimination of Violence against Women defines violence against women as "any act of gender-based violence that results in, or is likely to result in, physical, sexual or psychological harm or suffering to women, including threats of such acts, coercion or arbitrary deprivation of liberty, whether occurring in public or in private life."[1] As defined in the Declaration on the Elimination of Violence against Women, violence against women is a prevalent harm to the basic rights, freedoms, health, and welfare of women. It occurs in many settings and at many hands, including those of relatives, acquaintances, employers, and the state. It should be emphasised that violence against women is violence "directed against a woman because she is a woman or that affects women disproportionately."[2] Such violence takes many forms, among them murder; stabbing; beating; rape; torture; sexual abuse; sexual harassment; threats and humiliation; forced prostitution and trafficking. Violence may be physical, psychological, and sexual. It may be manifested through deprivation or neglect as well as through overt use of force or harassment.

In the Niger Delta, violence against women and girls continued unabated at least in the last ten years of the so-called democratic governance in Nigeria. During this period unimaginable brutality was perpetrated against women and girls in the region, for instance, in May 2009, the government forces engaged in an aerial bombardment of the communities that make up Gbaramatu kingdom of Delta state; the area bombarded included Kurutie, Kunukunuma, Kokodiagbene, Oporoza, Okerenkoko, Azama, Benikrukru and Ubefan.[3] These atrocities were committed with the excuse that they were attacking militant camps. Apart from the physical attack, women and girls have been raped by government forces and the police who are responsible for their protection. Women from this region have been maimed or sexually mutilated, subjected to humiliating strip searches, and often later killed or left to die.[4]

In the Niger Delta, armed groups have committed war crimes and crimes against humanity, including intimidation and humiliation of the womenfolk, and other atrocities have been committed against women in the region. As in most conflict situations, women's rights organisation in Nigeria have played a prominent role in addressing the women's rights violation in the Niger Delta area (Olukoya, 2002). Between 2000 and 2006, the National Network for Women in Niger Delta and the Niger Delta Women for Development Energy and Security helped and supported more than 2,000 women and girls who had been abducted by armed combatants. These were mostly women and girls from Gbaramatu kingdom, Odioma and Agge communities (Onduku, 2003). In 2005, the Odioma was completely razed down by the Joint Task Force. The action of the government through the Joint Task Force is a campaign of genocide against helpless women, children, and innocent indigenes of the Niger Delta. During the attack women were subjected to serious humiliation and some of them were raped. Most had acquired sexually transmitted diseases, and many became pregnant.[5]

It should be emphasised that a great deal of literature has explored the various intimidation, degradation and molestation the Niger Delta women and children suffered in the last decade. Let us state clearly that the plight of women in the Niger Delta has not received the attention it deserves. However, the condition of women will be a barometer for the progress and prosperous post-war communities in the Niger Delta. This is because women are the most severe victims of social deprivation. It has been suggested in various fora that a more concerted study of gender-based violence against women in the Niger Delta is required.[6] While this study does not attempt to integrate different directions of study into one, it does attempt to shed some light on the continuum discrimination against women and continued violence against women in the Niger Delta. The study also discusses the strategic and security implication of the Joint Task Force insurgencies in the region. Finally, the study suggests that for the interest of peace and stability, there is the urgent need to protect women from gender-based violence, including armed violence, whether committed by a state official, an abusive husband, a criminal, or an armed group. States should exercise "due diligence" to prevent, stop, investigate, punish, and ensure reparation for violence against women.

MILITANT INSURGENCIES: A CONTINUUM OF VIOLENCE AGAINST WOMEN

Violence against women has been described as the most extreme expression of the gender inequality that underscores social relations in the Niger Delta. This continuum of discrimination against women from the private to the public sphere; from the time of peace to a time of war, demonstrates the importance of the concerned non-governmental organisation in the Niger Delta especially during armed conflict, and its complementarity in relation to the work of human rights and development organisations in times of insurgencies (Ashton-Jones, 1988). Since the 1990s, the crisis in the Niger Delta has degenerated into a dangerous theatre of violent conflict, sustained by ethnic militias, tribal warlords, and misguided youths. The sociopolitical strife in the region include: kidnapping and sabotage and seizure of oil facilities while political assassinations have become a recurring decimal in the unfolding tragedy of the region (Ekine, 2000). Although the violence across the Niger Delta has manifested in different forms, in Warri it is seen as a conflict between Ijaw and Itsekeri ethnic militias, in Rivers State as a battle between Ijaw groups; it is essentially a fight for control of oil wealth and government resources. The violence in Port Harcourt has been perpetrated by two rival armed groups and their affiliates who battled to control territory and lucrative oil bunkering routes.[7]

These militias, private thugs, and government forces have been witnessed in full-blown conflict areas like the 1999 genocide in Odi and the continuous raids by the Nigerian military on villages and communities populated by innocent civilians. It is reported that thousands of innocent civilians, especially women, children, pregnant women, and the aged were killed in the attack. Several others numbering over 30,000 were trapped in the bush, swamps, and mangrove forest where they were hiding. The government forces routinely commit abuses against the civilians and hire out their services in conflict and after conflict from one community to the other, drawing their power from the "barrel of the gun" (arms) (Sha'aba, 1998).

In the last 8 years, reports say more women suffer disproportionately from the militant insurgencies and violence in the region. Government forces attacks, youth uprisings and communal revolts have also been recorded throughout the Niger Delta region claiming hundreds of lives and properties, running into several millions of naira. Examples of these include the murderous actions of the Joint Task Force against the Niger Delta people of Gbaramatu kingdom in Delta State, political assassinations and incessant violence by the tribal warlords and misguided youths (Olukoya, 2002). Sociopolitical and ethnic strife, including kidnapping, sabotage, and seizure of oil facilities have become a recurring decimal in the unfolding tragedy of the region. Under these scenarios, people act on primordial suspicions and sentiments; anarchy becomes the common currency. Women and children, being among the most vulnerable populations during times of these insurgencies and violence, continue to suffer from the consequences of these conflicts. Discrimination against women is both a cause and a consequence of the deprivations they suffer in wartime. It is imperative that humanitarian workers bear this in mind, and ensure that women are directly consulted and closely involved in all activities undertaken on their behalf.[8] Within the framework of its mandate, many non-governmental organisations in the region address these issues to the greatest extent possible, to ensure women's voices are heard in determining the needs of war-affected populations; such groups include: Kebetkache Women Development and Resource Centre, Women Light Foundation, Niger Delta for Justice, National Network for Women in Niger Delta, and the Niger Delta Women for Development Energy and Security.[9]

The armed conflict in Niger Delta region has dramatically increased. While the rural areas were previously the hardest hit, now the war has moved to the urban areas where 65 percent of the population lives, especially the marginalised neighbourhoods (Onduku, 2001). Diverse forms of violence overlap in this urban armed conflict, not only politically-motivated violence but also ethnically influenced. Nonetheless, the significant impact of the range of violence perpetrated within urban conflicts has not yet been acknowledged in analyses of the Niger Delta armed conflict. In recent times the urban armed conflict in the region has worsened due to the pervasive presence of government forces—the Joint Task Force, the ethnic militia groups. These delinquent gangs have reorganised under the control or influence of the paramilitaries or the guerrillas.[10]

Women experience this war as a personal drama because their sons, brothers, or other relatives often are involved in one of these armed groups. This situation fills them with feelings of impotence, anger, and fear. As the displaced women in the Niger Delta explained, "No mother wants bad things for her sons and daughters, but we do abandon our wards when danger looms."[11] They also pointed out that the militant insurgencies claim the lives of hundreds of innocent citizens, coupled with massive destruction of properties. The women further stated that they want to see an immediate deployment of peacekeepers to create a conducive environment for the free flow of people in the region. Countless women and girls have been shot and killed or injured in different parts of the Niger Delta. Millions more live in fear of armed violence against women. Two key factors lie at the heart of these abuses: the proliferation and misuse of small arms and deep-rooted discrimination against women (Okonto et al., 2004).

IMPACT OF THE INSURGENCIES ON WOMEN

The crises in the Niger Delta have become more violent and often result into mass movements of the civilian populations as people are forced to flee their homes. This has a disproportionate impact on women, first, as mothers, wives, and sisters; they suffered bereavement both in internecine conflicts and in the military's reign of terror in which thousands Niger Deltans were killed. Second, they were often the victims of the violence of security forces out to pacify an increasingly restive populace. Women were victims of rape, sexual slavery, flogging, and forced marriage. Third, many women were also direct activists in the confrontation with security forces and oil companies, paralyzing work.[12] At the height of the Ogoni crisis, many women and children were killed. For instance, many women and children were killed during the aerial attack of Okerenkoko, Kurutie, and Oporoza. Also many of them were maimed and killed when a group consisting mainly of women and children attempted to block work on a shell pipeline in Biara. Fourth, within communities, women especially widows and spinsters, were also the victims of violence by community members in the course of the crisis. At the same time other factors exist such as their care responsibilities and social restrictions on their mobility, that is, women at times may not be able to flee when they come under serious attack and so are at greater risk of abuse by the militants and the Joint Task Force (Nnanna, 2007).

The ethnic militia and the government forces put limits on people's movement setting up armed checkpoints and closing borders, creating situations where women are exposed to the risk of sexual violence. Sexual violence occurs across all socioeconomic and cultural backgrounds; women may be socialised to accept, tolerate, or rationalise it. A weak justice system, the lingering violence of the war, and an unwillingness to report instances compound the situation.[13] When armed groups and soldiers' raid communities for food and supplies, destroy, or poison their food-stocks or water, or prevent people moving around freely, or making a living, this also has a disproportionate impact on women. This is in large part because the burden of managing and providing for the household, caring for the elderly, for children and for people with disabilities frequently fall on women during conflict, especially when male relatives are more directly involved in fighting or are detained, injured, or killed.

Women of all ages have been sexually assaulted by different armed groups. Women have been turned into war booty: they are the prize for the strongest competitor or the instrument for punishing the loser. In the course of the armed conflict in the Niger Delta, tens of thousands of women and girls have been raped and sexually assaulted by combatant forces. Women and girls have been attacked in their homes, in the fields, or as they go about their other daily activities: for instance, the Joint Task Force attack on the people of Gbaramatu kingdom in Delta State and the 1999 genocide and rapes in Odi. Many have been raped more than once or have survived gang rapes. Girl child soldiers have also been the victims of rape and sexual violence. Rape has often been accompanied by other forms of torture. This is evident when rape is used as a form of provocation or to settle scores with the enemy (Olukoya, 2002).

It should be emphasised that large numbers of women and girls suffer directly and indirectly from armed violence. Although available data supports the widespread assumption that most direct casualties of the militant insurgencies are men, particularly young men, women also suffer disproportionately from psychological trauma. Not only do women carry the emotional and physical burden of caring for the whole family under difficult conditions but, in the process, they are more exposed to violence and often become victims of inadequate diets and infectious disease. Ironically, women's role as caregivers may affect their ability to receive assistance (Alidou and Turshen, 2000). Also the government forces attacks affect women's lives when they become the main breadwinners and primary caregivers when male relatives are killed, injured, or disabled by gun violence. Women are displaced and forced to flee their homes for an uncertain future. Displaced women often face starvation and disease as they struggle to fend for their families. Violence against women, whether committed with boots or fists or weapons, is rooted in pervasive discrimination which denies women equality with men. It occurs in a variety of contexts and cuts across borders, religions, and classes (Hemenway et al., 2002). This is not because violence against women is natural or inevitable, but because it has been condoned and tolerated as part of historical or cultural practices for so long.

Violence against women in the family and community, and violence against women as a result of state repression or armed conflict, are part of the same continuum. Much of the violence that is targeted against women in militarised societies, such as the one in the Niger Delta, is an extreme manifestation of the discrimination and abuse that women face in our society. Whatever the context or immediate cause of the violence, the state of anarchy in the Niger Delta invariably has the same effect; the state of acrimony in the region means more danger for women. When violence involves the use of weapons specifically designed to cause injury and death and which can fire bullets at high speed from a distance, sometimes at a rate of several bullets per second, then the risk to women's lives increases dramatically.

The prevalence of small arms that are affordable and easy to carry and use has changed the landscape of warfare, allowing women and children to be recruited as combatants (Charlotte Lindsey, 2002). Women are now been involved in armed conflict in the Niger Delta. Women and girls are also abducted into armed groups, or choose to join them, sometimes as a reaction to abuses they have suffered at the hands of the government forces (Nnanna, 2007). These developments have drawn women and girls ever closer into the violence of conflict, sometimes placing them in the ambiguous position of being simultaneously the perpetrators and victims of violence. Few women in some parts of the Niger Delta have traditionally participated in the public sphere only through their fathers and husbands, and have suffered social, legal, and cultural discrimination.[14]

Shocking as this is, it is even more difficult to comprehend the abuse and exploitation that women and girls have happened to suffer at the hands of humanitarian and peacekeeping personnel, the very people mandated to assist and protect them. In wartime women play many roles from actively bearing arms, to sustaining families, to leading peace movements. The resilience and courage many women demonstrate in the face of adversity belies the clichés that women are the most vulnerable in situations of armed conflict. Nonetheless, the outbreak of war can expose women to great risks, some common to the community as a whole, and others specific to their gender.[15]

PROTECTING WOMEN'S DIGNITY AND RIGHTS

The people of the Niger Delta, like in any other regions of the country, have economic, social, and cultural rights guaranteed by the Constitution which can be realised through legitimate agitations. The women's rights activists are, however, worried that a lot of unlawful activities including violence against women, rape, kidnappings, and deprivation are daily occurrences in the Niger Delta.[16] Under international law, states are obliged to protect women from gender-based violence, including armed violence. They must also take steps to prevent weapons falling into the hands of human rights abusers.

Violence against women is a prevalent harm to the basic rights, freedoms, health, and welfare of women. It occurs in many settings and at many hands, including those of relatives, acquaintances, and the state. Most forms of violence directed specifically against women were met with silence not only by the state but also by civil society and the human rights movement in Nigeria.[17] Though in recent times, some major human rights activists in the country have started addressing the problem of violence against women. In this last decade, the activities of the human rights groups have increased exponentially. This is because women's rights activists are using human rights instruments to combat violence against women and, in turn, the human rights movement is being enlarged and enriched by their approach.

International human rights law addresses the rights and dignity of all human beings, including women, men, and children. At all times and without discrimination, the women's human rights activists have ensured the development and implementation of international standards for the protection of women's human rights through direct advocacy in the Niger Delta.[18] Apart from the role of concerned individuals and human rights groups, it is very necessary that states should respect, protect, and fulfil human rights. The most fundamental human rights are "non-derogable," that is, they must be fully respected at all times, even during an emergency such as war. States must prevent, stop, investigate, punish, and ensure reparation for violence against women wherever it is likely to occur or has occurred, and whoever the perpetrators are, should be punished. In times of armed conflict, international humanitarian law (commonly known as the laws of war) offers additional protection, especially to those taking no active part in hostilities.[19]

The United Nations Convention on the Elimination of All Forms of Discrimination against Women (CEDAW), an international human rights treaty binding on all states which have joined it, prohibits all forms of discrimination against women. Gender-based violence against women is a form of discrimination, as explained by the Committee on the Elimination of Discrimination against Women. This organisation has been a leading group in the international human rights movement promoting women's human rights. Under its General Recommendation No. 19, it recognises that violence against women impairs women's right to enjoy basic human rights, including the right to life, the right not to be subjected to torture or ill-treatment, the right to equal protection under humanitarian law in times of armed conflict, and the right to liberty and security of the person.[20]

There is a growing acknowledgment that issues of gender need to be fully integrated into international work to stop the proliferation and misuse of small arms and that the specifics of armed violence have often been overlooked in some campaigns to address violence against women. It should be noted that there remains a significant gap between the international community's recognition that those who commit rape and other gender-based violence are legally liable and must be punished (Bunch, 1995). The Nigerian government and concerned authorities should also enforce international humanitarian and human rights law and insist that those who violate it are held accountable. The ongoing impunity of those who perpetrated violence against women in the Niger Delta in the recent Joint Task Force onslaught Delta is only one of many examples of failure by the federal government of Nigeria to investigate, prosecute, and punish those found responsible for acts of rape and sexual violence. This failure has contributed to an environment of impunity that perpetuates violence against women today. Whether the violence described is investigated and punished, and whether such acts are prevented in the future depends ultimately on the firm commitment of the major states in the Niger Delta and the federal government.[21]

In light of the foregoing, the plight of women whose lives are touched by the conflict in the Niger Delta, be they actively engaged in hostilities or inadvertently caught in the midst of conflict, can be improved only if the political exists. Let us be clear, if women continue to suffer in situations of armed conflict, it is not because there is insufficient law to protect them, rather because this law is insufficiently respected. The sooner the international community treats the protection of women as an obligation rather than an aspiration, the sooner we will witness concrete change.

THE WAY FORWARD—ENDING THE IMPUNITY AGAINST WOMANHOOD

Government has so far taken appreciable steps to tackle the Niger Delta issue, including dialogue with stakeholders, amnesty to militants, and the establishment of full fledged ministry to handle Niger Delta issues. These are no doubt important steps toward resolving the crisis in the Niger Delta. However, for these laudable government initiatives to succeed, governments at all levels must adopt a rights-based approach to development and women's protection in the Niger Delta. All the states and local governments in the region must ensure that they recover from the violent past, sexual violence, and exploitation. Safe houses, new laws, new partnerships, increased monitoring and additional public awareness of the crime against women and children and also work toward making concrete inroads to create a safer, more prosperous future for all women in the Niger Delta. Until the state's security and legal infrastructure are rebuilt, women's security is threatened inside and outside of the home, where they are subject to the rule of aggression rather than the rule of law.

The role of the international community is increasingly necessary in order to pressure nation-states to implement changes that will bring the womenfolks closer to social justice and a democratic state that can pursue political negotiations to end armed violence against women. The support of the international community is also invaluable for stopping the increase in human rights violations and impunity against womanhood in the Niger Delta (Igbatayo, 2001). Many human rights organisations not only in the Niger Delta but in other parts of the country have undertaken the task of forging an international network for women. Individuals can also help to put an end to the abuses and violation of women's rights by joining the international campaigns to stop violence against women. The Non-Governmental Organisations on their parts should also work out modalities to strengthen their efforts to increase awareness in local communities, working with traditional authorities and community leaders to educate and reach the mass of the people on the issue of women's rights and the evils of violence against women. Furthermore, there is the need to undertake a comprehensive review of the constitution to further the promotion and protection of women's rights so as to have the legal framework for the enhancement of the status and welfare of women.

Women throughout the world face systematic gender-based discrimination in laws, policies, and practices that deny them equal rights as human beings.[22] In many countries, women are regularly denied the right to life and security of person, full legal standing, health care, education, employment, inheritance, and freedom of movement. Women still do not have full access to economic and political decision-making processes in their various communities.[23] Too often, governments allow crimes against women to go unpunished, continuing a culture of impunity for family members, state agents, and others who discriminate against or commit violence against women. At the same time, the voices of women's rights groups combating such violations face enormous obstacles in reaching national and international decision-making institutions.

According to Article 4 of the United Nations Declaration on the Elimination of Violence against Women, "States should pursue by all appropriate means and without delay a policy of eliminating violence against women."[24] Human rights activists also believe that "states must promote and protect the human rights of women and exercise due diligence: to prevent, investigate and punish acts of all forms of violence against women, whether in the home, the workplace, the community or society, in custody or in situations of armed conflict."[25] Furthermore, a number of agencies should be well positioned to strengthen their work in the area of women, peace and security. The non-governmental organisations and other women's rights activists should also pay attention to women's psychosocial and trauma needs in the aftermath of war and support women leaders to build activist peace networks. The impunity that prevails for widespread crimes against women in the Niger Delta must be redressed. Accountability means being answerable to women for crimes committed against them and punishing those responsible.[26] In addition, the constitution of Nigeria must take into consideration the issue of violence against women and women must have full access to the rule of law.

CONCLUSION

This chapter examined the activities of the government and security forces against the backdrop of their violation of fundamental human rights of women in the Niger Delta. We have also argued that they are primarily responsible for the gender-based violence (including rape, sexual slavery, and forced pregnancy) committed against the tribal women of the Niger Delta. The region provides a stark example of lack of accountability of government to its people when it comes to the impact of their operations on women's rights. Violence against women, rape, and other forms of sexual violence such as forced prostitution have taken place repeatedly in various communities that have been invaded by the Joint Task Force and the militants in the region.

The government forces have unashamedly violated the fundamental rights of the people, especially that of women and children, in the name of maintaining peace in the region. The Nigerian government has failed in its obligation to respect and protect the rights of women in the Niger Delta. To break the cycle of violence and discrimination against women, it is vital for the federal government to take specific steps to readdress the activities and roles of the government forces in the Niger Delta.

NOTES

1. See United Nations Committee on the Elimination of Discrimination against Women, General Recommendation No. 19, *Violence against Women* (Eleventh session, 1992), UN Doc. HRI\ GEN\ 1\ Rev.1, para 6.

2. Women's Commission for Refugee Women and Children, The Gender Dimensions of Internal Displacement: Concept Paper and Annotated Bibliography, *Office of Emergency Programmes Working Paper Series*, UNICEF, 1998.

3. See Amnesty International, *Nigeria: Repression of Women's Protests in Oil-Producing Delta Region* (Index: AFR 44/008/2003).

4. Ibid.

5. Again Genocide in the Niger Delta—Ijaw National Congress Group Condemns Odioma Killings, *This Day*, Lagos, February 24, 2005.

6. Ibid.

7. For more, see A. Onduku (2001) Sustainable Development as a Strategy for Conflict Prevention: The Case of the Niger Delta. Online.

8. Reports by Human Rights Watch and Amnesty International document the escalating human rights crisis unfolding in the Niger Delta. *Human Rights Watch*, February 2005.

9. See Amnesty International, Nigeria: Repression of Women's Protests in Oil-Producing Delta Region (Index: AFR 44/008/2003).

10. Again Genocide in the Niger Delta—Ijaw National Congress Group Condemns Odioma Killings, op. cit.

11. Violence against Women: An Issue of Human Rights, *A Newsletter of the Office of Women in Development*, Summer 1997. Accessed online at www.usaid.gov/wid/pubs/nl.htm on January 3, 2010; see also UNIFEM, *Progress of the World's Women* 2002, Vol. II.

12. Niger Delta Women for Justice. Accessed online at www.ndwj/kabissa.org on January 15, 2010.

13. Amnesty International, Nigeria: Fight for Oil Wealth Fuels Violence in Delta, November 2004. See also Douglas, O. and D. Ola (1999), Defending Nature, Protecting Human Dignity: Conflicts in the Niger Delta, in *Searching for Peace in Africa: An Overview of Conflict Prevention and Transformation*. The Netherlands: European Centre for Conflict Prevention.

14. Again Genocide in the Niger Delta—Ijaw National Congress Group Condemns Odioma Killings, op. cit.

15. Human Rights Watch, UNHCR at 50: What Future for Refugee Protection? Accessed online at www.hrw.org/campaigns/refugees/pdf1.pdf, January 10, 2010.

16. See Amnesty International, *Nigeria: Repression of Women's Protests in Oil-Producing Delta Region* (Index: AFR 44/008/2003).

17. Women's Commission for Refugee Women and Children, *UNHCR's Policy on Refugee Women and Guidelines on Their Protection: An Assessment of Ten Years of Implementation*, May 2002.

18. Reports by Human Rights Watch and Amnesty International document the escalating human rights crisis unfolding in the Niger Delta. *Human Rights Watch*, February, 2005.

19. Human Rights Watch Overview. January 2004. Nigeria. Available at http://hrw.org/english/docs/2004/01/21/nigeri6976.htm.

20. Violence against Women: An Issue of Human Rights, A newsletter of the Office of Women in Development, Summer 1997, www.usaid.gov/wid/pubs/nl.htm; see also UNIFEM, Progress of the World's Women 2002, Vol. II.

21. Reports by Human Rights Watch and Amnesty International document the escalating human rights crisis unfolding in the Niger Delta. *Human Rights Watch*, February 2005.

22. The UNDP Human Development Report 2002 documents that gender inequality is universal—that although the extent of the inequality varies significantly, no country on earth treats women as well as it treats men.

23. Violence against Women: An Issue of Human Rights. A newsletter of the Office of Women in Development, Summer 1997, accessed online at www.usaid.gov/wid/pubs/nl.htm on January 11, 2010; see also *UNIFEM, Progress of the World's Women* 2002, Vol. II.

24. United Nations Committee on the Elimination of Discrimination against Women, General Recommendation No. 19, Violence against Women (Eleventh session, 1992), UN Doc. HRI\ GEN\ 1\ Rev.1, para 6.

25. Women's Commission for Refugee Women and Children, *UNHCR's Policy on Refugee Women and Guidelines on their Protection: An Assessment of Ten Years of Implementation*, May 2002.

26. See *Nigeria: Repression of Women's Protests in Oil-Producing Delta Region*, Amnesty International (Index: AFR 44/008/2003).

REFERENCES

Alidou, O., and Turshen, M. (2000), Africa: Women in the Aftermath of Civil War, *Race and Class* 41(4): 81. See also M. Davies, (ed.) (1994) *Women and Violence: Realities and Responses Worldwide*. London: Zed Books.

Ashton-Jones, N. (1988), *The ERA Handbook to the Niger Delta: The Human Ecosystems of the Niger Delta*. London: Environmental Rights Action.

Bunch, Charlotte (1995), Transforming Human Rights from a Feminist Perspective, in Julie Peters and Andrea Wolper (eds.) *Women's Rights, Human Rights: International Feminist Perspectives*. New York: Routledge.

Ekine, S. (2000), *Blood and Oil: Testimonies of Violence from Women of the Niger Delta*. London: Centre for Democracy and Development.

Hemenway D., Shinoda-Tagawa, T., and Miller, M. (2002), Firearm Availability and Female Homicide Victimization Rates among 25 Populous High-Income

Countries, *Journal of the American Medical Women's Association*, Spring 57(2). www.ogele.org/featureAs/features_nigerdelta.html accessed on January 13, 2010.

Igbatayo, S. (2001), Poverty Reduction and Sustainable Resource Management in the Niger Delta, *Proceedings of an International Conference on the Blueprint and Development Strategies for the Niger Delta*. February 26–28, 2001. World Environment Movement for Africa (WEMFA). Yenagoa.

Lindsey, Charlotte (2002), *Women Facing War*. Geneva: International Committee on the Red Cross.

Nnanna, Ochereome (2007), Nigeria: Clark, Niger Delta Overlord? *Vanguard*, October 8, 2007.

Okonto, Douglas, Von Kemedi, Ike Okonta, and Michael Watts (2004), Oil and Militancy in the Niger Delta: Terrorist Threat or Another Colombia? *Niger Delta Economies of Violence Working Paper* No. 4. See also A. Ekineh (2001) *Tears and Weeping of the Niger Delta*. London: Southern Solidarity Press.

Olukoya, Sam (2002), Women's Protests against Chevron Texaco Spread through the Niger Delta, *Corp Watch*, August.

Onduku, A. (2003), Confronting The Human Security Dilemma Towards Building Sustainable Peace in Nigeria's Niger Delta, presentation at the ceremony in honour of Ms Ibiba Don Pedro, the winner of the 2003 CNN African Journalist of the Year Award, at the Lambeth Town Council Building, London, Saturday, October 18.

Sha'aba, R. A. (1998), MOSOP and the Ogoni Struggle, in Omotoye Olorode et al. (eds.), *Ken Saro-Wiwa and the Crises of the Nigerian State*. Lagos: CDHR.

20

Gender, Environment, and Human Rights in the Niger Delta Region

Iwebunor Okwechime and Akin Iwilade

ABSTRACT

This chapter focuses on gender and the environment in Nigeria's oil-rich Niger Delta region. In doing so, it highlights the daily struggles of the inhabitants of the region, especially women, against state and corporate violations of their fundamental human rights, as well as their disempowerment through the destruction of the environment on which they depend for their livelihoods. Citing several cases of mass mobilization by the women against the oil companies, this chapter contends that the adverse consequences of oil industry activities on their sources of income and livelihood have forced the women of the Niger Delta to unite and engage the forces of global capitalism by exploring traditionally sanctioned avenues, through which they can fight for their rights and defend their environment.

In conclusion, this chapter notes that the struggle of the women of the Niger Delta against oil capital cannot be waged in isolation; rather, they must be fought through sustained international networking with their exploited and disempowered counterparts in other parts of the world.

INTRODUCTION

This chapter focuses on gender and environment in Nigeria's oil-rich, but volatile Niger Delta region. In doing so, it highlights the travails of the inhabitants of the region, especially women, and their struggles against successive Nigerian administrations and transnational oil corporations operating in their communities. Indeed, the travails and the struggles they engendered are visible in various ways: the destruction of the local economy, and therefore livelihoods, through the polluting activities of the transnational oil corporations, physical and sexual abuses (not to mention the psychological or mental trauma), extra-judicial murders and the reactive militancy with which the women have fought back. It is important to note, at this stage, that the women of the Niger Delta are not only up in arms against transnational capital and the Nigerian state, but also against their own menfolk who, by virtue of the patriarchal nature of the Niger Delta society, have shown little qualms in struggles of their women largely because of the material benefits they will obtain from the companies for undermining the women's struggle. As will be shown in the course of our analysis, the treacherous role of the men in the survivalist struggle against state tyranny and corporate exploitation has provoked into existence an alliance of the women and a large population of the youth and a small minority of the menfolk who have implicit belief in the cause for which their women have sworn to die.

To grasp fully the dynamics of gender and environment in the Niger Delta, we have focused analysis almost exclusively on women in this chapter advisedly because of the pivotal role that they play in the local economy. As indicated, the experience of the women of the oil minorities is unique among Nigerian women from other ethnic groups. It is known for a fact that 50 percent of the population of the oil-bearing communities is comprised of women. The women's dominance of the main economic activities of farming, fishing and trading in agricultural and other goods, casts them in a strategic role as the backbone of the communities in the Niger Delta. Unfortunately, it has become quite a struggle over the years for the women of this resource-rich region to engage profitably in these age-old economic activities in the face of the destructive operations of the oil industry to which their communities have played host over the past 50 years, but over which they have no control. It is precisely within this context that we can meaningfully understand the dynamics and the dialectics of gender and environment in the oil-rich, but ecologically fragile Niger Delta region.

For analytical convenience, the rest of this chapter has been organized into five separate but inter-related sections. In the premier section, we offer a conceptual explanation of the key terms such as gender, environment and the Niger Delta in the context of the chapter. In doing so, we link the issue of gender and environment in historical context. The purpose of this section is to highlight the fact that the people of the Niger Delta have always been conscious of their environment and have, therefore, been protective of that environment. Knowing full well that their subsistence is derived from the environment, they had, well before their encounter with the West, devised some environmental governance strategies which, for all practical purpose, had served their peculiar needs well and ensured that their environment was sustainably exploited. The second section explores the background to women's environmental rights struggle in the Delta region, particularly in the context of globalization. This section basically explores the political economy of the liberalization of the Nigerian economy under the neo-liberal market ideology and its impact on women in the oil producing communities. The discussion in this section dovetails into the analysis in the third section, which, in a nutshell, examines the role of structural adjustment programs in the intensification of environmental degradation in the Delta region. The penultimate section of the chapter highlights the travails of the women at the hands of transnational capital and a collaborating state. The fifth and final section concludes the argument and underscores its implications for our analysis.

CONCEPTUALIZING GENDER, ENVIRONMENT, AND THE NIGER DELTA

Gender

In the literature the term, "gender," is often used as a code word for women (Pettman, 1998:448). This perception of gender, presumed to have originated among the dominant male group, tends to devalue the roles and concerns of women at the expense of the men. A major consequence of this is that women are forced into conditions of dependence and are expected, according to Pettman, to be grateful for this protection, even when they do not wish it. In the grammatical context, gender has been defined as "the physical and/or social condition of being male or female, or the grammatical divisions of masculine, feminine and neuter into which nouns, adjectives etc. are divided in some languages."[1] In recent years, owing to increasing global attention that has been drawn to women's concerns, the concept of gender has expanded to the point that it is now commonly employed to describe "culturally defined, socially formed identities of men and women that are highly variable across cultures and are continually subject to change."[2]

For Enemuo, gender denotes, among other things, the different and unequal perceptions roles and relevance, as well as rewards, which a society assigns to men and women through its culture (Enemuo, 1999:227). Jev et al. argue in a similar vein when they speak of gender as the social relationship between men and women in which women have been systematically subordinated (Jev and Yomi, 2002:499). Olojede construes gender in terms of the social, economic and political differences between men and women: According to her:

> Gender is a complex and interacting construct representing struggles over the use and definition of power in the private and public realms. Like class analysis, gender is a fundamental category of political analysis, and not simply another independent variable representing biological sex. (Olojede, 2004:126)

In the light of the foregoing, it is possible to make the following important deductions. The first point is that the term "gender" is relative. In other words, we can speak of gender relations because women are involved. This simply implies that we do not, as Pettman puts it, experience our gender alone, or in isolation from other social identities.

It is specifically in this sense therefore that she describes gender as being constitutive of other social relations (Pettman, 1998:485). Moreover, the gendered nature of social relations has drawn attention to the important issue of inequality that exists between men and women in society. How do you explain the fact that women as a social category are marginalized in virtually every situation of power relation? Or how do we account for the fact that virtually every society tends to put a higher value on certain kinds of character or behavior associated with men? This is the context in which gender can be described as both relational and a power relationship.

Another conclusion to be drawn from the various definitions offered above is that the term "gender" is a social construction. This implies, as Euemuo has aptly observed, that "gender differences are created and sustained by society through its traditions, customs, conventions, mores, and the regulations" (Enemuo, op.cit. p. 227). In essence, therefore, gender as a sociocultural construct is variable across cultures and it is not immutable. The fourth point that the definitions above have highlighted relates to the fact that gender, as Jev et al. have pointed out, is a "psychological rather than a historical term" (op.cit. p. 499). Properly understood, sex is seen as biology; it refers, basically, "to the physical differences between men and women."[3] A final point that emerges from the foregoing is that the term "gender" can be male-biased or female-biased (Jev et al., op.cit., p. 499). This is largely because gender, as we have indicated, is socially and culturally constructed; and furthermore, varies from culture to culture.

We note, however, that in the specific case of the Niger Delta, relations between men and women have been marked by that what Fatton has described as "the hegemony of the male world-wide-view [who] has penetrated women's consciousness and debilitated the feminist struggle for emancipation" (Fatton, 1989:55). In particular, the issues of gender injustice and discrimination as they relate to the environment in the Niger Delta have been a major source of conflict and confrontation between the women, who constitute more than half of the population of the region, and the men whose worldview dominate the society on the one hand, and the oil companies and the Nigerian state on the other. Paradoxically, the women are in most cases excluded from negotiations that seek to resolve disputes or conflicts over control of or access to the environment.

As mentioned earlier, the Niger Delta, like most African societies, including Nigeria, is patriarchal structured. Professor E. J. Alagoa has posited that colonial rule dealt the death blow to the matrilineal system which was operating in parts of the Niger Delta. This, he argued, was because "the matrilineal system came into conflict with the patrilineal principles favoured by the new rulers" (Alagoa, 2002:40). He, however, observed by way of conclusion that the principle of descent through the female line did not by itself place women above men in public affairs. It meant, according to him, that the dominant male still identified himself through the lineage of his mother, and the maternal system remained significant in society as in religion (ibid.). Arguing in a similar vein, Okoh pointed out that even in those societies where inheritance and succession were through maternal descent, men ruled for women by proxy (Okoh, 2003:23). Though women in the Niger Delta have a history of activism, the goal, according to Mba, was far from seeking to "change the inequality in the traditional structure of gender relations" (Mba, 1992). Mba's assertion chimes with Alagoa's earlier observation that the matrilineal principles did not place itself above men in public affairs.

In the light of the foregoing, it is clear that the issues of gender as it relates to the Niger Delta cannot be understood outside of the context of the patriarchal traditions, culture and character of Nigerian society and the location of the Niger Delta within that context. It is therefore significant to note that the depredations of transnational capital on a largely non-capitalist society over the past fifty years has led the women to challenge the traditional structure of gender relations in the region. With the majority of the womenfolk in the region being largely illiterate, the onerous task of mobilizing the women has fallen to a generation of young, educated women. These women have been playing prominent vital roles in the various social movements that have been campaigning against the destruction of the Niger Delta environment by the transnational oil companies and a complicit Nigerian state. The preamble to the Resolutions of the First Niger Delta Indigenous Women's Conference held in Yenagoa in 1999 underline the determination of the women to challenge the *status quo*. According to the Preamble:

> the Niger Delta region has gone through several years of economic neglect by both the Federal government of Nigeria and the multinational oil companies operating in the region. Our environment has become devastated as a result of the exploration and exploitation of crude oil and means of livelihoods have been destroyed. (Agary and Agary, 2005)

In a fundamental sense, therefore, the environment is critical to an understanding of the dynamics of gender relations in the oil-producing Niger Delta region. For instance, apart from constituting more than half of the population in the region, women also dominate the traditional occupations, namely fishing, farming and trading. Moreover, it is known for a fact that the majority of the people living in the rural area are women children and the elderly (Ekine, 1999). Gender thus becomes the fulcrum of the discourse on human rights violations, disempowerment and conflict in the Niger Delta. Implicit in this assertion is that women in the oil-producing areas are doubly victimized as reflected in the ingrained patriarchal structures of their society and as demonstrated by their unique experience at the hands of transnational capital and the Nigerian state in the context of the political economy of international oil. As one of the leading women activists has noted, "the collective injustice against women is one which is often concealed by the general context of struggles and which ultimately results in plural disadvantages as many groups continue to bear the brunt of societal dislocations and remain invisible and neglected even in the face of so-called development, self-determination or autonomy" (Nkoyo, 2002).

Environment

The environment is the basis for peoples' existence. And any activity that ends to damage it ultimately spells doom for people, animals and plants that depend on it for their sustenance. The term "environment" is described as the natural world of land, sea, air, plants and animal.[4] According to Roberts:

> "The environment" refers to natural conditions, including land, air and water, inhabited by living organisms. It is the whole sum of the surrounding external conditions within which an organism, community or an object exists, and a product of the dynamic interaction between climate, soil types, microbes, plants, water, and animals. It is the surroundings of organisms, including biological, physical, and chemical factors. (Robert Nyemetu, 2004:87)

It can be gleaned from the above that, as a life-sustaining force, the environment needs to be protected against corporate activities as well as changing livelihood patterns that can undermine its sustainability, thereby imperiling the survival of future generations.

In the context of the Niger Delta, an interactive dynamics exist between the people, especially the women, and the environment. These interactive dynamics have existed since remembered time. And it is within this context that the struggle of the women of Delta region against oil company activities which are despoiling their environment should be located. It is known for a fact that, in the past, fishing, farming and trading were the major occupations of the women. It was common practice in the fishing communities for husbands, as a matter of obligation, to equip their wives with dug-out boats. Through this customary practice, the wives, it is argued, were empowered by the husbands to earn a living and to sustain the whole family, including the children and the husband himself. Similarly, in the upland Niger Delta, the dominant economic activity is farming though the people also engaged in subsidiary occupations such fishing, hunting, food processing, tools fabrication, carving and boat building (Robert Nyemetu, op.cit., p. 87). It is well established in the literature that trading was common among the people of the Delta. For instance, Alagoa has pointed out that the long distance trading across the Delta and into the hinterland was well established before the Portuguese arrived in the region at the beginning of the sixteenth century (Alagoa, 1976:100). However, a combination of factors ranging from urbanization, deforestation, oil industry activities, notably oil spills and gas flares, and soil erosion have wreaked havoc on the environment, thereby undermining the socioeconomic basis of women's existence in the region.

Oil industry activity is, by far, the most disruptive and destructive to the Niger Delta environment, as it devastates farmlands and fishing grounds. In the same breath, the oil industry alienates arable land for seismic activities. In a region where clean drinking water is in short supply, the pollution of the creeks and rivers poses serious threat to the health and well-being of the people. Of course, the fact that most of the people living in the rural communities bathe and defecate in the same creaks and rivers poses a health problem for the communities that live over water. A host of diseases that now afflict many of the inhabitants of the oil communities have been directly linked to the impact of oil exploration and production on the environment (Obianime et al., 2002).

The other level at which the environment plays a critical role in the lives of the people of Delta region is culture. To this end, the people had, well before the intrusion of adventurous Europeans, evolved environmental governance strategies as a way of protecting their environment. Thus, for an important example, certain forests are sacred and totems must not be hunted or killed, and some creeks and rivers, and by implication, certain species of marine life, are protected from fisher folks. Health-wise, the onslaught of the capitalist mode of production on a non-capitalist environment is visible in terms of the steady disappearance of local ways of taking care of infirm people in the communities. Over the years, oil company activities have destroyed most of the plants with medicinal properties which the locals have used since time immemorial to cure certain maladies that afflict them.

Finally, the advent of oil exploration and production activities have rendered extinct certain rituals based on local culture that bonds the people to their environment. In Ijaw land, for example, the age-long traditional baptism, where, three days after birth a child is taken to the river and dipped into the water and then fetched out at intervals, determined by the accompanying priest, is now extinct, thanks to the oil industry. This is because, in a situation where virtually all the rivers have become toxic, it would be foolhardy for parents to put their children through such potentially lethal performance. According to Keku, the obnoxious impact of oil exploration in the Niger Delta has not only robbed the people of their rights to existence and survival, but their right to traditional beliefs and practices (Maya, 2004:12). The importance women of the Delta region in attaching to their relationship with their environment is reflected in the following comment by an Ogoni woman activist, Diana Wiwa. According to her: "The loss of the fattening room and other traditions led the Ogoni women to make a conscious decision to organized against the oil industry on their land—a force they saw as being clearly responsible for cultural degradation in Ogoni" (Wiwa, 1997:13).

The Niger Delta

According to Roberts (2005:94),

> The Niger Delta is the huge fan of land fed by deposition from the Niger–Benue river system, which spreads out to reach the Atlantic Ocean on the coast of Nigeria. The Niger Delta lies just north of the Equator. It straddles latitude 50N, and extends into the Gulf of Guinea, dividing the Bight of Benin (to the West) from the Bight of Biafra (to the East). The NDES (Niger Delta Environmental Survey) defines the Niger Delta as the low-lying arcuate deltaic plan with a northern apex a little to the south of Onitsha at Aboh (5033°44″N, 603°38″E), a Western apex by the estuary of the Benin River (5033″E), and an eastern apex at Imo River Estuary (4027°16″N, 7035°27″E). In other terms, the delta is a triangle with its apex between Ndoni and Aboh, descending eastwards to the Qua Iboe River at Eket and West wards to the Benin River with its based along the Atlantic coast between the Bights of Benin and Biafra. The southern-most part of the Niger Delta is believed to be at Palm Point (4016°22″N, 6005°27″E), south of Akassa at the estuary of Nun River, one of the two major distributaries of the Niger River.

The Niger Delta is a heterogeneous, multicultural diverse region of 70,000 square kilometres (Saro-Wiwa, 1995:31) with over 20 different ethnic groups of Yoruba, Edo, Igbo, Izon, Igbo, Izon (Ijaw) and Cross River stock.[5] Several studies have shown that fishing, hunting, trading, farming and salt-making are the traditional occupations of the people.[6]

The Niger Delta is one of the three largest wetlands in the world and the largest in Africa (Manby, 1999). Quite apart from being hugely endowed with oil and gas deposits, fertile agricultural land, abundant rivers (as well as creeks) and fish, forest and human resources, the Niger Delta also supports a complex biodiversity and other biological and ecological features presently most diverse, sensitive and fragile in Nigeria (Onosode, 2003). According to the UNDP, cited by Roberts, the Niger Delta stretches over 560 km or approximately 75 percent of the coastline of Nigeria (UNDP, 2001:96). Three distinct ecological zones predominate in this region. These are the thick mangrove forests bordering the sandy coastal areas that in turn border the Atlantic coast. These are the fresh-water swamps and lastly, the dry land forests that support most of the farming.[7] As Robert further elaborates:

> Beyond this tripartite formation, the natural environment of the Niger Delta is divided primarily into two ecological zones, namely the "riverine" over half of the topography in the lower Delta which is crises-crossed by creeks and dotted with small islands, and the "upland" the rest of the upper delta. This is because the distinction between estuarine and brackish water zone is less obvious than between the brackish water and fresh water zones. The vegetation and other aspects of the ecosystem roughly follow this divide. We thus have the fresh water swamp forest vegetation in the upper delta and the mangrove in the lower delta. . . . [T]he distribution in the delta approximates this division: the drier land towards the head of the delta mainly support farming, the collection and processing of palm fruits, hunting and some fishing, while much further south, the riverine economy resolves essentially around fishing and trading. (Roberts, 2004:197)

Of the major ethnic groups in the region, namely the Ogoni, Urhobo and Itsekiri, the Ijaw nation constitutes by far the Delta's largest ethnic group, with over 5,000 communities from over 40 clans (Ijaw Youth Council, 1996:5), dispersed across six states, namely Ondo, Edo, Delta Bayelsa, Rivers and Akwa Ibom States. With over 800 oil-bearing communities, the Niger Delta has an estimated population of about 13 million people, some 4 million of whom are of Ijaw ethnic origin (Kemedi, 2003).

WOMEN AND ENVIRONMENTAL RIGHTS STRUGGLE IN THE CONTEXT OF GLOBALIZATION: THE BACKGROUND

Globalization places an especially heavy burden on women peasants and traders in the Niger Delta. The globalization of the oil industry has led to, among other things, the intensification of oil exploration and the further integration of the region into the market-driven global capitalist system. The consequence of this is well reflected in the increased environmental and social degradation, as well as widespread economic disempowerment among the women peasants and traders of the Niger Delta oil communities. Due to increased oil exploitation activities by the oil companies, huge tracts of arable land were annexed for oil industry-related activities, such as pipelines, flow stations, access roads and campsites for oil workers, among others. Furthermore, increased oil exploitation and production activities heightened environmental devastation, as land, water and air were polluted by oil spills, blow outs, seepages and gas flares. All this resulted in diminished productivity, thereby threatening the viability of the local economy in which women play a vital role. "Since farms are failing, palm trees are not bearing fruit, and fish are depleted," said Grace Ekanem, a women's group leader, "women are not only unable to feed their families, but cannot earn money to send their children to school or to afford medical treatment" (Esparza and Wilson, 1999).

It was against this background that the women mobilized themselves against the forces of globalization—the oil companies and the Nigerian state—demanding, among other things, an end to environmental degradation, community development and provision of economic empowerment programs, as well as employment for their children. Through their demonstrations, protests and sit-outs, the women have drawn the attention of the Nigerian state and human rights organizations to their plight. They have also largely succeeded in making the oil companies sign a series of memorandum of understanding (MOU) with them. At this point several questions are pertinent. How did poor, mostly illiterate, peasant women and traders unite and mobilize themselves against the forces of global capital? How did they overcome or transcend the constraints imposed by the patriarchal nature of their society? And what are the factors responsible for the relative success of these women-led protests over those of their male counterparts? These and other questions will be investigated in this study.

The year 1986 is remarkable, not just for the purpose of our analysis, but for the Nigerian state as well. It was the very year the military government of Nigeria under the disgraced dictator, General Ibrahim Babangida, officially adopted the Bretton Woods Institutions' imposed structural adjustment programs (SAP), despite the overwhelming groundswell of public opinion against the adoption of the program (Bangura, 1998). The year 1986 is also a landmark year in the sense that it flagged off, at least officially, the process of deregulation and trade liberalization, essential components of the adjustment program. Beyond the foregoing,1986 has a milestone significance in the contemporary political history of women's struggle in Nigeria, especially that of women in the Niger Delta.

In August 1986, a crowd of about 10,000 women from Ekpan in Uvwie Local Government near the oil city of Warri, mobilized themselves and laid siege to the premises and production facilities of the Nigerian National Petroleum Corporation (NNPC). Chanting and dancing in their accustomed manner, the women called on the NNPC and the oil companies operating in their community to provide social amenities for them, as well as jobs for their qualified sons and daughters. Prior to the Ekpan women's uprising, the Ogharefe women had in 1984 successfully organized a mass resistance protest against a subsidiary of the American oil multinational corporation, Pan Ocean. Following the example of the Ogharefe women, the Ughelli women (also in Western Niger Delta) organized a fierce anti-tax protest against the government. The anti-tax revolt came in the wake of the government's policy to levy taxes against women (Turner and Oshare, 1993). The taxation was necessitated by the parlous state of the national economy following the oil bust of the early 1980s and the consequent imposition by General Babangida's government of IMF loan "conditionalities." In the eyes of these women and their counterparts across the nation, the IMF and its adjustment policies were largely to blame for the hardship they were now in the throes of. To be sure, higher taxes, as Turner and Oshare have noted, constituted a key element in IMF adjustment packages (ibid). Thus, it was these anti-tax protests that supplied "the immediate atmosphere of popular, woman-centred mobilization within which the Ekpan women were moved to act" (Turner and Oshare, ibid.).

It is well to note that the protests against the imposition of structural adjustment conditions were not restricted to the oil-producing areas alone. True, similar protests and revolts were recorded in other parts of the country. However, those that occurred in the oil belt were unique in several respects. For example, in other parts of the country, mobilizations against the adjustment program were characterized by "instances of urban protest actions and anti-IMF riots" (Egwu, 1998). In the Niger Delta such protests not only originated from the countryside, but more importantly women (mostly peasants and traders) took the initiative. Explaining the reason for this is not difficult.

Women play a vital role in the local economy, as they constitute the bulk of the farmers, fisher folks and traders. However, the adjustment program threw up new contradictions whilst deepening old ones in the oil-producing communities. For example, the process of land alienation pursued by the state in the late 1970s under the rubric of the Land Use Act was reinforced by the SAP. According to Egwu, in the wake of economic crisis and SAP, land alienation and land grabbing became pronounced in the countryside (ibid.). By accelerating this process, he argued, structural adjustment impacted heavily on the agrarian and the land questions.

Nowhere was this "agrarian and land questions" more fiercely contested than in the oil-producing areas of the Niger Delta (Turner and Oshare, op. cit; Turner, 2001/2002). In the process of opening up the economy to private foreign investments, as dictated by the Bretton Woods institutions, huge tracts of cultivable land were parceled out to oil companies for oil exploration and production activities. Additionally, the attendant oil industry pollution devastated available arable land and water, the main sources of income for these rural women, the majority of whom were breadwinners of their families. Land hunger which consequently became endemic in the region, often resulted in inter-communal clashes. Grace Ekanem, a women's group leader in Akwa Ibom State, comments in this regard that women are not only unable to feed their families, but cannot even earn enough to send their children to school, or to afford medical treatment. "Women are now redundant" (Esparza and Wilson, op. cit., p. 10), she concluded. In other words, the women of Nigeria's oil-belt are economically disempowered, marginalized and excluded.

Apart from land hunger which the alienation of land by the Nigerian state engendered through the instrumentality of the Land Use Act, oil company operations further exacerbated the crisis of land shortage in the oil-producing areas. Oil pollution resulting from gas flares and oil spills have rendered the soil virtually infertile. In the words of a young female farmer:

> Since 1982 the soil has changed and crops well. It is not because of overuse because we know how to use our lands and our crops are rotated. It is because of the flares. The soil is now too hard-before a small child can turn the soil but now its too hard. The yield of crops very poor and there is lack of fish in this area. We have no help from Shell. They have brought pollution and no development. (Ekine, 2001)

The foregoing serves as the general context out of which the argument pursued in this study flows. In the next section, an attempt is made at a conceptualization of economic globalization, and highlighting the centrality of the multinational corporations as well as the role of IMF/World Bank initiated adjustment policies in the process. The aim, it should be stated, is to underscore the critical interface between globalization, multinational corporations and structural adjustment.

WOMEN UNDER STRUCTURAL ADJUSTMENT

The Structural Adjustment Program (SAP), in its form and content, falls within the rubric of economic globalization. It has its roots in neo-liberal thinking and belief in the (efficient) role of the market forces. The SAP came against the backdrop of the debt crisis of the early 1980s (Kiely, 1998). The early 1970s witnessed the collapse of the Bretton Woods system of fixed exchange rates, following the devaluation of the U.S. dollar against the price of gold. Consequently, a new system was to emerge which allowed for the operation of a system of floating exchange rates in the global economy. This period, 1973–1974, was characterized, incidentally, by the dramatic rise in the price of crude oil. The exponential rise in the price of oil translated into huge revenues for the oil-producing countries, mot of whom deposited these "windfall profits" (ibid.) in Western banks. The banks, in turn, loaned these monies to some developing countries, notably those from Latin American, at relatively low rates of interest.

In the early 1980s, the international financial system came under severe pressure, as many Western banks had lent far too much capital to some loan-seeking countries of the Third World. Saddled with increasing interest payments on their debts, these countries became unable to meet their debt obligations. In 1982, Mexico became the first in the long list of countries that were to declare a moratorium on their debt obligations.

A major outcome of the debt crisis was that the IMF and the World Bank, backed by governments committed to neo-liberal reforms, began to advocate policies that more or less reflected the neo-liberal paradigm (ibid.). Beyond advocating policies, Hoogvelt argues that they were also commissioned and dispatched to the frontiers of the global economy to exact payments from and supervise the credits to the Third World. According to her, the IMF and the World Bank have been able in this capacity "to profoundly affect the organization of production and trade in the periphery to the benefit of the core of the world capitalist system" (Hoogvelt, 1997:166). This was largely achieved through the instrumentality of the SAP. As she again observes:

> Structural adjustment is the generic term used to describe a package of measure which the IMF, the World Bank and individual Western aid donors have persuaded many developing countries to adopt during 1980s, in return for a new ware of loans. (ibid.)

SAP was the neo-liberal solution to what was largely perceived as the inefficient "orthodox" state-led development, including the Import-substitution Industrialization (ISI) program. It was the belief of the neo-liberal reformers that a sustainable strategy for Nigerian-type countries is the promotion of the private sector and the liberalization of their economies. The aim of SAP, as Leftwich notes, "was to shatter the dominant post-war, state-led development paradigm and overcome the problems of developmental stagnation by promoting open and free competitive market economies, supervised by minimal states" (Leftwich, 1993:607). According to Hoogvelt, the main conditionalities of IMF/World Bank proposals include "currency devaluation, deregulation of prices and wages, reduction of public spending on social programs and state bureaucracies, removal of food and other subsidies on basic necessities, trade liberalization, privatization of parastatal enterprises, and expansion of the export sector" (Hoogvelt, op. cit., p. 168).

In Nigeria, the adoption of SAP by the Babangida regime in June 1986 was largely occasioned by the national economic crisis. The crisis in question was, in large part, a function of the oil price shocks that occurred in 1982, and again in 1986, when crude oil prices fell below $15 per barrel

(Doyle, 2002). Summarizing the general economic situation surrounding the adoption of SAP by the Nigeria ruling class, Ake notes that:

> Between 1973 to 1978, during Nigeria's first oil boom, oil revenue grew quickly to more than 90 percent of Nigeria's export revenue. This increase was matched by increase public expenditure, which quadrupled between 1973 and 1975. By 1976 expenditure already exceeded revenue. During the second oil boom between 1973 and 1985, the surge in oil revenue elicited such profligacy that real income began to decline rapidly, as much as 60 percent between 1980 and 1983 when Nigeria recorded a negative growth rate of 6.7 percent and a budget deficit rising to 13 percent of GDP. Austerity measures instituted in 1982 and 1984 failed and the crisis depend, especially with the sharp fall in oil prices in 1986, the worsening of the terms of trade, debt service obligations and a sharp fall in imports and exports. (Ake, 2001)

The implementation of SAP was to place further pressure on the oil industry and, in consequence, the Niger Delta, the main site of oil exploration and production. For instance, it was expected that oil revenues would underwrite the whole adjustment program as well as the political transition program that was being supervised by the military government. In accordance with IMF conditionality rules and the reality of dwindling oil prices, state policy became a matter of direct disengagement from the oil industry, and the encouragement of private foreign and local investments in the industry.

In a bid to increase oil revenues under the SAP project, a memorandum of understanding (MOU) was signed between the government and the oil companies. Given the additional incentives that were included in the new MOU the oil multinationals intensified oil exploration and production operation in the Niger Delta. Consequently, the fragile Niger Delta environment came under severe environmental degradation leading to further impoverishment of the people, as they became increasingly unable to engage in their traditional occupations of fishing, farming and trading. This was the general condition under which the women of the oil-producing communities took up arms in defense of their environment. The state's response smacked of a classical rent collector: heavily armed troops were deployed to the restive communities, where women and young girls were beaten, abducted and raped (Manby, 2001).

The preceding amply demonstrates the role of SAP in the globalization of the Niger Delta environment. It also illustrates how adjustment, under the rubric of globalization, has detrimentally affected the peasants, especially the women of the Niger Delta oil communities. This is more so because "structural adjustment has helped to tie the physical economic resources of the African region more highly into serving the global system, while at the same time oiling the financial machinery by which wealth can be transported out of Africa and into the global system."

WOMEN: HUMAN RIGHTS VIOLATIONS, DISEMPOWERMENT, AND CONFRONTATION

> The environmental degradation of the Ogoni environment affects women more than men. This is because women do most of the peasant farming that is the main work of Ogoni people.

This assertion mirrors the experiences of rural women in the oil-producing communities. It also explains why women are usually found at the forefront of the struggle against environmental injustice and social neglect perpetrated by the transnational oil corporations, the most powerful proponents of globalization. The heavy burden which women now have to bear is underscored in a comprehensive report by a group of nine U.S. activists, academics and journalist after a ten-day fact-finding visit to the Niger Delta communities in September 1999. Commenting on the impact of loss of land and resources by the communities to oil company activities, the report notes that, "The diminished productivity and viability of local economies due to the environmental and social degradation caused by oil exploitation has affected the lives of women in unique ways" (Robinson, 1996:65). Since the great majority of the womenfolk have been marginalized and disempowered and are, as a consequence, unable to perform their traditional roles within their families, they have inevitably been forced to adopt alternative coping strategies. The harsh situation has forced many of them into prostitution as a means of survival (Esparza and Wilson, op. cit., p. 10). To be sure, this trend has generated its own contradictions within the households as well as within the larger society of the oil-producing communities. In many cases, for example, younger wives have reportedly abandoned their matrimonial homes and eloped with other men working for the oil multinationals. And for a society that is predominantly patriarchal, social mores have been severely undermined.

It should be noted, however, that the marginalization, disempowerment and exclusion of women in the Niger Delta did not begin with the introduction of economic adjustment. But insofar as it became a strong point for "indigenous feminists" (Turner and Oshare, op. cit., p. 330) to latch on to in their fight against environmental injustice in the 1990s, the mindless exploitation of nature (land, water and oil) by the forces of globalization alone can be held responsible. A 1993 World Bank Report on the impact of globalization on women lends credence to the experience of women in the Niger Delta (Ake, op. cit., p. 64). As a result of globalization, the report notes, the lot of women has steadily deteriorated: they must struggle, some times dangerously, to eke out an existence out of dwindling resources. Elaborating the reasons why Ogoni women have championed the struggle against increasing marginalization, disempowerment and repression in the Niger Delta oil communities, Diana Wiwa notes that:

> the constant acquisition of new territory for oil exploitation, and resultant pollution from the industry, has left the Ogoni women with no means to feed or support their families. Women have to go further away from home to find unpolluted water for their domestic chores. Their children have not received employment in the oil industry (a mere fifty Ogoni were employed until 1993, mainly as cleaners and drivers), making young men and women a continuing responsibility for their mothers long after they have been independent. These changes have brought a resultant rise of tension in the home. Testimonies of old women confirm that in the past there was less tension. (Wiwa, op. cit., p. 13)

What is underscored in this citation is that the women (and children also) are the most affected groups, they suffer most because, unlike their menfolk, they cannot easily migrate to the urban centers, to start life afresh. It underlines too the reason why the women have championed the fight-back from below against capital-driven globalization. Also, it highlights the emergence within the predominantly patriarchal culture of the Niger Delta, the reconfiguration of existing gender relations or what has been described as "gendered class alliance." This occurs "when women organized autonomously against the exploitation of oil corporations and local male dealers" (Turner and Oshare, op. cit., p. 330). Often, the alliance is reinforced when men forsake the male deal and join the ranks of the autonomously organized women to challenge capital and male dealers within their communities.

Following the example cited elsewhere of the Ogharefe and Ekpan women in 1984 and 1986, respectively, women from other parts of the region have confronted the oil companies, when their farms and fish ponds have been polluted. The Ogoni, the Egi and Eket women have at different times in the 1990s confronted the oil companies and voiced the demands of their communities to the companies (Saro-Wiwa, op. cit.). At times the demonstrations and protests turned bloody. As happened in April 1993 when a crowd of Ogoni women demonstrated peacefully against Wilbros, an American pipeline contractor firm working for Shell in the village of Biara. As Ken Saro-Wiwa reports:

> The women held twigs as they had been advised to do to indicate that they were protesting peacefully. The soldiers emptied their live ammunition on them. Eleven people were wounded, among them Mrs. Karalole Koregbara, a mother of five children who was shot in the left arm-it was subsequently amputated. (ibid., 156)

Furthermore, during the long drawn-out (1994–1999) military occupation of Ogoni in Rivers State and the one year-long militarization (1998–1999) of Ijawland in Bayelsa State, women were the worst victims of state-sponsored repression. For them, it was a double struggle in which they were raped and beaten, their husbands and sons killed or jailed, and their daughters either raped or taken away. Also, during this period, the women were constantly harassed by soldiers who extorted money from them and even prevented them from going to the farm or market. In most cases, trading activities became impossible, since market squares were constant targets, where goods were looted and/or set ablaze, and valuable personal effects as well as money carted away from homes (Wiwa, op. cit., p. 13).

Like their Ogoni, Umududja and Ijaw counterparts, the Egi women have had their fair share of confrontation with and repression at the hands of companies. In September 1998, the women took to the streets to protest against the activities of EIF, the giant French oil company. Their demands centered around the provision of basic social amenities such as water and electricity. During the protest, the women were quick to emphasize the stark contrast between their own residential areas and those of EIF workers, which were well supplied with basic amenities. The women also complained about the destruction of their farms and fish ponds by EIF and the consequent loss of their sources of income and food. Two months later, in November 1998, the Egi women were out on the streets once again. Despite the formidable presence of armed Mobile Police men numbering over a hundred, the women marched intrepidly toward the EIF gas installation plant and occupied it. They re-stated their earlier demands for water, electricity and compensation for loss of livelihood. Beyond this, the women also demanded the immediate release of Egi youths who had been detained. As a result of their pressure, "the youths were released, only to be charged in court" Turner et al., op. cit., p. 29). Barely one year later in August 1999, about five thousand women from the Egi women's movement laid siege to EIF's facility, shutting it for one day. This time, they demanded, non-violently, for clean air and water, as well as EIF's investment in community development projects. According to Esparza and Wilson, EIF's reaction was to deploy about forty local youths to whom it allegedly paid $2,000 each to aggressively break up the non-violent protest. Furthermore, EIF Oil Company is on record as having "paid the youth group representing the entire Egi community" (Esparza and Wilson, op. cit., p. 16). EIF's behavior is indicative of oil companies' insentivity toward host communities' plight and just demands, as well as attempts to divide and rule them, rather than investing in genuine and productive community development projects within their host community.

Today, the situation is much the same. The women of Niger Delta remain as marginalized and economically disempowered as ever, waiting for the dividends of globalization! Apparently impatient to wait any longer for promises from companies that treat them as cows to be milked, the women are again up in arms against the oil companies that made life miserable for them.

Thus, in July 2002, a two-week long sit-out protest was organized by hundreds of Itsekiri women from Ugborodo and Ogidigben when they occupied the Chevron-Texaco's Escravos Tank Farm, demanding, like their counterparts in other oil communities, the provision of basic social amenities such as water and electricity. They complained about the loss of their traditional occupations as a result of Chevron-Texaco's activities, which have devastated their farmlands and polluted their fishponds. The women also asked Chevron-Texaco to employ their children, so "that we the mothers will survive" (Awowede, 2002:44).

A few days later, following the resolution of the Escravos Tank Farm occupation, hundreds of aggrieved peasant women from the Ijaw communities of Gbaramatu and Egbema laid siege to four oil flow stations belonging, again, to Chevron-Texaco Oil Corporation. For almost two weeks, the women occupied the flow stations of Abiteye, Maraba/Otunana, Dibi and Olero creek. Like their counterparts from Ugborodo and Ogidigben, they charged Chevron-Texaco with neglect and environmental degradation. The Ijaw women, however, went one better than their Itsekiri counterparts. They demanded that each protester be paid, among other things, the sum of two million naira as recompense for the two-week long occupation, which according to the women, had cost each of them her trading and/or farming. A twenty million naira micro-credit scheme was also demanded by the women for each of the ten-odd communities that made up Gbaramatu and Egbema (Loc, op. cit). The Ijaw women later called off their siege, as did the women from the Itsekeiri communities of Ugborodo and Ogidigben, following the signing of a MOU between them and Chevron-Texaco.

Of great import in the women's anti-globalization struggle in Nigeria's Delta region is the direct, resolute and noncompromising attitude these grassroots women have adopted in their demands for environmental remediation and recompense. Given that the Niger Delta communities are predominantly patriarchal in nature, it becomes easier to appreciate the daring courage exhibited by these women. Indeed it is reasonable to suggest that these women peasants and traders decided to pick up the gauntlet in desperation and in defiance of their menfolk who habitually engaged in "male deals" with the oil companies at the expense of the communities (Turner and Oshare, op. cit.). It is also to be observed that the struggles of the Niger Delta women against the onslaught of economic globalization on their subsistence is a testament to the fact that even in patriarchal African societies, such as those of Nigeria's Delta region, there exist channels through which women can fight for their rights.

In the light of the preceding, it is clear that from the embattled Itsekiri communities of Ugborodo and Ogidigben to the Ijaw communities of Gbaramatu to the Urhobo women of Ekapan, all in Delta State, and to the Ilaje community in Ondo State, the women of Niger Delta are waging renewed battles against "anti-corporate, anti-war movement for globalization from below" (Turner and Brownhill, 2001:805). The following statements by Queen Uwawa and Christiana Mene, respectively, are instructive:

> for 38 years Chevron has been taking oil from Escravos (with) nothing to show for it, no development. We used to catch fish and crayfish for food, but that is not possible. The fishes and crayfish have gone away. They left because Chevron has polluted rivers and creeks. (Awowede, op. cit., p. 44)
>
> We want Chevron to employ our children. If Chevron does that we the mothers will survive, we will see food to eat. Our farms are all gone due to Chevrons pollution of our water. We used to farm cassava, okro, pepper and others. Now all the places we have farmed are sinking. That is why we told Chevron that Escravos women and Chevron are at war. (Loc, op. cit.)

The foregoing analysis has shown how globalization has blighted local subsistence production by destroying the physical environment of the people of Niger Delta, with grave consequences for the women of the region. The analysis has also demonstrated that women, especially the farmers and traders, have been hardest hit in the process. As a consequence and not surprisingly, they have been in the vanguard of demonstrations and protests against the devastation of the environment on which they depend for their livelihoods and survival. This struggle has, of course, led to some transformation in gender relations within the communities of the oil-producing region. The emergence of gendered class alliances amid long-established patriarchal structures has enormously strengthened the gathering of the wind of globalization from below.

CONCLUSION: TOWARD GENDER EMPOWERMENT, RESPECT FOR HUMAN RIGHTS, AND SUSTAINABLE DEVELOPMENT IN THE NIGER DELTA

In this chapter we have looked at gender and environment. In doing so, we laid bare the inevitable conflict that arises between women, whose very existence is tied to their environment, and the oil transnational corporations and the Nigerian State, whose object and the nature of the policies they pursue with respect to the Niger Delta environment are incompatible and contradictory to the people's perception of environmental security and sustainable development. Indeed, this contradictory perception of environmental governance strategies lies at the heart of the perennial confrontation between the women and the forces of global capitalism backed by the coercive instruments of the state. We noted that the women's fight to protect their environment has also brought them into conflict with their menfolk, who, on account of material benefits have, more often than not, sought to undermine the women's struggle. However, these "male-dealers," to adopt Terisa Turner's expression, have had to contend with the alliance of a majority of the youth in the region and a small, but growing minority of menfolk who have identified with the women in their struggle to protect the environment.

We located the background to the women's struggle in the context of the worsening national economic crisis engendered by the crisis in the global oil market. However, it was the hardships engendered by economic adjustment in the context of globalization that actually galvanized the women into action. For under SAP, as we have seen, the women experienced unprecedented levels of hardship, as their environment came under severe pressure, as the transnational oil corporations intensified their exploitation of oil and gas. Thus, vast tracts, of arable land were alienated by oil companies, as the Nigerian State was keen on the repayment of its debt to the IMF and the World Bank and other Western creditors. Oil spills, gas flares and other forms of oil industry-related pollution recorded huge increases during this period. And given the stated objectives of the state, and the forces of global capitalism, affected communities were hardly ever compensated.

We argued that for the women, it was a double struggle. For not only did they lose their farms and fishing grounds to oil industry-related projects and pollution, but they are also the most vulnerable to sexual abuse (rape and prostitution, for example) and daily harassment by security forces and oil workers—both local and expatriate. The fact that it is the women who lost their husbands, sons and daughters and, what is more, it is they who took care of the wounded and the maimed, inclined them to react in a militant fashion. Add to this the fact that some of them who had, under the unforgiving circumstances, struggled to send their children to higher institutions, only for them to be unemployed, fed the women with nothing but anger and bitterness. It is a truism that a country that neglects to invest in the welfare of its women is sitting on a time bomb. The oil companies have not done enough to improve the plight of the women in the region. Probably lost to them is the fact that women have a crucial role to play, both as mothers and wives, in the resolution of the lingering crises in the Delta. And they cannot prevail upon their husbands and sons to lay down their arms if they remain impoverished, neglected, abused and disempowered.

NOTES

1. *Cambridge International Dictionary of English* (1996) (Cambridge, UK: Cambridge University Press), p. 586.

2. Forum for African Women Educationists (FAWA) and UNESCO (n. d.) *Gender Analysis for Educational Policy Making*, Mimeo, p. 10.

3. *BBC English Dictionary* (1992) (London: Harper Collins Publishers), p. 380.
4. Constitutional Rights Project (CRP) Ibid., p. 7.
5. See, for example E. J. Alagoa's The Niger Delta States and their Neighbours, op.cit., and G. O. Onosodes (2003) *Environmental Issues and Challenges of the Niger Delta: Perspectives from the Niger Delta Environmental Survey* (Lagos: Lilybank Property and Trust Limited).
6. Constitutional Rights Project, op.cit., p. 12.
7. *Shell in the Niger Delta* (Ibadan: Kraft Books Limited).

REFERENCES

Ake, Claude (2001) *Democracy and Development in Africa* (Ibadan: Spectrum Books Limited).

Alagoa, E. J. (1976) The Niger Delta and their Neighbours, to 1800, in J. F. A. Ajayi and Michael Crowther (eds) *History of West Africa Volume One*, 2nd ed. (Harlow Essex: Longman Group Limited), p. 355; Alagoa, E. J. (1964) *The Small Brave City-State: A History of Nembe-Brass in the Niger Delta* (Ibadan: Ibadan University Press), p. 58; Roberts (2005) Environment and Livelihood in the Niger Delt," op. cit., p. 100.

Alagoa, E. J. (2002) God is Mother: A Historical Review of Women in the Development of Niger Delta Communities, in Nkparom Ejiwutu and O. I. Amakieri (eds) *Women in Nigerian History: The Rivers and Bayelsa State Experience* (Port Harcourt: Onyoma Publications Limited), p. 40.

Awowede, O. (2002) The Case against Chevron, *Insider Weekly*, August 19, p. 44.

Bangura, V. (1998) Recession and Nigeria's Foreign Policy, *Nigerian Journal of International Affairs*, Vol. 15, No. 1.

Doyle, Jack (2002) *Riding the Dragoon: Royal Dutch Shell and the Fossil Fire* (Boston: Environmental Health Fund).

Egwu, Samuel (1998) *Structural Adjustment, Agrarian Change and Rural Ethnicity in Nigeria* (Uppsala: Nordiska Afri-Kainstitutet).

Ekine, Sokrari (1999) Women in the Niger Delta: Violence and Struggle (website http:ndw.kabissa.org/Articles).

Ekine, Sokrari (2001) *Blood and Oil* (London: Centre for Democracy and Development).

Enemuo, C. Francis (1999) Gender and Women Empowerment, in Remi Anifowose and Francis Enemuo (eds) *Elements of Politics* (Lagos: Malthouse Press Limited), p. 227.

Esparza, E., and Monica Wilson (1999) *Oil for Nothing: Multinational Corporations, Environmental Destruction, Death and Impunity in the Niger Delta* (USA: Inkworks Press).

Fatton Jr., Robert (1989) *Gender Class and State in Africa*, in Jane L. E .Parpart and Ankie K. A. Hoogvelt (1997) *Globalization and the Post-colonial World: The New Political Economy* (London: Macmillan Press: Limited), p. 166.

Ijaw Youth Council (1999) *The Kaiama Declaration: Resolutions of the December*, 1998 All Ijaw Youths Conference held in the Niger Delta, Nigeria (Port Harcourt: Ijaw Council for Human Rights), p. 5.

Jev, Margret, Opuenebo and Yomi Oruwari (2002) Women and Gender Profile, in Ebiegberi Joe Alagoa and Abi A. Derefaka (eds) *The Land and People of Rivers State: Eastern Niger Delta* (Port Harcourt: Onyoma Publications), p. 499.

Kemedi, Demieri Von (2003) *Community Conflicts in the Niger Delta Petro-Weapon or Policy Failure?* Berkeley Workshop on Environmental Politics Working Paper No.WP 03–12, Institute of International Studies, University of California, Berkeley.

Kiely, Ray (1998) The Crisis of Global Development, in Ray Kiely et al. (eds) *Globalization and the Third World* (London: Routledge).

Koripamo-Agary, Timiebi A., and Kaine Agary (2005) Women and Environment in the Niger Delta, in Kayo de Fayemi, Stella Amadi and Ololade Bamidele (eds) *Towards an Integrated Development of the Niger Delta* (Lagos: Centre for Democracy).

Leftwich, Adrian (1993) Governance, Democracy and Development in the Third World, *Third World Quarterly*, 14 (3) p. 607.

Manby, Bronwen (1999) *The Price of Oil: Corporate Responsibility and Human Rights Violations in Nigeria's Oil–Production Communities* (USA: Human Rights Watch).

Manby, Bronwen, op. cit.

Maya, Emmanuel (2004) Oil Killed Ijaws Oldest Ritual, *Saturday Sun*, Lagos, June 19, p. 12.

Mba, Nina (1982) *Nigerian Women Mobilized: Women's Political in Southern Nigeria, 1900–1965* (Berkeley: Institute of International Studies, University of California).

Nkoyo, Tayo (2000) The Niger Delta Peoples and the 1999 Constitution: A Gender Perspective, in *"The Emperor Has No Clothes" Report of the Proceedings of the Conference on the Peoples of the Niger Delta and the 1999 Constitution*, Port Harcourt, November 2–4, p. 127.

Obianime, A. U., D. D. Datubo-Brown, and S. Raphael Oruamabo (2002) Health, in Ebiegbori Joe Alagoa and Abi A. Derefaka (eds) *The Land and People of River State: Eastern Niger Delta*, op. cit.; Anayochukwu Agbo (2001) The Haze, the Heat and Hurt, *Tell*, Lagos, July, 23.

Okoh, Juliana (2003) Feminism: An African Perspective, in Nkparom C. Ejiwutu and Amakieri O. I. Grabriel (eds) op. cit., p. 23.

Olojede, Iyabo (2004) Public Policy and Gender Politics in Nigeria, in Solomon Akinboye (ed) *Paradox of Gender Equality in Nigeria Politics* (Lagos: Concept Publications Limited), p. 126.

Onosode, op. cit.

Pettman, Jan Jindy (1998) Gender Issues, in John Baylis and Steve Smith (eds) *The Globalization of World Politics: An Introduction to International Relations* (Oxford, UK: Oxford University Press), p. 488.

Roberts, op. cit., p. 197.

Roberts, F. O. Nyemutu (2004) Environment and Livelihoods in the Niger-Delta, in Kayode Fayemi et al. (eds), op. cit., p. 87.

Robinson, Deborah (1996) *Ogoni: The Struggles Continues* (Switzerland: World Council of Churches), p. 65.

Saro-Wiwa (1995) *A Month and A Day: A Detention Diary* (Ibadan: Spectrum Books Limited), p. 185; CRP (Constitutional Rights Project) (1999) *Land, Oil and Human Rights in Nigeria's Delta Region* (Lagos: CRP), p. 31.

Staudt (eds) *Women and State in Africa* (London: Lynne Rienner Publishers), p. 55.

Turner and Oshare, op. cit. Also see Terisa E. Turner, et al. (2001/2002) Fightback from the Commons: Gendered Class Alliances and Petroleum Struggles in Nigeria's Oil-belt: 1980–2002, *Cambridge Review of International Affairs*, Vol. XIV, No. 3.

Turner, T., and Leigh S. Brownhill (2001) Gender, Feminism and the Civil Commons: Women and the Anti-Corporate, Below, *Canadian Journal of Development Studies*, Vol. XIV. No. 3, p. 805.

Turner, T., and M. O. Oshare (1993) Women's Uprising against the Nigerian Oil Industry, *Canadian Journal of Development Studies*, Vol. XIV, No. 3.

UNDP (2001) International Conference on the Development of the Niger Delta, Draft Issue Paper (Restricted); Roberts, op. cit., p. 96.

Wiwa, Diana (1997) The Role of Women in the Struggle for Environmental Justice in Ogoni, *Delta*, October 3, p. 13.

Bibliography

Abdullah, H. J. and I. Hamza (2003), Women and Land in Northern Nigeria: The Need for Independent Ownership Rights, in I. M. Wanyeki (ed.) *Women and Land in Africa: Culture, Religion and Realizing Women's Rights*. Cape Town: David Philip Publishers, pp. 133–147.

Abiodun, A. (1998), The Making of Political Parties. *The Guardian*, September 11.

Aderinto, F. O. A. and T. Fashoyin (eds.) (1986), *Manpower Development and Utilization in Nigeria: Problems and Policies*. Lagos: Lagos University Press.

Afonja, S. and B. Aina (eds.), (1995), *Nigerian Women in Social Change*. Ile- Ife, OAU Programme in Women Studies.

Agozino, B. and Ike Anyanike (2007), IMY AHIA: Traditional Igbo Business School and Global Commerce Culture. *Dialectical Anthropology*, Vol. 31, No. 1–3, pp. 233–252.

Aguda, A. (1985), A New Perspective in Law and Justice in Nigeria. Text of lecture delivered at NIPPS, Kuru, October 25.

Ake, C. (1981), *A Political Economy of Africa*. Essex: Longman.

Ake, C. (1985), The Future of the State in Africa, *International Political Science Review*, Vol. 6, No.1, pp. 105–114.

Ake, C. (1992), *The Feasibility of Democracy in Africa*. Ibadan: CREDU.

Ake, C. (1993), The Unique Case of African Democracy, *International Affairs*, Vol. 69, No. 2, pp. 239–244.

Ake, C. (1995), *Democracy and Development in Africa*. New York: Brookings Institute.

Ake, C. (2000), *Feasibility of Democracy in Africa*. Council for the Development of Social Science Research in Africa (CODESRIA), Dakar, Senegal.

Ake, C. (2001), *Democracy and Development in Africa*. Ibadan: Spectrum Books Limited.

Akinrinade, O. and J. K. Barling (eds.) (1989), *Economic Development in* Africa. London: London Printer Publishers Ltd.

Akinrinade, Sola, (1999), Democracy and Security in Africa: Towards a Framework of Understanding, *Journal of Contemporary African Studies*, Vol. 17, (July), p. 219.

Akintola, S. O. (2004), A Focus on Female Discrimination and Seclusion in Nigeria, Ife Juris Review, *A Journal of Contemporary Legal and Allied Issues*, Vol. 1 IFJR Part 2, pp. 312–320.

Ako-Nai, R. I. (2004), Organising for Change :Global Initiatives and the Growth of Women Interest Groups in Nigeria. Paper presented at the National Conference on Social Problems and Development and the Challenges of Globalisation, Organised by Department of Sociology and Anthropology, Obafemi Awolowo University Ile –Ife, Osun State.

Alagoa, E. J. (1964), *The Small Brave City-State: A History of Nembe-Brass in the Niger Delta*. Ibadan: Iba dan University Press.

Akrami, N. (2005), Prejudice: The Interplay of Personality, Cognition and Social Psychology. A doctoral dissertation from the faculty of the social sciences, Uppsala University, Sweden.

Alagoa, E. J. (1976) The Niger Delta and their Neighbours, to 1800, in J. F. A. Ajayi and Michael Crowther (eds,), *History of West Africa Volume One*, 2nd Ed. Harlow Essex: Longman Group Limited, p. 355.

Alagoa, E. J. (2002), God is Mother: A Historical Review of Women in the Development of Niger Delta Communities, in Nkparom Ejiwutu and O. I. Amakieri (eds.), *Women in Nigerian History: The Rivers and Bayelsa State Experience*. Port Harcourt: Onyoma Publications Limited, p. 40.

Alamveabee, E. I. (2005), *Gender Concepts and Issues in Nigeria*. Mankurah: Aboki Publishers.

Alemany, Cecilia, Nerea Craviotto, Fernanda Hopenhaym, Ana Lidia Fernández-Layos, Nerea Craviotto, Fernanda Hopenhaym, Ana Lidia Fernández-Layos, and Alice Schlegel (eds.), (1977), *Sexual Stratification: A Cross Cultural View*. New York: Columbia University Press.

Alidou, O. and M. Turshen (2000), Africa: Women in the Aftermath of Civil War", in *Race and Class* Vol. 41, No. 4, p. 81.

Amadiume, I. (1995), *Gender, Political Systems and Social Movements: A West African Experience*. Dakar, Senegal: CODESRIA.

Amadiume, I. (1995), Gender, Political Systems and Social Movements: A West African Experience, pp. 78– 89 in M. Mamdani and E. Wamba-dua-Wamba (eds.), *African Studies Movements and Democracy*. Dakar, Senegal: CODESRIA.

Amina, A. A. (1993), Women's Rights in Law and Practice: Special Welfare, in Akintunde O. Obilade, *Women in Law*, Southern University Law Center and Faculty of Law, University of Lagos, p. 235.

Amuwo, K. (2005), The Peripheral State: Critical Perspectives on the Structure and Role of the Public Bureaucracy. *Journal of Development and Alternative Area of Studies*, Vol. 24, No. 3–4, pp. 119–130.

Anheir, H. (2004), *Civil Society: Measurement, Evaluation, Policy*. London: Civicus.

Ankie, Hoogvelt (1997), *Globalization and the Post-colonial World: The New Political Economy*. London: Macmillan Press, p. 166.

Ann, S. (1974), *Planning for Development in Sub-saharan Africa*. New York: Praeger Publishers.

Aries, E. (1996), *Men and Women in Interactions: Reconsidering the Differences*. New York: Oxford University Press.
Ashiru, M. A. O. (2004), Preserving the Dignity of Women, in Ife Juris Review, *A Journal of Contemporary Legal and Allied Issues*, Vol. 1, IFJR Pt. 2, pp. 250–263.
Ashiru, M. A. O. (2007), Gender Discrimination in the Division of Property in Nigeria", *Journal of African Law*, Vol. 51, No. 2.
Ashton-Jones, N. (1988), *The ERA Handbook to the Niger Delta: The Human Ecosystems of the Niger Delta*. London: Environmental Rights Action.
Ate, Bassey (1992), The Presence of France in West-Central Africa as a Fundamental Problem to Nigeria, in Bassey E. Ate and Bola Akinterinwa (eds.), *Nigeria and its Immediate Neighbours: Constraints and Prospects of Sub-Regional Security in the 1990s*. Lagos: Nigerian Institute of International Affairs (NIIA)in cooperation with Pumark Nigeria Ltd., pp. 17–20.
Awake! (1998), *Will There Ever Be Human Rights For All*, Benin, Nigeria, November 22, p. 9.
Awe, B. (1977), The Iyalode in the Traditional Yoruba Political System, in Alice Schlegel (ed.), *Sexual Stratification: A Cross-Cultural View*. New York: Columbia University Press, pp. 144–160.
Awe, B. (1992), Saviours of their Societies, in *Nigerian Women in Historical Perspective*, Bolanle Awe (ed.). Lagos: Sankore Publishers Ltd., pp. 1–10.
Awe, B. (1994), *Nigerian Women in Historical Perspective*. Ibadan: Sankore/Bookcraft.
Awolowo, O. (1996), *Path to Nigeria Greatness*. Ibadan: Oxford University Press.
Awolowo, O. (2000), The Case Against Chevron, *Insider Weekly*, August 19, p. 44.
Ayandele, E. A. (1966), *Missionary Influence on Modern Nigeria, 1842–1914: A Political and Social Analysis*. London: Longman.
Ayeni-Akeke, O.A. (2008), *Foundation of Political Science*. Ibadan: Ababa Press.
Ayoade, J. A. A. (1997), *Nigeria and the Squandering of Hope*. An Inaugural Lecture delivered at the University of Ibadan. Ibadan: Vantage Publishers Limited, pp. 2–3.
Ayoob, Mohammed (1991), The Security Problematic of the Third World, *World Politics*, Vol. 43, No. 2. (January), pp. 257–283.
Ayoob, Mohammed (1995), *The Third World Security Predicament: State Making, Regional Conflict and International System*. Boulder, CO: Lynne Rienner.
Babatunde, Lawal (1996), *The Gèèlèèdéé Spectacle: Art, Gender, and Social Harmony in an African Culture*. Seattle: University of Washington Press.
Babayemi, S. O. (1987), The Role of Women in Politics and Religion in Oyo. Paper presented at the Institute of African Studies, University of Ibadan on Seminar on Women's Studies: The State of the Arts Now in Nigeria, November, 5.
Ball, Nicole (1988), *Security and Economy in the Third World*. Princeton, NJ: Princeton University Press, p. 388.
Ball, N. (1996), *Priority Tasks for Rebuilding War-torn Societies*. Washington DC: International Development Research Centre.
Bangur, V. (1998), Recession and Nigeria's Foreign Policy, *Nigerian Journal of International Affairs*, Vol. 15, No. 1.
Barber, B. R. (1984), *Strong Democracy: Participatory Politics for a New Age*. Berkeley: University of California Press.
Barikor-Wiwa, D. (1997), The Role of Women in the Struggle for Environmental Justice in Ogoni', *Cultural Survival Quarterly*, Fall.

Batliwala, Srilatha (2002), Grassroots Movements as Transnational Actors: Implications for Global Civil Society, *Voluntas: International Journal of Voluntary and Non-Profit Organisations*, Vol.13, No. 4, pp. 393-409.

Bayart, Jean-Francois (1986), Civil Society in Africa, in Patrick Chabal (ed.), *Political Domination in Africa*. Cambridge, UK: Cambridge University Press.

Berkowitz, Morton and P. G. Bock (1968), National Security, in David L. Sills (ed.), *International Encyclopedia of the Social Sciences*. New York: Macmillan, p. 40.

Bermeo, N. and P. Nord (2000), *Civil Society before Democracy*. New York: Rowman & Littlefield.

Blair, Tony (1999), Doctrine of the International Community. Excerpt of speech in Chicago, April 22, on occasion of NATO's 50th anniversary, p. 19.

Booth, K. (ed.) (1990), *New Thinking about Strategy and International Security*. London: Unwin Hyman.

Boserup, Ester (1970), *Women's Role in Economic Development*. London: George Allen and Unwin.

Boulding, E. (1977), *Women in the Twentieth Century World*. New York: John Wiley and Sons.

Bronwen, Manby (1999), *The Price of Oil: Corporate Responsibility and Human Rights Violations in Nigeria's Oil-Production Communities*. Human Rights Watch.

Bouta, T. and G. Frerks (2002), *Women's Roles in Conflict Prevention, Conflict Resolution and Post-Conflict Reconstruction: Literature Review and Institutional Analysis*. The Hague: Netherlands Institute of International Relations, www.clingendael.nl/cru/publications/publications_occ_papers.htm

Brown, Seyom (1998), World Interests and the Changing Dimensions of Security, in Klare and Chandrani (eds.), *World Security: Challenges for a New Century*, op. cit., p. 3.

Brume, F. (n.d.), Oil-pipeline vandalization in the Niger Delta: The way out. Urhobo Historical Society www.waado.org

Bruno, K. (February 6, 2002), The Whole World was Watching: New York Stages a Peaceful Protest against the World Economic Forum. CorpWatch.www.corpwatch.org.

Bryson, V. (1992), *Feminist Political Theory*. London: Macmillan Press Ltd.

Bunch, Charlotte (1995), Transforming Human Rights from a Feminist Perspective, in Julie Peters and Andrea Wolper (eds.), *Women's Rights, Human Rights: International Feminist Perspectives*. New York: Routledge.

Buzan, Barry (1991), *People, States and Fear—An Agenda for Security Studies in the Post- Cold War Era*. London: Harvester Wheatsheaf, p. 216.

Byrne, B. (1996), *Gender, Conflict and Development*, Vol. I: Overview, BRIDGE Report 34. Brighton: BRIDGE/Institute of Development Studies.

Campbell, Horace (2000), Peace Narrative and Education for Peace in Africa, in Adele Jinadu (ed.), *The Political Economy*, op. cit.

Campbell, J. (2010), *Electoral Violence in Nigeria*. Council on Foreign Relations, Center for Preventive Action, Contingency Panning Memorandum No. 9.

Charlton, E. and M. Sue (1984), *Women in Third World Development*. Boulder, CO: Westview Press Inc.

Chazan, Naomi (1992), Africa's Democratic Challenge, *World Policy Journal*, Vol. 9, No. 2, pp. 279–307.

Chen, M. A., J. Vanek, and M. Carr (2004), *Mainstreaming Informal Employment and Gender in Poverty Reduction*. London: Commonwealth Secretariat.

Chikwe, K. (2003), Prospects of Women in Meteorology, in *This Day Newspaper*, Saturday, May 24, p. 32.

Clapham, Christopher (2006), The Political Economy of African Population Change, *Population and Development Review*, Vol. 32, pp. 96–114.

Clark, Cindy and Sarah Rosenhek (2008), Implementing the Paris Declaration: Implications for the Promotion of Women's Rights and Gender Equality, commissioned by the Canadian Council for International Cooperation (CCIC) and developed by AWID and WIDE.

Cockburn, C. (1998), *The Space Between Us: Negotiating Gender and National Identities in Conflict*. London: Zed Books.

Cohen, J. and A. Arato (1992), *Civil Society and Political Theory*. Cambridge, MA: MIT Press.

Concepts of Gender and Gender Relations, www.genderfund.com.ua

Connell, R. W. (1987), *Gender and Power*. Stanford, CA: Stanford University Press.

Convention on the Elimination of All Forms of Violence Against Women (2008) and Accountability to Gender Equality in Nigeria: A Shadow Report. CEDAW.

Cooley, A. and J. Ron (2002), The NGO Scramble: Organisational Insecurity and the Political Economy of Transnational Action, *International Security*, Vol. 27, No. 1, pp 5–39.

Coquery-Vidrovitch, Catherine (1996), *African Women: A Modern History*. Boulder, CO: Westview Press.

Counts and Brown et al. (1999), *To Have and to Hit*. Chicago: University of Chicago Press, p. 77.

Cruz, F. A. (1992), New Perspective of Community Development. Discussion paper presented in Department of Agricultural Extension and Rural Studies (DAERS) Research, Extension, and Curriculum Planning. Workshop held on December 20. University of the Philippines Los Baños (UPLB), Philippines.

Davies, M. (ed.) (1994), *Women and Violence: Realities and Responses Worldwide*. London: Zed Books.

Deborah, S. D. and B. obert (eds.) (1976), *The Forty Nine Percent Majority: The Male Sex Role*. Reading, MA: Addison Wesley.

Deibert, J. Ronald (1997), Exorcismus Theoriae: Pragmatism, Metaphors and the Return of the Medieval in International Relations Theory, *European Journal of International Relations*, Vol. 3, No. 2 (June), pp. 167–192.

Demieri Von Kemedi (2003), *Community Conflicts in the Niger Delta Petro-Weapon or Policy Failure*? Berkeley Workshop on Environmental Politics Working Paper No. WP 03–12, Institute of International Studies, University of California, Berkeley.

Denis Ityaryar et al. (1992), *The State and Women in Nigeria*. University of Jos Press, p. 54.

Deudney, D. (1990), Environment and Security: Muddled Thinking, *Bulletin of Atomic Scientists*, Vol. 47, No. 3, pp. 22–28.

Diamond, Larry (1988), Introduction: Roots of Failure, Seeds of Hope, in Larry Diamond, Juan Linz, and Seymour Martin Lipset (eds.), *Democracy in Developing Countries: Africa*. Boulder, CO: Lynne Rienner Publishers.

Diamond, Larry (1999), *Developing Democracy toward Consolidation*, Baltimore, MD: Johns Hopkins University Press.

Diana, Wiwa (1997) The Role of Women in the Struggle for Environmental Justice in Ogoni, *Delta*, October 3, p. 13.

Dobel, J. P. (1978), The Corruption of a State. *American Political Science Review*, Vol. 72, No 3, pp. 958–973.

Doornbos, M. (1982), Ugandan Society and Politics: A Background", in G. N. Uzoigwe (ed.), *Uganda: The Dilemma of Nationhood*. New York: NOK.

Doyle, Jack (2002), *Riding the Dragoon: Royal Dutch Shell and the Fossil Fire*. Boston: Environmental Health Fund.

Dreze, J. and A. Sen (1989), *Hunger and Public Action*. New York: Oxford University Press.

Dworkin, Ronald (1977), *Taking Rights Seriously*. Cambridge, MA: Harvard University Press.

Easterly, W. and Serven Luis (2003), *The Limits of Stabilization: Infrastructure, Public Deficits and Growth in Latin America*. Stanford, CA: Stanford University Press and the World Bank.

Edelman, M. (1972), *The Symbolic Uses of Politics*. Chicago: University of Illinois Press.

Egwu, Samuel (1998), *Structural Adjustment, Agrarian Change and Rural Ethnicity in Nigeria*. Uppsala: Nordiska Afri-Kainstitutet.

Ekeh, Peter (1975), Colonialism and the Two Publics in Africa: A Theoretical Statement, *Comparative Studies in Society and History*, Vol. 17, No.1, pp. 91–112.

Ekine, S. (2000), *Blood and Oil: Testimonies of Violence from Women of the Niger Delta*. London: Centre for Democracy and Development.

Ekineh, A. (2001), *Tears and Weeping of the Niger Delta*. London: Southern Solidarity.

Elder Jr., G. H. (1995), The Life Course Paradigm. Social Change and Individual Development. In P. Moen, G. H. Elder Jr., and K. Luscher (eds.), *Examining Lives in Context* (pp. 101–139). Washington DC: American Psychological Association.

Emiola, A. (2000), *Nigerian Labour Law*. Ogbomosho, Nigeria: Emiola (Publishers) Limited, p. 43.

Enemuo, C. Francis (1999), Gender and Women Empowermnet, in Remi Anifowose and Francis Enemuo (eds.), *Elements of Politics*. Lagos: Malthouse Press Limited, p. 227.

Enemuo, F. (2005), Gender and Women Empowerment, in Remi Anifowose and Francis Enemuo (eds.), *Elements of Government*. Lagos: Sam Iroanusi Publications.

Engel, Merry Sally (2009), Rights, Religions and Community: Approaches to Violence against Women in the Context of Globalization", *Law and Society*, Vol. 35, No. 1, pp. 39–88.

Engels, F. (1884), *The Origin of the Family, Private Property and the State*. Enrich, XXI.

Eno, J. (2000), Women's Strategies for Peace: Gains and Losses in Sierra Leone, in *Report on the Workshop on Conflict Transformation in Africa: African Women's Perspectives*. London: International Alert and African Women for Research and Development (AAWORD), www.international-alert.org/pdf/pubgl/workshop.pdf

Equality@work (2001), An information base on equal employment opportunities for women and men, Geneva, ILO.

Esparza, E. and Monica Wilson (1999), *Oil for Nothing: Multinational Corporations, Environmental Destruction, Death and Impunity in the Niger Delta*. Ink-works Press.

Ezeaku, I. et al. (1990), *Socio Philosophical Perspective of African Traditional Religion*. Enugu: New Age Publishers.

Fadipe, N. (1970), *The Sociology of the Yoruba*. London: Oxford University Press.

Faseke, M. (1998), The Role of Women in Traditional Yoruba Society: A Review, in Ogunremi, Deji and Adediran 'Biodun (eds.), *Culture and Society in Yorubaland*. Ibadan: Rex Charles Publication in association with Connel Publications.

Fatton, Robert (1995), Africa in the Age of Democratization: The Civic Limitations of Civil Society, *African Studies Review*, Vol. 38, No. 2, pp. 67–99.

Federal Government of Nigeria (2004), *National Economic Empowerment Development Strategy*.

Federal Office of Statistics (2004), *Report of Nigeria Living Standard Survey 2003/2004*. Abuja: FOS.

Federal Republic of Nigeria (1999), *The Constitution of the Federal Republic of Nigeria*. Lagos: Federal Government Printer, pp. 892–893.

Federal Republic of Nigeria (2006), *National Gender Policy, Federal Ministry of Women Affairs and Social Development*.

Federal Republic of Nigeria (2008), *National Gender Policy: Strategic Implementation Framework and Plan*, Abuja.

Federal Republic of Nigeria, National Bureau of Statistics (2008), Women and Men in Nigeria, Facts and Figures 2001-2006, Vol. 2, September.

Fentiman, A. (1996), The Anthropology of Oil: The Impact of the Oil Industry on a Fishing Community in the Niger Delta. *Social Justice*. Vol. 23. Issue: 4. Crime & Social Justice Associates.

Ferguson, A. (2009), Empowerment, Development and Women's Liberation, in *The Political Interests of Gender Revisited*, A. G. JonasdoHir and K. B. Jones (eds.). Manchester, UK: Manchester University Press, pp. 84–101.

Ferris, E. (1993), *Women, War and Peace*, Life and Peace Research Report 14, Upsala: PRIO.

Fjeldstad, O. and J. Isaksen (2008), Anti-corruption Reforms: Challenges, Effects and Limits of World Bank Support. Background Paper to Public Sector Reform: What Works and Why? An IEG Evaluation of World Bank Support.

Forde, Daryll and G. I. Jones (1950), The Ibo- and Ibiobio-speaking peoples of South-Eastern Nigeria. London.

Fox, Jonathan (2000), Civil Society and Political Accountability: Propositions for Discussion, Working Paper, Notre Dame, Hellen Kelloggs Institute for International Studies, University of Notre Dame.

Fried, E. (1975), *Women and Men: An Anthropological View*. New York: Holt Rinehart and Winston.

Fukuyama, F. (1992), *The End of History and the Last Man*. London: Hamish Hamilton.

Garba, P. K. (1997), A Strategy for Empowering Women: Application to Trade Union Activities, pp. 244–276 in P. K. Garba, B. Akanji, and I. Isiugo-Abanihe (eds.), *Women and Economic Reforms in Nigeria*. Ibadan: WORDOC.

Galtung, J. (1995), Twenty-Five Years of Peace Research: Ten Challenges and Responses, *Journal of Peace Research*, Vol. 22.

Gana, A. T. (2005), The Democracy-Development Nexus, in A. T. Gana and Y. Omelle (eds.), *Democratic Rebirth in Nigeria*, Vol.1, Afrigov.

Garner, B. (2004), *Black's Law Dictionary*. New York: Thomas West Publishers, p. 1601.

Gender Empowerment and Sustainable Development in Africa'Iroko (1997), Vol. 2, No. 3, August.A Networking Publication of the Atlass Project.

Gender Issues in the World of Work (1995), ILO Gender Training for ILO Staff and Constituents for the Promotion of Equality for Women Workers, INT/93/MO9/NET, Geneva

GENDER ISSUES. An Occasional newsletter of National Coalition on Affirmative Acton (NCAA), an umbrella organization of over 100 NGOs across Nigeria working on women's rights and affirmative action. Vol. 1, No. 2, p. 10..

Gibbon, P. and Yusuf B. Ofstad (eds.) (1992), *Authoritarianism, Democracy and Adjustment: The Politics of Economic Reform in Africa*. Uppsala: Nordic African Institute.

Giles, W. and J. Hyndman (2003), *Sites of Violence: Gender and Conflict Zones*. Berkeley: University of California Press.

Glick, P. and S. J. Fiske (1996), The Ambivalent Sexism Inventory: Differentiating Hostile and Benevolent Belief about Men. *Psychology of Women Quarterly*, Vol. 23, pp. 519–536.

Glick, P. and S. T. Fiske (2001), An Ambivalent Alliance: Hostile and Benevolent Sexism as Complementary Justifications for Gender Inequality. *American Psychologist*, Vol. 35, No. 2, pp. 109–118.

Godwin, D. and D and J. Marlowe (1990), *Farms, Wives, Labour Force Participation, and Earnings Rural Sociology* Vol. 55, No. 1, Spring.

Group for the Defence of Women (2003), *Domestic Violence Against Women in Nigeria: A Nation-wide Survey*, Enugu, pp. 11–22.

Hall, W. W. (1862), Health of Farmer's Family, United States Department of Agriculture Annual Report.

Handbook on Women's Empowerment through Legal Awareness (2002), Gender and Development for Cambodia, Phnom Penh, Cambodia.

Hart, H. L. A. (1961), *The Concept of Law*. Oxford, UK: Oxford University Press.

Hawthorn, G. (1993), Liberalization and Modern Liberty: Four Southern States, *World Development*, Vol. 21, No. 1, pp. 1299–1312.

Hedley and Dorkeno (1992), *Violence Against Women*. Berlin: Adrienne Press, p. 61.

Hemenway, D., T. Shinoda-Tagawa, and M. Miller (2002), Firearm Availability and Female Homicide Victimization Rates Among 25 Populous High-Income Countries, *Journal of the American Medical Women's Association*, Vol. 57, No. 2, Spring.

Hobsbawn, E. and T. Ranger (eds.) (1983), *The Invention of Tradition*. Cambridge, UK: Cambridge University Press.

Hodges, A. (2001), Children and Women's Rights in Nigeria: A Wake-Up Call. A UNIFECS Publication, National Planning Commission, Abuja.

Holsti, K. J. (1998), The Problem of Change in International Relations Theory, Institute of International Relations, The University of British Columbia, Working Paper No. 26. December, pp.1–2.

Honsby, A. S. (2001), *Oxford Advanced Learners Dictionary*, 6th Edition. New York: Oxford University Press.

hooks, bell (2000), *Feminist Theory: From Margin to Center*. Cambridge, MA: South End Press.

Human Rights Watch (2007), Criminal Politics: Violence, "Godfathers" and Corruption in Nigeria, Vol. 19, No. 16 (A).

Human Rights Watch (May 1999), *Crackdown in the Niger Delta*, Vol.11, No. 2 (A).

Hyden, Goran (1992), Governance and the Study of Politics, in Goran Hyden and Michael Bratton (eds.), *Governance and Politics in Africa*. Boulder, CO: Lynne Rienner Publishers, p. 12.

Ibeanu, I. (2000), Ethnicity and Transition to Democracy in Nigeria: Explaining the Passing of Authoritarian Rule in a Multi-ethnic Society. *African Journal of Political Science*, Vol. 5, No. 2, pp. 45–65.

Iboro, E. N. (2010), Violence Against Women in Nigeria: The Factors and the Dynamics, in *The Constitution: A Journal of Constitutional Development*, Vol. 10, No. 2, p. 87.

Igbatayo, S. (2001), Poverty Reduction and Sustainable Resource Management in the Niger Delta, *Proceedings of an International Conference on the Blueprint and Development Strategies for the Niger Delta*. February 26–28. World Environment Movement for Africa (WEMFA).Yenagoa.

Igbuzor, O. (2005), *Perspective on Democracy and Development*. Lagos Abuja: Joe Tolani and Associates.

Ihnovbere, J. O. (2002), *Towards a New Constitution in Africa*, CDD Occasional Papers.

Ijaw Youth Council (1999), The Kaiama Declaration: Resolutions of the December 1998 All Ijaw Youths Conference held in the Niger Delta, Nigeria. Port Harcourt: Ijaw Council for Human Rights, p. 5.

Ilesanmi, T. M. (1998), The Significance of the Myths of Women in Socio-Political Role Sharing among Yoruba People, in Kolawole E. Modupe (ed.), *Gender Perceptions and Development in Africa: A Socio-Cultural Approach*. Lagos: Arrabon Academic Publishers.

ILO Geneva (2000), A Partnership of Equals. Bureau for Gender Equality.

Iroanusi, Sam O. (2000), The Making of the Fourth Republic. Lagos: Sam Iroanusi.

Isiugo-Abanihe, I. M. (1997), Women's Education and Structural Adjustment in Nigeria, pp. 156–174 in P. K. Garba, B. Akanji, and I. Isiugo-Abanihe (eds.), *Women and Economic Reforms in Nigeria*. Ibadan: WORDOC.

Itoro-Eze-Anaba (2009), Stopping Violence Against Women, 10 years after, *Vanguard*, Friday, December 18, at p. 44; www.vanguardngr.com (accessed December 18, 2009).

Jacobs, S., R. Jacobson, and J. Marchbank (eds.) (2000), *States of Conflict: Gender, Violence and Resistance*. London: Zed Books.

Jaquette, Jane S. and Gale Summerfield (2006), *Introduction*, in Jane S. Jaquette and Gale Summerfield (eds.), *Women and Gender Equity in Development Theory and Practice: Institutions, Resources and Mobilization*. Durham, NC: Duke University Press.

James, Jay Carafano and Nile Gardiner (2003), US Military Assistance for Africa, *Heritage Foundation*, (Oct. 15), p. 2.

Jinadu, L. Adele (2000), Introduction: The Dialectics of Democracy, Development, Peace and Security in Africa, in L. Adele Jinadu (ed.), *The Political Economy of Peace and Security in Africa—Ethno-Cultural and Economic Perspectives*. Harare: Africa Association of Political Scientists Books.

Johnson, S. (1921), *The History of the Yorubas from the Earlier Times to the Beginning of the British Protectorate*. London (reprinted 1956).

Johnson-Odim, Cheryl and Nina Emma Mba (1997), *For Women and Nation: Funmilayo Ransome-Kuti of Nigeria*. Urbana: University of Illinois Press.

Johnston, M. (1991), Political corruption: Historical conflict and the rise of standards. *Journal of Democracy*, Vol. 2, No. 4, p. 60.

Jones, S. (2000), *Feminist Theory and Christian Theology*. Minneapolis, MN: Augsburg Fortress.

Kabeer, N. (2003), *Mainstreaming Gender and Poverty Eradication in the Millennium Development Goals*. London: Commonwealth Secretariat.

Kabeer, N. (2007), Marriage, Motherhood and Masculinity in the Global Economy: Reconfigurations of Personal and Economic Life. Institute of Development Studies

(IDS) working paper 290, www.ids.ac.uk/ids/bookshop

Kaldor, Mary (ed.) (2000), *Global Insecurity: Restructuring the Global Military Sector*, Vol. III. London: Pinter.

Karliner, J. (February 6, 2002), Porto Allegre: Globalizing hope. CorpWatch.www .corpwatch.org.

Kauffman, L. (ed.) (1989), *Gender and Theory: Dialogues on Feminist Criticism*. Oxford, UK: Basil Blackwell Limited.

Kelley, H. H., J. G. Holmes, N. L. Kerr, C. E. Rusbult, and P. A. M. van-Lange (2002), *An Atlas of Interpersonal Situations*. New York: Cambridge University Press.

Kent, J. M. (1985), Gender Roles and Inequalities in Political Participation: Results from an 8 Nation Study, *Western Political Quarterly*, Vol. 36, No. 5.

Kiely, Ray (1998), The Crisis of Global Development, in Ray Kiely et al. (eds.), *Globalization and the Third World*. London: Routledge.

Klonoff, E. A. and H. Landrine (1995), A Measure of Life and Recent Sexist Discriminations in Women Lives. *Psychology of Women Quarterly*, Vol. 28, pp. 430–472.

Krishna, R. and C. Lovell.(1985), *Rural Development in Asia and the Pacific*. The Synopsis of ADB Regional Seminar in Asia and the Pacific, October 15–23. Asian Development Bank. Manila: Asian Development Bank.

Kuteyi, O. S. (2000), The Rights of Nigerian Women Under The Laws: Real or Myth. *Gender Issues and National Development*, Vol. 2, No 1, p. 1.

Leftwich, Adrian (1993), Governance, Democracy and Development in the Third World, *Third World Quarterly*, Vol. 14, No. 3, p. 607.

Leaper, C. (1994), Exploring the Consequences of Gender Segregation on Social Relationships, in C. Leaper (ed.), *Childhood Gender Segregation: Causes and Consequences, New Directions for Child Development*. San Francisco: Jossey-Bass, pp. 67–86.

Leaper, C. and H. R. Tenenbaum (2002), Are Parents Gender Schema Related to their Children's Gender-Related Cognitions. A Meta-Analysis. *Developmental Psychology*, Vol. 38, No. 4, pp. 615–630.

Lewin, K. (1936), *Principles of Topological Psychology*. New York: McGraw Hill.

Lindsey, Charlotte (2002), *Women Facing War*. Geneva: International Committee on the Red Cross.

Loescher, G. (1999), Refugee Movements and International Security, *Adelphi Papers 268, Brasseys*, London.

Lorand Matory, James (1994), *Sex and the Empire That Is No More: Gender and the Politics of Metaphor in Oyo Yoruba Religion*. Minneapolis: University of Minnesota Press.

Lott, B. (1987), Sexist Discrimination as Distancing Behaviour 1: A Laboratory Demonstration. *Psychology of Women Quarterly*, Vol. II, No. 1, pp. 47–58.

Love, Roy (2004), HIV/AIDS in Africa: Links, Livelihoods and Legacies, *Review of African Political Economy (ROAPE)*, No. 102, pp. 639–648.

Lyman, T. S. (2009), *Contemporary Political Ideologies: A Comparative Analysis*. Belmont, CA: Wadsworth.

Mafeje, A. (1971), The Ideology of Tribalism, *Journal of Modern African Studies*, Vol. IX, No. 2, pp. 252–262.

Mafeje, A. (1995), Theory of Democracy and the African Discourse: Breaking Bread with my fellow Travelers, in E. Chole and J. Ibrahim (eds.), *Democracy Processes in Africa*. Dakar: CODESRIA.

Mafeje, A. (1995), Demographic and Ethnic Variations: A Source of Instability in Modern African States, paper presented at the 8th General Assembly of CODESRIA, Dakar (June).

Magubane, B. (1969), Pluralism and Conflict Situations in Africa: A New Look, *African Social Research*, Vol. VII, No. 2.

Mama, A. (1997), Feminism or Democracy? State Feminist and Democratization, in J. Ibrahim (ed.) *Expanding Democratic Space in Nigeria*. Daka, Senegal: CODESRIA National Studies Service.

Mamdani, M. (1995), A Critique of the State and Civil Society Parading in Africanist Studies, in M. Mamdani, and E. Wemba-dia Wamba (eds), *African Studies in Social Movement and Democracy.*, Dakar: CODESRIA Book Series.

Manchanda, Rita (2001), Redefining and Feminizing Security: Making a Difference in Security Policies, *Economist and Political Weekly*, Vol. 36, No. 43, p. 4100.

Mann, D. S. (1984), No Way to Treat a Lawyer: Female Lawyers in South Carolina, *Women Lawyers Journal*, Vol. 70, No. 2, Winter.

Marger, M. (1992), Ethnic Policy", in M. Hawkesworth and M. Kogan (eds.), *Encyclopaedia of Government and Politics*. Vol. 2. London: Routledge.

Maya, Emmanuel (2004), Oil Killed Ijaws Oldest Ritual, *Saturday Sun*, Lagos, June 19, p. 2.

Mba, Nina (1982), *Nigerian Women Mobilized: Women's Political in Southern Nigeria, 1900–1965*. Berkley: Institute of International Studies, University of California.

Midgley, J. (1986), Community Participation: History, Concepts, and Controversies, in J. Midgley (ed.), *Community Participation, Social Development and the State*. London.

Mingst, K. A. (2004), *Essentials of International Relations*. New York: W. W. Norten and Company.

Moghadam, Valentine (2005), *The Feminization of Poverty and Women's Human Rights*, SHS papers in women's studies/gender research No. 2, UNESCO, July.

Mohmoud, F. A. (2004), Are Human Rights Universal? Issues of Gender and Culture, *African Notes.*

Mojúbàolú Olúfúnké, Okome (2001), African Women and Power: Reflections on the Perils of Unwarranted Cosmopolitanism, Jenda: Journal of African Culture and Women Studies, Vol. 1, No. 1.

Moser, C. and F. Clark (eds.) (2001), *Victims, Perpetrators or Actors? Gender, Armed Conflict and Political Violence.* London: Zed Books.

Mosteller, R. (1992), Child Abuse Reporting Laws and Attorney- Client Confidences: The Reality and the Specter of Lawyer as Informant. *Duke Law Journal,* Vol. 42, No 2.

Naanen, B. (1995), Oil Producing Minorities and the Restructuring of the Nigerian Federation: The Case of the Ogoni, *Journal of Commonwealth and Comparative Politics,* Vol. 33, No. 1.

National Bureau of Statistics (2004), *Poverty Profile of Nigeria.* Abuja: NBS.

National Planning Commission (2001), *Children's and Women's Rights in Nigeria: A Wake-Up Call.* A UNIFECS Publication, National Planning Commission, Abuja.

National Population Commission (1991).1991 Population Census Figures. Abuja: NPC.

National Population Commission, United Nation's Population Fund (2001), Gender and Sustainable Development. Nigeria Population Census 1991 analysis NPC Abuja, May.

Nelien, Haspels (2001–2003), Gender Equality at Work. Various Briefing Notes, BAO/EASMAT, ILO Bangkok.

Nelien, Haspels (2001), *Report of Workshop on Participation of Indigenous Men and Women in Development* (December 11–13, Chiangmai, Thailand), ILO/EASMAT.

Nelien, Haspels (2001), Training of trainers' (TOT) *Manual on Gender Equality at Work in Viet Nam,* Briefing Notes for Participants, ILO Bangkok.

Nelien, Haspels and Rosalinda Terhorst (2004), Women Workers Rights and Gender Equality: Easy Steps for Workers in Cambodia Bangkok, ILO.

Nelien, Haspels, Zaitun Mohamed Kasim, Constance Thomas, and Deidre McCann (2001), Action Against Sexual Harassment at Work in Asia and the Pacific, International Labour Office, Bangkok.

Nhiwatiwa, N. (1989), Keynote Report at the Inter-parliamentary Symposium on the Participation of Women in the Political and Parliamentary Decision-making Process. Reports and Conclusion Series, Report and Documents No.16, Geneva.

Nigeria Country Report (1995), *4th World Conference on Women,* Beijing.

Nkoyo, Tayo (2000), The Niger Delta Peoples and the 1999 Constitution: A Gender Perspective, in *The Emperor Has No Clothes: Report of the Proceedings of the Conference on the Peoples of the Niger Delta and the 1999 Constitution,* Port Harcourt, November 2–4.

Nnanna, Ochereome (2007), Nigeria: Clark, Niger Delta Overlord? *Vanguard,* October 8.

Nnoli, O. (1978), *Ethnic Politics in Nigeria.* Enugu: Fourth Dimension Publishers.

Nnoli, O. (1992), Reflections on Ethnicity and Multiparty Democracy in Africa, paper presented at the Bellagio Conference of Fellows of the Rockefeller Reflections Programme, September 21–26.

Nnoli, O. (1995), *Ethnicity and Development in Nigeria*. Aldershot, UK: UNRISD and Avebury.

Nnoli, O. (2000), Globalization and Democracy in Africa, in D. Nabudere (ed.) *Globalization and the Post-Colonial African State,* Harare: African Association of Political Science.

Nwabueze, B. O. (1978), *Constitutionalism in the Emergent States*. London: C Horsts and Co.

Nwabueze, B. O. (1982), *A Constitutional History of Nigeria*. Ibadan: Longman Press.

Nwankwo, O. (2011), *Reviewing the 50+ Years of Women's Participation in Politics in Nigeria*. WACSERIES, Vol. 2, No. 1.

Nwogugu, E. I. (1974), Problems of the Dissolution of Customary Law Marriages in Nigeria. A Seminar Paper on New Direction in African Family Law.

Nye, J. S. (1967), Corruption and political development: A cost-benefit analysis. *American Political Science Review*, Vol. 51, No. 2, pp. 417–427.

Oakley, A. (1997), Who is Afraid of Feminism: Seeing through the backlash, in M. Halambos, *Sociology: Themes and Perspectives*. Slough: University Tutorial Press Limited.

Obayelu, A. E. (2007), Effects of Corruption and Economic Reforms on Economic Growth and Development: Lessons from Nigeria. Paper Prepared for 2007 African Economic Conference. Retrieved from:www.adb_admin_pg/documents/AEC.org. Accessed July 20.

Obi, S. N. C. (1966), *Modern Family Law in Southern Nigeria*. London: Sweet & Maxwell.

Obi, S. N. C. (2003), Emergent Female Power in Popular Struggles in Nigeria: Women Movements in the Niger Delta. Paper presented at an international workshop on Emergent Actors in African Political Economy, organized by the Institute of Developing Economies, Tokyo, February 14–15.

Obianime, A. U., D. D. Datubo-Brown, and Raphael S. Oruamabo (2002), Health in Ebiegbori Joe Alagoa and Abi A. Derefaka (eds.) *The Land and People of River State: Eastern Niger Delta,* op. cit., Anayochukwu Agbo (2001) The Haze, the Heat and Hurt, *Tell,* Lagos, July, 23.

Obilade, A. O. (1993), *Women in Law*. Southern University Law Center and Faculty of Law, University of Lagos.

Oduyoye, M. (1986), *The State of Christian Theology in Nigeria, 1980-81*. Ibadan: Daystar Press.

Ogba, O. (2006), *Women for Ordination: An Analytical Look*. Ibadan: Daystar Press.

Ogundiya, I. S. (2009), Political corruption in Nigeria: Theoretical perspectives and some explanations. *The Anthropologist,* Vol. 11, No. 4, pp. 281–292.

Ogundiya, I. S. (2010), Corruption: The Bane of Democratic Stability in Nigeria. *Current Research Journal of Social Sciences,* Vol. 2, No. 4, pp. 233–241.

Ogungbe, M. O. (2003), *Nigerian Law: Contemporary Issues.* Essays in Honour of Sir, Chief (Dr.) Gabriel Osawaru Igbinedion, The Esama of Benin Kingdom & Chancellor, Igbenidion University, Okada.

O'Hare, A. M. Bernadette and David P. Southall (2007), First do no Harm: The Impact of Recent Armed Conflict on Maternal and Child Health in Sub-Saharan Africa, *The Royal Society of Medicine,* Vol. 100, No. 12, pp. 564–570.

Okeke, P. (1998), First Lady Syndrome: The [En] Gendering of Bureaucratic Corruption in Nigeria, *CODESRIA Bulletin*, Nos. 3&4.

Okonto, Douglas, Von Kemedi, Ike Okonta, and Michael Watts (2004), Oil and Militancy in the Niger Delta: Terrorist Threat or Another Colombia? Niger Delta Economies of Violence Working Paper No. 4.

Olarinde, E. S. (1997), *Contemporary Issues in Nigerian Legal System*. Nigerian Bar Association, Ibadan.

Olaseeni, O. O. (2004), The Nigerian Law of Abortion: The Need For a Change, in Ife Juris Review, *A Journal of Contemporary Legal and Allied Issues*, Vol. 1 IFJR Part 2, pp. 392–400.

Olojede, I. (2000), *Women's Interest Organisations: Encounters with the State on Issues of Good Governance*. Ibadan: Simlad Press.

Olojede, I. (2004), Public Policy and Gender Politics in Nigeria, in Solomon Akinboye (ed.), *Paradox of Gender Equality in Nigeria Politics*. Lagos: Concept Publications Limited, p. 126.

Olojede, I. (2009), Women: The Neglected Force in Public Administration. An inaugural lecture delivered at Lagos State University, Lagos, May 5.

Olojede, I. (2009), *Women: The Neglected Force in Public Administration*. Lagos: Fortune News Publication.

Olukoshi, A. (1997) Associational Life, in L. Diamond et al. (eds.), *Transition without End*. Ibadan: Vintage.

Olukoya, Sam (2002), Women's Protests Against ChevronTexaco Spread Through the Niger Delta, *CorpWatch*, August.

Olusi, O. J. (n.d.), Socio Cultural, Economic and Environmental Determinants of African Women's Poverty and Disempowerment: The Nigerian Example. International Fund for Agricultural Development.

Omoleke, I. I. and L. A. Bisiriyu (2004), Discrimination Against Women: An Overview of the Problem of Gender Inequality in The Public Service in Nigeria. A paper presented at the National Conference on Social Problems Development and the Challenges of Globalisation, Organised by Department of Sociology and Anthropology, Obafemi Awolowo University Ile-Ife, June 16–17.

Omololu, F. O. (1997), Women's Movements in the Context of Economic Adjustment: A Critique (pp. 66–82) in P. K. Garba, B. Akanji, and I. Isiugo-Abanihe (eds.), *Women and Economic Reforms in Nigeria*. Ibadan: WORDOC.

Omonubi-McDonnel, M. (2003), *Gender Inequality in Nigeria*. Ibadan: Spectrum Books Ltd.

Onduku, A. (2003), Confronting The Human Security Dilemma Towards Building Sustainable Peace in Nigeria's Niger Delta. Text of a presentation at the ceremony in honour of Ms Ibiba Don Pedro, the Winner of the 2003 CNN African Journalist of the Year Award at the Lambeth Town Council Building, London, Saturday, October 18.

Onifade, J. A. (1989), The Adequacy of Legal Rights of Women in Nigeria, in Akande and Osinulu, Voter Education For Nigerian Rural Women, Reports of Two Workshops.

Onokah, M. C. (2007), *Family Law*. Ibadan, Nigeria: Spectrum Books.

Onuoha, A. (1995), *Women and Children in Traditional African Societies*. Aba, Nigeria: Frontier Publications Ltd.

Opuenebo Jev, Margret and Yomi Oruwari (2002), Women and Gender Profile, in Ebiegberi Joe Alagoa and Abi A. Derefaka (eds.), *The Land and People of Rivers State: Eastern Niger Delta*. Port Harcourt: Onyoma Publications.

Oputa, C. (1997), Equal Rights Under the Law: A Myth or Reality, in *Contemporary Issues in Nigerian Legal System*. Nigerian Bar Association, Ibadan, pp 1–25 at p. 5.

Oputa, C. (2003), Equal Rights Under the Law: A Myth or Reality, cited by Adeniyi Olatunbosun, An Enquiry Into the Rights of Working Class Women in Nigeria. Nigerian Law: Contemporary Issues, Essay in Honor of Sir Chief (Dr.) Gabriel Osawaru Igeinedion, College of Law Igbinedion Univerity, Okada, Benin City, pp. 76–87 at p. 83.

Oquaye, M. (1996), Discrimination Against Women in Africa: An Agenda for Public Policy Reform. Paper presented at the Conference on Women and Development, United Nations, Institute de Formation et de Rechenche Demographiques (IF-ORD) University of Yaounde, February 5–7.

Orewa, G. O. (1997), *We Are All Guilty*. Ibadan: Spectrum Books Ltd.

Organisation for Economic Co-operation and Development's Development Assistance Committee (OECD DAC) (2007), Workshop on Development Effectiveness in Practice: Applying the Paris Declaration to Advancing Gender Equality, Environmental Sustainability and Human Rights, Dublin, Ireland, April 26–27.

Osaghae, E. (1986), Do Ethnic Minorities Still Exist in Nigeria?, *The Journal of Commonwealth and Comparative Politics*, Vol. 24, No. 2.

Osaghae, E. E. (1995), Amoral Politics and Democratic Instability in Africa: A Theoretical Exploration. *Nordic Journal of African Studies*, Vol. 4, No. 1, pp. 62–78.

Oyewumi, Oyeronke (1997), *The Invention of Women: Making an African Sense of Western Gender Discourses*. Minneapolis: University of Minnesota Press.

Oyo, N. (1997), Women Organisations and Political Development. Paper presented at the Center for Research Documentation Workshop on Women's Rights, Politics and Democratisation, Kano, November 26–28.

Palmer, I. (1985), *The Impact of Agrarian Reform on Women*. West Hartford: Kumarian Press. Paper presented at the Workshop on Practical Strategies for Enhancing the Participation of Women in the Political Decision Making Process. Center for Democratic Studies.Abuja, May 6–8,1991.

Pankhurst, D. (2000), *Women, Gender and Peacebuilding*, Centre for Conflict Resolution Working Paper 5, Department of Peace Studies, University of Bradford, August.

Parenti, M. (1967), Ethnic politics and persistence of ethnic identification, *American Political Science Review*, Vol. 61, No. 4.

Park, A. E. W. (1963), *Sources of Nigerian Law*, p. 51.

Pateman, C. (1970), *Participation and Democratic Theory*. Cambridge, UK: Cambridge University Press.

Pateman, C. (1997), Introduction to Gender Studies: An Overview of Concepts on *Concepts and Methods for Gender and Women's Studies in Nigeria*. Report of the Network for Gender and Women's Studies in Nigeria. N. 2.

Pereira, C. (2001), *Feminist Theories*. Presentation prepared for the Gender Institute, Social Science Academy of Nigeria, held at Ogun-Osun River Basin Development Authority Guest House, May 22. Alabata' Abeokuta.

Pettiford, Lloyd (1996), Changing Concepts of Security in the Third World, *Third World Quarterly*, Vol. 17, No. 2, pp. 289–304.

Pettiford, Lloyd and Melissa Curley (1999), *Changing Security Agendas and the Third World*, London: Pinter Publishers.

Pettman, Jan and Jindy (1998), Gender Issues, in John Baylis and Steve Smith (eds.), *The Globalization of World Politics: An Introduction to International Relations*. Oxford, UK: Oxford University Press, p. 488.

Pietila, K. (2002), *Engendering the Global Agenda: The Story of Women and the United Nations*. Geneva: UNCTAD/UG, LS/191.

Pratto, F. (1996), Gender Politics: The Gender Gap in the Bedroom, Cupboard, and the Cabinet, in D. M. Buss and N. M. Malamuth (eds.), *Sex, Power and Conflict: Evolutionary and Feminist Perspectives*, pp. 179–230). New York: Oxford University Press.

Procter, P. (1978), *Longman Dictionary of Contemporary English: International Student Edition*. England: Longman Group Limited.

Promotion of Equality for Women Workers (1950), INT/93/MO9/NET. Geneva Publications Inco.

Putnam, R. (1993), *Making Democracy Work: Civic Traditions in Modern Italy*. Princeton, NJ: Princeton University Press.

Ranger, T. (1994), The invention of tradition revisited: the case of colonial Africa, in P. Kaarsholm and J. Hultin (eds.), *Inventions and Boundaries: Historical and Anthropological Approaches to the Study of Ethnicity and Nationalism*, Occasional Paper No. 11, International Development Studies, Roskilde University.

Ranney, A. (1958), *The Governing of Men*. New York: Henry Holt & Company, p. 4.

Ransome-Kute, F. (1961), The Status of Women in Nigeria, *Journal of Human Relations*, No. 1.

Rawls, J. (1971), *A Theory of Justice*. Cambridge MA: Belknap Press of Harvard University Press.

Renninger, J. P. (1982), The Future of Economic Cooperation Schemes in Africa with Special Reference to ECOWAS, in T. Shaw (ed.), *Alternative Futures for Africa*. Boulder, CO: Westview Press; see also J. P Renninger, (1979) *Multinational Cooperation for Development in West Africa*. New York: Pergamon Press for UNITAR.

Report of the Fourth World Conference on Women (1997), Beijing, September 4–15. United Nations publication, Sales No.E.96.IV.13, chap. I, resolution 1, annex II.

Report on National Seminar on Action Against Sexual Harassment at Work, Malaysia (2001), jointly organized by Department of Labour, Ministry of Human Resources, Malaysia and International Labour Organization Bangkok and Geneva Offices.

Robert, D. (2004), Public Administration Politics and Change in the Principle of Government in Nigeria. Lagos: Mbeyi & Associates (Nig) Ltd.

Robinson, Deborah (1996), *Ogoni: The Struggles Continues*. Geneva: World Council of Churches, p. 65.

Rosaldo, M. Z. and L. Lamphere (eds.) (1975), *Women, Culture and Society*. Stanford, CA: Stanford University Press.

Rosenau, James (1990), *Turbulence in World Politics*. Princeton NJ: Princeton University Press.

Rosenbloom, D. H. and D. D. Goldman (1999), *Public Administration: Understanding Management, Politics & Law in Public Sector*. Singapore: McGraw Hill.
Ryan, S. (1995), *Peace-Building and Conflict Transformation in Ethnic Conflict and International Relations*. Dartmouth, NH: Dartmouth Publishing.
Saro-Wiwa (1995), *A Month and A Day: A Detention Diary*. Ibadan: Spectrum Books Limited.
Schulera, Margaret A., et al. (1997), *Women's Human Rights Step by Step*. Washington, DC: Women, Law and Development International Publications.
Schwarz, H. (1979), Ethnic Minorities and Ethnic Politics in China, in W. Peterson (ed.), *The Background to Ethnic Conflict*. Leiden: E. J. Baill.
Seidman, A. (1994), *Planning for Development in Sub-saharan Africa*. New York: Praeger.
Selener, D. (1997), *Participatory Action Research and Social Change*. New York: Cornell University.
Sen, A. (1981), *Poverty and Famines*. Oxford: Clarendon Press.
Serageldin, I. (1993), Making Development Sustainable. *Finance and Development* Vol. 30, No. 4.
Sha'aba, R. A. (1998), MOSOP and the Ogoni Struggle, in Omotoye Olorode et al., *Ken Saro-Wiwa and the Crises of the Nigerian State*. Lagos: CDHR.
Shaw, M. S. and J. Lee (2001), *Women's Voices Feminist Visions,Classic and Contemporary Readings*. New York: McGraw-Hill Higher Education Publishers.
Sklar, R. (1967), Political Science and Political Integration, *Journal of Modern African Studies*, Vol. V, No. 1.
Smith, Dan (1999), Women, War and Peace, in Ingeborg Breines et al., *Towards a Women's Agenda for a Culture of Peace*. Paris: UNESCO, pp. 57–74.
Snyder, M. C. and M. Tedasse (1995), *African Women and Development: A History*. Johannesburg: Witwatersr and University Press.
Sokrari, Ekine (1999), Women in the Niger Delta: Violence and Struggle; http:ndw. kabissa. org/Articles.
Sokrari, Ekine (2001), *Blood and Oil*. London: Centre for Democracy and Development.
Solomon, Hussein (1995), The Challenges of Global Change to International Relations Theory, *Politeia*, Vol. 14, No. 1, p. 43.
Solomon, Hussein (1999), Population Movements into South Africa: Trends, Outlook, Policies, Occasional Paper Series No. 2, *Foundation for Global Dialogue*, Braamfontein.
Solomon, Hussein and John Cilliers (1996), Sources of Southern African Insecurity and the Quest for Regional Integration, in Hussein Solomon and John Cilliers (eds.), *People, Poverty and Peace: Human Security in Southern Africa*. IDP Monograph Series, No. 4, June.
Srilatha, Batliwala (2002), Grassroots Movements as Transnational Actors: Implications for Global Civil Society, *Voluntas: International Journal of Voluntary and Non-Profit Organisations*, Vol. 13, No. 4, 393–409.
Stamp, P. (1983), *Technology, Gender and Power in Africa*. Ottawa : International Research Centre.
Strange, Susan (1996), *The Retreat of the State: The Diffusion of Power in the World Economy*. Cambridge, UK: Cambridge University Press.

Strickland, R. and N. Duvvury (2003), *Gender Equity and Peacebuilding (From Rhetoric to Reality: Finding the Way)*. Washington DC: International Centre for Research on Women.

Sunday Tribune Magazine (2002), Women in Power, Cover Choice of the Sunday Tribune, June 30, pp. 9–11.

Tadesse, M. (1992), The Role of African Women in the Informal Sector: Problems and Prospects. Background Document for the AAPAM 12th Roundtable Conference.

Terhorst, Rosalinda (1999), *Training Package for Awareness Raising about Legal Rights, Workers' Rights and Gender Equality*. Trainers' Manual, ILO Kathmandu.

Thomas, Caroline (1987), *In Search of Security: The Third World in International Relations*. Brighton, UK: Wheatsheaf Publishing House.

Thompson Drewal, Margaret (1992), *Yoruba Ritual: Performers, Play, Agency*. Bloomington: Indiana University Press.

Tickner, J. A. (1995), Re-visioning Security, in K. Booth and S. Smith (eds.), *International Relations Theory Today*. Cambridge, UK: Polity Press, pp.175–197.

Timiebi, A. Koripamo, Agary, and Kaine Agary (2005), Women and Environment in the Niger Delta, in Kayo de Fayemi, Stella Amadi, and Ololade Bamidele (eds.), *Towards an Integrated Development of the Niger Delta*. Lagos: Centre for Democracy.

Tjondronegoro, S. M. P. (1992). *A Sociological Evaluation of Participatory Approaches in Planned Rural Development: Some Experiences from Selected Third World Countries*, Mimbar Sosek Nomor 4, Juni. Bogor: Institut Pertanian Bogor.

Tocqueville, A. (1966/1835), *Democracy in America*. New York: Harper & Row.

Turner, T. and M. O. Oshare (1993), Women's Uprising against the Nigerian Oil Industry, *Canadian Journal of Development Studies*. Vol. XIV, No. 3.

Turner, T. and Leigh S. Brownhill (2001), Gender, Feminism and the Civil Commons: Women and the Anti-Corporate, Below, *Canadian Journal of Development Studies*, Vol. XIV, No. 3, p. 805.

Turner, T. et al. (2001), Fightback from the Commons: General Class Alliances and Petroleum Struggles in Nigeria's Oil Belt: 1980-2002, *Cambridge Review of International Affairs*, Winter 2001/2, Vol. XIV, No. 3.

Turshen, M. and C. Twagiramariya (eds.) (1998), *What Women Do in Wartime: Gender and Conflict in Africa*. London: Zed Books.

Uchem, R. N. (2001), Overcoming Women Subordination. An Igbo African and Christian Perspective: Envisioning an Inclusive Theology With Reference to Women. Dissertation.com Parkland, U.S.A.

Ugbodaga, K. (2003), Women Political Leadership: Overcoming the Barriers, in *Daily Times on Saturday*, August 2, p. 7.

United Nations (UN) (2002), *Women, Peace and Security*. Geneva: United Nations.

United Nations Children Education Fund (UNICEF) (2003). *Girls, Education and Development*. Geneva: UNICEF.

United Nations Development Program (2006), *Niger Delta Human Development Report*. Abuja: UNDP.

United Nations Development Programme (1999), *Nigerian Development Report, 1999*. Lagos: UNDP.

UNRISD (2005), *Gender Equality, Striving for Justice in an Unequal World*, Geneva.

Upadhyayam, A. S. (2003), Gender and Conflict Transformation: Focus on South Asia. Paper delivered at the workshop organized by the Canadian Committee on Women, Peace and Security and South Asia, October 20.
U.S. Arms Control and Disarmament Agency (USACDA) (1990), World Military Expenditures and Arms Transfers, Washington DC.
Uzoanya, E. P. (2002), Women Taking The Political Centre Stage, in the *Guardian Newspaper on Sunday*, October 13, pp. 20–21.
Valerie, B. (1992), *Feminist Political Theory: An Introduction*. New York: Macmillan Press.
Vandenberg, M. (2000), *Kosovo: Rape as a Weapon of 'Ethnic Cleansing*. New York: Human Rights Watch, www.hrw.org/reports/2000/fry/index.htm
Vasquez, J. A. (1996), *Classics of International Relations*. Upper Saddle River, NJ: Prentice Hall, p. 59.
Walzer, M. (1991) The Idea of Civil Society, *Dissent*, Vol. 38, No. 2, pp. 298–304.
Warren, M. (2001), *Democracy and Association*. Princeton, NJ: Princeton University Press.
Watt, S. (1991), The Renaissance of Security Studies, *International Studies Quarterly*, Vol. 35, No. 2, pp. 211–237.
Wescott, Joan and :Peter Morton-Williams (1962), The Symbolism and Ritual Context of the Yoruba Laba Shango, *Journal of the Royal Anthropological Institute of Great Britain and Ireland*, Vol. 92, No. 1, pp. 23–37.
Wilson, Joan H. (1989), The Negative Impact of the American Revolution, in *Major Problems in American Women's History*, Mary Beth Norton (ed.), 90–101. Washington, DC: D.C. Heath and Company.
Wirth, L. (2000), *Sociology: Themes and Perspectives*. London: Collins Publishers.
Wolfers, Arnold (1962), *Discord and Collaboration: Essays on International Politics*. Baltimore, MD: John Hopkins University Press.
Wolfinger, R. (1965), The Development and Persistence of Ethnic Voting, *American Political Science Review*, Vol. 59, No. 4.
World Bank (2003), World Development Indicators; www.worldbank.org/data.
World Bank (2006), *World Development Report 2006: Equity and Development*. Oxford, UK: Oxford University Press.
Wright, S. (1990). Development Theory and Community Development Practice. In H. Buller and S. Wright (eds.), *Rural Development: Problems and Practices*. Newcastle upon Tyne, UK: Atheneum Press Ltd.
Yerpes, Tito et al (2009), *Making Sense of Africa's Infrastructure Endowment: A Benchmarking Approach*. Policy Research Working Paper 4912, Washington, DC: World Bank.
Yolah, K. H. (1996), Socio-Cultural Factors Affecting Womens Advancement and Development. Paper presented at the Women Development Consultative Seminar at the Strategic Management Center, Lekki, Lagos, November 19.
Yukako, S. and P. Eloundou-Enyegue (2006), The Emergence of African NGO's: Functional or Opportunistic Response? *Africa Notes*, April/May.
Zivtev, L. (1991), *Doing Good: The Australian NGO Community*. North Stanley, New South Wales: Allen and Unwin.

Index

www.ingramcontent.com/pod-product-compliance
Ingram Content Group UK Ltd.
Pitfield, Milton Keynes, MK11 3LW, UK
UKHW012035150926
475560UK00001B/18

9 780739 177785